COMPARATIVE GRAMMAR
OF GREEK AND LATIN

COMPARATIVE GRAMMAR
OF
GREEK AND LATIN

By

CARL DARLING BUCK

THE UNIVERSITY OF CHICAGO PRESS

CHICAGO & LONDON

THE UNIVERSITY OF CHICAGO PRESS, CHICAGO & LONDON
The University of Toronto Press, Toronto 5, Canada

PREFACE

During the course of some forty years of lecturing on the Comparative Grammar of Greek and Latin I have written and re-written various chapters with a view to eventual publication. New material and new discussions necessitate constant changes in some regard, and, fortunately for our living interest in the subject, there is no time of stabilization.

I am undertaking here to set forth what now appear to me the most essential and best established facts, and what in my present judgment are the most probable views on such disputed matters as I have thought wise to touch upon. Argumentary discussion is avoided, and references to the views of others, whether those adopted or rejected, are omitted or relegated to the Appendix.

My obligations are to the whole body of scholars in the field rather than to any single book. For Greek the grammars of Brugmann-Thumb, Kühner-Blass and Smyth, and for Latin those of Lindsay, Sommer, and Stolz-Leumann have been of the most constant service. The manuals dealing with Greek and Latin together have long since ceased to be representative, with the exception of the recent work of Meillet and Vendryes, the excellent Traité de grammaire comparée des langues classiques.

The practice of combining the treatment of Greek and Latin comparative grammar, whether in lecture courses or in books, is not based upon a belief in a special Graeco-Italic linguistic unity within the Indo-European family. From the point of view of comparative grammar, Greek and Latin are simply two adjacent sister languages of the larger group, and the special relations between them are less striking than those between Latin and Celtic. But owing to the cultural relations, literary and other, between the two great peoples of classical antiquity, their languages are the common concern of the same body of scholars. For classical students each is the obvious and fitting complement of the other as a basis of comparison. Hence in treating the two together one avoids considerable repetition, and this I believe more than offsets the greater difficulties of arrangement. At least a common outline is the best introduction to the more intensive study of the historical development of either language.

For some of the topics the Greek and Latin history may be interwoven, for others the two sides of the picture are presented in separate paragraphs or chapters. In this matter of arrangement I have followed no principle other than that of practical convenience and clearness.

No acquaintance with Sanskrit, Gothic, Lithuanian, etc., is presupposed, but their forms are freely cited to vivify the reconstructions. Treatment of the Greek and Italic dialects lies outside the scope of the present work. Only some of their outstanding features or matters pertinent to the discussion are occasionally mentioned.

The title of the book is strictly a misnomer without the reservation "exclusive of syntax". For, with the exception of a few remarks in connection with inflection, there is no treatment of syntax (in the customary application of this term). This is not due to any mistrust of the comparative method as applied to syntax. This should show the relatively simple and crude structure out of which developed the sophisticated practice of the Greek and Roman writers. But, as it seems to me, the comparative treatment of Greek and Latin Syntax requires the repetition of a vast deal of illustrative detail which is adequately presented in the school grammars—much more such repetition of familiar facts than is required for the forms—so that for a book of this kind the space demanded would be disproportionate to the gain. However, the real excuse for the omission is perhaps, after all, my lesser interest in this field.

I have no apologies for adhering in the main to the order of treatment that is familiar in most grammars, while well aware of certain illogical aspects and inconsistencies.

Critics will find little or nothing in this book that is strikingly

new. But it reflects long years of experience in teaching the subject and of following critically, with some participation, its progress.

I am indebted to Professor Walter Petersen for assistance in
reading the proofs.

C. D. B.

Chicago

The several new printings have offered a welcome opportunity
to correct a number of annoying misprints and slips on the part
of the author. Many of these were noticed by myself and students
as soon as the book was in use. Others were pointed out by
friends. Without attempting to recall all cases of such assistance,
I wish to thank especially Professors Echols, Kent, Lane, Whatmough, and Mr. J. P. Cooke for the carefully prepared lists of
corrections which they were kind enough to send me.

A few other changes, such as were feasible, have been made.

But I have not introduced any such radical revision of reconstructed IE forms as some scholars would make, on the basis
of Hittite comparisons and theories of IE laryngeal consonants.
Furthermore, so far as I can see, such a revision will affect mainly
the reconstruction of Proto-IE (or "Indo-Hittite," cf. p. 15)
forms. Thus, if our familiar IE *dhē- is further analyzed into
*dhe + a laryngeal stop (or the like), the fact remains that
*dhē- is the immediate source of the root as it appears in G.
τίθημι, L. fēcī, Skt. dádhāti, Goth. gadēds (sb.), Lith. dėti, etc.
The remoter analysis would be needless for purposes of direct
comparison and would add to the student's burden. Or again, if
the inflectional system was actually less fully developed in IE
than is assumed, still the reconstructions are convenient as
formulaic expressions of the observed agreement, even when
this is so limited as that between certain middle endings in Greek
and Indo-Iranian.

C. D. B.

Chicago

CONTENTS

INTRODUCTION

PHONOLOGY

CONTENTS

CONTENTS

WORD FORMATION

APPENDIX

INDEXES

ABBREVIATIONS

Abbreviations of the names of Greek and Latin authors are those familiar in the lexicons.

The following are employed for languages and dialects:

Aetol. = Aetolian
Alb. = Albanian
Arc. = Arcadian
Arg. = Argolic
Arm. = Armenian
Att. = Attic
Av. = Avestan
Boeot. = Boeotian
Byz. = Byzantine
ChSl. = (Old) Church Slavic
Cor. = Corinthian
Corc. = Corcyraean
Cret. = Cretan
Cypr. = Cyprian
Cyren. = Cyrenaean
Dan. = Danish
Delph. = Delphian
Dor. = Doric
Du. = Dutch
El. = Elean
Epid. = Epidaurian
Eub. = Euboean
Fr. = French
G. = Greek
Gmc. = Germanic
Goth. = Gothic
Hitt. = Hittite
IE = Indo-European
Ion. = Ionic
Ir. = (Old or Middle) Irish
It. = Italian
L. = Latin
Lac. = Laconian
Lesb. = Lesbian
Lett. = Lettic
Lith. = Lithuanian

Locr. = Locrian
LG = Low German
Marruc = Marrucinian
ME = Middle English
MHG = Middle High German
ML = Mediaeval Latin
Meg. = Megarian
Mod.G. = Modern Greek
NE = New (= Modern) English
NHG = New (= Modern) High German
NIr. = New (= Modern) Irish
NWG = Northwest Greek
OE = Old English
OHG = Old High German
ON = Old Norse
OPers. = Old Persian
OPruss. = Old Prussian
Osc. = Oscan
Pael. = Paelignian
Pamph. = Pamphylian
Phoc. = Phocian
Praen. = Praenestine
Rhod. = Rhodian
Rum. = Rumanian
Russ. = Russian
Sab. = Sabine
SCr. = Serbo-Croatian
Skt. = Sanskrit
Sp. = Spanish
Sw. = Swedish
Teg. = Tegean
Ther. = Theran
Thess. = Thessalian
Umbr. = Umbrian
Vest. = Vestinian
W. = Welsh

INTRODUCTION

THE INDO-EUROPEAN FAMILY OF LANGUAGES

1. Greek and Latin are two of the sister languages which make up the great Indo-European[1] family, comprising most of the languages of Europe and some of Asia. The interrelations between the main branches, based on the points of contact between them, are mainly in accord with their relative geographical position, and are best exhibited in a scheme like the following. Omitted are Tocharian, Hittite, and some minor IE languages, for which see **13, 14, 15.**

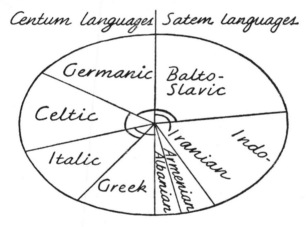

The vertical line separates the "centum" and "satem" languages, according to their treatment of the gutturals (**143**). This is the most striking and comprehensive feature of demarcation.

[1] The term Indo-European (hereafter IE), which appears to have been first used in 1813, and indicates the range from the languages of India in the east to the European in the west, is the one established in English and accords with what is most nearly the international usage. German scholars, after using "indoeuropäisch" for a time, have long since settled on "indogermanisch", whence "Indo-Germanic" in some English books, especially translations of German works. The term Aryan is also used, mainly by historians and ethnologists, in the same sense, but to philologists this generally connotes more specifically the Indo-Iranian branch of the family.

But the grouping which it shows is not to be understood as applicable in other respects or to be taken as a general classification of the IE languages.

Other important phenomena show other groupings. Indo-Iranian is distinguished from all the other branches in many respects, notably in the simpler vowel system (73.4). There are important points of agreement between Balto-Slavic and Germanic, notably the case-endings with *m* parallel to those with *bh* in the other branches (230.7); between Germanic and Celtic; between Celtic and Italic, so striking that some scholars believe in a period of special Italo-Celtic unity; between Italic and Greek, though certainly not sufficient to justify the old view of a Graeco-Italic unity.

All these relations are best explained by assuming that they reflect the germs of dialectic variation in the parent speech, the differentiation of the later more definite divisions beginning when they were still in geographical contact and in the relative positions indicated in the scheme above, these relative positions being substantially kept in their earliest spread.

What region was the common center, the home of the IE-speaking people, the "cradle of the Aryans" in popular parlance, has been a notorious subject of discussion, with theories ranging from the Scandinavian peninsula to central Asia. No conclusive evidence is available or likely to be forthcoming. But the best working hypothesis is that which favors the region extending north of the Black Sea and the Caucasus.

The period of IE unity can only be roughly estimated as around 3000 B.C. It is safe to say that by 2000 B.C. the main branches of the family had been differentiated and some of the IE-speaking peoples were on the march in the direction of their historical locations.

The more detailed classification is shown in the table and comments of the following paragraphs.

2. *Table of classification.*—Extant modern languages are in the last column.

		Vedic Sanskrit	Classical Sanskrit	Pāli, Prakrit dialects	
I. INDO-IRANIAN	Indic			Pāli, Prakrit dialects	Bengali, Hindi, Marathi, Gujerati, etc.
	Iranian	Avestan, Old Persian		Pahlavi, Sogdian, Sacian	Mod. Persian, Kurdish, Ossetan, Afghan, Baluchi, etc.
II. ARMENIAN				Old Armenian	Armenian
III. ALBANIAN					Albanian
IV. GREEK	East Greek	Attic-Ionic, Arcadian-Cyprian, Aeolic: Lesbian, Thessalian, Boeotian		The κοινή or Hellenistic Greek	Mod. Greek
	West Greek	NW Greek: Locrian, Phocian, Elean; Doric: Laconian, Argolic, Corinthian, Cretan, etc.			(Tsaconian dialect)
V. ITALIC	Latin-Faliscan	Latin, Faliscan		Vulgar Latin	French, Provençal, Catalan, Spanish, Portuguese, Italian, Rhaeto-Roman, Rumanian
	Oscan Umbrian	Oscan, Umbrian, Paelignian, Volscian, etc.			

VI. CELTIC	Gaelic		Old Irish	Irish, Scotch Gaelic, Manx
	Britannic		Old Welsh, Old Cornish, Old Breton	Welsh, Breton
	Continental	Celtic Inscriptions		
VII. GERMANIC	East Germanic		Gothic	
	North Germanic		Old Norse	Swedish, Danish, Norwegian, Icelandic
	West Germanic	Anglo-Frisian	Old English, Old Frisian	English, Frisian
		German { Low / High }	Old Saxon, Old Low Franconian, Old High German	Dutch, German
VIII. BALTO-SLAVIC	Baltic		Old Lithuanian, Old Lettic, Old Prussian	Lithuanian, Lettic
	Slavic	South Slavic	Old Church Slavic	Bulgarian, Serbo-Croatian, Slovenian
		West Slavic	Polabian	Bohemian, Slovak, Polish, Wendish
		East Slavic		Great Russian, White Russian, Ukrainian

3. *Indo-Iranian or Aryan.*—Indic and Iranian show a very close relationship, pointing to a period of special unity.

Certain forms that are clearly Aryan, either still undifferentiated Aryan or Proto-Indic (cf. *aika-* 'one' like Skt. *eka-* in contrast to Av. *aēva-*), occur in cuneiform records of western Asia dating from the 14th cent. B.C. These are the names of some of the kings of the Mitanni (that is, the dynasty was Aryan), of four of their gods, and a series of numeral compounds appearing in a Hittite work on horse-training. They constitute the earliest certain record not only of Aryan but of IE speech (Hittite, on which see **15,** is known from about the same date), though some proper names in still earlier cuneiform records are thought, not improbably, to be Aryan.

4. *Indic.*—The earliest form of Indic is that of the Vedic texts, of which the oldest is the Rigveda, a collection of hymns in extent slightly less than the Iliad and Odyssey together. Its date of composition is unknown, but may be fairly estimated as about 1000 B.C. The language of this and the other collections of hymns, with the prose works attached to them, is known as Vedic, and differs considerably from the later Sanskrit, much as Homeric from Attic Greek. But the comparison holds only for the relative antiquity of forms. Vedic and classical Sanskrit are not believed to rest on different local dialects, like Homeric and Attic. Classical Sanskrit is thought to be the result of literary evolution from Vedic, with elimination of obsolete forms and concessions to the spoken language, an artificial product not reflecting any local dialect.

Classical Sanskrit (or Sanskrit in the strict sense, for such was the application of the term *saṁskṛta-*'adorned, perfected') is the literary language in the form studied and fixed by the grammarians, especially Pāṇini in the 4th cent. B.C. It is the vehicle of a literature of vast extent, embracing all branches, and covering a period reaching down into the Middle Ages (or in a limited sense even to the present time). The masterpieces of lyric poetry and the drama are from the 6th cent. A.D., and some favorite texts for easy reading date from the 11th cent. A.D. and later. The position which Latin held in western Europe down through the Middle Ages, Sanskrit held in India—and beyond, for as a literary language it spread to Ceylon, Borneo, Java, and even to the Philippines. During all this time it remained substantially in the form fixed by the grammarians, much more stable than the written Latin of later periods.

But vernaculars, on a later stage of linguistic development, existed contemporaneously with the earliest classical Sanskrit and even in the Vedic period. From one of these, in the time of Buddha (died 480 B.C.), sprang Pāli, the sacred language of Buddhism. Others are called the Prakrit dialects. They are known from inscriptions and from their use in the Sanskrit drama (scenic Prakrit). Here they are employed, not like the dialects in Aristophanes to reflect the local speech of characters introduced, but with a curious social distribution. Only the gods and the leading male characters use Sanskrit, the leading female characters use a particular Prakrit which ranks highest in esteem, while the other characters use a variety of other Prakrits appropriate to their social rank. Pāli and the Prakrit dialects constitute what is known as Middle Indic, being on a stage midway between the ancient (Vedic and classical Sanskrit) and the modern Indic languages.

The modern Indic languages include Bengali, Hindi, Mahratti, and many others, some of them established literary languages. The languages of southern India, Tamil, Telugu, etc., are non-Aryan, Dravidian, though full of loanwords from Sanskrit.

Among the Indic derivatives is the language of the Gypsies, who are in origin wandering tribes from northwestern India. In spite of the great divergence of the Gypsy dialects and the large number of words adopted from the languages of the countries where they have lived, the main substratum is of obvious relationship to Sanskrit.

5. *Iranian.*—Iranian speech extended over the old Persian Empire east of Mesopotamia and Elam, namely from Media and Persia in the west to Bactria and Sogdiana in the northeast. The ancient Scythians, or at least their rulers as shown by their names in Herodotus, were also of Iranian speech. Records of Middle Iranian have been found in the present Eastern Turkestan and even farther east.

Two ancient Iranian languages are known.

Avestan (formerly called Zend by a misunderstanding), the language of the Avesta, the Zoroastrian Bible. Certain hymns known as the Gāthās show an earlier form of the language than that of the later portions. They belong to the time of Zoroaster (Zarathushtra), whose date is disputed but lies somewhere between 1000 and 600 B.C. The rest of the Avesta was composed at various later times, and may be taken as reflecting mainly the language of say 500–300 B.C. The final redaction was made under the Sassanian dynasty in the 4th cent. A.D., and was accompanied by a commentary in the language of that time, namely Pahlavi (see below). The extant Avesta is only a small part of the original. Just what part of Iranian territory was the home of the Avestan language is uncertain. There are some arguments in favor of Bactria (hence the name Old Bactrian once used by some scholars, but to be rejected as begging the question). It was clearly not Persia proper.

Old Persian, known from the cuneiform inscriptions of the Achaemenian kings, mainly of Darius I and Xerxes, and representing their official language, based on that of their home land, Persia proper. These inscriptions are trilingual, the versions being in order (1) Persian, (2) Elamite, (3) Babylonian. The Old Persian was the first to be deciphered, and this furnished the key to the decipherment of the other cuneiform scripts and the reading of Babylonian-Assyrian texts. The longest inscription, and one of the most important documents for history as well as for language, is that of Darius I at Behistun, the ancient Βαγίστανον ὄρος, southwest of Ecbatana.

Middle Iranian is represented by:

Pahlavi, the language of Persia in the Sassanian period (3d–7th cent. A.D.), known from inscriptions, the commentaries on the Avesta, and other religious texts.

Sogdian, known from Buddhist, Manichaean, and Christian texts discovered in Eastern Turkestan and farther east.

Sacian (?), known likewise from texts found in Eastern Turkestan, and formerly called North-Aryan (a misnomer, the language being clearly Iranian), now thought to be the language of the Sacae.

Modern Iranian is represented by Modern Persian (the only one with a literature of importance), the closely related Kurdish, the isolated Ossetan in the Caucasus, Afghan in Afghanistan, Baluchi in Baluchistan, several minor languages spoken on the Pamir Plateau, and an isolated relic of Sogdian.

6. *Armenian.*—The Armenians of IE speech were late comers in Armenia, which is known to have been occupied about 950–650 B.C. by a people which left records in a non-IE language. The Armenians are believed to be related to the Phrygians, but the records of Phrygian are so meager that it is not included in the classification and Armenian is given a place by itself. The language is full of Iranian loanwords, so that it was once mistakenly classed as Iranian. The earliest records are from the 5th cent. A.D. Much of the early literature consists of translations from Greek.

7. *Albanian.*—Spoken in the newly constituted state of Albania on the Adriatic coast, and in adjacent regions. There are also Albanian colonies, dating from the 15th cent. A.D. in Greece, southern Italy, and Sicily. Except for some meager records of the 16th and 17th centuries, the language is known only from recent times, and there has been no standardized written language until within these last few years. The largest element of the vocabulary is of Latin origin, and there are also great numbers of Greek, Slavic, and Turkish words. But there is a substratum of words and grammatical structure which is IE but not borrowed from any of these sources. This is doubtless a relic of the speech of some Illyrian or Thracian tribes which were almost but not quite Romanized. The present location of Albanian speech makes Illyrian origin seem the more natural, and this is the most widely current view. But against this, and in favor of Thracian origin, is the fact that Albanian is a "satem" language (**2, 143**), while Illyrian on the evidence of place names appears to belong to the "centum" group.

8. *Celtic.*—Celtic speech, now restricted to a small territory and small numbers, was in ancient times spread over a vast territory. Celtic-speaking tribes occupied not only the British Isles, Gaul, and part of Spain, but also central Europe, extending through Bohemia (which takes its name from the Celtic Boii) and present Austria, while the Galatians passed over into Asia Minor. Upper Italy (Gallia Cisalpina) was mainly Celtic about 400 B.C.

The old continental Celtic is known only from proper names and a few short inscriptions from Gaul and Italy. The better-known languages fall into the two groups Gaelic and Britannic, with Irish and Welsh the chief representatives of each.

Old Irish is known from the 8th cent. A.D. chiefly from glosses inserted in Latin texts by the Irish monks on the Continent. There is an extensive Middle Irish literature. Modern Irish is spoken by only a very small proportion of the population of Ireland, but is in process of revival. Manx and Scotch Gaelic are very closely allied to Irish.

Old Welsh is known from the 8th cent. A.D., and there is a large Middle Welsh literature. Modern Welsh is still very widely spoken in Wales. Cornish became extinct at the end of the 18th cent.

Breton, in the French province of Brittany, is not a relic of the old Celtic of Gaul, but was brought in by immigrants from England after the Anglo-Saxon invasion. Hence its close relationship to Welsh.

9. *Germanic.*[1]—Except for some brief runic inscriptions, the earliest record of Germanic speech is the Gothic Bible of Bishop Wulfilas, who lived in the 4th cent. A.D. The other remains of Gothic and of other East Germanic dialects are of small account.

Old Norse, representing the North Germanic branch, is known from runic inscriptions and the extensive Old Icelandic literature. By gradual differentiation arose the present Scandinavian

---

[1] The term Germanic accords with international usage, and is preferable to Teutonic. It is sufficiently differentiated from the narrower German. The latter is a substitute for the earlier Dutch (=NHG *deutsch*), after this had become restricted to the language of Holland.

languages, Swedish, Danish, Norwegian, and Icelandic. The Norwegian literary language is based upon and still very close to the Danish, the latter having been adopted in the long period of union between Norway and Denmark.

West Germanic falls into two divisions, the Anglo-Frisian and one that includes High and Low German with Dutch. Old High German, in various dialects (Franconian, Alemannic, etc.), is known from the 8th cent. on. Old Low German is represented by the Old Saxon of a 9th cent. poem, the Heliand. New High German, the present German literary language, or what we call simply German, is based mainly on the East Franconian dialect. The Low German speech of northern Germany survives in the local dialects, but is subordinate to the standard German literary language.

In the Netherlands a literary language developed, based chiefly on Low Franconian, namely the Dutch. The Flemish speech of northern Belgium is closely related and in the form restored to written use by the "Flemish movement" is virtually the same as Dutch.

The Anglo-Frisians (the Ingaevones of Tacitus and Pliny) once occupied the coast region from about the mouth of the Scheldt to Schleswig-Holstein inclusive. Frisian, the continental language most closely related to English, now survives chiefly in the West Frisian of the Dutch province of Friesland.

The Angles, Saxons, and Jutes, whose home was in the Schleswig-Holstein region, invaded Britain in the 5th cent. A.D. and brought their Germanic speech. Britain was still mainly Celtic. During the period of Roman occupation the country had been partially Romanized, especially the garrison towns, but not thoroughly like Gaul. The invaders settled in hordes, forcing the Celtic Britons ever farther west until most of the land was of Germanic speech, with little admixture of Celtic. For the amount of Celtic in English (apart from what came in through Latin) is insignificant, less than the number of Indian words in American English. But the later Danish invasions and occupation of the land north of the Saxon domain introduced a related Germanic, but Scandinavian, element, which resulted in a permanent mixture. The number of English words which reflect the Scandinavian rather than the true English form is very large.

The language was always called English, after the Angles, so even by the Saxon King Alfred. Hence Old English is the appropriate term for the language of this period, rather than Anglo-Saxon, which was a political term, apparently first used to distinguish the Saxons of England from those of the Continent. Most of the Old English texts are in the West Saxon dialect (King Alfred, the abbot Aelfric, etc.), which had the status of an official language (the earliest non-Latin official language in western Europe). The Anglian dialects are more meagerly represented (the Northumbrian Gospels, etc.).

After the Norman Conquest French was the language of the court, and the country swarmed with Norman officials, monks, and tradesmen. English ceased to be cultivated as a literary language and persisted only in the speech of the masses. But with the loss of Normandy and the other French possessions the interests of the ruling classes were centered in England and they came to feel themselves English. In the 14th cent. English emerged again as a literary language (Chaucer, Wiclif), and was substituted for French in the schools. This literary Middle English was based on the speech of London as then current in the court. Most of the inflectional system of Old English had been lost in the meantime, and much of the vocabulary replaced by French. Hence English is a Germanic language in the main line of descent, but in vocabulary and general character much less so than the other Germanic languages.

10. *Balto-Slavic.*—The Baltic and Slavic languages have so many points of striking agreement in form and vocabulary that they are properly grouped together, though the relationship is not nearly so close as that between Indic and Iranian. They were doubtless separated and pursuing their independent development long before the beginning of our era.

11. Of the Baltic languages the most important is Lithuanian, spoken in the present Lithuania. Between the 11th and 14th centuries A.D. the Lithuanian chiefs conquered much Russian territory and the old Grand Duchy of Lithuania once extended from the Baltic to the Black Sea. But this was only in small part of Lithuanian speech, and Lithuanian was not then employed as a written language. After the union with Poland the Lithuanians were submerged in Polish history. The earliest records of the language are from the 16th cent. A.D. Lithuanian is remarkable among living languages for the conservation of old forms and inflection, and hence is of great importance in IE comparative grammar.

Lettic, spoken in the present Latvia, is known from about the same period, but is on a later stage of linguistic development.

Old Prussian, once spoken in what is now East Prussia but extinct since about 1700 A.D., is known only from meager remains, mainly a catechism of the 16th cent. But it preserves some notable early forms, paralleled only in Gothic, early Greek, or Sanskrit.

12. The Slavs in the time of the Roman writers (the Venedi of Tacitus and Pliny) occupied the region northeast of the Carpathians in what is now southeastern Poland and western Russia. Hence they spread in all directions, the migrations west and south occurring between 200 and 600 A.D., after the great Germanic migrations. In the south they came into contact with Graeco-Roman civilization, and here arose the earliest Slavic states and the earliest form of written Slavic.

Slavic tribes on the Danube were in conflict with the Eastern Empire in the time of Justinian and in the 7th cent. were settled in Moesia and Thrace. Here they were conquered by a band of invaders of Asiatic origin, the Bulgars, who established the Bulgarian state, to become for a time a serious rival to the Byzantine power (cf. Bury, History of the Eastern Empire). These Bulgars, whose native tongue was of the Turkish family, adopted Greek as their official language. But they were soon absorbed in the mass of the Slavic population, so that the Bulgarian language is Slavic in all but name (just as French is Romance, though bearing the name of the Germanic Franks who founded the state).

Old Church Slavic is the language employed in their missionary work by the Slavic apostles, the brothers Constantine (Cyril) and Methodius, who lived in the 9th cent. They were Greeks of Thessalonica and no doubt had learned the language from the Slavs of the surrounding region, though their actual mission in 863 was to Moravia. The language is the early form of the Slavic that came to be known as Bulgarian (cf. above) and hence is sometimes called Old Bulgarian.

Church Slavic is the earliest recorded form of Slavic and for a long time it was the only written or literary language among the Slavs, for whom it held the same position as Latin in the West. Moreover, while not identical with the primitive undifferentiated Slavic, it comes so near to reflecting this that it serves as the main representative of Slavic in comparative grammar, and is the foundation of Slavic linguistics.

The other South Slavic languages, besides the Church Slavic and the modern Bulgarian, are Serbo-Croatian and the closely connected Slovenian, now united in the present Yugo-Slavia.

The West Slavic languages are: Bohemian (Czechish) with the closely connected Slovak, now united in the present Czecho-Slovakia; Polish in Poland; Wendish or Sorbian, spoken by a small Slavic enclave in Germany northeast of Dresden; some minor dialects, partly extinct. (After the Germanic migrations Slavs occupied the land as far west as the Elbe and even beyond, and in the time of Charlemagne all this region, including Berlin, Leipzig, etc., was still Slavic. Later it was gradually Germanized. Wendish is a surviving relic.)

East Slavic is represented by Russian in its various forms, namely: Great Russian, the standard Russian; Little Russian or Ukrainian in the south; White Russian in the region adjacent to and partly in the present Poland.

13. Several other languages, not included in the foregoing classification, are known from meager remains, only sufficient to show that they belong to the IE family.

Phrygian is known, apart from proper names and glosses, from a few old inscriptions in an archaic Greek alphabet and some others of Christian times. It is believed that the Phrygians, with the Trojans, and the later Armenians, were closely akin to the Thracians, constituting a Thraco-Phrygian group.

Lycian, known from numerous inscriptions, is now believed to be IE, and even Lydian, Carian, etc., seem to have some remote IE affinities.

Thracian is known from proper names and glosses, and there is one obscure inscription believed to be Thracian. Cf. above under Phrygian.

Illyrian is known mainly from proper names. Languages for which Illyrian origin is claimed or disputed are Venetic and Messapian in ancient Italy, Macedonian, and Albanian.

Macedonian, that is, the native speech of the Macedonians as distinguished from the Attic κοινή which they came to adopt as their official language, is known from proper names and rather numerous glosses in the Greek lexicographers. Their language was certainly not Greek in the sense of being a regular Greek dialect co-ordinate with the others. It may be regarded as a sort of detached Greek with independent development and mixture with Illyrian—or as Illyrian with Greek mixture. Which is the more fundamental relation cannot be determined from the scanty evidence.

14. *Tocharian.*—This is a newly discovered IE language which has come to light in writings found in Eastern Turkestan[1] and dating from the 7th and 8th centuries A.D. It appears in two dialects known as A and B. The name Tocharian rests on the evidence that the language is that referred to in a MS as toχri, and the further identification with the Τοχαροί (in Bactria) of Strabo, Skt. *Tukhāra-*, Chin. *Tu-ho-lo*. The material is only partially published and interpreted, but its IE character is obvious and un-

---

[1] The expeditions (British, French, German, etc.) which were conducted from 1900 on in Eastern Turkestan and partly in the western provinces of China proper brought to light an astounding mass and variety of new linguistic material. The manuscripts represent three religions (Buddhist, Manichaean, and Christian), a dozen different languages or dialects, and a still greater variety of scripts. The languages hitherto unknown are the Tocharian and two new Middle Iranian languages, Sogdian and Sacian (see above, 5).

questioned. The remarkable fact, for a language in this region, is that the language is IE but not Indo-Iranian. In the treatment of the gutturals it goes with the "centum" group (cf. above, **1**), and the vowel system is European rather than Aryan.

15. *Hittite.*—The decipherment of the cuneiform records of the Hittites, whose empire in Asia Minor flourished about 1450–1200 B.C., shows that their official language was one of IE descent, though with a large admixture of non-IE vocabulary. It presumably is the language of conquerors of IE speech, mixed with that of the old native Hittite element, the "Proto-Hittite" or better distinguished simply as "Hattic", which is also preserved in some records. Closely related to the cuneiform Hittite are the hieroglyphic Hittite and Luwian.

While the IE affinity of the official Hittite is now undisputed, a question has arisen as to the precise nature of the relationship— namely whether Hittite is co-ordinate with the other branches of the IE family, or whether, as some are convinced, it represents an offshoot from an early form of IE antedating the differentiation of the other branches, in which case one would refer the relationship to a Proto-IE (called also "Indo-Hittite") period.

GREEK

OUTLINES OF THE EXTERNAL HISTORY

16. Archaeological discoveries have carried back the history of Greek lands, in the matter of material civilization, to periods far antedating any written records and long before the arrival of the historical Greeks of IE speech.

The population of the Neolithic Age, lasting till about 2500 B.C., is of unknown affinities, though presumably akin to that of the Danubian region.

In the early period of the Bronze Age, about 2500–2000 B.C., known as Early Helladic in mainland Greece, Early Cycladic in the Cyclades, and Early Minoan in Crete, the population was, there is reason to believe, akin to that of Asia Minor, constituting what is conveniently called Aegean. Many names are survivals from this period, notably those with -νθ-, as Τίρυνς, -υνθος, Κόριν-θος, Ἐρύμανθος, etc., similar to the numerous *nd*-names of Asia Minor.

Actual records of pre-Greek speech are found in outlying regions. The language of the undeciphered Cretan script was undoubtedly pre-Greek, and some specimens of this script have been found in mainland Greece. There are three "Eteocretan" inscriptions from eastern Crete written in the Greek alphabet, two of them as late as the 4th cent. B.C. An archaic inscription of Lemnos is in a form of Etruscan.

Whether the Greek invasion began about 2000 B.C., corresponding to the break between the Early and Middle Helladic periods, or some centuries later is disputed. But it is reasonably clear and now pretty generally admitted that at least from the beginning of the Late Helladic, that is, the Mycenaean period (*ca.* 1600–1200 B.C.), the dominant element of the population was Greek. This is indicated by working back from the historical period and allowing time for the prehistoric movements to be inferred from the relations of the Greek dialects. For the Doric invasion of about the 12th cent. B.C. was only the last of these prehistoric waves of Greek invasion, and must have been preceded by several centuries of Greek occupation. The identification of Hitt. *Aḫḫiyawā* with *Ἀχαιϝᾱ (cf. Ἀχαιϝοί, whence L. *Achīvī*), and of certain other proper names as Greek, in Hittite records of the 14th and 13th centuries B.C., is contested. But there are other reasons for believing in the early Greek occupation of parts of Asia Minor and Cyprus.

17. *Some general characteristics of Greek.*—From the time of the earliest records Greek appears, not as a unified language, but in numerous dialects. The differentiation of the larger dialect groups goes back to a remote period before the Greeks had entered Greece. Nevertheless there are many distinctive features common to all the Greek dialects, from which is to be inferred a period of common development, a relatively unified Greek language. Of such general characteristics some involve retention of the old in

contrast to changes elsewhere, while others are innovations, and
of these latter many are exclusively Greek while some have parallels elsewhere. Some of the most striking are as follows:

Phonology.—Preservation in large measure of the old vowel
system, with the old diphthongs (**73.**2), and of gradation (**117** ff.);
pitch accent, with special laws regarding position, recessive accent
in finite verb (**218–20**); αρ, ρα and αλ, λα from IE ŗ, ļ (**114**); α, αν from
IE ņ (**115**); prothetic vowel before init. ρ, etc. (**106**), three series
and three orders of stops, the latter including voiceless aspirates
(**128–30**); labials, dentals, and gutturals from IE labiovelars
(**151–53**); ʿ from IE init. *s* (**161**) and *y* (**177**); loss of intervocalic *s*
(**164**); loss of IE *y* as a separate sound, its union with preceding
consonant forming new groups (**181** ff.), and its development
initially in some words like *dy*, as in ζυγόν (**177**); change of τ
tó σ before ι, though in part only dialectic (**141**); loss of final stops
(**211.**1); change of final *m* to ν (**211.**2).

Inflection, word-formation, syntax.—System of five cases, with
merging of the genitive and ablative, and of the dative, locative,
and instrumental (**228**); dat. pl. in -σι (**230.**10); retention of IE
dual (**227**); genitive absolute construction (abl. abs. in Latin,
loc. abs. in Sanskrit, dat. abs. in Balto-Slavic); pers. pron. pl.
ἄμμες, ἡμεῖς, etc. (**299**); ν-stem forms in τίς, τίνος, etc. (**309**); retention of subjunctive and optative in distinctive uses (**326**), and
of aorist and perfect in distinctive uses (**327**); κ-perfect (**406**);
aor. pass. in -ην, -θην (**401**); σθ-forms in middle endings (**344.**5);
masc. ā-stems, especially -τᾱς, -της (**484**); productive type of
nouns in -ευς (**452**); formation of comparatives in -ιων, -ιων (**293**);
comparative and superlatives in -τερος, -τατος (**294**); great productivity in noun composition (**516**) and in varieties of denominative verbs (**363**).

Vocabulary (quoted in Attic forms).—εἷς 'one' (**313.**1), λέγω
'say', θέλω 'wish', βούλομαι 'choose', ποιέω 'make', θάλαττα 'sea',
ξένος 'stranger', δίκη 'right, legal action'. These and many others
constitute a distinctive Greek vocabulary.

18. *External influence upon Greek.*—The place names with -νθ-,
like Τίρυνς, Τίρυνθος, Κόρινθος, etc., have already (**16**) been noted

as survivals of the earlier Aegean occupation. The influence of this Aegean speech was doubtless considerable, at least in vocabulary, but cannot be proved in detail, since our knowledge of Aegean speech is so slight. The lack of a satisfactory IE etymology for a given Greek word is no proof that it is not of IE origin; it merely invites the suspicion that it may be a loanword. Nevertheless there are many common words, for articles of commerce, plants, etc., and some titles (τύραννος, ἄναξ, βασιλεύς), for which pre-Greek, Aegean origin is altogether probable.

Phoenician influence was not limited to the alphabet, which was adopted by the Greeks from the Phoenician traders. Various words for articles of commerce, clothing, measures, etc., were adopted. But some words common to Greek, Latin, and Phoenician, as those for 'wine', may be from a common Aegean source.

Latin influence begins only in the Hellenistic period, and other influences much later, so that these have no bearing upon classical Greek.

19. The Greeks of the heroic age, the period portrayed in Homer, were speakers of the "Old Hellenic" dialects representing the Attic-Ionic, the Aeolic, and the Arcadian-Cyprian groups, of which the last two have important characteristics in common and very probably represent divisions of a larger group co-ordinate with the first or Ionic in the wider sense. For a remoter period, the assignment of these groups to a particular series of waves of migration is somewhat speculative. But there are some grounds for the hypothesis that the earliest wave was the Ionic, covering Attica and the shores of the Saronic Gulf, and perhaps considerable parts of central Greece and the Peloponnesus. However this may be, the situation in the period preceding the Doric invasion was as follows.

Northern Greece beyond Attica and except in the far northwest was Aeolic—not only Thessaly and Boeotia which remained Aeolic in speech, with some West Greek admixture, but also Locris, Phocis, and southern Aetolia, as indicated by tradition, Mycenaean remains, and some linguistic evidence. Aeolic speech was carried to Lesbos and the adjacent coast of Asia Minor, where it survived in its purest form.

Most of the Peloponnesus was occupied by those whose speech survived the Doric invasion in the inland Arcadia. From the eastern Peloponnesus (the later Doric lands, not of course from the later Arcadia) it was carried to Cyprus, where it remained dominant, the dialects of Cyprus and Arcadia being most closely akin; also to Pamphylia, where it remained in a more mixed form; and to Rhodes, Crete, Thera, etc., where some scattered traces of it survived in its later Doric. There are also some survivals in the Doric of Laconia and Argolis.

The West-Greek-speaking tribes were entirely out of the picture in the heroic age, and presumably located in the northwest. The Doric invasion which followed was part of a general West Greek expansion, which affected northern Greece scarcely less than the Peloponnesus; and brought about a greatly changed distribution of dialects—the one we know in the historical period. Phocis, Locris, and Aetolia became West Greek, and there is a strong West Greek admixture in Boeotian and Thessalian, so that these dialects share in some of the important West Greek characteristics (notably $\delta\acute{\iota}\delta\omega\tau\iota = \delta\acute{\iota}\delta\omega\sigma\iota$, etc.), while retaining distinctive Aeolic characteristics. The West Greek admixture is greater in Boeotian than in Thessalian. In the Peloponnesus the dialects of Elis and Achaea are nearest to the Northwest Greek dialects of Locris and Phocis. Megara, Corinth, Argolis, Laconia, and Messenia became Doric. Doric speech was carried from Argolis and Laconia to Rhodes, Thera, Crete, etc., and the southern part of Asia Minor; from Corinth to Corcyra and the Acarnanian coast, to Sicily, etc.

The relationship between the Doric and the Northwest Greek dialects is very close. In fact, the general characteristics of the Doric dialects as a whole are common also to the Northwest Greek, in other words are really West Greek.

20. The classification of the Greek dialects has been indicated in the preceding paragraph, and is given in summary in the table

(2). We know these dialects mainly from the thousands of inscriptions, rather than from Greek literature, which shows only a few of them and would give no idea of the actual linguistic diversity. For Greece was as decentralized in language as in politics. As there was no unified Greece as a state, but only a number of city states and changing leagues, so there was no standard Greek language, but only a series of local dialects. Not only in early times, but also, in most parts of Greece, long after Attic had become the norm of literary prose, each state employed its own dialect, both in private monuments of internal concern and in those of a more external or interstate character, such as decrees in honor of foreigners, decisions of interstate arbitration, and, in general, communications between different states. Many of the dialects remained in common written use down till about 200 B.C., and some till the beginning of our era, though more or less mixed with Attic. How long they may have survived in spoken form, especially in remote districts, no one can say. Eventually they were replaced by the κοινή (22) both as the written and spoken language and from this is descended Modern Greek. The only exception is the present Tsaconian dialect, spoken in a small portion of Laconia, which is in part the offspring of ancient Laconian.

21. The literary dialects are mainly the result of literary evolution. They came to be characteristic of certain classes of literature, and their rôle once established, the choice of one or the other usually depended upon this factor rather than upon the native dialect of the author.

The language of Homer is Old Ionic, but with an admixture of undoubtedly Aeolic forms. These can only be explained as survivals from an earlier period of Aeolic lays. There was to be sure some actual mixture of dialect in the region near the border of Aeolic and Ionic, as in Chios. But the mixture in Homer is of a very different kind and cannot possibly be regarded as reflecting any natural spoken dialect. It is a literary mixture.

The Homeric language was closely imitated in all later epic poetry; it was followed in the main by Hesiod and by the elegiac and iambic poets like the Ionian Archilochus, the Athenian Solon, the Megarian Theognis, etc.; and to some extent it influenced all Greek poetry.

Alcaeus and Sappho employed their native Lesbian, with some traces of epic forms. Their language was imitated by Theocritus in three of his idyls, and certain of their Lesbian forms were used by other lyric poets and even in the Doric choral lyric.

The language of the choral lyric is Doric, whether the poet is a Boeotian like Pindar, or an Ionian like Simonides and Bacchylides. This Doric, however, is not identical with any specific Doric dialect. It is rather a conventionalized Doric, an artificial composite, showing many of the general Doric characteristics, but with elimination of local features and with some admixture of epic and Lesbian forms. The language of Alcman is more nearly the local Laconian. A Sicilian literary Doric appears in the scanty fragments of Epicharmus and Sophron, and later in Theocritus. There are fragments of Doric prose by writers of Magna Graecia.

Corinna of Tanagra, whose fame was scarcely more than local, used her native Boeotian. The Boeotian, Megarian, and Laconian dialects appear in crude caricature in Aristophanes.

The earliest prose writers were the Ionic philosophers and historians of the 6th cent. B.C., and in the 5th cent. not only Herodotus, but Hippocrates of Cos, a Dorian, wrote in Ionic. In the meantime, with the political and intellectual supremacy of Athens, Attic had become the recognized language of the drama, and before the end of the 5th cent. was also employed in prose. The earlier prose writers as Thucydides, like the tragedians, avoided certain Attic peculiarities which were still felt as provincialism, as the native ττ and ρρ (πράττω, ἄρρην) for which they used the σσ and ρσ of Ionic and the majority of dialects, while later writers conformed to the Attic ττ, ρρ. Attic became the established language of literary prose.

22. Hellenistic Greek, or the κοινή, which was spread by the Macedonian conquests over a vast new territory and was permanently established in places which became leading centers of Greek civilization, is unquestionably based in the main upon Attic, with some Ionic influence (e.g. both ττ and σσ frequent).

But owing partly to the natural development of all living speech, even in Athens itself, and partly to its wide currency among non-Attic Greeks, this Hellenistic Greek became something quite different from the Attic of the older Attic writers. "Atticism" was a protest against the innovations, an attempt to hold fast to the old Attic tradition and conform to the language of the great Attic writers. Lists were made of expressions which were to be approved as Attic as contrasted with those to be rejected as Hellenistic. Thus "νεῖν καὶ νήχεσθαι 'Αττικοί. κολυμβᾶν "Ελληνες." The latter is the Modern Greek word for 'swim', and so in many other cases the Hellenistic words are those that survived, just as the words disapproved by the Roman grammarians as vulgar are those that survive in the Romance languages. The language of the New Testament is Hellenistic Greek, with considerable variation in the degree of colloquialism.

Hellenistic Greek is the source of Modern Greek. Many Latin words were adopted, some in the early centuries of Roman rule, others in the early Byzantine period when the court at Constantinople was Latin-speaking. In later times some Slavic and many Turkish words were borrowed. But mixture in vocabulary is common to most of the present European languages. There were also changes in pronunciation, in syntax, and in the meaning of words, similar to the changes that have taken place in the other European languages. The present spoken language is naturally quite different from ancient Greek, but it is its lineal descendant in the same sense that Italian is a modern form of Latin.

23. *The extent of Greek-speaking territory.*—Long before 1000 B.C. Greek speech covered the Greek mainland, the Aegean islands including Crete, the western coast of Asia Minor, Pamphylia on its southern coast, and a part of Cyprus. Before 500 B.C., after the period of western colonization, southern Italy and a large part of Sicily were Greek, and there were flourishing Greek colonies on the northern African coast (Cyrene, etc.) and on the Mediterranean coast of Gaul and Spain. Other colonies covered the northern coast of the Aegean and the shores of the Black Sea. The Macedonian conquests left some knowledge of Greek in some even distant parts of the East, and Greek became the language of the educated classes in Syria, Palestine (so in the time of Christ, when the vernacular was Aramaic), and Egypt, where it remained the official language even under Roman domination. The Hellenization of interior Asia Minor belongs mainly to the Byzantine period.

Southern Italy and Sicily, and the Greek colonies in Gaul and Spain, were eventually Romanized, but not fully until well into our era. After the Arab conquests the whole northern fringe of Africa and the lands on the eastern Mediterranean became Arabic in speech. Slavic peoples occupied much of the previously Hellenized Thrace and Macedonia. The Turkish conquests made Asia Minor Turkish in speech, except for the Greeks on the coast and in a few scattered communities in the interior, and in the last years these Greeks have been expelled.

Thus the present Greek-speaking territory, except for the loss of the Asia Minor coast, is substantially what it was in the old Greek world before the western colonization and the Macedonian conquests.

ITALIC. LATIN AND THE ITALIC DIALECTS

OUTLINES OF THE EXTERNAL HISTORY

24. In contrast to Greece, which in the historical period was a country of one language though many dialects, Italy was still a land of many languages—non-IE, IE but not of the Italic branch, and those that were sister languages to Latin but not dialects of it.

Etruscan, the language of that people which had the most profound influence upon early Roman civilization, is certainly not IE in the usual sense, though there may be some remote connection, as in the case of Lydian. The tradition of the Lydian origin of the Etruscans (Hdt. 1. 94) may be substantially true. There are about eight thousand Etruscan inscriptions, most of them mere epitaphs, but a few of some length. The force of certain suffixes and the meaning of a few words are known, but the language as a whole still resists interpretation.

Ligurian, along the Gulf of Genoa, is now believed to be IE, intermediate between Italic and Celtic. The linguistic material is very scanty—local and tribal names, together with the "Lepontic" inscriptions, from the region of the North Italian lakes, which probably represent a form of Ligurian.

There are nearly two hundred short Venetic inscriptions from the land of the Veneti at the head of the Adriatic, and about as many Messapian from Calabria. Both are IE, and perhaps belong with Illyrian. A few short inscriptions from the region of Picenum, erroneously called Old Sabellian, are unintelligible and of unknown relations.

Celtic tribes, which poured in from the north and sacked Rome in the early 4th cent. B.C., settled in northern Italy, Gallia Cisalpina. Greek colonies occupied nearly the entire southern portion of Italy, and this "Magna Graecia" remained Greek in speech until late times.

25. The languages that constitute the Italic branch of the IE family fall into two distinct groups, Oscan-Umbrian and Latin-Faliscan.

The Oscan-Umbrian group, so named from its two most important members, includes also the minor dialects of central Italy, as Paelignian, Marrucinian, Vestinian, Volscian, Marsian, Sabine, etc.

Oscan, though the name comes from the Campanian Oscans, was the language of all the Samnites. In one of the *Samnite* wars the Roman consul sent out spies acquainted with the *Oscan* language (Livy 10. 20). The Oscan inscriptions, over two hundred in number, are from Campania, Samnium, northern Apulia, Lucania, Bruttium, and some written by the Campanian Mamertines in Messana. Most of them date between 200 B.C. and the social war in 90–89 B.C.

Umbrian is known mainly from the Iguvinian Tables, seven bronze tablets from the ancient Iguvium. They contain an account of the ceremonies of the Atiedian Brothers, similar in general character to the Roman Acta Arvalium.

Oscan and Umbrian are written partly in the native Oscan and Umbrian alphabets, both derived from the Etruscan, and partly in the ordinary Latin alphabet,[1] a few Oscan inscriptions also in the Greek alphabet.

26. Oscan-Umbrian has much in common with Latin, reflecting a period of common Italic development. The inflectional system is substantially the same in broad outlines and in many details: the same types of declension and conjugation; the merging of ablative and instrumental; extension of the ablative singular in -*d* from the *o*-stems to the other declensions; partial fusion of *i*-stems and consonant-stems (going farther in Latin than in Oscan-Umbrian); use of the interrogative-indefinite pronoun as relative; fusion of aorist and perfect, and of subjunctive and optative; formation of . imperfect indicative and imperfect subjunctive; the gerundive. In phonology, the change of the aspirates to fricatives (also Greek, but later) and especially of *dh* to *f*. In vocabulary, common words for 'say' as L. *dīcō,* Osc. *deicum* (in other IE languages 'point out', and different words for 'say'), or 'law' as L. *lēx*, Osc. *ligud.*

27. There are many striking differences between Oscan-Umbrian and Latin, in general more radical than those between the Greek dialects. Thus, to mention only a few:

Phonology.—*p* and *b* in contrast to L. *qu* and *v* from the labio-velars (**151, 152**), as Osc. *pis* 'quis', Umbr. *benust* 'venerit'; retention of Italic medial *f* in contrast to L. *b* or *d*, as Umbr. *tefe* 'tibi', Osc. m e f i a í 'mediae'.

Inflection.—Nom. pl. of *ā*-stems in -*ās*, of *o*-stems in -*ōs;* infinitive in -*om*, as Osc. *ezum,* Umbr. *erom* 'esse'; different formation of the future and the future perfect, as Umbr. *ferest* 'feret',

---

[1] In quoting Oscan and Umbrian it is customary to distinguish the forms written in the native alphabets and those written in the Latin alphabet by some difference in type, here as Osc. f a k i i a d 'faciat', but *factud* 'facito'. The signs í and ú in Oscan words, as p í d 'quid', p ú d 'quod', transcribe certain differentiated forms of the letters i and u that denote differences in quality. Marks of quantity are not supplied, even where the length of the vowel is beyond question, as in Osc. gen. sg. e i t u a s (cf. L. *pater familiās*), gen. pl. *egmazum* (L. -*ārum*).

benust 'venerit'; an *f*-perfect and others, but none corresponding to the L. *vī*-perfect.

Vocabulary.—*her-* 'velle', *toutā-* 'civitas, populus', *medes-* 'ius', *pŭr-* 'ignis', *ner-* 'vir, princeps'.

Oscan is the most conservative of all the Italic dialects, and is rivaled only by Greek in the retention of the inherited vowel system with the diphthongs intact.

28. Faliscan, the language of the district of Falerii in southeastern Etruria, is known from a number of short inscriptions. It is closely related to Latin.

Latin, though in name the language of Latium, is in reality, as we know it, the language of the city of Rome. There were other local dialects in Latium, of which we have some indications in the case of Praeneste and Lanuvium.

29. The earliest Latin is that of some inscriptions, but this material is very meager, almost insignificant compared to what we have for Greek. The oldest is that on the gold fibula from Praeneste, of about 600 B.C., reading *Manios med fhefhaked Numasioi* 'Manius made me for Numerius'. The forum inscription of about 500 B.C. is so fragmentary that only a few words are certain. The Duenos inscription of the 4th(?) cent. B.C. is a puzzle. There are many short inscriptions of the 3d cent. B.C. The earliest inscription of considerable length, and the most important one for Early Latin, is the Senatus consultum de Bacchanalibus (SC de Bacch.) of 186 B.C.

The literary remains of Early Latin comprise the fragments of Livius Andronicus, Naevius, and Ennius, the prose of the elder Cato, and the comedies of Plautus and Terence.

30. *Expansion of Latin.*—The spread of the Latin language followed, at longer or shorter interval, the advance of the Roman power. It first displaced the local dialects of the rest of Latium and those of the neighboring Sabines, Aequians, Marsians, Volscians, etc., later the Umbrian, Etruscan, Venetic, Celtic, etc., later still the Oscan, and last of all the Greek in the south. By 100 B.C. Italy was mainly of Latin speech, except for the Oscan and Greek in the south. But already before this, Latin had been carried beyond Italy by the Roman conquests—to Spain, southern Gaul, Illyria. In these and the lands later occupied Latin displaced the native languages, except in the East where Greek with its old prestige held its own.

31. *Vulgar Latin.*—The Latin spoken over this vast Romanized territory was not the formal Latin of the classical writers. It was the more colloquial, popular, or vulgar Latin, which shows itself to some extent in Plautus and Terence, and, after being submerged in the classical period, reappears in Petronius, who exhibits it intentionally, and in various writers of the early Christian centuries, who reveal it unintentionally.

Among the more important of these sources are: some of the early Christian Fathers, as Tertullian; the older Latin versions of the Bible, the so-called *Itala*, preceding the vulgate; a veterinary treatise, the *Mulomedicina Chironis;* the *Peregrinatio ad loca sancta* of the Spanish (?) nun Aetheria, written in the late 4th cent. A.D. (or, some think, the 6th); the *Historia Francorum* of Gregory of Tours; various chronicles and documents of the Merovingian period in France.

The authors of these works did not deliberately choose to write in colloquial as contrasted with classical Latin. Gregory of Tours apologized for his ignorance of correct Latin. Even the scribes of the Merovingian formulae, some of them a hopeless jumble for the Latinist, were trying to write as good Latin as they could. There is no document before the emergence of French, Italian, etc., which can be trusted as a full and faithful representation of the current vulgar Latin speech. The latter merely shows through, but that it does unmistakably. Confusion of spelling discloses the changes in pronunciation. The main skeleton of Latin structure remains, but cases are often confused, prepositional phrases encroach on the old genitive and dative, and periphrastic expressions for tenses and moods begin to appear. Changes in the meaning of words, anticipating their modern uses, are conspicuous, such as *mittō* 'throw, put' (cf. Fr. *mettre*, It. *mettere*) *demoror* 'dwell' (cf. Fr. *demeurer*), etc.

In the time of Charlemagne the knowledge of literary Latin was revived, and from this time on the written Latin, though far from classical, is much less instructive for vulgar Latin than that of the preceding period.

32. This Vulgar Latin, from which the Romance languages have sprung, is conveniently so called, to distinguish it from the classical Latin. But it is not to be pictured too precisely, as if it were the Latin of a single social class and the same everywhere. It was, rather, a composite of the speech of all classes, and subject to growing local differences, but always more or less influenced by the literary language.

The fact that the countries were Romanized at widely different periods, so that the Latin first carried to Spain was different from that carried to other regions by the later conquests, or again that the peoples of the different countries were of diverse speech, have been considered by some scholars as the fundamental factors in the differentiation of the Romance languages. In theory they might well be so, but there is little concrete evidence to support this. The assumption of an early development of markedly distinct African Latin, Spanish Latin, etc., has proved largely illusory. It appears rather that, owing to the extensive intercourse between all parts of the empire and the centralizing influence of the Roman organization, the language remained fairly uniform during the first centuries of our era.

It was after the virtual collapse of the Western Empire about A.D. 400, when it was overrun by invaders, when there was no longer any strong centralizing force and knowledge of literary Latin became almost extinct, that the tendencies toward linguistic variation had full sway. Not a few languages at first but a great number of dialects emerged.

33. By new centralizing forces, political and ecclesiastical, larger groups were formed, and within these, from dialects of regions enjoying political or intellectual supremacy, arose the great literary languages—French from the dialect of Paris, Italian from that of Florence, Spanish from that of Castile. In the south of France, Provençal gained the position of a literary language and for centuries resisted the domination of French. In Spain, Catalan resists the domination of (Castilian) Spanish and is reckoned a distinct language. Portugal remained outside the political unification of the rest of Spain, and so developed its own literary and national language. The Rhaeto-Roman dialects in parts of present Switzerland and northeastern Italy are a series of numerous dialects which cannot be reckoned as either French or Italian dialects, and of which some are used locally as written languages, as Romansh, Upper and Lower Engadine, Ladin, Friulian.

Rumanian reflects not so much the short-lived Roman occupation of Dacia as the much longer and more intensive Romanization of Illyria. The Romanized inhabitants were submerged by the invading Slavs and adopted a vast number of Slavic words. Rumanian was not written until the 16th cent. A.D., and then in the Slavic (Cyrillic) alphabet, which was not finally replaced by the Latin alphabet until 1873. In spite of the strong Slavic admixture in the vocabulary, the language is clearly a derivative of Latin, and is of especial interest to the student of vulgar Latin because, in contrast to the western Romance languages, it was completely cut off from influence of the literary Latin until modern times.

Besides the language of present Rumania (called more specifically Daco-Rumanian), a form of Rumanian is spoken by the Vlachs in the northern part of present Greece.

The Latin of the Dalmatian coast also developed into a special dialect, of which a relic survived in the island of Veglio until 1898.

The various forms of Rumanian, the Dalmatian, and the large Latin element in Albanian, together represent the Latin as it developed in the Balkan region.

34. *External influence upon Latin.*—The earliest influence, in language as in civilization, was that of the neighboring Etruscan. The name of Rome is thought by many scholars to be of Etruscan origin, though the evidence is by no means conclusive. An Etruscan medium is probably an important factor in the transmission of the alphabet (**69**), and certainly in the distortion of a number of Greek words, especially proper names (cf. G. Γανυμήδης, Etr. *Catmite*, L. *Catamitus*). L. *persōna* seems to be a derivative, through a denom. *personāre*, of a *persō, -ōnis*, from an Etr. φερσυ which appears written beside a masked figure, this φερσυ being possibly a mutilation of G. πρόσωπον. Etruscan origin is for one or another reason, for example the form of the suffix, probable in the case of a number of Latin words, where with our slight knowledge of the Etruscan vocabulary it is not possible to point to the Etruscan form.

By far the most extensive and persistent influence was the Greek. Many words were borrowed at a very early period by way of commerce or from the Greeks of Magna Graecia, often in a form earlier than that familiar in literary Greek and early enough to take part in certain Latin phonetic changes. Thus G. *ἐλαιϝά (ἐλαία) became *olaivā, olīva (**80**.6), 'Aχαιϝοί Achīvī, τάλαντον talentum (**110**.1), etc. The early loanwords generally reflect the ā of Doric, etc., as māchina from μᾱχανά not Att.-Ion. μηχανή. In the later period literary Latin is full of words borrowed from literary Greek, and the influence extends to syntax and style.

A few Latin words are shown by their forms to be borrowed from some dialect of the Oscan-Umbrian group, as *bōs* 'ox', *popīna* 'cookshop' beside *coquīna* (**155**.6), *rūfus* 'red' beside *ruber* (**140**).

There are several of Celtic origin, notably for various kinds of vehicles, as *carrus, raeda, petorritum, carpentum*, etc. There are some of Germanic origin in late Latin, as *burgus* 'castle'.

SOME GENERAL FEATURES OF
LINGUISTIC HISTORY

35. The history of language is one of change. Every living language is in process of change, imperceptible at a given moment, but conspicuous when one compares different periods. The change may be in the form of words, in their meaning, or in structure.

Changes in form are due mainly to certain regular phonetic processes affecting the speech sounds, but also in part to the analogical influence of other words. To understand the former, it is necessary to have some knowledge of the mechanism of speech and the classification of speech sounds.

MECHANISM OF SPEECH AND CLASSIFICATION
OF SPEECH SOUNDS

36. Speech sounds (hereafter called simply "sounds") are vibrations of air produced by the organs of speech (their genetic aspect) and perceived by the organs of hearing (their acoustic aspect). The production and perception are co-ordinated through the motor and auditory centers in the brain, and it is this combined mental image which is the element of continuity in the history of a sound. For the sound once uttered vanishes. When we speak of the change of a given sound, as of $\bar{a}$ to $\bar{o}$, as if it had an independent life of its own, we are merely employing a convenient figure of speech.

It is the genetic aspect that is the main basis of the classification of sounds and will be considered in the following.

The number of distinct sounds that can be produced by the organs of speech is infinite, and those actually employed in language would run to many hundreds. But in any one language there is only a limited number, usually between the limits of thirty and sixty. These are the pattern sounds or "phonemes" of the particular language.

37. The lungs, controlled by the chest and abdominal muscles, act like bellows and furnish the stream of air. This passes up through the windpipe to the chamber at the top, the larynx, in which are situated the vocal cords, and hence to the mouth and nose, which act as resonance chambers of variable shape.

The vocal cords are not like violin strings, but are the edges of two folds of membrane, more like the edges of flaps of rubber. They may be drawn together and made tense by muscular action, so that they are set in vibration. In breathing they are left open, and in the production of some sounds they are equally inactive, while in others they vibrate. According as there is or is not vibration of the vocal cords, sounds are classified as "voiced" ("sonant") or "voiceless" ("breathed", "surd"). The vowels are voiced, and so usually the liquids and nasals. The stops and fricatives (cf. below), including the sibilants, occur in pairs, voiceless (also with stronger aspiration) and voiced (also with weaker aspiration), as English *p:b, t:d, f:v, s:z*, etc. The vibration can be felt by putting one's finger on the "Adam's apple", or more clearly through the skull when the ears are covered tight by the hands. Contrast the *s* of *sin* with the *z* of *zero*, each pronounced by itself without following vowel.

The vocal cords are also subject to alterations in length and tensity, with consequent variation in the frequency of vibrations. These constitute differences in pitch (tone, intonation), which in our own current speech (as distinguished from song) are observed mainly in sentence modulation, as in the rising tone of interrogation, but in some languages as ancient Greek and Sanskrit are the dominant elements of word-accent.

Apart from the action of the vocal cords, the distinguishing characteristics of our sounds are the result of overtones produced in the resonance chambers of the mouth or nose. Of these two the less important and the simpler is the nose. This functions only in the nasal sounds produced when the nasal passage is left open. If the stream of air is cut off in the mouth and issues only through the nose we have nasal stops like *m* or *n*. If the air issues through both nose and mouth we have nasal vowels as in French. The nose is a rigid chamber, not subject to alteration in shape, and the difference between the various nasal sounds is caused by different mouth positions.

In distinction from the nasals, all other sounds are "oral". The nasal passage, open in breathing, is cut off by raising the velum or soft palate, and the mouth alone acts as the resonance chamber. Owing to the mobility of the jaws, lips, and especially the tongue, the chamber of the mouth may assume a great variety of shapes, resulting in as many different sounds.

Of the consonants some are formed with complete closure, by which the stream of air is wholly blocked, followed by a sudden release of the breath, as, for example, *p* with closure of the lips. These are called "stops" ("explosives", "mutes"). The nasal consonants are stops, so far as concerns the passage of the breath through the mouth (the closure is the same for *m* as for *p*), but the flow of breath through the nose is continuous.

The release may be followed by an added puff of breath, as in *uphill*. Then we have aspirated stops (aspirates). Our English initial stops in words like *pen* are distinctly aspirated by comparison with the French.

Others are formed with close approximation (not complete closure) and resulting friction, as *f* with friction between the lower lip and upper teeth. These are called "fricatives" ("spirants").

The distinctions so far made, as stop, fricative, nasal, voiceless, or voiced, may be conveniently called "orders", as contrasted with the "series" (or "classes") depending upon the position where the closure or friction takes place.

Between lips and throat there is a continuous range of possible points of contact. A rough division of this into three main areas and the recognition of three series, labial, dental, and guttural (palatal), is the general basis of classification, and sufficient for some languages. But labials include bilabials, as *p*, *b*, *m*, and labiodentals, as *f*, *v*. The dental stops, *t*, *d*, differ considerably in different languages, as the French, which are pure dentals, from the English in which the tongue touches the gums back of the teeth; and sometimes there are two distinct series in the same language, as in Sanskrit. The area back of the dental is the most extensive, and "guttural", used here as the general term, covers the greatest diversity. There is some difference between the gutturals of English *card* and *kin*, much more between those of German *kann* and *Kind* or *doch* and *ich*, and frequently one must recognize two distinct guttural series, a front ("palatal", "praepalatal") and back ("velar").

The series as represented in English are then:

Labials.—The bilabial stops, voiceless *p*, voiced *b;* the labiodental fricatives, voiceless *f*, voiced *v;* the nasal *m*.

Dentals.—The stops, voiceless *t*, voiced *d;* the (interdental) fricatives, written *th*, voiceless in *thin*, voiced in *then;* the nasal *n*.

Gutturals.—The stops, voiceless *k*, *c* (as in *cat*), voiced *g* (as in *get*); the guttural nasal [ŋ],[1] as in *ink* [iŋk],[1] *finger* [fiŋgə(r)], *ring* [riŋ]. There is no guttural fricative, of which German *ch* is an example.

The "sibilants" form a special class of fricatives and are so named from their acoustic character, rather than from the manner of production. In the voiceless *s* of *sin* and the voiced *z* of *zero* (often written *s* as in *rose*) the tongue forms a narrow channel through which the breath is projected onto the teeth, with a resulting hissing sound. In the voiceless [š] of *shake*, *sure* and the voiced [ž] of *azure*, the channel is broader and the stream of air more spread out.

The "liquids", as the term is now applied (it has no precise descriptive value), are *l* and *r*. The *l* is produced by touching the tip of the tongue to the palate, leaving openings at the sides through which the breath passes. For the *r* the sides of the tongue form the contact, leaving a channel down the middle through which the breath passes over the tip of the tongue. But in both there are several variable factors, and there is the greatest variety among the *l*- and *r*-sounds of different languages.

The vowels are produced without closure or friction. Their differences depend upon the various shapes of the resonance chamber caused by the position of the lips and tongue. The lips may be rounded or unrounded. The tongue may be raised high in the front of the mouth or in the back, or it may lie flat; its position may be intermediate. Hence vowels are distinguished as rounded or unrounded, and by extremes as front or back and as close (high) and open (low). Thus the *u* of *pull* is a close (high) back rounded vowel, while the *i* of *pit* is a close (high) front unrounded vowel. The French *u* and the German *ü* are front rounded vowels. Open and close are relative terms and one speaks of an open or close *o* or an open or close *e*.

---

[1] Here and in the following square brackets are sometimes used to enclose phonetic transcriptions (in accordance with a current practice), but the brackets are omitted where there seems to be no danger of ambiguity.

The symbols are mostly those of the International Phonetic Association, now widely employed. But [y], not [j], for the *y* of *yet;* [ü], not [y], for the Fr. *u;* [š] and [ž] for the sibilants of *ship, azure;* the macron for length of vowels.

The semivowels, *w* of *wet* and *y* of *yet*, are produced with virtually the same position as the vowels *u* and *i*, but with a rapid glide to the following vowel, so that they have the function of consonants.

The *h* is merely a strong breathing. There is no independent mouth position, which is that of the coming vowel.

38. A classification of the Greek and Latin sounds is given here for further illustration of the preceding. More detailed

	CONSONANTS				
	Bilabial	Labiodental	Dental	Guttural	
Stops	π *p* β *b* φ (*ph*)		τ *t* δ *d* θ (*th*)	κ *k, c, qu* γ *g* χ (*ch*)	voiceless voiced voiceless aspirate
Nasals	μ *m*		ν *n*	γ *n* (+gutt. stop)	voiced
Fricative		(late φ) *f*	(late θ)	(late χ)	voiceless
Sibilants			σ *s* (late ς) *z*		voiceless voiced
Liquids			λ *l* ρ *r*		voiced voiced
Semivowels	(ϝ) *u*-cons.			*i*-cons.	voiced

Breathing ᶜ *h*

Compound consonants ψ = *ps*   ζ = *zd*   ξ = *ks*   x = *ks*

	VOWELS				
	Back Rounded	Back Unrounded	Front Rounded	Front Unrounded	

Close (high)	ου *ū*
	     u
	 ο *ō*
			ῠ (Att.) (*y*)	ῐ *ī*
				     i
				 ε, ει *ē*	

Open (low)	ω *o*	ᾰ ᾱ		η *e*	

Diphthongs

αι, (early ει), οι   αυ, ευ, (early ου)   ᾳ, ῃ, ῳ
ae, au, oe   (ei, eu, ui rare)

statements regarding Greek and Latin pronunciation will be made in various parts of the phonology, for example, on the qualitative difference between long and short vowels in **96, 97.**

VARIETIES OF PHONETIC CHANGE

39. According to the relation between the earlier and later sound, without regard to any special conditions governing the change, the following types of phonetic change may be noted:

VOWELS

1. Change in quantity. Lengthening and shortening of vowels.
2. Changes in quality, as

    Rounding, as $\bar{a} > \bar{o}$ in NE *home* from OE *hām*, *a* to open *o* [ɔ] in NE *all*, *water*, $a > u$ in L. *occupō*.

    Unrounding, as $u > [\Lambda]$ in NE *but* (in contrast to *pull*).

    Fronting, as Fr. *u* in *lune* from L. *lūna*, or Att. *v*. If fronting is followed by unrounding the result is *i*, as in the modern pronunciation of G. *v*.

    Raising (low to high, or open to close), as $\bar{o} > [\bar{u}]$ and $\bar{e} > [\bar{\imath}]$ in NE *doom*, *meet;* (raising and fronting) $\bar{a} > [\bar{e}]$ in NE *name*, G. $\bar{a} >$ Att.-Ion. *η*, L. $a > e$, *i* in *acceptus*, *accipiō*.

    Lowering (high to low, or close to open), as $e > [a]$ (before *r*) in *heart* (cf. NHG *Herz*), *parson* (from L. *persōna*), G. dial. $\pi a \tau \acute{a} \rho a = \pi a \tau \acute{e} \rho a$.

3. Change of diphthongs to monophthongs, as in L. *oinos* > *ūnus*, *deicō* > *dīcō*, Gmc. **ainas* (cf. Goth. *ains*) > OE *ān* 'one'.
4. Change of monophthongs to diphthongs, as OE *ī*, *ū* > [ai], [au] in NE *mine*, *mouse*.

CONSONANTS

5. Change in series, as in NE *laugh* (cf. NHG *lachen*), Osc. *pod* = L. *quod*, Rum. *lapte* from L. *lacte*.
6. Change in order, as $b > p$ in L. *scrīptus* (*scrībō*), $p > m$ in L. *somnus* (from **swepnos*), $p > b > v$ in Fr. *rive* (from L. *rīpa*). The Germanic shift of stops ("Grimm's Law") consists of changes in order within the same series, as $p > f$, $bh > b$, $b > p$, $t > [\theta]$, $dh > d$, $d > t$, etc. (**133**).
7. Change in order and series, as in Italic $dh > th > [\theta] > f$ (**129.**$_3$). $s > z > r$ ("rhotacism", **166**).
8. Among other consonant changes are $l > r$ or $r > l$ (mostly dissimilation, **40.**$_9$).

    $s > h$, as in G. ἑπτά:L. *septem* (**161**).

    $y > h$, as in G. ἧπαρ:L. *iecur* (**177**).

    $gh > h$, as in L. *vehō*:G. ὄχος (**148**).

The change of any consonant to *h* is really its loss (that is, the elimination of its distinctive articulation) with merely its breath impulse remaining. This too may be lost, as the *h* from original intervocalic *s* in Greek (**165**) and eventually the initial *h* (**168**).

40. According to various special conditions under which the change takes place the following types are important:

VOWELS

1. Vowel quantity affected by following consonants, as in Latin lengthening before *ns*, etc. (**99**), shortening before *nt*, etc. (**100**), or in English lengthening before *ld* (OE *ald* > *āld* > NE *old*).
2. Vowel quality affected by following or preceding consonants, as L. *e* > *i* before *n*+guttural (**79.**1), *o* > *u* before *nc*, *mb*, etc. (**82.**1), *e* > *o* after *sw* (**80.**2), NE *a* > [ɔ] before *ll*, etc., or.after *w* (*call, water*).
3. *Anaptyxis.*—This term (ἀνάπτυξις 'unfolding') is commonly applied to the evolution of a vowel out of certain consonant groups, mostly such as contain a liquid or nasal, as in L. **pōclom* > *pōcolom, pōculum* (**107**), Osc. *aragetud* from **argentōd*, NE *Henry* in three syllables, as often in Shakespeare.
4. Syncope, that is, total loss of a vowel, in unstressed syllables, as in L. *dexter, caldus, nec* (**108**). When it is a final vowel that is lost, this is also called "apocope".
5. Weakening of vowels in unstressed syllables, as in L. *adigō, comprimō* (**110**), or in the unstressed syllables of NE *human, purpose* [ə], *added, honest, image* [lax *i*].
6. Assimilation of vowels in adjacent syllables, as in L. *nihil* from **ne-hil* (**79.**2). The German "umlaut" in *Mann*, pl. *Männer; Gott*, pl. *Götter; Fuchs*, pl. *Füchse*, is partial assimilation, namely fronting before the front vowel of the next syllable. So in NE *man*, pl. *men; goose*, pl. *geese; mouse*, pl. *mice* (OE *mūs*, pl. *mȳs*), where the vowel of the second syllable, to which that of the first was partially assimilated, was later lost.

   a. The Greek "epenthesis" in βαίνω from **βανιω, χαίρω from **χαριω (**188**) is somewhat similar, but here it is only the consonantal ι that has this effect on the preceding vowel.

CONSONANTS

7. Consonant affected by following vowel, as G. τ > σ before ι (**141**). So the "palatalization" of a guttural before a front vowel, often with its further development to [tš], [š] or [ts], [s], as in It. *cento*, Fr. *cent*, etc., from L. *centum*, or in NE *chin cheese* (cf. NHG *Kinn, Käse*).

8. Assimilation of consonants
   1) Of contiguous consonants
      a) Assimilation of the first to the second, best described as "anticipatory", but commonly called "regressive" (because the action is regressive, that of the second upon the first).
      L. *scrībtos (scrībō) > scrīptus (assim. in order only, "partial") > It. scritto (in series also, "complete").
      IE *swepnos > L. somnus ("partial") > It. sonno "complete").
      b) Assimilation of the second to the first, commonly called "progressive" (because the action is progressive). G. *ἀλι̯os > ἄλλos, L. *ferse > ferre, *velse > velle.
   2) Of non-contiguous consonants
      a) Regressive: IE *peṇqʷe (Skt. pañca) > L. *quenque, quīnque.
      IE *peqʷō (Skt. pac-) > L. *quequō, coquō.
      OFr. cercher (whence NE search) > Fr. chercher.
      b) Progressive: Skt. *çasin- (cf. NHG Hase) > çaçin.
9. Dissimilation of consonants, mostly of non-contiguous consonants, especially liquids.
      a) Regressive, change (or sometimes loss) of former. Dissim. of aspirates in G. τίθημι, etc. (132).
      L. quīnque > vulg. L. cinque (Fr. cinq, etc.).
      G. *ἀλγαλέος (ἄλγος) > ἀργαλέος.
      L. peregrīnus > late pelegrīnus (cf. NE pilgrim).
      G. φρᾱτρίᾱ > dial. φᾱτρίᾱ (loss).
      b) Progressive, change (or sometimes loss) of latter. G. κεφαλαλγίᾱ (ἄλγος) > later κεφαλαργίᾱ. L. *Flōrāria (from *Flōsāsia) > Flōrālia. ME marbre (Fr. marbre from L. marmor) > NE marble. G. ϝρήτρᾱ > dial. ϝρήτᾱ (loss).
10. Transposition of consonants
   1) Of contiguous consonants
      G. (*τι-τκ-ω redupl. pres. like γί-γν-ομαι) > τίκτω. L. *vepsā > vespa, like OE wæps > NE wasp. OE āscian and ācsian, NE ask and dial. ax.
      Cf. the transposition of liquid and vowel. OE þridda > NE third, L. formāticum > Fr. fromage, G. προτί > dial. πορτί.
   2) Of non-contiguous consonants
      G. *σπεκτομαι (cf. L. speciō) > σκέπτομαι, late L. parabola > Sp. palabra.
11. Development of new consonant out of certain groups. G. *ἀνρός > ἀνδρός, *ἀ-μροτος > ἄμβροτος (201.1). L. *ēmtos (emō) > ēmptus, *sūmsī (sūmō) > sūmpsī (195). L. camera (with syncope) > Fr. chambre (NE chamber), OE þunor, gen. þunres > NE thunder, vulg. L. essere (with syncope) > OFr. estre (Fr. être).

12. Loss of consonant in group. G. *γεγράφσθαι > γεγράφθαι, *διδάκσκω > διδάσκω, L. quīnctus > quīntus, *torctos (torqueō) > tortus. NE castle, hasten, with t lost in pronunciation.

13. Haplology, loss of one of two successive similar syllables. G. ἀμφιφορεύς (Hom.) > ἀμφορεύς, L. *sēmi-modius > sēmodius, late L. īdōlolatria (from G. εἰδωλο-λατρεία) > idolatria, G. τετράδραχμον > τέτραχμον.

14. Changes in external combination ("sentence combination", "sandhi"). Many changes are conditioned by the relation of a word to the rest of the sentence. The same word may show differences of form according as it is emphatic or unemphatic or according to the preceding or following word. Thus OE ān 'one' (the numeral), when unemphatic and used for the indefinite article, became an and this again gives the "sentence doublets" NE an and a according as the next word begins with a vowel or consonant. Here belong such matters as elision, crasis, and the change of final consonant in combination with the initial of the following word. There is much of all this in colloquial speech, only a small part of which is commonly represented in the writing. Cf. the pronunciation of this year, don't you with the same consonant changes that are observed in the interior of a word in mission, nature; or the pronunciation of and as [n̠] in bread and butter; or the French "liaison", as vous [vu] but vous [vuz] avez.

    a. There is a great difference in the degree to which such changes are noted in the written language. In classical Sanskrit they were brought to a rigid system which must have been highly artificial. In the Celtic languages certain mutations of consonants are regularly observed, as W. *pen* 'head' interchanging, according to the preceding word, with *ben*, *phen* (pronounced *fen*) and *mhen*. But in general such changes are most frequently indicated in the older and cruder writings, and in the gradual standardization of a written language the tendency has been to disregard such variations in the form of a word and establish a single spelling. This process may be observed in detail in comparing Greek inscriptions of different periods (cf. **214**.6).

PHONETIC LAWS. SCOPE, REGULARITY, AND
CAUSES OF PHONETIC CHANGE

41. *Scope.*—Phonetic laws are not to be understood as laws of universal validity like certain physical laws. There are no such laws applicable to all languages or even to all periods of the same language, though of course many changes do recur in different languages and periods. The phonetic laws are merely empirical formulae of observed regularity in a given language or dialect at a given period. Even with this limitation they differ in scope, some being generic and others conditioned.

Generic changes are the sweeping changes not subject to more special conditions, like that of OE $\bar{a}$ to $\bar{o}$ in NE *home, bone, stone*, etc., or of G. $\bar{a}$ to Ion. η.

Conditioned changes are those subject to special conditions of surrounding sounds, position (as initial, medial, final), accent, etc., like those surveyed in **40** and many others.

42. *Regularity.*—The phonetic changes, whether generic or conditioned (but always within the same language or dialect and period), show a remarkable regularity, far greater than can be observed in any other phase of linguistic development or anywhere else in the domain of humanistic studies. This is evident from the mere fact that the great majority of phonetic changes need not be given for a particular word only, but can be stated in formulae that cover whole masses of words. The progression of stops in Germanic ("Grimm's Law") is only an especially conspicuous and large-scale example of the "laws", named after their discoverers or more often nameless, that are observed in the historical study of all languages.

The famous postulate of the "invariability of the phonetic laws", that is, that the phonetic laws as such under like conditions are without exceptions, is now less fervidly discussed than in the years following its first assertion (by Leskien in 1876). The factors involved in "like conditions" are more complicated than was once realized. Nevertheless, this postulate may still be maintained as essentially true, and in any case has served its purpose as a protest against the assumption of casual, mere chance, exceptions, and as a working hypothesis guiding procedure. Great progress has been made, and continues, in the explanation of apparent irregularities. Many such still remain unexplained, and in this book in many instances it has been thought preferable merely to state the apparently conflicting facts rather than to repeat complicated and doubtful explanations. But this is not to doubt that there should be some explanation.

43. *Cause of phonetic change.*—Why does a sound change at all and why does it change in one direction rather than in another? As is so often the case in other branches of science, what seems to the layman the simplest question, one to which a prompt and precise answer is expected, may be the most difficult. There is in fact no generally accepted single cause of phonetic change. There are various theories, various alleged causes, of which one or another may be regarded by certain scholars as the dominant one, but no one of which is an adequate, compelling cause.

The geographical theory, influence of climate.—This is an old and popular view, but without scientific support. The same phonetic changes that have been attributed, with some plausibility in an individual case, to a warm or cold climate or to a mountainous or flat country, respectively, are observed to occur also under the opposite conditions. Furthermore, countless phonetic changes have occurred where there was no change of geographical conditions.

The ethnographic or substratum theory.—Certain changes have been attributed to the retention of native speech habits after a people has adopted a new language, as in the case of the adoption of Latin by the Celtic-speaking Gauls. This is plausible in theory, but there is scarcely a bit of concrete evidence for such direct influence that is generally accepted. Some more indirect effect upon the adopted language, from the inherited temperament of the people adopting it, may be assumed. But the influence of national temperament upon language, while one feels that there must be such influence, is something too vague to be definitely proved. Many of the suggestions along this line are romantic and fantastic, as when certain changes are attributed to a certain people's love of liberty (why not all changes and among all peoples?). Whatever kernel of truth there may be in the substratum theory, its scope is certainly exaggerated by those who make it the primary factor in phonetic change. Countless changes have occurred in periods of a language when no racial mixture could be involved.

There are various theories connected with the acquisition of language by children. But there is no substantial evidence that the permanent phonetic changes originate with children.

The ease theory, economy of effort.—This is the most seductive theory, since it contains an element of truth that is open to everyone's observation. Many of the conditioned changes, such as the assimilation of consonants, are plainly in the direction of easier co-ordination, a less abrupt shift of articulation. But even here it is no compelling cause. L. *octō* gives It. *otto*, but the *ct* was pronounced without difficulty by the Romans for hundreds of years and has not been assimilated in the other Romance languages (though undergoing various other changes, as in Fr. *huit*, Sp. *ocho*, Rum. *opt*), and in G. ὀκτώ (now ὀχτώ) the guttural has remained unassimilated for thousands of years. For the generic changes, which move in every direction and sometimes through a complete cycle (cf. NHG *Vater*, with change of original $t > þ > ð > d > t$), there is no tangible ground for assuming easier articulation.

WRITING AND ITS RELATION TO SPEECH

44. Writing has its ultimate origin in art, in the crude pictures which sprang from the impulse to artistic expression in prehistoric man. The use of pictures to convey messages or record events was adventitious, and picture writing arose independently in different parts of the earth. It was extensively employed by the American Indians and was understood by those of different tribes, being quite independent of the spoken language.

For in pure picture writing the picture stands for an object or idea, and not the word for it in any particular language. So long as this relation holds, whether or not the pictorial form remains obvious, it is an ideogram. But the sign may come to be felt as representing the·familiar word for the idea, and the ideogram becomes a phonogram. Thus a crude picture of the sun in the heavens will convey the same idea, no matter whether one's own word for it is *sun*, *sōl*, ἥλιος, or what not. It may be conventionalized and lose all resemblance to the object, and still remain an ideogram for the sun. When it comes to be felt as representing the group of sounds making up the word for it in a given language, namely, if we take the English word for illustration, [sʌn], it is now a phonogram. But as a pure phonogram for [sʌn] it is ambiguous, as it may represent *sun* or *son*. To determine which, one must combine with the phonogram a determinative or classifier, for example a "heavenly body" determinative for *sun* or a "human being" determinative for *son*. Such a combination of phonograms and determinatives is characteristic of Egyptian hieroglyphics, Assyrian cuneiform, and Chinese writing.

The evolution of the phonogram from the ideogram is the most significant step in the history of writing, the one which first brings writing into relation to speech. The syllabary and alphabet are successive simplifications of the phonogram (but the imaginary illustration of a phonogram chosen above, [sʌn], would be already adapted to a syllabary system). The simplified syllabaries like the Cyprian with signs for the single consonant plus vowel, and eventually the alphabets, developed mostly according to the acrophonic principle, as if the phonogram for [sʌn] became the sign for [sʌ] and then for [s].

The distinction between ideogram and phonogram, syllabary or alphabet, must not be confused with that of the external form of the writing, namely pictorial or linear (in which the pictorial origin is no longer obvious). The Egyptian hieroglyphics continued pictorial in form, but certain of the pictures constituted an alphabet of 24 letters, which was employed as early as 3000 B.C. Conversely Assyrian and Chinese writing are linear in form, but not alphabetic.

The classification from two points of view may be illustrated by the table.

	Pictorial	Linear
Ideogram	*Egyptian Mexican*	*Assyrian Chinese*
Phonogram.......		
Syllabary		*Old Persian Sanskrit Cyprian*
Alphabet.........		*Phoenician, Greek, etc.*

45. The ideal alphabet for a given language is one in which there are as many letters as there are distinctive sounds (phonemes) in that language—one letter for each sound, one sound for each letter. But this is far from the actual situation. In the adaptation of an alphabet it usually happens that some letter serves for two or more similar sounds and conversely some letters are used superfluously. Furthermore, when changes in pronunciation take place, the spelling may or may not be changed accordingly. When the spelling remains unchanged, regardless of change in sound, this is known as "historical spelling". If there were only uniform generic changes of sound, this would merely result in new but equally fixed values for the letters. But the actual result is usually different new values for some of the letters.

Greek spelling has remained substantially historical down to the present day. In Latin some of the early changes in sound were reflected in the spelling (as *oe* to *ū*, *ei* to *ī*), but after this the spelling remained almost fixed. English spelling rests on an early mixture of Old English and French spelling, followed by various orthographical reforms inconsistently applied, with many letters not pronounced, some of these once pronounced in English (as the *k* in *knight*, the *l* in *calm*), some etymologically correct but never pronounced in English (as the *b* in *debt*), some not even etymologically justified (as the *s* in *island*), all together resulting in the most unphonetic and irregular spelling conceivable. So far is it from the ideal of alphabetic writing that we have, for example, some ten different spellings, six of them common, for the sound [ī] (*me, fee, sea, field, conceive, machine; key, quay, people, Caesar*), and some five different sounds for the letter *a* (*man, was, name, father, sofa*). Among the modern European languages French is only second to English in unphonetic spelling, while German, Italian, and Spanish have a relatively phonetic spelling.

46. *Spelling pronunciation.*—The normal relation between spelling and pronunciation is of course that spelling is intended to represent the pronunciation and should conform to it. But as the written form of a language becomes standardized and is felt as authoritative, its influence may be such that the spelling reacts on the pronunciation, resulting in what is known as "spelling pronunciation". Thus ME *langage* came to be spelled *language* with the etymologically correct *u* and is now pronounced accordingly. ME *parfit* came to be spelled etymologically *per-fect* and is now so pronounced. The present pronunciation of *servant, merchant,* etc., and the American pronunciation of *clerk, Derby* in contrast to the British is spelling pronunciation, counteracting the early change of *er* to *ar* which once prevailed in *servant, merchant,* etc.

There is a great deal of such spelling pronunciation in English and in other modern languages. The influence of the written language, with its wide diffusion since the invention of printing, is of course much greater than in ancient times. Yet even then there may well have been cases of spelling pronunciation, especially in the much school-mastered Latin, and certain facts are perhaps best explained by this assumption (**198***b*, **212.3***a*).

ANALOGY

47. Analogy, the influence exerted by mental associations, is one of the potent factors in language. It affects the form of words, their meaning (semantic analogy), construction (syntactical analogy), and the creation of new words. It is considered here in its effect on the form of words. Forms that are for any reason commonly associated in the mind are subject to analogical influence. The association may be one of function or of meaning, and under the latter head it may be due to identity or similarity of meaning, or to contrasted meaning, since opposites are also naturally associated in the mind, or to the fact that words belong to similar semantic groups. Sometimes a partial agreement in form may lead to a fanciful association, a popular etymology, which may further affect the form. Or the relation of certain dialect or sentence doublets may be imitated in other words. The association is the fundamental factor, and any classification of types, like the following, is merely one of convenience. The term "leveling," since differences are thus leveled out, is often applied, especially to the first two of the following types.

48. 1. *Functional analogy, or external grammatical analogy.*—Analogy between forms of corresponding function, as like cases, tenses, etc. The child or illiterate, who knows nothing of case or tense by name, feels the same association between forms used in like situations, and is inclined to say *see'd,* *teached, hitted* conforming to the familiar type. So *knowed, blowed* for *knew, blew,* while the similar *snowed* for earlier *snew* has long since been established, as *swelled, slept* for older *swoll, slep.* Or conversely after the analogy of the inherited *drive, drove,* etc., we have now *strive, strove* for earlier *strived,* and frequently *dive, dove* instead of *dived.* The old gen. sg. ending of *o*-stems, as OE *dæges* 'day's', was extended by analogy to all declensions; likewise the nom. pl. ending *-s,* which did not belong originally to neuters like OE *word,* nom. pl. *word* (cf. L. *verbum, verba*), but is now the general sign of the plural. In Greek and Latin *o*-stems the pronominal ending *-oi* was extended to nouns, which originally had *-ōs* (**240.**1). L. gen. pl. *-ōrum* is formed after the analogy of *-ārum* (**240.**2); acc. sg. *-im* mostly replaced by *-em* after the analogy of consonant stems (**260.**4). G. Σωκράτης, acc. Σωκράτη, but also Σωκράτην after the analogy of Θουκιδίδης, Θουκιδίδην, etc., of the first declension. Vulg. L. *essere* after the analogy of *legere,* etc. The history of Greek and Latin inflection is full of such examples of functional analogy.

2. *Internal grammatical analogy.*—Analogy between different inflectional forms of the same word. Thus *roofs, hoofs* have their *f* after the analogy of the singular, in contrast to the inherited relation in *wife, wives, shelf, shelves;* similarly *deaths, births* [-θs] in contrast to *paths, mouths* [-ðz]. The past tense *swore* was once pronounced like *sore* (cf. *sword* as pronounced), but the *w* was restored by the analogy of *swear.* The past tense of *sing* was once sg. *sang,* pl. *sung,* then one form or the other was generalized; cf. NHG *war, waren,* with extension of *r* from plural to singular, in contrast to NE *was, were.* L. *honōs* was replaced by *honor,* with *r* after *honōris,* etc. (**255**). G. ἕπεται instead of *ἕϝεται after ἕπομαι (**154.**1). Numerous other examples will appear in the discussion of inflection.

A similar association exists between derivatives of the same root, where the relationship is obvious, and especially between compounds and the words of which they are composed, the latter often resulting in what is known as "recomposition." Cf. the occasional pronunciation of *forehead* like *fore* and *head* instead of the normal [fɔrəd]. For Latin prepositional compounds the normal vowel weakening of the root syllable and the consonant assimilation are both frequently counteracted by the influence of the simple verb or the separate prefix, respectively, as *conlocō* in place of a normal phonetic *collicō* (cf. **111, 189**).

3. *Congeneric analogy.*—The association between words of the same semantic group, such as numerals, words of relationship, of color, etc., may effect analogical change. Skt. *patis* 'lord, master' (G. πόσις) when used as 'husband' has gen. sg. *patyur* with *-ur* from gen. sg. *pitur, mātur,* etc., of the inherited group with suffix *-ter-.* Hom. υἱάσι has α after πατράσι, etc. G. dial. ὀκτώ with ʿ or ὀπτώ with π, after ἑπτά. Late L. *October* after *September, November, December.* The pronunciation of NE *February* with omission of

the first *r*, though starting as dissimilatory loss (**40**.9), owes its much greater frequency than the corresponding loss in *library* to the support of *January*.

4. *Analogy between words of contrasted meaning.*—Late L. *sinexter* for *sinister*, after *dexter*. Vulg. L. *grevis* (whence OFr. *gref*, ME, NE *grief*) for *gravis*, after *levis*. NE *female* for *femell* (ME, OFr. *femelle*), after *male*. Cf. the analogical creations like **G.** ἐμποδών 'in one's way' after ἐκποδών (ἐκ ποδῶν) 'out of the way', ἀνδράποδα 'captives, slaves' after τετράποδα 'quadrupeds' (the two constituting the booty in men and beasts).

5. *Blending, also known as contamination, or as telescoping of words.*— Many blends may be observed as unconscious momentary lapses, as *remaindants* (*REMAINDer+remnANTS*), and many more are deliberately created for picturesque effect, as *whirlicane* (*whirlwind, hurricane*), *insinuendo* (*insinuate, innuendo*), *happenstance* (*happening, circumstance*), *Popocrats* (once very familiar for an actual fusion of Populists and Democrats; in France the Jacobins came to be called *Jacoquins* after *coquin* 'rascal'). But any such blend may lose its ephemeral character and become a generally accepted form. Blending occurs also in inflection, as L. *iocineris* (**iecinis, iecoris*, **251**), and in syntax.

6. *Popular etymology.*—Some resemblance in form may suggest a relationship, resulting in a further assimilation in form. OE *utemest* (*ut-em-est*, with double superlative ending; cf. L. *-imus*, G. *-ιστος*) gives NE *utmost*, as if formed from *most*. OE *brӯd-guma* lit. 'brideman' (*guma* cognate with L. *homō;* cf. also NHG *Bräutigam*) gives NE *bridegroom*, as if formed from *groom*. In *sovereign* from ME, OFr. *souverain*, late L. *superānus*, the spelling is from *reign*. *Sparrow grass* for *asparagus* was once in common use.

7. *Analogical extension of sentence or dialect doublets.*—In the speech of southern England and New England, where *r* has been lost before a consonant and when final, unless followed by a word beginning with a vowel, there are natural sentence doublets like *fear* [fīə] but *fear* [fīʳr] *of it*. Hence by analogy *idea* but *idea-r of it*. Similarly in colloquial French, after the analogy of doublets like *vous* [vu] but *vous* [vuz] *aussi*, also *moi* but *moi-z aussi*. So in Greek the *ν*-movable spread from some inherited doublets to certain categories of forms (**215**).

Those whose vernacular pronunciation of *new, duty* is [nū], [dūti] but who have learned to substitute the standard [nyū], [dyūti], may on occasion extend the substitution to words like *noon, do*. In German dialects where *ü* is pronounced [i], the familiar substitution of [ü] in speaking the standard language is often wrongly extended, e.g. in *trieb* just as in *trüb*. Such "overcorrection" is the principle of the "hyper-Doric" or "hyper-Aeolic" forms that sometimes occur in late specimens of the Greek dialects. The equivalence of *ā* to Att.-Ion. *η* was so widespread that *ā* was sometimes substituted where the proper Doric or Aeolic form was also *η*, as in ᾱμισυς, ἔφᾱβος for ἥμισυς, ἔφηβος.

SEMANTICS

49. Change in meaning is known as "semantic change" (G. σημαντικός, from σημαίνω 'signify'), and the study of meanings as "semantics" (analogous to *physics*, etc.; the more cumbersome *semasiology*, adj. *semasiological* are also used).

The meaning of a word may remain stable for thousands of years, as has been the case with the words represented by NE *father, mother, son, daughter, sun, night*, the numerals, and many others. But much more frequently there is some change, and the change may move in any direction and to any extent, so that without the intermediate stages we should sometimes be at a loss to discover any relation between the earliest-known and latest meaning.

The associations underlying semantic change are too complex to admit of any rigid classification with a pigeonhole for every change. Many a change may be viewed from more than one angle. In a sense every word has its individual semantic history. But understood as selected points of view and by no means exhaustive, there are certain types which it is helpful to observe.

50. The two most general types of semantic change, both from the point of view of scope, are generalization or extension of meaning, and specialization or restriction of meaning.

1. *Generalization.*—Late L. *molīna* 'machine for grinding, gristmill' (cf. *molō* 'grind') is the source of OE *myln*, NE *mill* now generalized in *sawmill*, *steel mill*, etc. OE *ber-ern* lit. 'barley-place', but actually 'storehouse for any farm produce', hence NE *barn*, now even *car barn*. Skt. *go-pa-* lit. 'cowherd' but actually '-herd, protector'. So G. βου-κόλος 'cowherd', but βουκολέω used also with reference to goats or horses, hence even ἱππο-βουκόλος 'horse-herd'.

Words of such broad general meanings as 'do, make', 'go', 'thing', 'very', etc., show generalization from more specific notions. Thus:

'Do, make': L. *faciō*, also OE *dōn*, NE *do*, from IE **dhē,-* 'place, put' in G. τίθημι Skt. *dhā-*, etc. G. πράττω, πρήσσω, in Homer often 'pass through' (cf. πέρα 'beyond'), hence 'get through, accomplish, do'. G. ποιέω in Homer mostly 'construct, build', denom. of **ποι-ϝο-*, from IE **qʷei-* in Skt. *ci-* 'arrange in order, construct', ChSl. *činŭ* 'arrangement, order', *činiti* 'arrange', whence also 'do' in Boh., Pol., etc. Mod.G. κάνω, replacing the above as the common word for 'do, make' from G. κάμνω 'toil, work' (cf. Hom. κάμε 'wrought').

'Go': NE *went*, orig. past of *wend*, cf. NHG *wenden* 'turn'. G. ἔρπω 'creep, move slowly' (cf. L. *serpō*), is in some dialects simply 'go'. L. *ambulō* 'walk' is used colloquially for 'go' in Plautus and so commonly in late Latin, whence Fr. *aller*. Rum. *merge*, the regular word for 'go', is from L. *mergō* 'dip, sink', the stages being 'sink, disappear, go away, go'.

'Thing': G. χρῆμα orig. 'what is needed' (cf. χρή 'it needs'). L. *rēs* orig. 'property', like Skt. *rās* 'goods, riches'. This was displaced in vulgar Latin by *causa* 'cause, lawsuit, subject of dispute', whence finally any 'matter' or 'thing', as It., Sp. *cosa*, Fr. *chose* (or in Rumanian by *lucru* from L. *lucrum* 'gain'). Similarly OE *þing* 'judicial assembly' and 'thing', NE *thing*.

'Very': L. *valdē* lit. 'strongly' from *validus* 'strong'. Fr. *très* from L. *trāns* 'across, beyond' (cf. NE *through, thoroughly*, NHG *durchaus*). NE *very*, orig. adj. 'true' from OFr. *verai* (Fr. *vrai*), from an extension of L. *vērus* 'true'. NHG *sehr*, cognate with NE *sore* (cf. *sore afraid*).

2. *Specialization.*—NE *deer* orig. any 'animal', like NHG *Tier*. NE *hound* orig. any 'dog', like NHG *Hund*, L. *canis*, etc. G. πρόβατα in Homer and elsewhere 'domestic quadrupeds', in Attic only 'sheep'. L. *pecora* 'domestic quadrupeds', It. *pecora* 'sheep'.

L. *emō* orig. 'take, obtain' (hence *dēmō* 'take away', etc.), but specialized to 'obtain in trade, buy'. Similarly It. *comprare* 'buy', Fr. *acheter* 'buy', NE *purchase*, all from 'get, obtain'. Conversely G. ἀποδίδωμι in aor. mid. 'sell', and NE *sell* orig. 'give, offer' (cf. OE *sealde his ancennedan sunu* 'gave his only begotten son').

L. *carō* orig. 'a cut (cf. κείρω 'cut, shear'), portion' (cf. Umbr. m e s t r u k a r u 'maior pars'), specialized to 'portion of flesh', then simply 'flesh, meat'. NE *meat* orig. 'food' (so Goth. *mats*, OE, ME *mete*, and so *meat and drink* in NT).

NE *sermon* from L. *sermō* 'discourse' as specialized in church writings. L. *ōrō, ōrāre* orig. 'speak', then 'plead' and mostly 'beseech, pray'.

L. *speciēs* 'look, appearance', hence 'form, kind', in late Latin used frequently of the prepared forms of natural products, hence 'goods, wares' especially 'spices, drugs', hence with different further specializations Fr. *épice* 'spice', NE *spice*, Fr. *épicier* 'grocer', It. *spezeria* 'drug store'.

3. Many words show highly specialized uses in certain contexts or situations. A stone is one thing to a builder, another to a jeweler. *Play* differs according as one is thinking of a child, a game, the stage, or a machine. So L. *māteria* is naturally in certain situations 'building material, timber', but was not completely specialized like Sp. *madera* 'wood'. These occasional specializations are not on a par with those in which the specialized use has become the dominant one, but they show how the latter started.

4. The history of a given word may show successively a specialization and generalization from a new center. NE *starve* orig. 'die' (cf. NHG *sterben*) specialized (already in OE) to 'die of hunger', then extended to 'suffer from hunger' and figuratively even 'be in urgent need', so that in *starving for sympathy* neither 'death' nor 'hunger' is involved.

51. There are many other semantic changes which, while they may also involve extension or restriction or both in succession, may be considered from a different point of view than that of scope, as more specific types of shift within certain groups of ideas or in certain directions. They include figurative uses similar to those known by the old stylistic terms "metaphor", "metonymy", etc. But the term "faded metaphors" is misleading if it implies that they originated in conscious rhetorical or poetical creation. They are rather the natural result of unconscious association and are common to speech everywhere. The poet's metaphor is merely a further step along the same line, in being fresh and striking, in contrast to such transfers as are commonplace and belong to normal everyday speech, like "mouth of a river".

There is no end to the number of groups that one might abstract from the complex relations of ideas, but the following kinds of transfer or interchange may be noted:

1. *Extension owing to similarity of form or relation to other parts*, as in *foot* of a mountain, *mouth* or *arms* of a river, is common everywhere.

2. *Interchange of application to space or time* is usual in words for 'long', 'short', 'before', 'after', etc. But one or the other application may be preferred or become dominant. L. *brevis* 'short' in space or time, but from it NE *brief*, as adj. now mostly of time. L. *ante* 'before' of place or time, but more commonly of time, while in *prae*, *prō* the local use prevails or others derived from it.

Prepositions originally denoting relations of place or time may develop all sorts of secondary uses, which sometimes prevail over the earlier. L. *ante* remains 'before' of place or time, while *prō* is mostly, 'in behalf of', 'in place of', etc. Conversely G. πρό remains 'before' in place or time, while ἀντί is mostly 'in place of, instead' ('before, in front of' in some early inscriptions). L. *ob* orig. local 'in front of', etc. (Osc. ú p , *op* 'at' or like L. *apud*), but mostly 'because of, for the sake of'. 'Concerning' is expressed by prepositions meaning 'from' (the point of view), as L. *dē;* 'about' as L. *circum*, G. περί (so OPers. *pariy*), also ἀμφί in Hom. and in Cretan, NE *about;* 'over', as G. ὑπέρ, L. *super*.

3. *Interchange of application to size, quantity, or number, mainly between the last two.*—Note the varying distribution in the following:

	Size 'large'	Quantity 'much'	Number 'many'	Size 'small'	Quantity 'little'	Number 'few'
G........	μέγας	πολύς	πολλοί	μικρός	ὀλίγος	ὀλίγοι
L........	magnus	multus	multī	parvus		paucī
It........	grande	molto	molti	piccolo	poco	
Fr........	grand	beaucoup		petit	peu	

In these examples quantity and number go together as against size, except in the case of L. *parvus* 'little' in size or quantity, but *paucī* 'few'. But in vulgar Latin *parvus* was displaced by *poucus* for quantity and by other words for size.

4. *Extension or transfer from subjective to objective, or conversely.*—L. *tristis* 'sad' of persons, but also of things that make one 'sad'. NE *pitiful* orig. only of persons full of pity, now only of things that excite pity ("pitifull sight"). L. *sēcūrus* orig. only of persons 'without care', then also of things that are 'secure, safe'. G. δύσκολος 'hard to satisfy, difficult' of persons only, but in the NT δύσκολόν ἐστι 'it is difficult'.

Conversely OE *fǣr* 'danger' (as NHG *Gefahr*), but now *fear*. L. *poena* 'punishment' is the source of NE *pain*, L. *mercēs* 'reward' of NE *mercy*.

5. *Interchange owing to similarity of condition or result, or to some natural sequence.*—Growing things are green, and 'green' and 'unripe' so commonly coincide that we may say "blackberries are red when they are green". Only a person could be literally *dis-mantled,* now used of a fortress. L. *dīlapidō* lit. 'scatter stones', but actually 'destroy, waste', whence NE *dilapidate* (use affected by wrong idea of its history). What 'seems good' or 'is pleasing' is given approval, hence the technical terms for voting approval, G. ἔδοξε (δοκεῖ 'seems good'), in dialects also ἔαδε (ἀνδάνω 'please'), L. *placuit* (*placeō* 'please'). 'Lack' of anything leads to notions of 'necessity', or 'wish'. NE *want* orig. a noun 'lack', then verb *it wants* (*lacks*), *he wants* (=*lacks*) *food, he wants* (=*wishes*) *food, he wants* (=*wishes*) *to do it*. G. χρηΐζω 'lack, need', also 'desire', in some dialects=θέλω 'wish'. Osc. f a k i i a d   k a s i t 'faciat oportet', where k a s i t in form=L. *caret* 'is without, lacks'. L. *fallit* 'tricks, deceives', then 'escapes notice', and in later development 'fails, lacks' (cf. NE *fail*) and Fr. *il faut* 'it is necessary, must'.

6. *Material and product.*—L. *penna* 'feather' was used (late) for a 'quill pen' in contrast to the *calamus* 'reed pen', hence NE *pen* as an instrument of writing of whatever material (similarly NHG *Feder* 'pen', wholly isolated

in feeling from *Feder* 'feather'). One name of the papyrus plant is the source of G. βίβλος 'book', another of the general European word for 'paper'. NE *box* is from L. *buxum* 'boxwood'. G. ἀργυρίς orig. 'silver cup', but simply 'cup' in πίνειν ἐξ ἀργυρίδων χρυσῶν. It. *campana* 'bell' goes back to 'Campanian bronze' (cf. *aes Campānum, vāsa Campāna*).

In such cases there is a complete shift of meaning from material to a special instrument or product, so that the word persists after the use of the original material has become obsolete, and there is nothing incongruous in speaking of a 'gold pen', a 'tin box', or 'paper' made of pulpwood. Conversely in some cases the name of a material is derived from an early use which later becomes insignificant, as NE *rubber* from *rub* (*rubber* was an eraser), or *graphite* from G. γράφω 'write', but now more important as a lubricant.

7. *Extension or transfer from one to another sense perception.*—This is the linguistic side of what the psychologists call "synaesthesia". The IE word represented by NE *sweet* (Skt. *svādus*, etc.) was doubtless applied primarily to taste, but also commonly to smell and hearing ('sweet smell', 'sweet voice'), while G. ἡδύς, L. *suāvis* were still further extended to 'pleasant', and in the literal sense mostly replaced by γλυκύς, *dulcis*, these too being extended in use. L. *clārus* 'clear' orig. of hearing (*vōx clāra;* cf. *clāmō*, G. καλέω 'call'), but as commonly of sight (*nox clāra*). A shift of application from hearing to sight is seen in OHG *hel* used only of sound 'clear, loud', but NHG *hell* used nearly always of sight 'clear, bright'. Note the extensions involved in NE *loud colors, warm colors, sharp taste*, etc.

A given sense perception and its stimulus, what is perceived, may or may not be expressed by the same or related words. NE *I taste, smell,* and *it tastes, smells,* a person's sense of *taste, smell* and an apple's *taste, smell*. But the second, objective use prevails in L. *sapiō, sapor* 'taste' (subjective *gustō, gustātus*) and G. ὄζω, ὀσμή, L. *oleō, odor,* 'smell', though the subjective ὀσφραίνομαι, *olfaciō* are related. A similar relation between 'hearing' and 'what is heard' appears in G. κλύω, Skt. *çru-* 'hear' and G. κλέος, Skt. *çravas* 'fame', Slav. *slovo* 'word', L. *clueō* 'be heard, be spoken of'.

8. *Extension or transfer from physical to mental.*—G. φόβος 'flight' in Hom., later 'fear'. G. τρέω 'flee' and 'fear', L. *terror* 'fear' from the same root **ters-* **tres-*, also in Skt. *tras-* 'tremble' and related to **trem-* in L. *tremō* 'tremble'. L. *horror* 'shaking, horror' from 'bristle up', this meaning appearing in the verb *horreō* and the cognate Skt. *hṛṣ-*, the latter developing otherwise, through 'be excited' to 'be glad'. G. θυμός 'spirit, anger', etc., with complete transfer from the physical ebullition of its cognates L. *fūmus*, Skt. *dhūmas* 'smoke'. NE *glad*, orig. 'bright' or 'smooth' (cf. NHG *glatt*, L. *glaber* 'smooth').

'Understand' is expressed by G. ἐπίσταμαι lit. 'stand on' somewhat like NE *understand*, NHG *verstehen*, NG καταλαβαίνω from G. καταλαμβάνω 'seize upon', It. *capire* from L. *capiō* 'take', Fr. *comprendre* from L. *comprehendō* 'lay hold of, grasp', etc., just as NE *grasp* is also so used, but without loss of its literal sense.

Latin words that are only occasionally used without transferred meaning may retain only the latter in their derivatives, as in NE *eager, suggest, abject, dejected, afflicted* from L. *ācer, suggestus, abiectus, dēiectus, adflictus.* Similar uses, but without loss of the literal sense, in NE *keen, put before* (or *put up to*), *cast down.*

9–10. *Degeneration or ennobling of meaning: pejorative or meliorative development.*—Use of words *in malam partem* or *in bonam partem*, in a bad or good sense. All this has to do with the important matter of the emotional value of words. A word like NE *old* may be used as an opprobrious epithet or one of affection, according to the tone and circumstances. NE *temper* may be good or bad, only the latter in "he shows temper". NE *deserts*, what one deserves, may be rewards or punishments, only the latter in "he gets his deserts".

But often the meaning becomes settled in one direction or the other. So NE *retribution* now only in an unfavorable sense, though Benjamin Franklin once sold something "for a reasonable retribution". G. τῑμή mostly 'reward, honor', sometimes 'penalty', but from the same root ποινή 'penalty' rarely 'reward', while the formally equivalent Slav. *cěna* is only 'reward'. G. ταπεινός lit. 'low-lying' is 'low, mean, base' in the classical period, but acquires a favorable sense 'lowly, humble' in the NT and church writings.

Some examples of a striking shift in one direction or the other are given under the separate heads.

Pejorative.—NE *knave* orig. 'boy, servant', as NHG *Knabe; villain* orig. 'belonging to one's country estate' (L. *villa*); *hussy* from OE *hūswīf* 'housewife'; *stink* from OE *stincan* 'have a smell' good or bad; *silly* from OE *sælig* 'fortunate, happy' (cf. NHG *selig* 'happy, blessed'). It. *cattivo* 'bad', Fr. *chétif* 'vile', NE *caitiff*, from L. *captīvus* 'captive'. G. ἰδιώτης 'private person' becomes an 'ignorant person', L. *idiōta*, whence NE *idiot.*

Meliorative.—NE *knight* orig. 'servant', as NHG *Knecht*, then 'king's servant, retainer.' NE *nice* once 'foolish, stupid' from OFr. *nice*, L. *nescius* 'ignorant'. It. *vezzoso* 'charming' from L. *vitiōsus* 'faulty, vicious'. Rum. *învaţ* 'accustom, teach' from vulg. L. *invitiāre* 'accustom to a fault' (*vitium*). L. *caballus* 'packhorse, nag' rises in the scale, supplanting *equus*, and is the source of all the Romance words for 'horse', Fr. *cheval*, etc., and the derivative words like *chivalry.*

52. *Some special causes or factors in semantic change.*—The great majority of semantic changes arise from natural associations inherent in the relation of the ideas, regardless of any outward circumstance. But there are also some special factors to be noted.

1. A certain association may be natural to a particular social or occupational class, and this special class meaning become the generally accepted one.

In church circles G. ἐκκλησία 'assembly' was an assembly of the faithful, the 'church' as a body (only so in NT), later as the building, Fr. *église*, etc. G. πρεσβύτερος 'older' became the *priest*. L. *sermō* 'discourse' was a religious discourse, *sermon*, *praedicāre* 'proclaim' became 'preach', and *persōna* 'person' became in English the *parson*.

In military circles L. *arma* 'fittings' became (defensive) 'arms', *classis* 'class' was an 'army' or usually a 'fleet'. G. τάξις 'arranging' became 'battle array' or 'body of soldiers', in late times also a 'military expedition', whence NG ταξίδι 'journey'.

In legal terminology G. δίκη 'usage, right' (as in Hom.; orig. 'direction, way', from δείκνῡμι 'point out') became 'lawsuit, trial'. L. *causa* 'cause' became 'lawsuit' and its subject, whence later, emerging from its legal application, any 'matter, thing', It. *cosa*, Fr. *chose*, etc. (similarly NE *thing*; cf. **50**.1).

In commercial circles 'take, obtain' became 'buy' in L. *emō*, etc., and 'give' became 'sell' in NE *sell*, etc. (cf. **50**.2).

Among hunters the favorite 'wild animal' of the chase was the *deer*, and the 'dog' was of course a hunting dog, *hound* (cf. **51**.2).

From L. *minor, -ārī* 'threaten' arose vulg. L. *mināre* a technical farmer's term for 'drive cattle' (so still Rum. *mîna*), and through this Fr. *mener* 'lead'.

2. The association may start from the verbal context. So in the familiar cases of ellipsis like (*via*) *strāta* 'street', (*ōrātiō*) *prō(r)sa* 'prose', (*sōl*)*oriēns* 'orient', etc. Words added to a negative for emphasis may absorb the negative force so as to be used alone in the same way, as Fr. *pas, point, plus, rien* from *ne pas*, etc., or NG τίποτε 'nothing', ποτέ 'never'.

The radical changes often observed in the meaning of prepositions started in certain phrases where the transition was easy. So that in NE *with* formerly 'against' (cf. NHG *wieder*) then replacing the older *mid* (cf. NHG *mit*), probably started in phrases like *fight with*.

3. Cultural changes may underlie the semantic changes. The history of words goes hand in hand with the history of things, with the changing conditions of material and intellectual life. This is most apparent in cases like *pen* or *paper*, or in the vicissitudes of the Roman *dēnārius* orig. a silver coin of ten asses (*dēnī*), but fluctuating at different periods between a gold coin and a 'copper'. *Oil* (from L. *oleum*) was originally olive oil, among the Greeks and Romans an important article of food, also used for cleansing the body (predecessor of the modern soap), also used in lamps. This last use became

the most widespread, while at the present time its use as fuel or lubricant dwarfs all others in magnitude.

4. *Semantic borrowing: translation words.*—Besides the borrowing of words from another language, there is frequently the borrowing of meaning. In such cases one speaks of semantic borrowing in contrast to the borrowing of the actual words, or of translation words in contrast to loanwords. In Latin there are hundreds of loanwords from Greek. But there are also many cases in which not the word itself but a certain meaning was borrowed, transferred to the Latin word which corresponded in its literal sense. That is the Romans expressed certain notions by literal translations of the Greek. Such was their whole grammatical terminology. For 'case' the Greek grammarians used πτῶσις 'fall' (thought of as 'fall, deflection' from the nominative), which the Roman grammarians accordingly rendered by *cāsus* 'fall'. For the physical 'world' the Greek philosophers introduced the term κόσμος from the 'orderly arrangement' of the heavens. But in later times κόσμος meant 'adornment', and the Romans familiar with this use rendered κόσμος 'world' by *mundus* 'adornment' (cf. adj.: *mundus* 'neat, elegant').

As Greek influenced Latin, so Latin, which was for centuries the literary language of western Europe, influenced the other European languages as they came into literary use. In the Romance languages and in English for the most part the Latin words were adopted. (The Romance languages are full of loanwords from Latin, that is, words borrowed from the literary language in contrast to those that were inherited through the spoken language. Such loanwords are distinguishable because they do not show the phonetic and semantic changes which the inherited words have undergone. Contrast the Fr. *frêle*, NE *frail* with Fr., NE *fragile*, from L. *fragilis*, but the second a late borrowing from literary Latin.) But in German frequently not the word but a meaning was borrowed. As L. *nāvis* 'ship' was used also for the 'nave' of a church, so NHG *Schiff*. L. *expressiō* in its secondary sense 'expression' was rendered by the literally corresponding *Ausdruck*, similarly *conscientia* 'conscience' by *Gewissen*.

Fr. *beau-père*, orig. a term of polite address, then 'father-in-law' (also 'stepfather'), is the model of Dutch *schoonvader* 'father-in-law'. Fr. *arrière pensée*, lit. 'back-thought', but used for 'mental reservation', is imitated in NHG *Hintergedanken*.

The examples given are of semantic borrowing through literary influence. But the same thing happens in the speech of bilinguals, as among German Americans who say *ich gleiche es* after English *I like it*, since *gleich* and *like* so generally correspond.

5. The fondness for picturesque expression, for something fresher or more vigorous than the commonplace usages of the language, is an important factor. It shows itself in colloquial speech and runs riot in its extreme form,

the slang of the day. The expressions may be of only ephemeral vogue without permanent effect. But any widespread colloquial use may in time become the accepted one.

L. *testa* 'potsherd', easily applied to the 'skull', was the colloquial vulgar Latin word for 'head' (cf. *bean* in current slang), mostly displacing *caput* in its literal sense, hence It. *testa*, Fr. *tête* 'head'.

L. *fābulor* was the colloquial equivalent of *loquor* as early as Plautus, and in vulgar Latin displaced the latter (hence Sp. *hablar*), itself partly displaced later by a derivative of late L. *parabola* 'word', this from G. παραβολή 'parable' and 'saying' (hence It. *parlare*, Fr. *parler*). G. λαλῶ 'chatter, prattle' is simply 'speak' in the NT.

L. *mandūcō* 'chew' was commonly used for 'eat' in vulgar Latin, hence It. *mangiare*, Fr. *manger* 'eat'.

G. τρώγω 'gnaw, nibble, feed on', used mostly of animals but also of men, had become the regular word for 'eat' for the author of John (who puts it in the mouth of Jesus, John 13. 18), as it is in Modern Greek.

STRUCTURE

53. The greatest differences in structure appear when one compares languages of totally different families. One speaks of "isolating" languages like Chinese, in which there is no formal grammar, no formal distinction of parts of speech, of cases or tenses, the relation of words being expressed by the order. Or of "agglutinative" languages like Turkish, in which there is a complex structure, a wealth of formative elements but so loosely put together that the joints are apparent (as if NE *un-truth-ful-ly* were representative). But the types of structure are so various that no simple classification will cover them.

The IE languages are classed as "inflectional". The term is not truly descriptive of the difference between them and those called "agglutinative". For just as there is agglutination in the IE languages (**56**), so conversely there is plenty of inflection in Turkish (or Finnish, with fifteen case forms). The difference lies rather in the greater fusion of stem and formative elements in the so-called inflectional languages, and the term "fusional", that has been suggested, would be more appropriate.

54. While the IE family as a whole and historically belongs to a single structural type, yet even here very considerable changes of structure have taken place in the course of time, and between the structure of Sanskrit, Greek, or Latin and that of present English there is as great a gulf as between languages of unrelated families. There has been a general trend, notably in most of the modern European languages, from the highly inflectional to a more analytic structure. The number of formal categories has been reduced, and their place taken by prepositional phrases, auxiliary verbs, or word order.

Of the three IE genders, the neuter has been lost in the Romance languages (likewise in Lithuanian), the feminine in Danish (except in a pronoun). In English almost the sole relic of formal gender distinction is the singular of the pronoun *he, she, it,* where it is virtually one of natural gender, and the old grammatical gender of nouns and adjectives has wholly disappeared.

Of the three IE numbers, the dual was lost in Latin (and Italic) in prehistoric times, in Greek before the time of the NT. In the earliest Celtic and Germanic it is confined to a few forms and later disappeared. It survives today only in Lithuanian and two minor Slavic languages.

The eight IE cases were reduced to seven in Balto-Slavic, six in Latin, five in Greek, four in early Germanic, and (for the noun) two in present English, only one in most of the Romance languages. In present English the adjectives have no distinction of gender, number, or case.

Of the voices, the old middle and passive have been largely replaced by periphrastic expressions.

Of the moods, the subjunctive and optative were merged in Latin, the subjunctive was lost in classical Sanskrit, the optative in late Greek. In Germanic the subjunctive and optative were merged, as in Latin, and of this subjunctive there is very little left in present spoken English.

In contrast to the six or seven tenses of Greek and Latin, there are only two simple tenses, present and past, in English and the other Germanic languages, all the others being periphrastic. In the Romance languages there is a greater number, but of these the future and conditional are of periphrastic origin.

In English the loss of inflection has gone so far that there is little left of formal distinctions between the parts of speech. Hence the high degree of convertibility, as noun used as verb or conversely, noun as adjective, adjective as adverb, etc. The sentence "her eyes like angels watch them still" has been quoted as one in which all but two of the words might be used in the function of two or more parts of speech; and of the two apparent exceptions, *angels* has been actually used in print as a verb (like *mothers*), and *them* may be an adjective pronoun in illiterate speech.

55. *Evolution of structure: origin of the formative elements.*— It was once held that there was a regular sequence of structural development, from isolating to agglutinative, from this to inflectional, and from this, by what was thought of as a process of decay, to the analytical. Language was represented as being built up through thousands of years to the perfected type of Greek and Latin, only to degenerate subsequently from that high mark. But there are various difficulties with this old view, and the matter is certainly not so simple.

The last step, that from inflectional to more analytical, is one of observed fact in European languages (**54**), only one must reject the implication that this is a retrograde movement. For, while the intrinsic merit of different types of structure is always a delicate question, only with difficulty freed from prejudice in favor of the type of one's own native language, there is much more to be said for the thesis that the modern development is on the whole one of continued progress. It seems, for example, to be a positive gain to eliminate grammatical gender and the wealth of different case forms after these have been rendered superfluous by the use of prepositions which express the relations more exactly.

The stock example of an isolating language, Chinese, is anything but a primitive language, if viewed as a vehicle of thought; and again there is some evidence that its type of structure is not original, but the result of development from a more formal type, just as is the relatively simple type of present English which in many respects resembles that of Chinese. Conversely many languages of primitive peoples show an astonishing complexity of structure and would far outshine Greek or Latin if this were a measure of merit. This fact and the modern European tendency toward a more analytical type have led some scholars to reverse the old sequence, maintaining that there has been a continuous movement from complex to simple structure and that man's earliest speech was of complex structure. This is far too strong a generalization in the other direction. Among languages of primitive peoples there are some of the most complex, but others of the simplest structure, so that as a whole they prove nothing. There is still no good reason to reject the natural hypothesis that primitive speech was of a simple isolating structure, only superficially resembling the modern analytic type, the one reflecting primitive fragmentary thinking, the other the developed analytic thinking.

56. *Agglutination*, or the union of once independent words, was once regarded as the only possible source of the formative elements. Not only this, but the attempt was made to apply this theory in detail to the IE formative elements, to derive the case-endings, personal endings, tense signs, etc., from actual words. This attempt has long since, for the most part, been given up as futile. For these endings, suffixes, etc., had already become simple formative elements in the IE period, and their generation belongs to a period much more remote, so that whatever connection there might be with independent words had long since ceased to be in evidence. Only for a very few of the suffixes that go back to the parent speech is connection with independent words reasonably clear. All this is nothing against the theory of agglutination, only against the too optimistic and speculative application.

For agglutination is a process that is undeniably attested in the historical period. So characteristic a suffix as the NE adverbial *-ly*, originally and still in part also adjectival, goes back to a word *līc* 'body, form', as in OE *eorþ-līc*, a possessive compound meaning 'having the form of the earth', hence *earthly*. The suffixes of NE *wis-dom, child-hood, friend-ship, up-ward* go back to the use in compounds of OE *dōm* 'judgment, authority, rank', *hād* 'rank, condition', *-scipe* from *scieppan* 'create, fashion', *-weard* from *weorþan*, 'become' orig. 'turn'; while in NE *truth-ful, three-fold, fear-less*, the origin is still obvious. The Romance adverbial suffix, It. *-mente*, Fr. *-ment*, goes back to L. abl. sg. *mente*, as It. *veramente*, Fr. *vraiment* from L. *vērā mente*. The Romance future and conditional rest on vulgar Latin periphrastic combinations of the infinitive with forms of *habeō*, as fut. It. *canterò*, Fr. *chanterai* from *cantāre habeō*.

57. So agglutination is an actually attested source of formative elements, and there is no good reason to doubt that it was an important source in prehistoric times. But it was an error to regard it as the only possible source. For it can be shown that formative elements may have become such in quite other and more accidental ways, by what is known as "adaptation". In NE *ox, oxen* the *-en* is a sign of the plural, just as much as the usual *-s*, and one that is very productive in NHG plurals (*Knaben, Taten*, etc.). But it is in origin nothing but a part of the word stem which was formerly present in the singular also. That is, of the OE nom. sg. *oxa*, gen. sg. *oxan*, etc., nom. acc. pl. *oxan*, gen. pl. *oxna*, etc., the *oxa* became *ox* and the other singular forms disappeared, leaving only *oxen* in the plural, so that by contrast it has all the value of a plural sign. The NHG *-er* in *Kinder, Bücher*, etc. (both types combined in NE *children*), is of similar origin, being a form of the old *es*-stems. It is just as if L. *genus, genera* were to lose their final syllables, leaving *gen, gener*.

Adaptation is an important factor in the history of suffixes, in the productivity of certain types. From some particular word a suffix may acquire a certain association and become productive with a new force. The inchoative force of L. verbs in *-scō* (which is not prominent in the corresponding type elsewhere) may have started from *crēscō* 'grow'. Of the numerous G. derivatives in *-ιᾱ* some happened to denote an ailment as ὀφθαλμίᾱ 'disease of the eyes', ναυτίᾱ 'seasickness'. From these were formed denominatives as ὀφθαλμιάω, ναυτιάω, and the association of *-ιάω* with ailment became so strong that there followed ὀδοντιάω, λαρυγγιάω, λιθιάω 'suffer from toothache, sore throat, or gallstones' and many others.

THE INDIVIDUAL LÁNGUAGE[1]

58. *Language and dialect.*—These are not absolute, but relative, terms as commonly employed. They do not represent rigidly definable degrees of speech variation, as if we could say that if two forms of speech differ by so much they must be distinct languages, but if by only so much they must be only distinct dia-

---

[1] The preceding sections, 35–57, deal with questions of language as an institution; the following, 58–63, with matters concerning languages as linguistic units. The French have a neat distinction between *le langage* 'language' and *la langue* 'the language'.

lects. Certain German "dialects" are much farther apart than the Danish and Swedish "languages".

We generally use the term "language" of a literary and national language, and "dialect" of a form of speech that is subordinate from a cultural point of view. Dutch is linguistically co-ordinate with the Low German dialects of northern Germany. It is only by reason of certain historical factors that the former gained the status of a literary and national language, while the latter are subordinate to the High German language. We speak of Oscan and Umbrian as Italic dialects, though linguistically they are co-ordinate with Latin, and in fact the Romans themselves spoke of the *lingua Osca*. We speak of the Greek dialects, but in the older period all Greek speech was divided into dialects. For that time "the Greek language" is only an abstraction, or a composite. (In fields where there are no literary languages, like that of the American Indian languages, the terms "language" and "dialect" are used with more reference to larger or smaller differentiation. But even here no rigid definition is possible.)

The term dialect is also an elastic term in scope. It may refer to the speech of a considerable area, or that of a single town, or even that of a certain social stratum. We speak of the New England dialect or that of Boston; or for ancient Greece of the Ionic dialect, of the (Ionic) Euboean dialect, or the (Euboean) Eretrian dialect.

In any detailed study of dialects one finds that the different peculiarities rarely cover precisely the same territory. The "isoglossal lines" marking their respective areas overlap. But a certain combination of peculiarities is characteristic of a given region and constitutes a well-marked dialect.

59. *Differentiation of languages.*—Language is in constant process of change, and there is a natural tendency to even individual variation. This centrifugal tendency is held in check by the centripetal force of social contact.

When one language breaks up into two or more, this is due to some disturbance of that social contact which makes for unity. Such disturbance may come about in two ways.

There may be abrupt and complete severance by migration. Migration is not in itself a cause of linguistic change, in fact the language of the migrating people may prove more conservative than that of the people remaining at home, as in the case of Icelandic compared with Norwegian. But after the separation the changes, for changes are bound to occur in language, proceed independently on each side, resulting in gradually increasing divergence. In modern times, with the unifying influence of an established literary language, the printing press, and ease of communication, migration may lead to only minor differentiation without disrupting the general unity of the language. But this does not apply to earlier periods.

Many cases of language differentiation are the result of known migrations in the historical period, as the colonization of Iceland from Norway or that of Britain by the Anglo-Saxons from the Continent. Many more are the result of migrations that must have just as certainly occurred in prehistoric times. Migration explains both the differentiation and the resemblance, and migration in turn is a safe inference from a close relationship between geographically separated languages or dialects. Thus, in the case of the Greek dialects, the peculiar features common to Arcadian and the distant Cyprian are so striking as to leave no doubt that Cyprus was colonized from a part of the Peloponnesus where the dialect at that time was that which survived in the historical Arcadian (19).

Migration has doubtless been the principal factor in language differentiation, and there is no objection in principle to representing language relationships by pedigree schemes analogous to genealogical tables. But the relations are often too complex to be represented adequately in such a way, and many of the once popular schemes have been discarded as too elaborate and arbitrary.

But language differentiation may also come about without the abrupt severance, by gradual disintegration of a language spread over too large a territory to hold together in the absence or loss of a strong centralizing force. Changes start from one point or another, each spreading over adjacent teritory, so that there are countless local varieties of speech with differences that are slight between adjacent points, great between extremes. By geographical, political, and social factors new centers of influence gather about them larger groups, between which there is greater differentiation in speech, and eventually well-defined dialects or languages arise. It is thus that vulgar Latin broke up after the collapse of the Roman Empire and the loss of the centralizing force of Roman and literary Latin (32)—not as if it had been first divided neatly into Italian, French, etc., and then each of these into Italian dialects, French dialects, etc.

60. *The evolution of a standard literary language.*—This is the culmination of the centralizing process. Just as minor local dialects yield to that of an important center, which becomes the norm for a certain district, so of these larger units some one dialect becomes the basis of a standard literary language for a whole country or people. This is not due to any intrinsic merit of this dialect as such, any superiority over other dialects from the linguistic point of view, but solely to external circumstances, usually the political or intellectual supremacy of its center. The speech of Rome absorbed the minor dialects of the rest of Latium and spread hand in hand with the advance of the Roman power. Among the many dialects of France, the speech of Paris, the political and intellectual center, gained a dominant position at an early period and by the 13th cent. was firmly established as the literary language (and to some extent even an international language), though it was resisted for some centuries in the south. So the English literary language is based on the speech of the upper classes in London of Chaucer's time, the Italian on that of Florence in Dante's time, etc. Not that every local peculiarity of these centers was necessarily adopted or maintained, for in a sense they were also centers of compromise. But their regional dialects formed the main basis.

In the case of Greek and of German the evolution of a unified literary language was slow and complex compared to that of Latin or French. For both Greece and Germany remained decentralized linguistically as well as politically until a late period in their respective histories. In Greece the dialect of Athens, owing to its intellectual supremacy, became the standard of literary prose and finally overcame the long-continued linguistic diversity (**18–20**). In Germany it was not till the early 16th cent. that a literary standard, in the official documents of the Saxon and imperial courts, was popularized by Luther, and even after that it was slow in winning general acceptance.

61. *The linguistic results of mixture of population.*—When a country is conquered or partly occupied by a people of different speech from that of the native population, the two languages for a time exist side by side. But ultimately, in most cases, there results a single language, which, while it may contain a greater or less degree of mixture, is quite definitely the survival of one or the other. Either the language of the conquerors prevails over the native language or conversely. The two opposite results are determined by complex factors, not by numbers only.

The language of the native population prevails over that of the conquerors. This has happened time after time in the historical period. The Franks who conquered the Romanized Gauls and gave their name to the country of France lost their Germanic speech and adopted the Romance speech of their subjects, which henceforth came to be called French. The Normans of Normandy lost their Norse speech within a few generations and adopted French. This the Norman conquerors of England carried with them and kept for some centuries while in close contact with Normandy, but eventually gave up in favor of the native English. For the language which emerged from the conflict, though showing a heavy admixture of French in vocabulary, was, in its main line of descent, English in fact as in name. The Swedish founders of the Russian state, the Asiatic Bulgars who gave their name to the Slavic Bulgaria, the Manchu conquerors of China, all adopted the language of the native population. In all these cases the conquerors formed only a minority of the population, and moreover either from the outset had lost contact with their kinsmen or eventually became primarily identified in their interest with their new home.

The language of the conquerors prevails over that of the native population. The most notable example is the spread of Latin in the Roman Empire, as in Gaul at the expense of the native Celtic. Here the country was filled with Roman officials, soldiers, and tradesmen, and large colonies of veterans were established. Although the Romans were a minority in actual numbers, they remained a part of the great Roman organization, with all the prestige of the Roman name and the Latin language, which the Gauls themselves were ambitious to share. The case of the Anglo-Saxon invaders of England is very different in circumstance, for they were not backed by a powerful state organization or by an established literary language. But they came in hordes and in successive waves, and, driving back the Celts or enslaving some, they solidified their position over a gradually increasing territory—much as did the English long after in North America in relation to the Indians.

The spread of the IE languages involves a similar imposition of the language of invaders upon the earlier native population of India, Greece, Italy, etc. The circumstances are all veiled in obscurity. But obviously the situation could have had no resemblance to that of the Roman domination in western Europe. For these IE-speaking invaders were not part of an organized state nor did they have a written language. They cannot have been merely small bands of warriors, or, according to all analogies in history, they would have been absorbed linguistically. However much of physical and mental superiority we ascribe to them, we must also assume that they came in considerable numbers with their families, a people on the march, and gradually solidified their position as did the Anglo-Saxons in England.

62. *Language and race.*—Between language and race, as a distinct physical type, there is no necessary connection. "The Latin races", an absurdity to the anthropologist, is only a popular phrase for the peoples (not races) speaking languages of Latin descent. Linguistic and racial classifications cut right across each other, and much confusion has resulted in the past from the use of a term like Celtic now of a linguistic, now of a racial group. Often a people adopts the language of another, as in the cases mentioned in the preceding section and many others. Race is usually more persistent than language, but not always. The Magyars of Hungary have kept their non-IE language, but are no longer racially distinct from their neighbors. Most of the linguistic groups are of mixed race. The French are descended from Gauls, Romans, and Germans, and neither of these elements was a distinct race. Of the three major racial types of Europe, known as Nordic, Alpine, and Mediterranean, all three are represented among the French, the first two among the Germans, the last two among the Italians, etc. The Greeks were of mixed race even in ancient times. The IE linguistic family includes people of diverse race, very largely no doubt because of mixture with conquered peoples. But it is by no means certain that even the IE-speaking people before its dispersion was a distinct race. It may have been already racially mixed. For the racial types, as determined by skull measurement and other physical criteria, go back to extremely remote periods. They have little bearing on the grouping of peoples in the earliest historical or the near-historical period.

63. *Language and nationality.*—A people or nationality is rarely a distinct race in the anthropological sense (**62**), nor is it necessarily a nation in the political sense. The ancient Greeks were not a united nation, but they were conscious of a common nationality. The evidence of this they found in their common descent, language, religion, and customs (Hdt. 8. 144). Of these criteria the first was only a matter of belief, of legend. Of the others the most tangible and definite was the community of language, despite the persistent diversity of dialects.

The Romans, with all their knowledge and admiration of the Greek language, upheld officially the prestige of Latin. The use of Greek in the Roman senate was frowned upon and on occasion definitely prohibited. Cicero was blamed for addressing the Syracusan assembly in Greek. Aemilius Paulus at the assembly of Amphipolis made his formal proclamation to the Macedonians in Latin, which was then repeated in Greek by the praetor (Livy 45. 29).

And so in subsequent European history language has been the most conspicuous mark of nationality, the one of which a people is most conscious and to which it is most fanatically attached— one to be defended against encroachment and conversely the first object of attack on the part of a power aiming to crush out a distinction of nationality among its subject peoples. Several of the 19th-cent. nationalistic revivals, which have finally led to independent statehood, had their beginnings in the field of language and literature. With a few exceptions (as Belgium, Switzerland) the present European nationalities are essentially language groups, for which language is the accepted criterion of nationality.

PHONOLOGY

THE GREEK AND LATIN ALPHABETS

64. The Greek alphabet is derived from the Phoenician, and the Latin from the Greek, probably through the medium of Etruscan. The origin of the Phoenician alphabet was long disputed, but its ultimate Egyptian source is now pretty well established by the discovery of a connecting link in the early Semitic inscriptions found on the Sinai peninsula. These Sinaitic inscriptions, dating from the early second millennium B.C., show an alphabet based upon selected Egyptian hieroglyphics, to which were given the Semitic names of the objects represented, as *daleth* for the 'door' picture, and then the alphabetic value of their respective initials, as the *d* of *daleth*. This alphabet was then the source, in principle at least, if not in all details, of the North Semitic alphabets including the Phoenician. But see now Appendix, p. 369.

The pedigree may be outlined as follows:

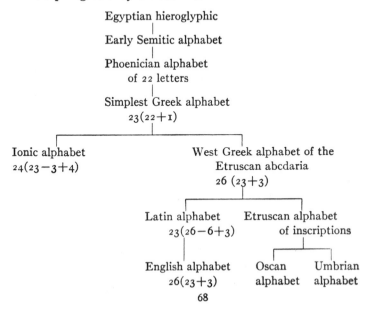

Egyptian hieroglyphic
|
Early Semitic alphabet
|
Phoenician alphabet
of 22 letters
|
Simplest Greek alphabet
23(22+1)

Ionic alphabet
24(23−3+4)

West Greek alphabet of the
Etruscan abcdaria
26 (23+3)

Latin alphabet
23(26−6+3)

Etruscan alphabet
of inscriptions

English alphabet
26(23+3)

Oscan
alphabet

Umbrian
alphabet

65. Table of the Phoenician, Greek, and Latin alphabets.[1]

I Semitic (Hebrew) Names	II Phoenician Alphabet[2]	III Primitive Greek Alphabet[3]	IV Early Attic Alphabet	V Ionic Alphabet[4]	VI Greek Names	VII West Greek Alphabet of Etrusc. Abc.[5]	VIII Latin Alphabet[6]	IX Latin Names
Aleph				A	ἄλφα		A	a
Beth				B	βῆτα		B	be
Gimel				Γ	γάμμα		C	ce
Daleth				Δ	δέλτα		D	de
He				E	εἶ, ἒ (ἒ ψιλόν)		E	e
Wau					ϝαῦ, διγάμμα		F	ef
Zayin				I (Z)	ζῆτα		G	ge
Cheth				H = η	ἦτα		H	ha
Teth				Θ	θῆτα			
Yod				I	ἰῶτα		I	i
Kaph				K	κάππα		K	ka
Lamed				Λ	λά(μ)βδα		L	el
Mem				M	μῦ		M	em
Nun				N	νῦ		N	en
Samekh				Ξ	ξῦ, ξεῖ (ξῖ)			
Ayin				O	οὖ, ὸ (ὸ μικρόν)		O	o
Pe				Π	πεῖ (πῖ)		P	pe
Tsade					σάν			
Qoph				P	κόππα		Q	qu
Resh				Σ	ῥῶ		R	er
Shin				T	σίγμα		S	es
Tau				Υ	ταῦ		T	te
				Φ	ὺ (ὺ ψιλόν)		V	u
				X = χ	φεῖ (φῖ)		X	ix
				Ψ = ψ	χεῖ (χῖ)			
				Ω	ψεῖ (ψῖ)		Y	y
					ὦ (ὦ μέγα)		Z	zeta
	22	23	23	24 (23 − 3 + 4)		26 (23 + 3)	23 (26 − 6 + 3)	

[1] Phoenician writing was from right to left, likewise the earliest Greek. The letters are given in their old retrograde form in cols. II, III, IV, VII.

[2] Forms of the Moabite Stone (early 9th cent. B.C.) with some variant forms, put first, of the earliest Byblos inscription (13th cent. B.C.).

[3] Reconstructed from a composite of the earliest alphabets of Crete and Thera, in which, however, the Ꟛ is lacking (only M = σ) and the Ꟛ rare.

[4] Given here in its developed form, as it appears in the standard Greek alphabet. The ϝ and ϙ occur in very early inscriptions, also a form of the san.

[5] From the abcdarium of Marsiliana.

[6] The six losses are those shown by the five blank spaces and also the I replaced by the G; the three additions are the G, Y, and Z. The zeta is counted first among the losses and again as an addition.

66. The Phoenician alphabet is now known from as early as about 1000 B.C. Through the Phoenician traders it became familiar to the Greeks. Just where and when it was first adopted and adapted to the Greek language cannot be determined, perhaps in the 10th or 9th cent. B.C. The earliest records were doubtless on perishable material, such as merchants' accounts on papyrus. The earliest surviving writings, such as the scrawls on the rock in Thera, can be dated only roughly, but are probably of the 8th cent. B.C. or possibly even earlier.

Phoenician writing was by consonants only. The fundamental feature of the adaptation to Greek, the innovation that is common to all the local Greek alphabets from the earliest times, is the use of certain Phoenician letters to express the Greek vowels. The signs for the light breathings, the *aleph* and *he*, were used with the value of the vowels in the names, that is, to express α and ε. The *ayin*, a sign for the glottal fricative which probably caused the following vowel in the name to have an *o*-like quality, was used to express o. The *yod*, not needed for a consonantal *y* which did not exist in Greek, was used to express the corresponding vowel, the ι. But the *wau* was needed both in its original consonantal value of *w* and to express the corresponding vowel *u*, and the result was a differentiation. The Ϝ, which must reflect some variant form of the Phoenician letter, was given the original value and alphabetic position of the latter, while Υ agreeing with the usual form of the *wau* in Phoenician inscriptions, served for the vowel *υ* and was added at the end of the alphabet—thus making up the Greek alphabet of 23 letters in place of the Phoenician of 22 letters.

Phoenician had more signs for sibilants than were needed in Greek, and while they were all kept at first, their uses and their names were confused. Either M(σάν) or Ϻ was preferred, according to locality, to express σ. The Ι and Ξ were used for a time with various values (e.g. Ther. ΞΕΥΜ = Ζεύς).

Of the two signs for a guttural voiceless stop, Κ and Ϙ, the latter was used only before o (or ρο as in Λοϙρός) or υ, and was eventually given up.

Phoenician furnished a sign for only one of the Greek aspirates, namely ⊕. The others were expressed by ΓΗ and ΚΗ or ϘΗ.

This primitive Greek alphabet, as given in column III of the table, is the one employed in the archaic inscriptions of Crete, Thera, and Melos, with some omissions (F only in Crete, Ɪ only in Thera and rare, Ϡ lacking in all three places, M being preferred for σ).

67. All the other local Greek alphabets, from the time of the earliest records, have two or more of the so-called supplementary letters. They all have Φ for the labial aspirate and either X or Y for the guttural aspirate. Thus with the inherited ⊕ the series of aspirates was filled out. Later and much less general was the use of a single letter for the κσ and πσ combinations, suggested by the use of the inherited I for σδ or τσ. The κσ was more widely expressed by a single letter (Ɪ or X) than was the πσ (Y or some other rare forms), and neither, for example, in the old Attic alphabet (ἔδοχσε, ἔγραφσε).

The alphabets fall into two main classes according to the value of the supplementary letters.

I. East Greek alphabets: X = χ.
   1. Ionic (and Corinthian) alphabet: X = χ, also Ɪ = ξ and Y = ψ.
   2. Old Attic: X = χ, but no Ɪ or Y.
II. West Greek alphabets: Y = χ, also X (but sometimes XϠ or YϠ) = ξ.

The origin of the supplementary letters and the explanation of the divergent local values of the X and Y has been the subject of endless discussion. One point which is now clear is that the West Greek, guttural, value of the Y is the original and that the letter is simply a variant form of the Phoenician *kaph*, the source of the κάππα. Its early form V agrees in fact precisely with the *kaph* in the Byblos inscriptions, while that on the Moabite Stone is more like the earliest form of the Greek κ. That is, it did not develop as a Greek variant of κ, but reflects a Phoenician variant, which very likely reached Greece by another route. On the origin of the Φ and X there is no agreement, but a plausible view is that they are both derived from the one inherited aspirate sign, the ⊕,

the ⊕ by omission of one of the cross lines, the X (or +) by omission of the circle.

Both Y and X had originally guttural value. In the West Greek alphabet Y was preferred for the simple guttural aspirate, while the X was used, perhaps first in XΣ and then alone, for the κσ combination. In the East Greek alphabet, where the old Ξ was used with the κσ value, the X was used for the guttural aspirate, and the left-over Y was then arbitrarily employed for the πσ combination, as a pendant to the Ξ for κσ.

68. The source of what became the standard Greek alphabet was the Ionic alphabet, more specifically the form that developed at Miletus. This was of the East Greek type, as described above, and was further characterized by the addition of Ω, in origin a variant form of O (in some other local alphabets other types of variants appear, as ☉ = ω), and by the use of H for the vowel. For the H (early ⊟) had originally the value of the spiritus asper, and so in the other alphabets. But in the East Ionic dialect this sound was lost and the letter was then employed for the vowel η, which in the other alphabets was not differentiated from ε but expressed equally by the E. Apparently the H was at first used only for the η from ᾱ, and then also for the general Greek η. For some inscriptions of the Ionic islands show such a difference, as Νικάνδρ⊟ μ'ἀνέθΕκεν in an archaic Naxian inscription.

After the general adoption of the Ionic alphabet, the spiritus asper was commonly left undesignated (as in Attic inscriptions ΕΓΤΑ in place of the earlier ΗΕΓΤΑ), or else indicated by some differentiated form of the H. So sometimes the old ⊟ = ' in contrast to H = η. The halved H, namely ⊢, occurs in the Heraclean Tables and some other inscriptions. It was used in MSS as a diacritical sign placed over the vowel, then also ⊣ as a pendant to it, whence later ᶜ and ᶦ, and the ' and ' of our current texts.

The Ionic alphabet was officially adopted in Athens in 403 B.C., and not much later replaced the old native or "epichoric" alphabets in other parts of Greece. But the ϝ (sound and letter had long since disappeared in Ionic) was retained for a time where it still survived as a sound.

The *wau*, *koppa*, and *san*, which disappeared from the alphabet, were maintained as numeral signs, the *wau* for 6 in a form that later became identified with the στ- ligature, the "stigma", the *koppa* for 90, and the *san* for 900 in the form known by the late name of σαυπί.

69. The Latin alphabet is derived from a West Greek alphabet. Such an alphabet was that employed in the Chalcidian colonies of southern Italy, Cumae, etc., and it was formerly taken for granted that the Romans got their alphabet from this source. But it is also the alphabet of the abcdaria found in Etruscan territory, those long known from Formello and Caere, and the more recently discovered and most perfect specimen, the ivory tablet of Marsiliana. This Greek alphabet introduced by the Etruscans (from what immediate source is not clear) is the basis of, but differs from that of, the later Etruscan abcdaria and the actual Etruscan inscriptions, in which several of the letters are lacking and another characteristic letter ($8 = f$, agreeing with a Lydian letter of the same value) appears. This Etruscan alphabet of the inscriptions is the source of the Oscan and Umbrian alphabets, with their $8 = f$, lack of O, etc., though they contain some survivals of the older and fuller alphabet. It cannot of course be the source of the Latin alphabet.

But it is a probable view that the fuller alphabet of the early abcdaria became known to the Romans through the Etruscans. This supplies a nearer source than the alphabets of the Chalcidian colonies in the south, and fits in with the well-known intensive Etruscan influence on early Rome. Furthermore, certain features of Etruscan writing help to explain some peculiarities of the Latin, notably the value of C as contrasted with that of its source, the Greek gamma (the form ⟨ or C is common in Greek inscriptions of various regions and is that of the Formello and Caere abcdaria).

It is characteristic of Etruscan that it had no voiced stops, or at any rate only a single order of unaspirated stops, perhaps midway between the two orders of Latin (hence the fluctuation in the transcription of Etruscan names). The B and D were not used in Etruscan inscriptions. Of the three letters for guttural stops,

C, K, ?, all were employed for a time, but all with the value of a voiceless stop, the differentiation being rather according to the following vowel, as CE, KA, ?V (similarly in an early Faliscan inscription CE, KA, ?O). The restriction of ? to the position before *o* or *u* was inherited from the Greek and was favored by the name ϙόππα ; the preference for KA was favored by the name κάππα; both names perhaps already reduced to *ka, qu.* But the C was the preferred form and except in the earliest inscriptions was used almost exclusively.

So in early Latin inscriptions, without regard to the distinction of voiceless or voiced stops in the actual speech, Q, before O or V (vowel or consonant), as QVOI or QOI=*quoi*, EQO=*ego*, PEQVNIA, etc.; K especially, though not exclusively, before A, as KAPIA, PAKARI, but also SAKPOS and Praenestine FHE-FHAKED; C especially before E, as RECEI, FECED, but with growing tendency to prefer this in general, with value of *c* or *g*. Eventually the Q was given up before O and vocalic V and kept only in the group QV where V had the consonantal value, as QVOD, QVIS, etc.; K, continuing to occur for some time before A, was finally restricted to KALENDAE, especially its abbreviations KAL. or K., and K.=*Kaesō;* a differentiated form of C, namely G, was introduced to distinguish the voiced stop, and C=*g* survived only in the abbreviations C.=*Gaius* and CN.=*Gnaeus.*

The new G took the position in the alphabet of the old I (Z) which, though not actually attested, was according to tradition formerly in use, presumably for the *z* that must have been intermediate between the original invervocalic *s* and the historical *r*, as Osc. -*azum*=L. -*ārum.*

In the 1st cent. B.C. Z, and likewise Y (the other form of V, which was already represented by L. V), were borrowed with their current Greek forms and values and placed at the end of the alphabet.

The fricative *f* was denoted at first by FH (FHEFHAKED on the Praenestine brooch), as in early Etruscan (FH occurs also in early Greek inscriptions, but here with the value of a voiceless *w* or *hw* from IE *sw*, **162**), and then by the simple F.

Other differences between the Latin and the standard Greek alphabet in values are the West Greek value of the X in contrast to that of the X in Ionic, and the retention of the original value of the H in contrast to the new vowel value of the Ionic H. Differences in the forms of the letters, as in the case of the Latin D, L, P, R, are without significance. They merely reflect divergent preferences among variant forms, and those that prevailed in Latin can also be found in Greek inscriptions.

Three Greek letters which were not used in the Latin alphabet served as numeral signs:

⊙ = 100, whence the usual C, as if the initial of *centum*.

Φ, ∞ = 1,000, later M as if the initial of *mille;* halved it gave D = 500.

Ѵ, ⊥, L = 50.

The Latin alphabet is the source of the English (as of most other European alphabets). The increase from 23 to 26 letters is due to the differentiation of I into I and J, and of V into U, V, and W. Of these the earliest differentiation is that of the W, which is simply VV, W, appearing in Latin inscriptions from the 1st cent. A.D. on, especially in the representation of Germanic or Celtic names, as VVITILDES = *Witildis* (*CIL* 12. 2095), but also sometimes in Latin words. The J and U reflect cursive forms of the old I and V. In early modern texts a common practice was to use *v* initially but *u* medially, as *vnto*, but *fugitiue*. It was not until the 16th cent. that the difference in form came to be used to distinguish the vowel and consonant. This modern practice, as regards the *u* and *v*, is for convenience often applied to Latin, and so in this book.

70. *The Greek names of the letters.*—The majority of the Greek names are obviously the Semitic names taken over with some phonetic modification (as the spread of final -α and especially -τα).

But the names of the sibilants were mostly new, as ζῆτα modeled on ἦτα, θῆτα ; ξῦ after μῦ, νῦ, or ξεῖ after πεῖ, φεῖ, etc.; σίγμα (relation to Sem. *samekh* doubtful). Only the σάν appears to reflect the Sem. *shin*, and it was originally applied to either form of the σ. In most of the statements (Hdt. 1. 139, etc.) that it was the Doric name corresponding to the Ionic name σίγμα there is no implication that it was applied only to the form M. But there is some evidence that in late times it was applied to this less familiar form (which, like the old ϙ, was used as a brand on horses; cf. σαμφόρᾱς, κοππατίᾱς), and it is convenient to follow this in modern practice.

The early name of the Ϝ was Ϝαῦ, though this is attested only in the late spelling βαῦ, and that in a Roman grammarian. The later name, δίγαμμα, was based on the form of the letter.

The πεῖ reflects Sem. *pe*, only pronounced with a long vowel, that is, ē written ει (**96**). This convenient monosyllabic name of a stop was the model for the names of the added φεῖ, χεῖ, and ψεῖ and the Ionic ξεῖ. These are the correct spellings (with ει = ē), as attested in Attic inscriptions and elsewhere, while πῖ, φῖ, etc. (usually followed in modern practice), are late, reflecting the late pronunciation of ει. For the vowels, ἄλφα and ἰῶτα reflect the Sem. names, and so the ἦτα, only here with η from the Ionic value of H. The ε, ο, υ, ω were simply named by their sound, with lengthening in the monosyllables, namely εῖ (that is, ē, and in this case virtually inherited from the Sem. name), οὖ (that is, ō), ῦ (with ' as regularly for initial υ, **167**), and ὦ. Later names are ἒ and ὂ, and still later (Byzantine) ὂ μικρόν, ὦ μέγα (since ο and ω had become identical in sound), and ἒ ψιλόν, ῦ ψιλόν, these last meaning 'simple ε', 'simple υ' in contrast to the diphthongs αι and οι which had come to have the same pronunciation as ε and υ respectively.

71. *The Roman names of the letters.*—The Greek names as a whole were not retained in Italy. They were replaced, perhaps first among the Etruscans, by monosyllablic names representing the simple sound of the letters in the case of the vowels, or, for the consonants, the sound supported by a vowel, usually *e*, following the stops, preceding the others.

For the vowels this was merely an extension of what was also the Greek practice in the names of ε, ο, and υ. The Greek name πεῖ gave the *pe*, and this, supported by the first syllable of βῆτα and δέλτα, was followed by *be*, *ce*, *de*, *te* and the late *ge;* while *ka* accords with the first syllable of κάππα and the prevailing use of *k* before *a;* and *qu* both with the normal Etruscan and the prevailing Latin use of *q* before *u.*

The letters for the continuous sounds, that is the nasals, liquids, and fricatives, were perhaps at first, like the vowels, named by their sounds, that is with syllabic *m, n, l,* etc., which appear to have been frequent in Etruscan. But the attested Latin names are with a preceding supporting *e,* as *em, en, el, er, ef, es.* The name of the *x,* namely *ix,* shows inversion of the Greek name in its late form ξῖ, probably due to the fact that no Latin word begins with *x.* The *h* was often called "aspirationis nota" (because of the Greek '), but the name *ha* is attested. Of the late additions to the alphabet, the Z and Y, the Z was known by its Greek name, namely as *zeta,* and the name of Y, though not clearly attested, was either *hy* (with the ' of the name *ȳ*) or *y,* in either case the sound of the Greek *v.*

The Latin names are the source of those current in English and the other West European languages. The vowels alone (*a, e, i,* etc.) and as finals (*be, de, ka,* etc.) were pronounced long and took part in the regular changes of long vowels in English since Chaucer's time. The divergence of *ar* from *el, em, en* is due to a 14th-cent. regular change of *er > ar* (which was not counteracted by spelling pronunciation as in *servant,* etc., **46**). The name of the new letter *j* took the vowel of the name of the following *k* and was thus distinguished from the name of *g;* that of *v* followed the analogy of *be, ce,* etc.; that of *w* is from its origin double *u.* The name of *x* became *ex* instead of *ix,* after *es,* etc. The name of *z* remains *zed* in British usage, but in U.S. usage becomes *ze* after *pe, te,* etc. For *h* the old *ha* was replaced by *ah* and this came to be written *ach* (like *nichil, michi* in late texts, **152***a*), hence French *ache* and the English name now commonly spelled *aitch.* For *y* the old name would in late Latin (when the special sound of the *y* was lost, **76***c*) not be distinguished from that of *i.* It was sometimes called *y graeca,* as now *y grec* in French. The English name *wī* (attested *ca.* 1200 A.D.) goes back to a name *VI* (pronounced *uī* in two syllables, then *wī*), which is based on the form Y as if a union of V and I. It is thus analogous in source to the Greek name digamma for the Ϝ and to the English name of *w*.

VOWELS AND DIPHTHONGS

72. The normal correspondences of the vowels and diphthongs, exclusive of the long diphthongs (**94**) and the syllabic liquids and nasals (**113–15**), may be surveyed in the accompanying table.

IE	G.	L.	Skt.	Lith.	ChSl.	Goth.	OE
i...........	ι	*i*	*i*	*i*	*ĭ*	*i(aĭ)*	*i*
ī...........	ῑ	*ī*	*ī*	*y*	*i*	*ei*	*ī*
u...........	υ	*u*	*u*	*u*	*ŭ*	*u (aú)*	*u*
ū...........	ῡ	*ū*	*ū*	*ū*	*y*	*ū*	*ū*
e...........	ε	*e*	} *a*	*e*	*e*	*i (aí)*	*e*
o...........	ο	*o*		} *a*	*o*	*a*	*œ*
a...........	} *a*	*a*					
ə...........			*i*				
ē...........	η	*ē*	} *ā*	*ė*	*ě*	*ē*	*ǣ*
ō...........	ω	*ō*		*uo, ō*	} *a*	*ō*	*ō*
ā...........	*ā, η*	*ā*		*ō*			
ei...........	ει	*(ei) ī*	} Aryan *ai* Skt. *e*	*ei, ie*	*i*	*ei*	*ī*
oi...........	οι	*(oi, oe) ū*		} *ai, ie*	*ě*	*ai*	*ā*
ai...........	αι	*(ai) ae*					
eu...........	ευ	} *(ou), ū*	} Aryan *au* Skt. *o*	} *au*	*u*	*iu*	*ēo*
ou...........	ου					} *au*	*ēa*
au...........	αυ	*au*					

73. Notes to the preceding table.

1. The *ə* (inverted *e*) is a conventional symbol for a vowel which has the same representation as IE *a* in the European languages, but appears as *i* in the Indo-Iranian branch, and moreover differs from IE *a* in its relation to other vowels in the system of vowel gradation (**124**). Its precise quality is of course unknown, but for convenience we may give it the sound of the final vowel in NE *sofa*, and call it the IE "obscure vowel".

2. The Greek vowels and diphthongs reflect most nearly those of the parent speech. They are in fact identical, if we except the merging of IE *a* and *ə*, and bear in mind that the η from *ā* and the changed pronunciation of the *υ*-vowels are Attic-Ionic but not general Greek. Furthermore, the Greek vowels were notably stable in quality, showing relatively few changes due to special conditions of position, accent, surrounding consonants, etc.

This applies to Greek of the classical period. Since then there has been a wholesale shift in the pronunciation of vowels and diphthongs, as radical as that which has taken place in English.

3. In Latin the principal change, so far as appears in the table, is the monophthongization of most of the diphthongs, which were still preserved in early Latin (the bracketed forms in the table). But the vowels in Latin have undergone the greatest variety of secondary changes under special conditions, especially in medial and final syllables, so that the representation given in the table is actually maintained only to a limited extent. In general, the original vowel system is as greatly disguised in Latin by secondary changes as it is transparent in Greek.

4. The relative simplicity of the Sanskrit vowel system results from the loss of the difference in quality between the original *e*-, *o*-, and *a*-vowels, whether short, long, or the first element of a diphthong. This is characteristic of the whole Indo-Iranian branch. In the case of the diphthongs, the resulting *ai* and *au* remained in Iranian, but in Sanskrit became monophthongs, *e* and *o*. These were long vowels, but, as there were no short *e*'s and *o*'s, they are not marked long in the usual transcription of Sanskrit, which is followed in this book.

5. In the Balto-Slavic branch, and also in the Germanic, the difference in quality between the *a*- and *o*-vowels was lost (except that in Lithuanian IE *ō* and *ā* are only partly merged). The letter *y* denotes *ī* in Lithuanian, but in Slavic a peculiarly modified *u*. Lith. *ė* is a long close *e*. Slavic *ě* is an open *e;* *ĭ* and *ŭ* are weak vowels of obscure quality.

6. In Gothic *ei* denotes *ī;* *ai* and *au* denote diphthongs, but also under certain conditions open *e* (the value of Greek *αι* at the time of Wulfilas) and *o* (these latter cases it is customary now to differentiate by writing *ai*, *au*). OE *æ* had about the value of *a* in *man.*

i, ī[1]

74. IE *i*. Hom. *ἴδμεν*, Skt. *vidma*, Goth. *witum*, OE *witon* 'we know', NE *wit;* G. *ἰδεῖν*, L. *videō*.

G. *τί*, L. *quid*, Skt. *cid*   G. *ἵστημι*, L. *sistō*, Skt. *tiṣṭhāmi*

a. In Latin, *i* > *e* (as *u* > *o*, **76**a) before *r* arising from *s* (**164**).
serō from **si-sō*, with reduplication as in *sistō*
cinis, gen. sg. *cineris* from **cinises*
Falerii from **Falisii* (cf. *Faliscus*)

[1] This and similar headings refer to the IE sounds. A few examples of the normal representation, which might be multiplied, are given first, followed by an account of the special changes. The Latin vowel changes in medial syllables are treated together under a separate head (**110**); likewise several of those in final syllables (**112**), but some are included in the discussion of the several vowels or diphthongs. For phonetic terms and classification of sounds, see **36–40**.

The asterisk, which is used to indicate prehistoric, reconstructed word forms (IE, Greek, Italic, Germanic, etc.), is omitted as cumbersome and unnecessary in the case of assumed IE sounds or groups of sounds, likewise case endings, personal endings, suffixes, and the like.

b. In Latin, final *i* (unless lost, **108**) >*e.*

ante from **anti* (cf. *anti-cipō*) : G. ἀντί, Skt. *anti*[1]

nom.-acc. sg. n. of *i*-stems, as *mare* from **mari*

c. For *ācer* from **ācris*, *ter* from **tris*, see **109**.

75. IE *ī*. G. *ĩs*, L. *vīs*   L. *vīvus*, Skt. *jīvas*, Lith. *gyvas.*

u, ū

76. IE *u*. G. ζυγόν, L. *iugum*, Skt. *yugam*,[2] Goth. *juk.*

G. ἐρυθρός, L. *ruber*, Skt. *rudhiras.*[2]

a. In Latin, *u*>*o* before *r* arising from *s* (**164**), like the parallel change of *i*>*e* (**74***a*).

forem from **fusēm*, with *fu-* as in *fuit*, etc. (but *nurus* from **snusu-*, with *u* kept, perhaps because of following *u*)

b. Dissimilatory change of L. *u* (through *ü*) to *i* between *l* and a labial.

lubet, *libet*:Skt. *lubh-* 'desire'   *clupeus*, *clipeus*:G. καλύπτω

c. G. *v* (and likewise *ū*) had originally the plain *u*-sound and this was retained in many dialects. But in Attic it changed from a back rounded to a front rounded vowel like Fr. *u* from L. *ū* (**39**.2) or NHG *ü*. In late times (1st cent. A.D. and later, according to locality) it lost even the rounding and became identical with *ι*, as it is in Modern Greek.

In Latin the early loanwords from Greek had *u*, but in the first cent. B.C. *y* was introduced to represent the current Greek sound. In vulgar Latin this came to be pronounced like *i*, and the *y* was merely a variant spelling of the same sound, often found in words which did not have *v* in Greek, as *ydolon* (from G. εἴδωλον), or were not even of Greek origin.

77. IE *ū*. G. μῦς, L. *mūs*, Skt. *mūs*, OE *mūs.*

G. θῦμός, L. *fūmus*, Skt. *dhūmas*, Lith. *dūmai*, ChSl. *dymŭ* (all meaning 'smoke, vapor' except G. θῦμός, which is used only of mental ebullition, 'soul, spirit, anger', and so is semantically related to L. *fūmus* as is conversely L. *animus* 'soul, spirit' to G. ἄνεμος 'wind')

[1] The colon is used here as a sign of comparison, to be interpreted as 'to be compared with', 'cognate with'.

[2] Sanskrit nouns and adjectives are quoted here in the nominative singular, to conform with the practice for Greek and Latin. In Sanskrit grammars and dictionaries they are quoted in the stem form, as *yuga*, *rudhira*. When quoted in the stem form in this book a hyphen is added to make this plain, as *yuga-*, *rudhira-*. Sanskrit forms are given without marks of accent except where the accent is pertinent to the matter under discussion; also usually without definitions, it being understood that the meaning is in substantial agreement with that of the Greek and Latin forms to which they are compared.

e

78. IE *e*. G. φέρω, L. *ferō*, Skt. *bharāmi*, OE *beran*.

G. ἐστί, L. *est*, Skt. *asti*, Lith. ἐsti, Goth. *ist*

G. γένος, L. *genus*, Skt. *janas*

79. *e*>*i* in Latin.

1. Before a guttural nasal, that is, before *n*+guttural stop and before *gn* (**198***b*).

tingō from **tengō*: G. τέγγω

lingua, dingua (**142**) from **denguā, *dn̥ĝhwā* (cf. **115**): OE *tunge*

quīnque (vowel length from *quīnctus*, **99**.2) from **quenque, *penque* (**40**.8): G. πέντε

lignum from **legnom*: *legō*   *dignus* from **degnos, *decnos*: *decet*

Cf. NE *think* from OE *pencan*, and NE *England, English* as pronounced.

2. *Miscellaneous*.—The factors involved include assimilation, and weakening (as in **110**.3) due to proclitic or enclitic use, but are too complex to be fully understood.

Preposition *in* and verbal prefix *in-*: G. ἐν

Negative prefix *in-* from **en-, n̥-* (**115**).

nihil from **ne-hil* (*ne* as in *ne-fās*)

mihi, tibi, from **mehei, *tebei* (**298**.3)

similis, simul (early *semol*), *simplex* (but *semel, semper*), all from **sem-*

vitulus: G. dial. ἔταλον 'yearling', ἔτος 'year'

3. In medial syllables (**110**), and in final syllables before final *s* or *t* (**112**).

80. *e*>*o* in Latin. Before *w*, after *w* (mostly consonant +*w*), or before *l*, but subject to further conditions only partly understood, the vowel of the following syllable being often a factor. The main facts are as follows.

1. *ew*>*ow* (cf. *eu*>*ou*, **92**).

novus from **newos*: G. νέ(ϝ)ος Skt. *navas* (OE *nēowe*, Skt. *navyas*, from **newyos*)

novem from **newn̥*: G. ἐννέα, Skt. *nava* (**313**.9)

a. This is an Italic change. Cf. Osc. N ú v l a n a m : L. *novus*, and Umbr. n u v i m e : L. *novem*. In *brevis, levis* the *ev* is not from IE *ew* but from *eghw, egʷh* (**153**).

2. *swe* > (*swo*, hence by **170**) *so*.

somnus from *swepnos:Skt. *svapnas*, OE *svefn* 'sleep, dream'
(G. ὕπνος from *supnos, with weak grade, **119**.3)

soror from *swesōr:Skt. *svasar-*, OE *sweoster*

socer, socrus from **swekro-*, etc.: G. ἑκυρός, ἑκυρά (ἑ- from σϝε-, **162**),
Skt. çvaçuras, OE *sweger* 'mother-in-law'

3. *que* > (*quo*, hence by **170**) *co*.

coquō from *quequō, *pequō* (**40**.8): G. πέσσω, Skt. *pac-* (but *quīnque, queror*, etc.)

4. *dwe* > (*dwo*, hence by **172**) *bo*.

bonus from *duonos, duenos* (but *bene*)

5. *we* > *wo*, **vomō** from *wemō:G. ἐμέω, Lith. *vemti*.

a. **homō**, though apparently from early *hemō* (cf. *nēmō* from *ne-hemō),
is more probably an inherited form with *o*-grade (cf. Osc. h u m u n s , Umbr.
komonus). No such change in *emō, premō*, etc.

6. Before a "guttural *l*", that is, before *l* when

a) Followed by a back vowel, *a*, *o*, or *u*

b) Followed by another consonant (except *l*)

c) Final

volō, volt (later *vult*) from *welō, *welti, in contrast to *velim, velle*

colō (through *quolō, **170**) from *quelō, in contrast to *inquilīnus*
(with regular weakening of *e* > *i*, **110**.3)

olīva, an early loanword from G. ἐλαίϝᾱ (*elaivā > *olaivā > *olīva*,
with *ai* > *ī* as in *occīdō*, etc., **110**.5)

simul, early *semol*, from *semel:Umbr. s u m e l

Certain exceptions, as *celsus, gelu, helvus*, admit of various
explanations.

o

81. IE *o*. G. πόσις, L. *potis*, Skt. *patis*.

G. ὀκτώ, L. *octō*, Skt. aṣṭāu   G. δόμος, L. *domus*, Skt. *damas*

82. *o* > *u* in Latin.

1. Before *nc, ngu, mb*, and *l*+cons. (except *l*).

hunc, early *honc*, from *hom-ce

uncus: G. ὄγκος   *unguis*: G. ὄνυξ

umbō, umbilicus: G. ὀμφαλός   *multa* 'fine', early *molta*

But *longus*, though one would expect the same change before *ng* as before *nc, ngu*.

2. In final syllables ending in any consonant.

dolus, dolum, dōnum, from *-os, -om* 　　*illud* from *-od* (kept in *quod*)
legunt from *-ont* 　　*cōnsul* from *cōnsol*

3. In medial syllables before *l* (but *o* kept after a vowel, *fīliolus, alveolus*) and before two consonants.

pōculum from *pōcolom* 　　*cōnsulō* from *cōnsolō*
leguntur from *legontor* 　　*euntis* from *eontis*: G. ἰόντος

4. The change to *u*, as in 1, 2, 3, took place in the historical period. The earlier *o* appears regularly in inscriptions down to about 200 B.C.

So *honc, molta, praifectos, sacrom, dōnom, pōcolom, cosentiont*

The SC de Bacch. of 186 B.C. has *-us, -um, -unt*, but *o* before *l* in *tabolam, consoluerunt, cosoleretur*.

5. But after *u*, vowel or consonant, the change to *u* did not take place until considerably later. The forms of Plautus and Terence were (*dolus, dōnum, legunt*, etc., but) *volt, volnus, mortuos, servos, relinquont, sequontur, quom*. This spelling in fact remained, though probably the pronunciation changed sooner, until about the middle of the 1st cent. B.C. The earliest example of *u* in such cases is *suum* beside *suom* in an inscription of 45 B.C., and the spelling *o* is often found much later, especially in *volt, volnus*.

6. When finally *servos* became *servus*, the consonantal *u* of *qu* was lost before the new *u*, and *equos, relinquont, sequontur, quom* became *ecus, relincunt, secuntur, cum*, which are the proper forms of the Augustan period. Later *qu* was restored by analogy of the other forms, as *equus* after *equī*, etc., similarly *relinquunt, sequuntur*. But the more isolated conjunction *cum* remained (*quum* is only a very late spelling, to be disregarded).

At a time when the conjunction was written *quom* but already pronounced as *com*, the preposition *com* was also frequently written *quom* in inscriptions.

7. Quite different from the preceding regular changes, and not

well understood as to the precise conditions and period, is the change of *o* to *u* before *m* in some words (in contrast to *domus*).

humus: Umbr. *hondra* 'infra', G. χθον-

umerus, from *omesos: Umbr. loc. sg. *onse*, Goth. *ams*

numerus: G. νόμος

Likewise obscure, perhaps dialectal, *o* > *u* before *r* + cons. in some words, as *furnus* (*fornus* rare) beside *fornāx* (*furnāx* rare), *formus*, etc.

83. Other changes of *o* in Latin.

1. *vo* > *ve* before *r* + cons., *s* + cons., or *t*, about 150 B.C.

Early *vortō, vorsus, vorrō, voster, votō* > later *vertō, versus, verrō, vester, vetō*

2. *ov* > *av* in some words, but conditions in contrast to *novus, novem*, etc., obscure.

cavus (vulg. Lat. also *covus*, Port. *covo*): G. κόοι 'hollows' (Hesych.)

caveō: G. κο(ϝ)έω   *faveō* beside early *fove*   *lavō*: G. λό(ϝ)ω

3. Final *o* > *e*.

2 sg. imperat. pass. *-re*: G. -σο

4. *o* > *e*, *i* in medial syllables, **110.2.**

a

84. IE, *a*. G. ἄγω, L. *agō*, Skt. *aj-*.

G. ἀγρός, L. *ager*, Skt. *ajras*, Goth. *akrs*

G. ἀπό, L. *ab*, Skt. *apa*, Goth. *af*

a. *a* > *e*, *i*(*u*) in medial syllables, **110.1**; > *e* in final syllables, **112.**

ə

85. IE ə. See **73.1** and **124.**

G. πατήρ, L. *pater*, Goth. *fadar*, Skt. *pitar-*

G. στατός, L. *status*, Skt. *sthitas*

ē

86. IE *ē*. G. τίθημι, ἔθηκα, L. *fēcī*, Skt. *dhā-*.

G. πλήρης, L. *plēnus*, Skt. *prātas*

L. *sēmen*, Lith. *séti* 'sow', OE *sǣd* 'seed'

ō

87. IE ō. G. δῶρον, L. dōnum, Skt. dānam.

G. γνωτός, L. nōtus, Skt. jñātas

G. φέρω, L. ferō, Skt. bharāmi

a. A change of ō to ū is observed in L. fūr (cf. G. φώρ) and cūr from early quōr.

ā

88. IE ā. Dor. (etc.) ἴστᾱμι, Att.-Ion. ἴστημι, L. stāre, Skt. sthā-.

Dor. (etc.) μᾱ́τηρ, Att.-Ion. μήτηρ, L. māter, Skt. mātar-

Dor. (etc.) φᾱ́μᾱ, Att.-Ion. φήμη, L. fāma

Dor. (etc.) and Att. οἰκίᾱ, γενεᾱ́, χώρᾱ, Ion. οἰκίη, γενεή, χώρη

The change of ā to η is peculiar to Attic-Ionic, complete in Ionic, in Attic except after ε, ι, and ρ. The ā remains in all other dialects, not merely in Doric, but for the sake of brevity one may speak of the "Doric" ā or "Dor." μᾱ́τηρ, etc.

In Greek words in their familiar, that is, their Attic-Ionic form, we have then to distinguish, for example in the two syllables of μήτηρ, between the special Attic-Ionic η from ā and the general Greek η from IE ē, which is the same in the other dialects (but written Ε until the introduction of the Ionic alphabet, **68**). The difference may be determined from (1) the forms of other dialects, (2) the cognates in Latin, etc., (3) sometimes even within Attic-Ionic from the weak form of the root (τίθημι, θετός, but ἴστημι, στατός).

Some kinds of secondary ā were of sufficiently early origin to take part in the change to η, while others developed subsequently to the period when the change took place and so were unaffected. Thus ἔφηνα from ἔφᾱνα from *εφανσα, but πᾶσα from πάνσα from *παντια, or τᾱ́ς from τάνς. See **204**.

Apparent exceptions to the familiar rule for Attic are due to various causes. κόρη, δέρη, κόρρη are from *κορϝη, δερϝη (Arc. κόρϝᾱ, δέρϝᾱ), κόρση. χορηγός follows the analogy of στρατηγός etc. λοχᾱγός is a Spartan term, kept by Attic writers.

The change of ā to η was a gradual one, and there was once a period, still reflected in some inscriptions of the Ionic islands (**68**), when the new vowel was not yet fully identical with the general Greek η, that is, it was even more open. But in general the η in both syllables of Att.-Ion. μήτηρ had the same sound. In the best period it was a very open ē (somewhat as in NE *there*), in Hellenistic times a close ē, and in the early centuries of our era it became identical with *i*, as it is in Modern Greek.

ei

89. IE *ei* = G. ει, L. *ī* (early *ei*).

G. δείκνῡμι, L. *dīcō*, early *deicō*, Osc. *deicum*, Goth. *ga-teihan* 'announce'

G. εἶμι, Skt. *emi*, L. 2 sg. *īs*   G. πείθω, L. *fīdō*

1. In Greek, as early as the 5th cent. B.C., the diphthong had become a monophthong ę̄, that is, a long close *e* in contrast to the open η (**88, 96**). (The vowel in NE *late*, etc., is more or less diphthongal, ē^i or *ei*, and so offers a convenient approximation to either the earlier or the later value of G. ει.) But the spelling ει was unchanged, and came to be used to denote also the ę̄ which had never been a diphthong (**96**).

a. In Roman times ει became identical with *ī*, but the spelling still remained and was sometimes used for original *ī* as τειμή = τῑμή.

2. In Latin, *ei* was a real diphthong in the earliest period, but became ẹ̄ (closer than the inherited ē), later *ī*. In the time of Plautus and Terence it was identical with the sound resulting from *ai* in medial and final syllables (**91**) and from *oi* in final syllables (**90**), but was still distinct from *ī*. The spelling in all such cases was *ei*, or occasionally *e*, e.g., in the SC de Bacch. *deicerent, inceideretis*, nom. pl. *foideratei* (never *i* in such forms, and conversely never *ei* for *ī* as later). By the middle of the 2d cent. B.C. the sound had become identical with *ī*, the spelling fluctuated between *ei* and *i*, and the former, being now merely a sign for *ī*, was also used for *ī* which had never been a diphthong, e.g. *audeire*. This spelling *ei* is frequent in inscriptions down to the time of Cicero, and even in the Augustan period was not wholly obsolete.

a. The intermediate *ẹ̄* serves to explain the relation of *seu* to *sīve* from *sei-ve*. Beside the intermediate *sẹ̄ve* arose *sẹ̄u* (cf. *nec, neque*), whence with the regular vowel shortening (103), *seu*. Similarly *neu* from *nei-ve* (but can also be from *nē-ve*), *ceu* from *cei-ve;* also *deus* from *dẹ̄os*, beside *dīvus*, both from *deiwos* (170*a*).

oi

90. IE *oi* = G. οι, L. *ū* (early *oi, oe; oe* retained in some words), but *ī* (early *ei*) after *v* and in final syllables.

G. οἰνή 'ace', L. *ūnus*, early *oinos, oenus*, Goth. *ains*

L. *commūnis*, early *comoinem*, Osc. m u i n i k a m , Goth. *gamains*

L. *cūrō*, early *coiravēre*, Pael. *coisatens*

G. οἶδα, οἶκος, οἶνος, L. *vīdī, vīcus, vīnum*

nom. pl. *o*-stems, G. -οι, L. *-ī* (early *-eī*)

dat. pl. *o*-stems, G. -οις, Osc. *-ois*, L. *-īs* (early *-eis*)

a. It is probable that the monophthongization in *ūnus*, etc., had already taken place by the time of Plautus (cf. the pun *Lȳde, lūdō*, etc.), though the earliest inscriptional examples of the spelling *u* are somewhat later (*utier* in a Scipio epitaph, precise date uncertain; *usura* 146 B.C.). The old spelling *oc* remains frequent in inscriptions until about the middle of the 1st cent. B.C., and Cicero in the laws for his ideal state purposely wrote *oenus, coerari*, etc. Since *ū* also comes from *ou* (92) the archaizing spelling sometimes shows *ou* instead of *oe*, as *couraverunt*.

b. The normal change to *ū* was not observed in certain words, which persisted only in the archaic form. Thus, in legal terminology *foedus* 'treaty' and *poena* 'penalty' (but *pūniō*, which was less technical); *Poenus* the old official title (while the common term *Poenicus* became *Pūnicus*); *moenia* 'walls' which was thus kept distinct from *mūnia* 'duties' (while the more general word for 'wall' *moerus* became *mūrus*); also *foedus* 'foul' for less obvious reasons (perhaps it was for a time only a literary word, though later adopted in popular speech, as in Petronius and as shown by its survival in Romance).

c. In *poena*, etc., the diphthongal pronunciation of *oe* (about as in NE *coin*) was probably maintained in educated speech until a late period. But eventually it became a close *ē*, as *ae* became an open *ē* (91). Hence the frequent confusion in spelling, in late inscriptions and in manuscripts, between *oe, ae*, and *e*.

d. In medial syllables there are no clear examples of change to *ei, ī* as in final syllables, parallel to that of *ai* in medial syllables (91), as might be expected. Rather *oi* was kept by recomposition (as mostly *o*, 111) and developed as in initial syllables, e.g. *commūnis*, *sēcūrus*, etc. Some regard *pōmērium* as an example of weakening with retention of the intermediate *ę̄* before *r*. But more probably the form, though the generally accepted one, represents the late pronunciation of *pōmoerium* (above, *c*).

e. L. *coepī* is from *co-ēpī* (so sometimes in early Latin) with *ēpī* to the rare *apiō*, like *cēpī* to *capiō*. Change to *coepī* (in contrast to *coēgī*) is due to the fact that the word was not felt as a compound and to the influence of the early L. pres. *coepiō*, this from **co-ipiō*, **co-apiō* (by **110.**1).

L. *oboediō* beside *audiō* (in contrast to *clūdō*, *inclūdō*, **110.**5) is puzzling, with only a complicated and doubtful explanation.

L. *nōn* is from early *noenum*, this from *ne oinom* (cf. NE *not*, short form of *nought*, from OE *nowiht* 'no-thing'). The peculiar phonetic development is obscure, but doubtless connected in some way with the unaccented use.

ai

91. IE *ai* = G. αι, L. *ae* (early *ai*), but *ī* (early *ei*) in medial and final syllables.

G. αἴθω, L. *aestus*, *aedēs* (orig. 'hearth'), Skt. *edhas* 'fuel'

G. λαιός, L. *laevus*   G. σκαιός, L. *scaevus*

L. *caedō*, but perf. *cecīdī*, cpds. *incīdō* (early *inceidō*), etc. (**110.**5)

L. dat. pl. *ā*-stems, *-īs* (early *-eis*), from *-ais* = Osc. *-ais*, G. -αις.

a. The spelling *ae*, which replaced *ai* early in the 2d cent. B.C., merely indicates that the second element of the diphthong had a more open quality than *i* in other positions, as is true also of the corresponding NE diphthong in *ride*, etc. The same holds for the *oe* from *oi* (**90**).

L. *ae* remained a diphthong in educated urban speech down to imperial times, as appears from statements of the grammarians and from loanwords like OHG *keisur* from L. *Caesar*. But the monophthongization to an open *ē* was earlier in colloquial speech, and eventually prevailed, with resulting confusion of spelling between *ae* and *e*. In *pre-hendō* (in contrast to *prae-* in other compounds) this pronunciation was favored by the assimilating influence of the *e* in the succeeding syllable.

eu, ou

92. IE *eu*, *ou* = G. ευ, ου, L. *ū* (early *ou*).

G. ζεῦγος, L. *iūmentum* (early *iouxmenta*)

G. λευκός, λοῦσσον, L. *lūx*, *lūna*

G. εὔω, L. *ūrō*, from **eusō* (**164**, **167**)

L. *dūcō*, early *doucō*: Goth. *tiuhan* 'lead', IE **deukō*

G. σπεύδω beside σπουδή, etc. (**119.**3)

1. In Greek the two diphthongs are kept distinct at all periods. But ου, as early as the 5th cent. B.C., had become a monophthong, first ō, that is, a long close o (in NE *boat*, etc., the vowel is close, but more or less diphthongal, ōᵘ or ou), then ū (with the same change as in NE *doom*). But the spelling remained unchanged, and ου came to be used also to denote the same sound in cases where it had never been a diphthong (**96**).

a. G. ϝευ became ϝει by dissimilation in εἶπον, ἔϝειπον from *ἐϝευπον: Skt. *avocam*, IE *e-we-uqʷom* (reduplicated aorist with weak grade of *weqʷ-*, Skt. *vac-*), and ἀείδω, *ἀϝείδω, from *ἀ-ϝε-νδω:Skt. *vad-*.

2. In prehistoric Italic, *eu* became *ou*, just as *ew* became *ow* in *novus* (**80.**1), and so was merged with original *ou*. The *ou* is preserved in early Latin (as in Oscan), but had become ū by about 200 B.C. The spelling *ou*, however, still appears in the SC de Bacch. of 186 B.C. and often later.

a. L. *līber*, early *leiber*, cognate with O. L ú v f r e í s 'Līberī', G. ἐλεύθερος, shows a dissimilatory change (*ou* > *oi* > *ei*) between *l* and *b*, analogous to that seen in *libet* from *lubet* (**76***b*).

b. L. *eu* never represents IE *eu*, but is always of secondary origin, as in *seu, neu, ceu* from *sei-ve*, etc. (**89.**2*a*), or in *neuter*, i.e. *ne-uter*, which remained trisyllabic till a late period.

c. L. ū also comes from *ovi, ove*, with syncope of the second vowel, as *prūdēns* from *pro-v(i)dēns* (*videō*), *nūndinae* (*noundinum* in SC de Bacch.) from *nov(e)n-dinai* (*novem*), *nūntiō* from *noventiō* (*novus*) *nūdus* from *nov(e)dos*, this from *nogʷedos* or the like (:Goth. *naqaþs*, NE *naked*).

d. But a different development is seen in *mōtus, vōtus* from *movetos, *vovetos* (cf. *monitus* to *moneō*), *nōnus* from *novenos* (*novem*), *cōntiō* from *coventiō*, and some others. This is perhaps due to the influence of *moveō, voveō, novem*, etc., but there is difficulty with this and all other explanations offered.

au

93. IE *au* = G. αυ, L. *au*, but ū in medial syllables.
G. αὔξω, L. *augeō*, Goth. *aukan*   αὖ, αὖτε, L. *aut, autem*
L. *claudō*, but *inclūdō*, etc. (**110.**5)

a. The pronunciation ō for *au*, as *Clōdius* for *Claudius*, was common in vulgar Latin, but even the Romance languages point to the long persistence of diphthongal *au* as the normal pronunciation.

LONG DIPHTHONGS

94. The existence of IE long diphthongs, that is, diphthongs with the first vowel long, as *ēi, ēu*, etc., is most clearly shown by the Indo-Iranian *āi* (IE *ēi, ōi, āi*) and *āu* (IE *ēu, ōu, āu*) as distinct from *ai* (IE *ei, oi, ai*) and *au* (IE *eu, ou, au*). The Skt. *āi, āu* in the transcription followed here had really become simple *ai, au* (and are now frequently so transcribed), but were still kept distinct from the Indo-Iranian *ai, au* which became Skt. *e, o* (**73.**4).

The final long diphthongs are preserved in Greek, as dat. sg. *-āι, -ηι, -ωι* (*-ᾳ, -ῃ, -ῳ*, **95**). Otherwise in Greek and Latin (and the other European languages) the long diphthongs are changed in one of two ways, the conditions determining which being obscure. They show either

1) Shortening of the first element, resulting in a diphthong of the ordinary type, or

2) Loss of the second element, resulting in a simple long vowel. This appears also sometimes in Sanskrit and probably dates in part from IE times.

IE **d(i)yēus*, Skt. *dyāus*, (1) G. Ζεύς, (2) L. *diēs, diem*, Skt. acc. sg. *dyām*, G. Ζῆνα, Ζηνός etc., based upon acc. sg. **Ζην*

IE **gʷōus*, Skt. *gāus*, (1) G. βοῦς, (2) Dor. βῶς, L. *bōs*

IE **rēis* (stem **rēi-*, cf. Skt. gen. sg. *rāyas*), (2) Skt. *rās*, L. *rēs*

IE instr. pl. of *o*-stems, *-ōis*, Skt. *-āis*, (1) G. dat. pl. *-οις*, Italic dat.-abl. pl. *-ois* (Osc. *-ois*), whence L. *-īs* (**90**)

IE dat. sg. of *o*-stems, *-ōi*, G. *-ωι*, (1) Osc. *-oi*, L. *-oi* in *Numasioi* (**29**), (2) L. *-ō*

95. Except for the final *-āι, -ηι, -ωι* (**94**), the Greek long diphthongs are of secondary origin, the result of contraction, as κληίς, from κλη(ϝ)ίς, κλᾱ(ϝ)ίς (cf. L. *clāvis*), crasis as Ion., Dor. ὡυτός from ὁ αὐτός, or of analogical formation, as the augmented forms like ᾔτησα (αἰτέω), ᾤκησα (οἰκέω), ηὔξησα (αὐξάνω), or subj. λέγηις, λέγηι.

In Attic in the 4th cent. B.C. ηι became ē, written ει as κλείς. So too in the augmental forms, in the dative singular, and in the subjunctive, the spelling ει prevailed for a time (in 3d-cent. Attic inscriptions ΕΙ is more than twice as common as ΗΙ); but in those categories $\eta\iota$ was restored by analogy, e.g. $\tau\iota\mu\hat{\eta}\iota$ by the influence of $\tau\iota\mu\dot{\eta}$, $\tau\iota\mu\hat{\eta}s$, etc.

Finally the ι of $\bar{a}\iota$, $\omega\iota$, and the restored $\eta\iota$ ceased to be pronounced, and especially after 100 B.C. the spelling of Attic inscriptions fluctuates between AI and A, HI and H, ΩI and Ω.

The spelling with iota subscript, $\kappa\lambda\hat{\eta}s$, $\ddot{\eta}\tau\eta\sigma a$, $\lambda\dot{\epsilon}\gamma\eta$, which is usual in our literary texts, and which we shall resume from this point, has no authority in antiquity. It is a late Byzantine device for indicating a vowel which had historical but no longer any phonetic value.

The difference between the earlier and later value of the long diphthongs is reflected in Latin in words borrowed at different periods, as *tragoedus* ($\tau\rho\alpha\gamma\omega\iota\delta\delta s$), but *rapsōdus* ($\dot{\rho}a\psi\omega\delta\delta s$).

GREEK SECONDARY $\bar{e}$ AND $\bar{o}$: "SPURIOUS DIPHTHONGS"

96. Greek ϵ and o, in many dialects, including Attic-Ionic, differed in quality from η and ω, being close vowels, while η and ω were open. (The difference was at least as marked as that in French between the close e and o of *été, beau* and the open e and o of *mère, encore;* η and ω were perhaps as open as e and o in NE *there, forty*). Consequently the long vowels which came from ϵ and o by contraction or compensative lengthening, since they retained the same quality, were not identical with η and ω, but were $\bar{e}$ and $\bar{o}$, the latter becoming $\bar{u}$ (just as in NE *doom*, etc.), and were designated by $\epsilon\iota$ and $o\upsilon$ after these original diphthongs had come to have the same phonetic values (89.1, 92.1).

$\tau\rho\epsilon\hat{\iota}s$ from *$\tau\rho\epsilon\underset{\iota}{}\epsilon s$ (**178**) $\epsilon\dot{\iota}\mu\dot{\iota}$ from *$\dot{\epsilon}\sigma\mu\iota$ (**203.**2)

gen. sg. *-ου* from *-οιο* (**179.**1)   acc. pl. *-ους* from *-ονς* (**204.**4)

a. In Attic and Ionic inscriptions the usual spelling was E and O until after 400 B.C., though occasional examples of EI (especially EI$\mu\dot{\iota}$) and OV are much earlier.

b. In some dialects secondary $\bar{e}$ and $\bar{o}$ were identical with η and ω, hence $\tau\rho\hat{\eta}s$, $\dot{\eta}\mu\dot{\iota}$, gen. sg. *-ω*, acc. pl. *-ωs*.

c. Whether $\epsilon\iota$ or $o\upsilon$ in any given case is a genuine diphthong or spurious may be determined from various criteria. Thus in the infinitive $\lambda\epsilon\dot{\iota}\pi\epsilon\iota\nu$ the first $\epsilon\iota$ is genuine, the second spurious, as shown by

1) The early spelling λEIπEν.

2) Dialectic $\lambda\epsilon\dot{\iota}\pi\eta\nu$.

3) For the root syllable by λέλοιπα, ἔλιπον, with the regular interchanges of *ei* (**119**.2), in contrast to ἔφθορα, ἐφθάρην beside φθείρω from *φθεριω.

4) For the infinitive ending by the absence of ι in the contracted forms like τιμᾶν from τιμάειν, in contrast to 3 sg. τιμᾷ from τιμάει with genuine ει.

d. An early change of ε̄ to ῑ occurs in Att. χῑ́λιοι = Ion. χείλιοι (**203**.2), ῑμάτιον beside εῖμα.

QUALITATIVE DIFFERENCE BETWEEN SHORT AND LONG VOWELS

97. In Greek, as already noted (**96**), ε, ο were close, η, ω open vowels. For the other vowels there is no evidence as to difference in quality.

In Latin there is no evidence of difference in quality between *a* and *ā*. But otherwise the short vowels were open, the long vowels close. This is known from statements of Roman writers and from the development in the Romance languages. For in vulgar Latin the difference in quantity disappeared, while the difference in quality persisted. The Romance languages (with some reservations which need not be explained here) reflect a vulgar Latin vowel system related to the older as shown in the accompanying tabulation, with illustrations from Italian.

	L.		Vulg. L.	It.		L.		Vulg. L.	It.
decem	*e*	....	*e*	*diece*	*bonus*	*o*	......	*o*	*buono*
fēcit	*ē*	⎫		*fece*	*dōnum*	*ō*	⎫		*dono*
quid	*i*	⎬	*ẹ*	*che*	*supra*	*u*	⎬	*ọ*	*sopra*
quī	*ī*	....	*i*	*chi*	*lūna*	*ū*	......	*u*	*luna*

a. The same relation as in Latin obtained in Oscan, Umbrian, and in Oscan the original *ē*, *ō* had become so close that they were regularly written *i*, *u*, e:g. *licitud* = L. *licētō*.

This relation, rather than that in Greek, is the more usual one in general and holds good for the English vowels. Thus the short [ĭ], [ŭ] of *did, full* are relatively open, the long [ī], [ū] of *deed, fool* relatively close, and the latter are from earlier close [ē], [ō] as the spelling still shows.

b. The contrast between It. *detto* from *dictus* and *scritto* from *scrīptus* illustrates the nature of the Romance evidence for Latin hidden quantity. It is an inference from quality to quantity.

Other evidence for hidden quantity, which may conveniently be mentioned here, is as follows:

1) Statements of Roman writers, as one of Cicero covering cases like *cōnsul* (**99**.1*a*).

2) Spelling in inscriptions, the apex over the vowel, and *ei* or I longa for *i*. But there is no consistency in the practice and there are many errors.

3) Greek transcriptions.

4) Etymology.

5) Treatment in compounds, long vowels not being subject to the weakening in medial syllables (**110**), e.g. *adāctus* beside *āctus* in contrast to *adfectus* beside *factus*.

Often there are several kinds of evidence combined. But there are also many doubtful cases where the evidence is meager or conflicting.

LENGTHENING AND SHORTENING OF VOWELS IN GREEK

98. 1. The simplification of various consonant groups containing a nasal or liquid is attended by lengthening of the preceding vowel (see **188**.2, **201**.3, **203**.2, **204**.2, **205**.2).

2. Long vowels were shortened in prehistoric Greek before a nasal or liquid+consonant. So regularly before *ντ*, as in pple. γνόντες from *γνω-ντες, or 3 pl. Dor. ἔγνον from *ἔγνω-ντ. But long vowels arising later by contraction or analogy were not affected, e.g. τιμῶντες, φέρωνται.

3. Long vowels are shortened before other vowels in various dialects, most commonly η before *o* or *ω* in Attic-Ionic. So gen. pl. βασιλέων from βασιλήων (Hom.), Att. ἕως from ἠώς (Hom., Hdt.). When the second vowel is short it may be lengthened, resulting in what is known as "quantitative metathesis". This is peculiar to Attic-Ionic and most uniformly observed in Attic, e.g., νεώς 'temple' from νηός (Hom.; Dor. νᾱός), λεώς from ληός (Hom. has the non-Ion. λᾱός), gen. sg. βασιλέως from βασιλῆος (Hom.; βασιλέος in later Ionic), and similarly acc. sg. βασιλέᾱ from βασιλῆα.

Homer often shows the older forms (as sometimes Hdt.), but also in many cases the shortening and quantitative metathesis, as gen. sg. -εω from -ηο beside Aeol. -ᾱο, or gen. pl. -εων from -ηων beside Aeol. -ᾱων. No brief statement can cover the details.

LENGTHENING OF VOWELS IN LATIN

99. 1. The simplification of certain consonant groups, as *sn, sd,* etc., and final *ns*, is attended by lengthening of the preceding vowel (see **202**.1, 3).

2. Vowels were regularly lengthened before *ns, nf, nx,* and *nct,* as in *cōnsul, īnfrā, iūnxī, iūnctus.*

a. Aside from statements like that of Cicero, *Orator* 159, that *in* and *con* were pronounced with long vowels when compounded with words beginning with *s* or *f,* or those of various grammarians for *amāns, dēns,* etc., the long vowel is very frequently indicated in inscriptions by the use of the apex or the I longa e.g. CÓNSVLES, ÍNFRA, CONIV́NXIT, IV́NCTA.

b. There was a tendency in some quarters to lengthen a vowel before *r*+consonant, and this seems to have become the accepted pronunciation in a few words, as *fōrma, ōrdō, ōrnō,* and perhaps *quārtus.*

c. A similar locally or socially restricted tendency to lengthen a vowel before *gn* will account for Priscian's statement that words ending in *gnus, gna, gnum* had a long vowel in the penult and for the occurrence of I longa in *signum, dignus, ignis, privignus.* But even in these words the Romance and other evidence points to *sĭgnum, dĭgnus,* etc., and in most words, like *magnus,* which with all its great frequency in inscriptions never appears with the apex, there is no justification for assuming a long vowel. In *rēgnum* the long vowel is original, as in *rēx, rēgis.* So in a few others.

d. The long vowel in the perf. pass. pple. of most roots ending in *g,* as *lēctus, rēctus, tēctus, āctus, tāctus, pāctus,* from *legō, regō,* etc., and of some of those ending in *d,* as *vīsus, fūsus, ēsus, cāsus,* from *videō,* etc., is regarded by many scholars as due to a lengthening which attended the change of the voiced consonant to a voiceless. But vowel lengthening on such a basis seems improbable, and furthermore it is not observed in *strictus, fissus, scissus, sessum.* Forms like *lēctus* may perfectly well contain the inherited *ē*-grade of the root which is seen in *lēgī, rēx, rēgis, ēdī, ēst,* etc., and *vīsus, fūsus* the form of the root that appears in *vīdī, fūdī;* and even those with *ā,* as *āctus* and *cāsus,* may be formed from *āg-, cād-,* etc., though these forms are not otherwise extant in Latin.

SHORTENING OF VOWELS IN LATIN

100. Long vowels were shortened in prehistoric times before a nasal or liquid+consonant. So regularly before *nt* or *nd,* as pres. pple. stem *amant-, vident- (amāns, vidēns,* by **99.**2), gerund. *amandus, videndus,* formed from the verb stems *amā-, vidē-.*

a. But changes in the historical period led to the existence of long vowels in this position, as *cōntiō* from *coventiō* (**92.**2*d*), *nūntiō* from **noventiō* (**92***e*), *ūndecim* from **oino-decem, prīnceps* from **prīmo-caps,* etc. There is evidence that in such words also the vowel was eventually shortened (e.g. *contio* in grammarians, *undecim, nuntiō* to be inferred from Fr. *onze, annoncer*), but probably not in the classical period.

101. Long vowels were regularly shortened before final *m*, *t*, *nt* (*nt* under **100**), and, except in monosyllables, before final *r* and *l*.

amābam, *-bat*, *-bant* beside *-bās*, *-bāmus*, *-bātis*, and *amābar* beside *-bāris*, etc.
amat, *amant* beside *amās*, etc.
pres. subj. *legam*, *legat*, *legant*, *legar* beside *legās*, etc.

And so in all verb forms in which the tense stem ended in a long vowel, as shown by the second singular, etc.

nom. sg. *pater*, *māter*: G. πατήρ, μήτηρ
nom. sg. *victor* etc.: G. -τωρ
nom.-acc. sg. neut. *animal*, *exemplar* beside gen. sg. *animālis*, *exemplāris*
acc. sg. of the first and fifth declensions, *-am*, *-em* from *-ām*, *-ēm*
gen. pl. *-um* from *-om* (**82.**2), this from *-ōm*: G. -ων

a. The shortening before final *t*, *r*, *l* began in iambic words (**102**), and in Plautus occurs only in such, and not always then. Forms like *vidēt*, *amōr*, etc., are even found in later poetry.

102. "*Iambic shortening*".—There was a marked tendency in colloquial speech, as reflected in early poetry, to shorten the final syllable, especially a final long vowel, in iambic words, thus changing the word rhythm from ⏑ – to ⏑ ⏑. This shortening was permanently effective in certain words.

bene, *male*, *modo*, *cito* beside *altē*, *prīmō*, etc. (**511.**4)
duo from **duō* (**313.**2) *ego*: G. ἐγώ
nisi, *quasi* from *nisī*, *quasī* (earlier *nisei*, *quasei*)
likewise *mihi*, *tibi*, *sibi*, *ibi*, *ubi* though here the poets continued to use also the older *mihī*, etc., at will

a. In Plautus we find also many instances like gen. sg. *boni*, abl. sg. *malo*, nom. pl. *viri*, imperat. *ama*, *mone*, *abi*, nom. sg. *homo*, 1 sg. *volo*. But the divergence thus created between forms of the same inflectional category (e.g. gen. sg. *boni*, but *prīmī*) was contrary to the tendency to uniformity within the same category, and the long vowel was restored as the normal in all these classes. Only in a few imperatives that were isolated by their interjectional use, as *ave*, *cave*, *puta*, the popular pronunciation with short vowel was generally accepted.

Forms like *homo*, *volo* are occasionally employed by poets of the later Republican and Augustan periods, and from Ovid on short *o* is more and more frequent, even in non-iambic words as *esto, ergo, octo.* By the 4th cent. A.D. the grammarians recognized final *ō* only in the dative and ablative singular and in the monosyllables *dō, stō.*

In Plautus the tendency to iambic shortening shows itself also in cases like *velĭnt, volŭptātēs,* etc. The details belong to the study of Plautine prosody.

103. Long vowels were generally shortened before another vowel. So *pius* from *pīus, seu* from **sēu* (**89.**2*a*), *fuit* from *fūit,* gen. sg. *reī, fideī* from *-ēī,* which was retained after *i,* as in *diēī, faciēī; deesse* from *dē-,* and likewise *dehinc, dehīscō,* for the weak *h* (**149**) did not prevent the shortening (cf. also *prǎ-eunte, prehendō*). But the long vowel was retained in some words, notably in the forms of *fīō* (except *fierī, fierem,* etc.). For the pronominal genitives the pronunciation *ūnīus, illīus,* etc., was the one which was regarded by the Romans as correct (perhaps owing to the influence of *eius, cuius,* etc.), though *ūnius, illius,* etc., were also familiar and often occur in poetry.

a. A final long vowel was sometimes shortened when an enclitic element was added. So *si quidem, tu quidem* beside *sī quidem, tū quidem* (with *sī, tū* restored by analogy) and always *quasi* from **quāsī* (probably from **quam-sei*) and *hodiē* from **hō-diē.*

CONTRACTION OF VOWELS IN GREEK

104. The prehistoric loss of intervocalic *y* (**178**) and *s* (**164**), and the later loss of intervocalic *ϝ* (**174**) produced a great variety of vowel combinations which generally underwent contraction. A table of the regular contractions in Attic may be found in a Greek grammar, and need not be repeated here. Most of them are illustrated in the inflection of the contract verbs. The following points may be noted here:

1. *ι* and *υ* unite with a preceding vowel to form diphthongs, as 2 sg. *εἶ,* from **ἔ(σ)ι.*

2. Like vowels contract to the corresponding long, whereby *ε+ε* and *o+o* give spurious *ει, ου,* but in some dialects *η, ω* (**96**).

3. In the combination of an *o*-vowel with an *a*- or *e*-vowel, the *o*-quality prevails, as *ω* from *a+o* or *o+a,* or spurious *ου* from *ε+o* or *o+ε. a+ε* gives *ā* (but Doric *η*), while *ε+a* gives *η.*

4. The contraction of *ε+o* to (spurious) *ου* (*φιλοῦμεν*) is Attic

only. In other dialects εο is uncontracted, or appears as ευ, especially in Ionic. Even in Attic εο and εα are uncontracted (1) when from εϝο, εϝα, as ἠδέος, ἠδέα, (2) in dissyllabic words, as θέος, ἔαρ.

5. The Attic-Ionic change of ᾱ to η (88) preceded the contraction, e.g. ᾱ+ω became first ηω, whence εω, ω, and ᾱ+ε became ηε, whence η. In the other dialects the result of contraction was ᾱ, e.g. gen. pl. 1st decl. -ᾱν = Att. -ῶν.

6. Certain irregularities of contraction are due to analogy, e.g. acc. pl. ὀστᾶ from ὀστέα, ἁπλᾶ from ἁπλόα, influenced by the α of the regular ending in δῶρα, etc.

7. Homeric forms like ὁρόω, ὁράασθαι are thought by some to represent an intermediate stage between ὁράω, ὁράεσθαι and ὁρῶ, ὁρᾶσθαι, one in which the vowels were assimilated but not yet contracted. But no such forms are attested by the inscriptions of any dialect, and the prevailing and more probable view is that they are artificial. After the contracted form had become current, the necessary metrical value was restored by a process of "distraction" (ᾱ to αα, ω to οω, etc.) instead of by a restoration of the original uncontracted forms.

CONTRACTION OF VOWELS IN LATIN

105. Contraction of vowels in Latin is less extensive and also more obscure in its results than in Greek. The principal occasion of contraction was the loss of intervocalic *y* (**178**), while in Greek not only *y* but also *s* and *w* were lost between vowels; *h* and *v* were sometimes lost between like vowels; some compounds of *dē-*, *pro-*, and *co-* with words beginning with a vowel show contraction.

1. Like vowels contract to the corresponding long vowel. So *trēs* from **treyes* (Skt. *trayas*), *cōpia* from **co-opia*, *nēmō* from **ne-hemō* (**80.**5), *nīl* beside *nihil*. The diphthong *ae* absorbs a following *e* or *i*, as in *praemium* from **prae-emium* (*emō*), *praebeō* beside *prae-hibeō*.

2. Unlike vowels. *dēgō* from **dē-agō*, *cōgō* from **co-agō*, *prōmō* from **pro-emō*, *cūrō*, etc. (denominatives of first conj.) from *-āyō* (but *-eō* uncontracted). *sōl* from **sāol*, **sāvol*, **sāvel* (cf. Goth.

sauil, G. dial. ἀϝέλιος), but *mālō*, *Mārs* with *ā* under the influence of the parallel uncontracted forms *māvolō*, *Māvors*.

In the denominatives of the first, second, and fourth conjugations part of the forms are the result of normal contraction (as in Greek), but others probably not (see **371, 373, 376**).

PROTHETIC VOWEL IN GREEK

106. A prothetic vowel, usually ε, sometimes α or ο, appears regularly before ρ, when this represents an original initial *r*, and less commonly before initial λ, μ, ϝ.

ἐρυθρός:L. *ruber*, Skt. *rudhiras*, Eng. *red*

ἔρεβος: Goth. *riqis* 'darkness', Skt. *rajas* 'mist, darkness'

ἐλεύθερος:L. *liber*   ἀλίνω:L. *lino*

ἀμέλγω:L. *mulgeō*, Skt. *mṛj-* 'wipe', Eng. *milk*

εἴκοσι from *ἐϝικοσι beside Dor. ϝίκατι:L. *vigintī*

Hom. ἐέρση from *ἐϝέρση:Skt. *varṣas* 'rain'; similarly Hom. ἐέργω

(Att. εἴργω), ἔεδνα, ἐέλδωρ, etc.

a. In ὄνομα (L. *nōmen*, Skt. *nāma*), the initial vowel belongs to a fuller form of the stem, perhaps also in ἀνήρ (Skt. *nar-*, Osc. *ner-*), and some others.

An ι, apparently prothetic, appears in ἴσθι, (cf. Av. *zdī*), ἰκτῖνος (cf. Skt. *çyenas*), and a few others. The first reminds one of vulg. L. *ispiritus* (Fr. *esprit*), etc., but is an isolated case in Greek.

ANAPTYXIS IN LATIN

107. In Latin an anaptyctic vowel (**40.**3) develops regularly in the case of the groups *cl* and *bl*, where it takes on the quality of the following vowel.

pōculum, early *pōcolom*, from **pōclom*

facilis from **faclis*   *stabulum, stabilis* from **stablom, *stablis*

Occasionally a vowel is developed in other groups of consonants, and especially in borrowed words, as *mina* from μνᾶ. In Greek the second vowel of ἕβδομος, dial. ἕβδεμος is anaptyctic.

VOWEL SYNCOPE IN LATIN

108. In languages with a stress accent, like English, an unaccented short vowel is often suppressed. So in NE *chapter* from *chapiter*, *captain* from *capitain*, colloquial and poetic *ev'ry* beside more formal *every, gen'ral* beside *general*, and countless others. Such syncope of short vowels is unknown in ancient Greek with its pitch accent, but is very common in Latin. As in English, this occurred at various periods in the history of the language; and, apart from the fact that the vowel was unaccented, under diverse conditions too complex to admit of any precise formulation. In most cases the older form was definitely displaced by the syncopated form, but sometimes both forms were in use.

Syncope occurred most extensively in the prehistoric period (and so under the older accentual system when all words were stressed on the initial syllable, **221**), and left no trace of the unsyncopated form. Thus *dexter* from **déxiteros* (cf. δεξιτερός), *rettulī* from **ré-teluli, quīndecim* from *quīnque* and *decem, prīnceps* from **prīmo-caps;* in final syllable, in *mors, pars, mēns, mōns,* etc., from **mortis* (Skt. *mṛtis*), etc.; final vowel, in *ab, sub* (G. ἀπό, ὑπό, Skt. *apa, upa*), personal endings *-t, -nt* from *-ti, -nti* (**337, 340**).

Parallel forms in related words: *superus* but *suprā, suprēmus, īnferus* but *īnfrā, validus* but *valdē* (*valide* in Plautus).

Parallel forms of the same word: *calidus* and *caldus, solidus* and *soldus, surrigō* and *surgō; neque* and *nec, atque* and *ac* (in Plautus also *nemp* beside *nempe,* etc.).

a. Among the probable factors determining the presence or absence of syncope may be mentioned: quality of the vowel, *i* being the shortest of all vowels and the one which is oftenest lost; position in open or close syllable, cf. *dexter* from **dexiteros,* but *sinister;* quantity of following syllable, cf. *superus,* but *suprā, suprēmus;* familiarity of consonant group resulting from syncope, cf. *caldus,* but not *frigdus* until late. But the complexity of factors and the variety of cross currents make it impossible to lay down any precise rules. The parallelism of *calidus* and *caldus* was like that of *every* and *ev'ry* in English, *caldus* being the colloquial form, frequently appearing in poetry, while *calidus* was preferred in more formal speech, though Quintilian in his time regarded it as pedantic.

Syncope was further extended in late vulgar Latin, e.g. *frigdus* (It. *freddo,* Fr. *froid*) from *frīgidus,* and still further in the several Romance languages, most of all in French, e.g. *chambre* from *camera,* still unchanged in Italian.

109. Syncope is frequent in the case of final *-ros* and *-ris*. The resulting *-rs* becomes *-r* (**200.2, 212.6**), as in *vir* from **viros, puer* from **pueros*. If a consonant precedes, the *r* becomes syllabic and then -er, as in *ager* from **agros* (G. ἀγρός), *sacer* from *sakros* (in forum inscr.), *Alexander* from Ἀλέξανδρος, *ācer* from **ākris*, etc. So also, even in accented syllables, *ter* from **tris* (G. τρίς, Skt. *tris*), *testis* 'witness' orig. 'third party' from **tristis*, *cernō*, *certus* from **krinō*, **kritos* (G. κρῑ́νω from **κρινι̯ω*, κριτός). The more special conditions for these last (as contrasted with *tribus*, etc.) are obscure.

VOWEL WEAKENING IN LATIN

110. In languages with a stress accent, an unaccented short vowel, instead of being wholly lost (**108**), may suffer a change of quality, which under these conditions is known as weakening (**40.**5). In Latin the weakening took place in the preliterary period, under the old accentual system of initial accent (**221**). It is mainly in the direction of raising and in part fronting of the vowels, as $a > e$, $o > e$, $e > i$. Long vowels were not affected, but diphthongs were, through the change in quality of their first element. The earliest change was that of a, and in part o, to e, after which this e together with original e was further changed to i under certain conditions. More specifically the changes in medial syllables are as follows:

1. a becomes e, and this is further changed to i before a single consonant except r, also (by **79.**1) to i before ng, and (by **80.**6, **82.**1) to u before l+consonant.

*perfactos > perfectus   **perfaciō > *perfeciō > perficiō*
*talantom (τάλαντον) *> talentum*   **peparai > peperī*
*cecadai > *cecedei > cecidī   **attangō > *attengō > attingō* (**79.**1)
*insaltō > *inseltō > īnsoltō (**80.**6) *> īnsultō* (**82.**1)

a. In the history of *attingō, cōnfringō, īnsultō, inculcō*, etc., only the first step, resulting in **attengō, *inseltō*, etc., belongs properly under the head of weakening, which did not affect further the *e* in these forms any more than in *perfectus* or elsewhere before two consonants. The subsequent steps are due to the fact that the weakening to *e* took place early enough to bring these forms under the action of certain other phonetic laws which affected both accented and unaccented vowels, namely those stated in **79.**1, **80.**6, **82.**1.

The retention of *e* in *peperī*, contrasted with *cecidī*, as of orig. *e* in *congerō*, contrasted with *adsideō* (3), is due to the fact that *r* often tends to lower a vowel (**39.**2), or, as here, to prevent its raising.

2. *o* before a single consonant except *l* becomes *e*, which remains after *i*, otherwise is further changed to *i*.

*socio-tās > societās   **novo-tās* (cf. G. νεότης) *> novitās*
*in-(s)locō > īlicō   **hosti-potis > *hospet(i)s > hospes* (*e* kept in final syllable), gen. *hospitis*

a. Before *l* or two consonants *o* remained well into the historical period, when it became *u* (**82.**3).

3. *e*, unless preceded by *i*, becomes *i* before a single consonant except *r*.

*atteneō > attineō   **conregō > corrigō*
*adsedeō > adsideō   **compremō > comprimō*
But *congerō*, etc.

4. Instead of the weakening to *i* before a single consonant, as stated in 1, 2, 3, we sometimes find *u*, whence in part later *i*, before *p, b, f*, or *m*, especially when the influence of these labials was supported by rounded vowels in the surrounding syllables.

Thus, from the root *cap-* (*capiō*), *occupō* beside *occipiō, anticipō, aucupis* (*auceps*) beside *prīncipis* (*prīnceps*), *mancupium*, later *mancipium*

Further *contubernālis* (*taberna*), *surrupuit*, later *surripuit* (*rapiō*)
proxumus, optumus, maxumus, later *proximus*, etc.
possumus, volumus beside *legimus*, etc.
aurufex, pontufex, later *aurifex, pontifex*.

a. It is impossible to formulate the conditions more precisely, or to distinguish always between phonetic and analogical change. Analogy tended to the generalization of *-imus* in the superlatives, and in the first plural ending which was further supported by the second plural *-itis* (lacking in the case of *volumus, possumus, quaesumus*). Presumably *documentum, monumentum*, but *tegimentum* represent the normal phonetic relation, while *monimentum, docimentum, tegumentum* are analogical.

In cases like *optumus, optimus* the spelling with *u* prevails in early times, while after some fluctuation the spelling with *i* became the standard. Quintilian and others state that the sound was intermediate between *u* and *i*, from which it is inferred that it was like Fr. *u* or Ger. *ü*. But if so, it is remarkable that the spelling with *y*, which was introduced to represent this sound in Greek words (**69**), was not also employed in words of this class. It is more probable, though not the usual view, that we have to do with an ordinary *u* in the early *maxumus* (as obviously in the persistent *occupō*) and with an ordinary *i* in the later *maximus*, the alleged intermediate sound being imaginary, suggested by the fluctuation in spelling.

5. *ai* becomes *ei*, *ę̄*, whence *ī; au* becomes (probably *ou*, whence) *ū; av* and *ov* become *u*.

*incaidō>inceidō (SC de Bacch.), *incīdō*
*inquairō>inquīrō   **inclaudō>inclūdō*   **adcausō>accūsō*
*ēlavō>ēluō   *dē novō>dēnuō*

111. Exceptions to the foregoing rules are mostly due to analogical influence.

1. In compounds the influence of the simplex may cause the retention or the restoration of its vowel, that is recomposition (**48.**2). This may be actual recomposition in the historical period, as in *ēnecō* (*necō*) replacing early *ēnicō*, or *consacrō* in inscriptions of imperial times for usual *consecrō*, or late composition as in *circumagō* beside *adigō*, etc., or the continuous retention of the original vowel, as in *adlegō*, *intellegō* beside *colligō*, *dēligō*, or *adhaereō*, *exaudiō* contrasted with *inquīrō*, *inclūdō*. Compounds of verbs containing *o* in the root syllable never show the weakening, e.g., *abrogō*, *conlocō*, *admoneō*.

2. Besides recomposition, there are other types of analogical influence, e.g. *integer* (from *tag-* of *tangō*), instead of **intiger*, under the influence of the oblique cases *integrī*, etc., where the *e* before two consonants is regular. The frequent interchange of *e* and *i* (from *a* or *e*), as in *prīnceps*, *prīncipis*, *mīles*, *mīlitis*, and especially *artifex*, *-ficis*, etc., has led to *iūdex*, *iūdicis*, *index*, *indicis*, instead of **iūdix*, **indix* (*-dic-s*). Compounds of *gradior*, *gressus* (**121**), have *-gredior* (not *-gridior*), *gressus* with generalization of the *e*.

3. In some cases the assimilative influence of the vowel of the preceding syllable has been a factor in preventing weakening, e.g., in *alacer* or gen. sg. *anatis* (*anas*), *segetis* (*seges*), *tegetis* (*teges*), etc., contrasted with *principis*, *mīlitis*.

4. A few compounds show syncope instead of weakening, as *pergō* from **per-regō*, *surgō* beside early *surrigō*, rarely *porgō* beside *porrigō*. So, apparently, with vocalization of a preceding

consonantal *u* or *i*, *-cutiō* (whence also *-cussi*, *-cussus*) in compounds of *quatiō*, as *percutiō*, etc., and *-iciō* in compounds of *iaciō*,
as *adiciō*, etc. But for the last we have also early *adieciō*, *reieciō*
(first syllable long as in *eius*, that. is, *eiius*, **179**.2), and such
forms are reflected by *adiciō*, *reiciō* with first syllable long in
poetry.

112. The vowel changes in final syllables agree only partially
with those in medial syllables.

The weakening of *a* to *e* is seen in *prīnceps* (*cap-*), *artifex* (*fac-*),
etc., also in *cornicen* (*can-*), *oscen*, etc. (not -*cin, for even a single
consonant when final makes a closed syllable).

An *e* remains before a final nasal, as in *nōmen* (but *nōminis*),
decem (but *decimus;* yet also *ūndecim*, etc,); but it becomes *i* before
final *s* or *t*, as gen. sg. *rēgis* from *-es* (**245**.2), 2 sg. *legis*, 3 sg. *legit*
from *-esi*, *-eti* (**332, 349**). Secondary *-es* from *-ets*, as in *mīles*,
hospes (*hospotis > *hospets) was not affected.

Other changes in final syllables have been mentioned elsewhere,
as that of *o* to *u* (**82**.2), or *ai* and *oi* to *ī* (**90, 91**), final *i* to *e* (**74b**).

SYLLABIC LIQUIDS AND NASALS

113. Liquids and nasals are sounds of such sonority that, while
they usually have the function of consonants and so are normally
ranked as such, they may also have the function of the ordinary
vowels, that is, they may be pronounced so as to form a distinct
syllable without the aid of other vowels. This is the case in many
languages, and so in English in the unaccented syllables of words
like *able, hidden, bottom*, in which the vowels which appear in the
spelling are no longer pronounced, but only the *l, n, m*. Such
sounds are assumed for the parent speech, and are best termed
"syllabic"[1] liquids and nasals and distinguished from the corresponding consonants by the symbols *ŗ, ḷ, ṇ, ṃ*. And whatever the
precise phonetic character of the sounds in the parent speech,

[1] If we chose to define vowel and consonant solely by their difference of function
in the syllable, we might speak of "vowel" liquids and nasals. There is no very
serious objection to this, and in fact the Sanskrit *r* and *ḷ* are regularly known as
"vowels". But it is preferable to hold to the traditional application of the term
vowel, and to use "syllabic" where it is simply a matter of syllable-making function.

which is of small consequence, the symbols $ṛ$, $ḷ$, etc., are those which best represent the essential facts of their historical relations.

For the sounds in question were (1) related to r, l, etc., in precisely the same way as i to y or u to w (e.g., acc. sg. ending m after vowels, $ṃ$ after consonants), and (2) were reduced forms of fuller er, el, etc. (or re, etc.), parallel to i beside ei or u beside eu, as will be made clear in the discussion of vowel gradation (**117, 118**).

In the position before a vowel, and in part before y or w, the development in some of the IE languages is different from that before a consonant. We shall speak of antevocalic $ṛ$, etc., for which many scholars use a different symbol, as $ₑr$ or the like.

In the accompanying table "+vow." is to be understood as covering in part, and certainly for Greek, the position before y or w.

IE		G.	L.	Skt.	Lith.	Gmc.
$ṛ$	+cons.............	αρ, ρα	*or*	$ṛ$	*ir*	*ur, or*
	+vow.............	αρ	*ar*	*ir, ur*		
$ḷ$	+cons.............	αλ, λα	*ol*	$ṛ$	*il*	*ul, ol*
	+vow.............	αλ	*al*	*ir, ur*		
$ṇ$	+cons.............	α	*en*	*a*	*in*	*un*
	+vow.............	αν	*an*(?)	*an*		
$ṃ$	+cons.............	α	*em*	*a*	*im*	*um*
	+vow.............	(αμ)	*am*(?)	*am*		

114. IE $ṛ$ and $ḷ$. G. καρδίᾱ, κραδίη, L. *cor*, gen. *cordis*, Lith. *širdis*, Skt. *hṛd* (though this last does not agree in the initial consonant).

G. θάρσος, θράσος, Skt. *dhṛṣ-* 'dare', OE *dorste* 'durst'

L. *poscō* from **porscō*, Skt. *pṛcchāmi* 'ask', NHG *forschen*

L. *mollis* from **moldwis*, Skt. *mṛdus*

G. πλατύς, Skt. *pṛthus*   ἔσταλμαι beside στέλλω, etc. (**119.**5)

The conditions governing the interchange of αρ, αλ and ρα, λα

before consonants are not determined. In some words the difference is one of dialect, but not in most.

G. βαρύs, Skt. gurus, Goth. kaúrus 'heavy' (aúr = or)

G. βάλλω from *βάλι̯ω beside βέλos (**119.**5)

L. carō originally 'a portion, a cut': G. ἐκάρην aor. pass. of κείρω

a. It is uncertain whether L. pariō (from a weak grade of *per- in Lith.
periu 'brood, hatch') or morior (beside mors: Skt. mṛtis) represents the normal
Latin development of ṛ before y, since either may be explained by the analogy
of other forms.

b. In a few words IE ṛ, ḷ seem to be represented by G. υρ, υλ, L. ur, ul (and
similarly Lith. ur, ul, instead of ir, il). G. ἄγυρις, ἀγύρτης beside ἀγείρω
(*ἀγερι̯ω), ἀγορά, etc. L. mulier probably related to mollis (above). The
setting up of IE ᵘṛ, ᵘḷ (that is, ṛ, ḷ with u-timbre) is a convenient device for
grouping such cases, though not an explanation.

115. IE ṇ and ṃ. IE negative prefix *ṇ- (the weak form of IE
*ne in Skt. na, L. ne-fās), G. ἀ-, before vowels ἀν- (ἄ-πιστος, ἄν-υδρος),
Skt. a-, before vowels an- (a-kṛtas, an-udras), L. in- (from en-),
Germanic un- (NE un- beside the borrowed L. in-).

IE *dekṃ, G. δέκα, L. decem, Skt. daça, Goth. taíhun, Lith. dešimt

IE *ḱṃtom, G. ἑκατόν, L. centum, Skt. çatam, Goth. hund, Lith.
šimtas

IE -ṃ, acc. sg. ending of consonant stems (beside -m of vowel
stems), G. -a, L. -em (Skt. -am after analogy of vowel stems)

IE -ṇs, acc. pl. ending of consonant stems (beside -ns of vowel
stems), G. -as, L. -ēs (from -ens), Skt. -as, Goth. -uns

IE -ṇtai, -ṇto, 3 pl. mid. endings after consonants (beside -ntai,
-nto after vowels), G. -αται, -ατο, Skt. -ate, -ata

G. βάσις, βατός, Skt. gatis, gatas, L. con-ventiō, Goth. ga-qumþs,
from IE *gʷṃ- weak grade of *gʷem- in Skt. gam-, Goth. qiman

So also G. βαίνω (*βανι̯ω) from *gʷṃyō, and perhaps L. veniō (or
from *gʷemyō?), for which see also **196.**

a. It is a disputed question whether ṇ before vowels is represented in Latin
by en (as before consonants) or by an (parallel to ar from ṛ before vowels).
The latter view is preferred here. So maneō from *mṇ- beside *men- in G.
μένω, and the difficult canis: G. κύων, κυνός, apparently a blend of *ḱwṇ-
and ḱun-.

116. IE r̥̄, l̥̄, n̥̄, m̥̄. There is evidence that there existed in the parent speech certain sounds which, whatever their precise phonetic value, are genetically related to r̥, etc., precisely as ī to i or ū to u. The symbols r̥̄, etc., are those best adapted to reflect this situation and, though discarded by many scholars, will be retained here. Like ī and ū, the r̥̄, etc., resulted from contraction of the weak grades of dissyllabic stems, that is, r̥ə, etc., which might also remain uncontracted and appear in Greek as αρα, etc., as θάνατος beside Dor. θνᾱτός (see **126**).

Their representation is as follows:

Skt..............	ĭr, ŭr	ā (ām)
G...............	ρᾱ, λᾱ or ρω, λω	νᾱ, μᾱ (Att.-Ion. νη, μη)
L...............	rā, lā	nā, mā

Skt. ūrṇā, Dor. λᾱνος, L. lāna (Goth. wulla, Lith. vilna, etc.)

Dor. τλᾱτός, L. lātus (*tlātos beside tollō)

Skt. stīrṇas, L. strātus, G. στρωτός　　Skt. jātas, L. nātus

Dor. θνᾱτός, κμᾱτός, δμᾱτός beside θάνατος, κάματος, ἐδάμασα

a. The Greek correspondence to Skt. ĭr, ŭr has been much disputed. It is assumed here that it is normally ρᾱ, λᾱ, parallel to the νᾱ, μᾱ. But forms like στρωτός, βλώσκω, βιβρώσκω, βρωτός seem also to belong here (rather than from IE *strō-, etc., for which there is no evidence, as there is for IE ǵnō-, G. γνω-), and are perhaps to be explained by their relation to o-forms like ἐστόρεσα, ἔμολον, though these also are puzzling (**127b**).

VOWEL GRADATION

117. The term vowel gradation (for which the brief German "ablaut" is also familiar) is applied to certain alternations of vowel which recur in the several IE languages and must have originated in the parent speech—such, for example, as are seen in G. πείθω, πέποιθα, ἔπιθον, L. fīdō, foedus, fīdēs, or in NE drive, drove, driven, all pointing to IE ei—oi—i. They are to be distinguished from those alternations which, however regular, have arisen under the special phonetic laws of a particular language, as in L. faciō, adficiō, adfectus (**110**), where one may at most speak of a secondary vowel gradation.

The inherited vowel gradation arose under the accentual and other conditions of the parent speech, conditions which affected every syllable of the word, whether belonging to the root or to a formative element. Hence the gradation, while most conspicuous in the root syllables, is by no means confined to these. Thus we find gradation in the root *ter-* and likewise in the suffix *-ter-*. To cover all such cases one may use "stem" ("base" has also been introduced in this connection) as a general term for the syllable (or, in some cases the group of syllables, **126**) involved. It is customary to cite the stems in what is believed to be the "normal" or fundamental grade.

Vowel gradation is a conspicuous and vital feature in the interrelations of Greek forms, as it is also in Sanskrit and in the Germanic languages, where it still pervades the forms of the strong verbs, as in NE *drive, drove, driven,* or *sing, sang, sung.* In Latin, on the other hand, vowel gradation has been to a considerable degree eliminated by the generalization of one or the other grade, and while it is still reflected by certain occasional alternations, it has ceased to play any such significant rôle as in Greek.

118. The *e*-series. By far the most prevalent gradation is that which falls under the *e*-series, in which the normal grade contains *e*. This series is then to be further subdivided, according as the normal grade contains simple *e* between stops, e.g. *pet,* or *ei, eu, er, en,* etc. (or *ye, we, re,* etc.), in which the *e* is followed (or preceded) by an element which is itself capable of syllabic function. The general scheme is as shown in the accompanying table.

STRONG		WEAK			LENGTHENED	
e-Grade	*o*-Grade	Reduced Grade		Zero Grade	*ē*-Grade	*ō*-Grade
1. *e*	*o*	*e*		o	*ē*	*ō*
		+vow.	+cons.	+vow.		
2. *ei*	*oi*	*i*	*i*	*y*	*ēi*	*ōi*
3. *eu*	*ou*	*u*	*u*	*w*	*ēu*	*ōu*
4. *er*	*or*	*r̥*	*r̥*	*r*	*ēr*	*ōr*
5. *el*	*ol*	*l̥*	*l̥*	*l*	*ēl*	*ōl*
6. *en*	*on*	*n̥*	*n̥*	*n*	*ēn*	*ōn*
7. *em*	*om*	*m̥*	*m̥*	*m*	*ēm*	*ōm*

a. It is to be understood that we may have, for example, *we* (*wo*, etc.) as well as *eu,* with the same weak grade *u,* or *re* (*ro,* etc.) as well as *er,* with the same weak grade *r̥*. Before a vowel we have *ey* (*oy,* etc.), *ew* (*ow,* etc.) instead of *ei, eu.* Such alternatives are omitted from the table, in order not to make it still more cumbersome. But they are represented in some of the illustrations to follow.

For much of the material the differences under the weak grade may be ignored. In the first subdivision the reduced grade, as p_et, is somewhat problematical and assumed only for some few forms (121). In 2–7, if the stem ends in a consonant (a stop or s; there are no original roots in -ein-, -eil- or the like), there is only one form of the weak grade, namely that given in the central column. Thus G. λιπ-, φυγ-, weak grade of λειπ-, φευγ-.

If the stem ends in ei, eu, etc., and a consonant follows, the weak grade can likewise be only i, u, etc., as in G. ἴ-μεν, Skt. i-más beside εἶ-μι, ê-mi. But if a vowel follows, the weak grade may be either i, u, $ŗ$, etc., or y, w, r, etc. While this is only a matter of syllabic function, and is in part conditioned by the preceding consonants, and so not strictly a matter of gradation, it is customary and sometimes convenient to call the former the reduced grade and the latter the zero grade. Thus with reduced grade (R) G. κλύω beside e-grade in κλέ(ϝ)ος (cf. Skt. aor. açruvam, 3 sg. perf. mid. çuçruve), ἐρρύην (e-grade in ῥέ[ϝ]ω), ἔβαλον (e-grade in βέλος, Arc. δέλλω), ἔκτανον (e-grade in κτείνω from *κτενι̯ω), etc., but with zero grade (Z) G. ἤγρετο, ἀγρόμενος (e-grade in ἀγείρω from *ἀγέρι̯ω), ἔπλετο, -πλομενος (e-grade in πέλομαι), ἔπεφνον (e-grade in θείνω from *θενι̯ω), etc.

119. The most commonly occurring grades are the *e*-grade, the *o*-grade, and the weak grade, so examples of these will be given first. One must bear in mind the representation of IE $ŗ$, $ņ$, etc. (**114, 115**), and, for the Sanskrit comparisons, the merging of IE *e* and *o* in *a* (**73**.4) and the consequent loss of distinction between the *e*- and *o*-grades.

e-Grade	*o*-Grade	Weak Grade
1. G. πέτομαι	ποτή	ἐπτόμην, πτερόν
Skt. pátāmi		paptúr
G. ἕπομαι (*σεπ-, **161**)		ἑσπόμην
L. sequor	socius	
Skt. sáce		saçcúr
G. ἔχω (*σεχ-, **161a**)	ὄχοι	ἔσχον
2. G. πείθω	πέποιθα	ἔπιθον
L. fīdō	foedus	fidēs
G. δείκνυμι		δίκη
L. dīcō		dictus, abdicāre
Skt. dekṣyámi		diṣṭás, diç-
G. λείπω	λέλοιπα, λοιπός	ἔλιπον
G. στείχω	στοῖχος	ἔστιχον
Goth. steiga	staig	stigans
NE drive	drove	driven
	(o = OE ā, Goth. ai, IE oi)	

e-Grade	o-Grade	Weak Grade
3. G. πεύθομαι		ἐπυθόμην
Skt. bódhāmi	bubódha	buddhás
Goth. biudan	bauþ	budans
L. dūcō		ductus, dux
G. φεύγω		ἔφυγον
G. σπεύδω	σπουδή	....
G. χέ(ϝ)ω	χο(ϝ)ή	κέχυται
Skt. svapnas, L. somnus (*swepnos)		G. ὕπνος
4, 5. G. δέρκομαι	δέδορκα	ἔδρακον
Skt. ádarçam	dadárça	ádṛçam, dṛṣṭás
G. δέρω	δορά	δέδαρμαι, δαρθείς
G. τρέπω	τέτροφα, τρόπος	ἔτραπον
L. precor	procus	poscō from *porscō
Skt. praçnás		pṛcchāmi
G. στέλλω	στόλος	ἔσταλμαι
G. βέλος	βολή	βάλλω
6, 7. G. τείνω (*τένι̯ω)	τόνος	τέταμαι, τατός
Skt. tántum		tatás
G. θείνω (*θένι̯ω)	φόνος	πέφαμαι, ἔπεφνον
Skt. hántum	ghanás	hatás
G. μένω	μονή	μίμνω
G. ἐγενόμην, γένος	γέγονα, γόνος	γίγνομαι, γεγάμεν
L. genus		gignō
NE drink	drank	drunk

120. Further examples, with inclusion of the ē- and ō-grades are:

e-Grade	o-Grade	Weak Grade	ē-Grade	ō-Grade
1. L. pedis	G. ποδός....	....	L. pēs	Dor. πώς¹
	Skt. padás......	....	Skt. pāt	Goth. fōtus
3. { G. ἔπος (ϝέπος).......	ὄψ, L. vocō	....	....	L. vōx
{ Skt. vácas............		uktá	....	vāk
4. { G. πατέρα..........	ἀπάτορα	πατρός, πατράσι	πατήρ	ἀπάτωρ
{ Skt. pitáram........		pitṛé, pitṛ́ṣu	pitā́	....
6. G. φρένα............	ἄφρονα	φρασί(Pind.) ἀρνός, κυνός	φρήν ἀρήν	ἄφρων κύων

¹ Att. πούς (ου=secondary ō) cannot directly represent any inherited grade. It is a new analogical form, for which the special model is uncertain.

121. The reduced grade of the type *pₑt* is assumed as the source of certain otherwise anomalous forms, such as L. *quattuor*, Hom. πίσυρες, beside τέσσερες, Skt. *catvāras* with IE *e* in the first syllable, L. *pateō* beside G. ἐπέτασα, G. ἵππος beside L. *equus*, L. *magnus* beside G. μέγας, L. *gradior* beside *gressus*, etc. Further, G. νύξ, νυκτός beside L. *nox, noctis*, and some other instances of υ in connection with liquids and nasals, are brought under this head by some. The problem of these and still other occasional anomalies in the *e*-series is too uncertain for further discussion here.

122. *Conditions and causes.*—Since vowel gradation was already an accomplished fact in the parent speech, the result of processes which took place well back in its history, it is natural that the precise conditions and causes of these remote processes should be involved in obscurity.

One phase, however, is reasonably clear, namely the relation of the weak to the strong forms. The normal grade was weakened in the syllable preceding the accent, at a period of the parent speech when the accent had a considerable element of stress. In Sanskrit, where the position of the IE accent is best preserved, this relation between accent and gradation is most apparent. Cf. pres. 1 sg. *émi* but 1 pl. *imás* (G. εἶμι, ἴμεν with secondary accent), infin. *étum* but perf. pass. pple. *itás*, pres. *bódhāmi* but *tudámi* (cf. G. λείπων, φεύγων but λιπών, φυγών, the old accent being preserved in the pple. and infin.), perf. 1 sg. *véda* but 1 pl. *vidmá* (G. οἶδα, ἴδμεν with secondary accent).

a. It is true that the Sanskrit (as the Greek) accent was one of pitch, and one does not readily connect vowel weakening with a pitch accent. But there is no objection to the view that, while Sanskrit preserves the IE position of the accent (as confirmed by other evidence) and probably the character of the accent in the latest IE period, this accent at a remoter period of the parent speech was one of greater stress. At any rate one cannot reasonably deny the very extensive evidence of an original relation between gradation and accent. It does not follow that this relation was kept intact and is to be observed in all categories of forms. Even in the parent speech there were doubtless many subsequent shifts, so that a weak grade might come to be accented or conversely.

b. The qualitative change of *e* to *o*, and of *ē* to *ō*, is of obscure origin. A relation between vowel quality and accent is observed in certain Greek types, as φρήν, pl. φρένες, but ἄφρων, ἄφρονες, πατήρ, πατέρες, but ἀπάτωρ, ἀπάτορες, ποιμήν but δαίμων, ῥητήρ but ῥήτωρ. But generally no such relation holds, and the accent (in this case one of pitch) can at the most have been only one of a variety of factors.

c. The lengthened grades occur mainly, though not exclusively, in final syllables, especially the nominative singular of consonant stems. The lengthening (of *e* to *ē*, whence also *ō*) probably started as some kind of compensative lengthening, but the more precise conditions are altogether obscure.

123. The *a*- and the *o*-series. An original *o*-series is a somewhat doubtful assumption, to cover certain groups of cognates in which *o* appears not alternating with *e* or *a*, and so as if representing the normal grade, the only other grade, and that rare, being *ō*.

So G. ὄϝις, οἶς, L. *ovis*, Ir. *oi, oe*, Skt. *avis*

G. ὄσσε, ὄψομαι, L. *oculus*, Skt. *akṣi*, etc.

G. ὄζω, ὄδωδα   L. *fodiō, fōdī*

The *a*-series is of more consequence, but rare compared to the *e*-series, and apart from the normal and weak grades the material is so meager as to leave doubt as to the full constitution of the IE series. Some examples of the actual alternation are as tabulated.

G. ἄγω	ὄγμος		ἀγωγή	
L. *agō*		*ambāges*		
Skt. *ájāmi*				*pari-j-man*
G. ἄκρος	ὄκρις			
L. *aciēs*	*ocris*	*ācer*		
G. αἴθω				
L. *aedēs*				
Skt. *edhas*				*iddhás*
G. αὖος, Lith. *sausas*				Skt. *çuṣkas* (for **suṣkas*)

a. A Greek alternation of *a* with *ā* (Att.-Ion. *η*) may be assigned to either this or the *ā*-series (ἵστημι, στατός, etc., **124**). It is usual in verbs like ἁνδάνω (perf. Hom. ἔᾱδε; cf. ἡδύς, Dor. ᾱδύς), λαμβάνω (λήψομαι, εἴληφα), λανθάνω (λήσω, λέληθα), etc. Since roots of the *e*-series show the weak grade in corresponding nasal infix presents (**354.**6), as πυνθάνομαι beside πεύθομαι, it is natural to assume that here too it is the weak grade in the present, that is, λαβ-, etc., beside strong grade λᾱβ-, and accordingly in the *ā*-series. But it is difficult to reconcile certain Sanskrit forms (as *svād-, svad-*, not *svād-, svid-*). One must take the Greek alternation as it stands, without regard to its relation to the IE series, which from the point of view of internal Greek relations is not important.

124. The $\bar{e}$-, $\bar{a}$-, and $\bar{o}$-series. These three series, of which the first is next in importance to the e-series, are typically represented in the gradation of the roots of τίθημι, ἵστημι (ἵστᾱμι), δίδωμι, namely IE *dhē-, *stā-, *dō-. The weak forms appear either in a zero grade, in which the vowel is wholly lost, or a reduced grade, in which the long vowel is reduced to IE $ə$. In Greek and Latin it is nearly always the reduced grade which appears, even in forms where Sanskrit has the zero grade. But in Greek, instead of having uniformly $a =$ Skt. i from IE $ə$ (**85**), we commonly find $ε$ or o where the normal grade has η or ω, probably by qualitative assimilation to the latter.

If the long vowel was preceded by y or w, the reduced grades $yə$, $wə$ were usually contracted to $\bar{\imath}$, $\bar{u}$. So the opt. mood-sign, strong -$y\bar{e}$-, weak -$\bar{\imath}$- (**419**). But in Greek there are also some forms pointing to uncontracted $yə$ (or $iə$). So fem. suffix, -$y\bar{a}$-, nom. sg. -$\bar{\imath}$ in Sanskrit, etc., but -ια in Greek, as φέρουσα from *φέροντια : Skt. bharantī (**237**). Cf. also G. πρία-σθαι : Skt. krī-ṇā-mi.

If the normal grade contained a long diphthong, as $\bar{e}i$, $\bar{o}i$, $\bar{e}u$, etc., the reduced grades $əi$, $əu$ were usually contracted to $\bar{\imath}$, $\bar{u}$ (but $əy$-, $əw$- before a vowel). Owing to the loss of the second element in the long diphthongs before a consonant (**94**), the resulting alternation might be $\bar{e}:\bar{\imath}$ or $\bar{o}:\bar{\imath}$, or $\bar{o}:\bar{u}$, etc.

The general scheme is as tabulated, in which $\bar{a}^x$ may stand for IE $\bar{e}$, $\bar{a}$, or $\bar{o}$.

STRONG		WEAK	
Normal Grade	$\bar{o}$-Grade	Reduced Grade	Zero Grade
$\bar{a}^x$.............	$\bar{o}$	$ə$	o
$y\bar{a}^x$.............	....	$(yə)$ $\bar{\imath}$	i
$w\bar{a}^x$	....	$(wə)$ $\bar{u}$	u
$\bar{a}^x(i)$.............	....	$(əi)$ $\bar{\imath}$	i
$\bar{a}^x(u)$	....	$(əu)$ $\bar{u}$	u

a. The forms that are put here under reduced grade are the more common forms of the weak grade in categories where roots of the e-series show the zero grade (Skt. hitás parallel to çrutás, etc.) and are classed by some as zero grade, in which case the forms put here under zero grade would have to be a sort of "infra-zero" grade. But the above classification seems on the whole preferable, especially in connection with dissyllabic stems (**126**).

125. Examples of the ē-, ā-, and ō-series.

STRONG		**WEAK**	
Normal Grade	ō-Grade	Reduced Grade	Zero Grade
1. G. τίθημι	θωμός	θετός, τίθεμεν	
L. fēcī		faciō	
Skt. dádhāmi		hitás	da-dh-más
G. ἵημι	Dor. ἕωκα		
G. ῥήγνῡμι	ἔρρωγα	ἐρράγην	
2. G. ἵστημι (ἵστᾱμι)		στατός, ἵσταμεν	
L. stāre		status	
Skt. tíṣṭhāmi		sthitás	
G. φημί (φᾱμί)	φωνή	φαμέν, φατός	
L. fārī		fateor	
3. G. δίδωμι, δῶρον		δοτός, δίδομεν	
L. dōnum		dare, damus	
Skt. dádāmi		adita	da-d-más
4. IE *dhē(i-)		*dhǝy-, *dhī-	
Skt. ádhāt		dháyati, dhītás	
G. θῆσθαι, θῆλυς			
L. fēlō, fēmina		fīlius	
IE pō(i-)		*pī-	
Skt. pắtum		pitás	
G. πῶμα		πῑ́νω	
L. pōtus			

126. *Dissyllabic stems.*—It has already been remarked that every syllable of a word was subject to gradation in the parent speech. Generally, however, it is possible to consider the gradation of each syllable separately, that is, to treat the subject on the monosyllabic basis, as has been done in the preceding paragraphs. This is simpler and no less scientific, and therefore preferable. But in certain cases it becomes necessary to hold in view two syllables, since they clearly form a unit in relation to the weak form.

Thus in Sanskrit, if we find çrótum:çrutás but bhávi-tum:bhū-tás (and similarly in so many other instances that the relation cannot be accidental), it is obvious that as u is the weak grade of o (IE eu), so is ū of avi (IE ewǝ). Again we find çvā-tras:çū-nas, etc., from which it appears that ū is also the weak grade of vā (IE wā͡ˣ, cf. 124).

Similarly in stems containing a liquid or nasal we find in Sanskrit hártum: hṛtás, but cáritum:cīrṇás, and práti:pūrṇás, pūrdhí, showing that as ṛ is the weak grade of ar, so is īr or ūr the weak grade of ari or rā; hántum:hatás, but jánitos:jātás, damitá:dāṁtás, showing that as a (IE ṇ) is the weak grade of *an*, so is *ā* or *āṁ* the weak grade of *ani, ami* (or *nā, mā*). For the European correspondences to Skt. *ir, ūr, ā, āṁ*, see **116**.

The dissyllabic stems are probably, in their remote origin, extensions of monosyllabic stems. At any rate we sometimes find parallel series of related forms, some belonging to dissyllabic, some to monosyllabic stems. So Skt. *stáritave, stīrṇás*, but also *stártave, stṛtás;* Skt. *janitár-*, G. γενέτης, γνήσιος, but also γένος, γόνος, γίγνομαι, etc. (**119**.6); G. ἔβλην, but also βάλλω, βέλος, βολή. To assume that the latter are derived from dissyllabic stems with loss of *ə* before another vowel is unnecessary.

The general scheme of possible gradations is as tabulated (*ā^x*=IE *ē, ā*, or *ō; S*=strong, *R*=reduced, *Z*=zero grade). It serves to bring into relation with one another the forms of a given stem that are scattered through the IE languages. It is not anywhere maintained as a definite system, like that illustrated in **119**, and is represented only by *disiecta membra*. In the individual language a given stem may be represented almost exclusively by one or two grades. So IE **bhū̆-, *plē-, *ĝnō-* cover nearly all the Greek and Latin forms of these stems.

¹ S+R	² R+S	³ Z+S	⁴ Z+R	⁵ R+R	⁶ RR	Z
eyə	iā̆ˣ	yā̆ˣ	y̆ə	i̯ə	ī	i̯, y
ewə	uā̆ˣ	wā̆ˣ	wə	u̯ə	ū	u̯, w
erə	rā̆ˣ	rā̆ˣ	rə	r̥ə	r̥̄	r̥, r
elə	lā̆ˣ	lā̆ˣ	lə	l̥ə	l̥̄	l̥, l
enə	n̥ā̆ˣ	nā̆ˣ	nə	n̥ə	n̥̄	n̥, n
emə	m̥ā̆ˣ	mā̆ˣ	mə	m̥ə	m̥̄	m̥, m

Examples¹

¹ S+R	² R+S	³ Z+S	⁴ Z+R	⁵ R+R	⁶ RR	Z
Skt. bhávitum	Lith. búvo	L. -bā-	Skt. -bhwa-	Skt. ábhuvam	Skt. ábhūt / G. ἔφῡ	G. φύσις / L. futūrus
		Skt. çvātrás / G. πᾱμα		G. κύαμος, κνέω	Skt. çūnás / G. κῦρος	
		Skt. práti / G. πίμπλημι / L. plēnus			Skt. pūrṇás / Lith. pilnas	G. πίμπλαμεν
G. τελαμών			G. τάλαντον	G. τάλαντον	G. τλᾱτός / L. lātus	G. τέλαμεν / L. tollō
Skt. jánitos / G. γενέτης		G. γήσιος			Skt. jātás / L. nātus	G. γίγνομαι
		Skt. jñātum / G. γιγνώσκω / L. nōscō	L. cognitus		L. gnārus	
				G. ἐδάμασα	Skt. dāmtás / G. δμᾱτός	

¹ Including some forms in which ə is lost before, or replaced by, another vowel.

127. For Greek and Latin relations, much of the intricate and in part problematical theory of gradation in dissyllabic stems, as briefly sketched in the preceding paragraph, may be disregarded. But the matter cannot be wholly ignored, since certain parts of the system play an important rôle in Greek.

It is sufficient to recognize in Greek, beside forms that may be classified on the monosyllabic basis (**118 ff.**):

1. *Dissyllabic stems.*—These may reflect, from the scheme in **126**:
   a) $S+R$, as τελαμών
   b) $R+R$, as τάλαντον
   c) Or, under various analogical influences, may differ from either, as ἐκάλεσα, ἐστόρεσα
2. *Monosyllabic stems ending in* η (gen. G. η), ᾱ (Att.-Ion. η, but cited here in the ᾱ-form), *or* ω.
   a) $Z+S$, as πίμπλημι, πλῆτο, ἔβλην, γιγνώσκω
   b) RR, as δμᾱτός, τλᾱτός; here also probably (**116a**) στρωτός, βρωτός

Examples of parallel forms of the two types, as thus classified from the point of view of Greek, are:

τελαμών...................... ἔτλᾱν, τλᾱτός
ἐτάλασα, τάλαντον

κέλαδος...................... κλητός
ἐκάλεσα

ἐστόρεσα...................... στρωτός
βάραθρον .... βιβρώσκω, ἔβρων
γενέτης...................... γνήσιος
θάνατος .... θνᾴσκω, θνᾱτός
κάματος...................... κμᾱτός
ἐδάμασα, πανδαμάτωρ.......... δμᾱτός.

a. For the function of such forms in Greek it is immaterial just how they are to be aligned in the IE system, whether, for example, the *tlā-* of G. τλᾱτός and L. *lātus* is RR or $Z+S$ of a **telə-*, and further whether the στρω- of G. στρωτός and the *strā-* of L. *strātus* is RR or $Z+S$. It is more important to observe that the forms of type 1 (above) are mainly responsible for the futures like τενέω, βαλέω (**390**) and the aorists like ἐκάλεσα, ἐδάμασα (**397**.4)—and that those of type 2 (above) are notably productive in various tenses of the verb and in derivatives, as, for example, in ἔβλην, βέβληκα, βλητέος, βλῆμα.

For the existence of these two types beside forms which show the simple monosyllabic stem, as γενέτης, γνήσιος beside γίγνομαι, γένος, γέγονα, see **126**.

b. There is no satisfactory explanation of the *o* in ἐστόρεσα, and in ἔμολον, ἔπορον, ἔθορον, ἔτορον (beside βλώσκω, πέπρωται, θρώσκω, τιτρώσκω), for which we should expect *ἔμαλον, etc. (cf. βάραθρον beside βιβρώσκω).

CONSONANTS

STOPS

128. The IE stops are classified as follows, according to series and orders (**37**):

Series: labial, dental, palatal, labiovelar, and plain velar

Orders: plain voiceless (*p*, *t*, etc.), plain voiced (*b*, *d*, etc.), voiced aspirate (*bh*, *dh*, etc.), and voiceless aspirate (*ph*, *th*, etc.)

a. Although three distinct guttural series are here set up, no more than two are required from the standpoint of Greek and Latin, or of any single IE language. The reality of a third guttural series, the plain velars, in the parent speech may be questioned, and ultimately no doubt it belongs with one of the other two, as even these two may be one in ultimate origin. In fact the precise situation in regard to the gutturals in the IE period is an unanswerable problem. But the third series offers at least a convenient formula for a certain set of correspondences which does not agree with those of the other two (see **144**).

b. The third order is represented by voiced aspirates in Sanskrit, voiceless aspirates in Greek, fricatives in Italic, elsewhere by simple stops. From this variety it is impossible to infer with certainty the precise phonetic value of the antecedent sounds in the parent speech. Nor is this of vital importance. We follow the usual designation and notation, as representing the most probable hypothesis and at any rate a convenient formula.

c. The fourth order, of voiceless aspirates, is assumed to cover the cases, comparatively infrequent, in which we find Skt. *ph*, *th*, etc., instead of the usual *bh*, *dh*, etc., answering to the Greek aspirates. So Skt. *sphal-*: G. σφάλλω, Skt. *vettha*: G. οἶσθα. But Skt. *th* also appears where we have simple *t* elsewhere, as Skt. *sthā-*: G. ἵστημι, L. *stō*; Skt. *pṛthus*: G. πλατύς; Skt. *panthās*: G. πόντος. The voiceless aspirates will be disregarded in the later survey of the series.

ORDERS

129. Examples of the different orders will be given under their respective series. But certain matters affecting the corresponding orders of all series are discussed here.

1. The voiceless stops are the most persistent. They remain such except in Germanic (**133**).

2. The voiced stops also remain such in classical Greek and Latin. But G. *β, γ, δ* eventually became voiced fricatives, as in Modern Greek where *β* = NE *v*, *δ* = NE *th* in *then*, *γ* = NHG *g* in *Tage* or (before front vowels) = NE *y* in *yet*. This change took place at an early period in some dialects, but in standard Attic and the κοινή probably not until the 1st cent. A.D. or later.

Latin intervocalic *b* also became a fricative in the early centuries A.D. (**173**).

3. The IE voiced aspirates (as assumed above) became voiceless aspirates in prehistoric Greek and Italic, and so were merged with the infrequent IE voiceless aspirates. They remained such in classical Greek, only later becoming fricatives (**130**). But in Italic a change to fricatives took place, at least initially, in prehistoric times; together with a change of the dental fricative (= NE *th* in *thin;* here represented by *θ* in its later value) to the labial fricative *f;* and a weakening of the guttural fricative (= NHG *ch;* here represented by *χ* in its later value) to *h*. That is, where we have *f* or *h* in both Latin and Oscan-Umbrian we assume the following prehistoric steps:

$$bh > ph > f$$
$$dh > th > \theta > f$$
$$gh > kh > \chi > h$$

a. In the medial position, where we also find *f* in Oscan-Umbrian, but *b* or *d* in Latin (**137, 140**; also *g* after *n*, etc., **148**), the steps leading to the latter are disputed. But probably these too have passed through the stage of the fricatives *f, θ, χ* (as above in third place). G. λίτρα, name of a Sicilian coin, is explained as a Sicilian loanword representing a prehistoric Italic **līθrā*, whence L. *lībra*.

130. *The Greek aspirates.*—G. *θ, φ, χ* were true aspirates, that is, voiceless stops followed by a distinct aspiration, as in NE *hot-house, up-hill, back-hand*, except that in these latter the stop and the *h* are in different syllables. (So a better parallel would be the Danish *t, p, k*, which are strongly aspirated; the English

and German initial stops are also somewhat aspirated, as compared with the pure stops of the French.) In archaic Greek
inscriptions before the introduction of the signs for φ or χ, the
latter were expressed by ΓΗ, ΚΗ or Ϙ Η (**66**). The Romans transcribed the Greek aspirates, first by *t*, *p*, *c*, then more exactly
by *th*, *ph*, *ch* (**131**).

Eventually θ, φ, χ became fricatives, as in Modern Greek,
where θ = NE *th* in *thin*, φ = *f*, and χ = NHG *ch* in *ach* or in *ich*
(the latter if a front vowel follows). There are indications that
this change took place at an early period in some dialects, e.g. in
Laconian where a fricative θ is to be inferred from its representation by σ. But in standard Attic and the κοινή the pronunciation
as fricatives did not prevail until sometime in the early centuries
A.D. The significant transcription of φ by Latin *f*, instead of *ph*,
is not found till the 1st cent. A.D., and is not usual till the 4th
cent. A.D.

131. *Aspirates in Latin.*—In Greek proper names and other
loanwords from Greek, θ, φ, χ were represented by *t*, *p*, *c* in the
early inscriptions, and so pronounced in the time of Plautus. But
after about 150 B.C. they were represented by *th*, *ph*, *ch*, and the
correct pronunciation of the aspirates was so highly esteemed in
polite speech that it became the fashion to introduce the aspirates
also in a number of native Latin words, in some of which this was
no doubt favored by a fancied Greek origin. Cicero (Orator 48.
160) states that he yielded to popular usage, against his own better knowledge, in the case of *pulcher*, *triumphus*, etc., while he
persisted in *sepulcrum*, *corona*, *lacrima*, etc. Quintilian (1. 5. 20)
also speaks of the excessive use of aspirates, as in *chorona*, *praecho*,
chenturio. Inscriptions and manuscripts show many examples of
the aspirates, most frequently in *pulcher*, which was established
as the approved spelling.

a. Similarly in English, after the *th* was reintroduced in *theater*, *throne*,
etc., it was extended to some words which were indeed of classical origin but
had no *th* in Latin or θ in Greek, e.g. *anthem* from OE *antefn* this from G.
ἀντίφωνα, *author* from OFr. *autor*, L. *auctor*.

The view held by some that there was a native Latin development of aspirates, independent of Greek influence, is unnecessary.

132. *Dissimilation of aspirates in Greek.*—Aspirates in successive syllables are avoided, the former regularly losing its aspiration. So in the reduplicated forms of roots beginning with an aspirate, as τί-θημι, τέ-θηκα, πέ-φευγα. The first aspirate remains unchanged when the second has lost its aspiration in combination, hence the apparent transfer of aspiration in θρίξ, gen. τριχός (*θριχ-); ταχύς comparative θάττων (*θαχ-); τρέφω, fut. θρέψω (*θρεφ-).

There are many exceptions, where the aspirate is retained under the analogical influence of other forms, as in the aor. pass. ἐχύθην, ἐφάνθην, etc., and imperat. φάθι, τέθναθι. In these categories dissimilation· is observed only in case of identical aspirates, as aor. pass. ἐτέθην, ἐτύθην (θύω), and aor. pass. imperat. σώθητι, etc., for *σωθη-θι, with dissimilation of the second, instead of the first, aspirate.

a. In Sanskrit there is a similar dissimilation of aspirates, but these were voiced, in contrast to the Greek voiceless aspirates. In Latin there is no such dissimilation. Hence, from roots containing two aspirates, we have such an initial correspondence as π=Skt. b=L. f.
πεύθομαι, Skt. *bodhāmi* from IE *bheudh-   πείθω, L. *fīdō* from IE *bheidh-

133. *"Grimm's Law".*—The notable difference which is observed between the stops of Greek or Latin words and those of their English cognates is the result of a general Germanic shift, often referred to briefly as "Grimm's Law". This was a shift of the order, within each series. It took place in the prehistoric period of Germanic and underlies all the languages of this group. English reflects substantially this early shift, while High German has undergone a second shift. In the following diagram, as in the tables given later, certain divergences, due to special accentual conditions ("Verner's Law") or combinations, are ignored.

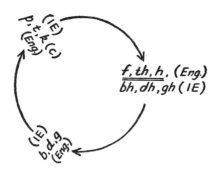

THE LABIAL AND DENTAL STOPS

134. The normal representation of the labial and dental stops may be surveyed in the accompanying table.

IE	G.	L.	Osc.-Umbr.	Skt.	Lith. and ChSl.	NE
p	π	*p*	*p*	*p*	*p*	*f*
b	β	*b*	*b*	*b*	*b*	*p*
bh	φ	*f* initially *b* medially	*f*	*bh*	*b*	*b(v)*
t	τ	*t*	*t*	*t*	*t*	*th*
d	δ	*d*	*d*	*d*	*d*	*t*
dh	θ	*f* initially	*f*	*dh, h*	*d*	*d*
		b medially (before or after *r*, before *l*, or after *u*) *d* medially (except as above)				

135. IE *p*. G. πατήρ, L. *pater*: Skt. *pitar-*, NE *father*.
G. πούς, L. *pēs*: Skt. *pāt*, NE *foot*

136. IE *b*. G. βάρβαρος: Skt. *barbaras* 'stammering'.
L. *dē-bilis*: Skt. *balam* 'strength'

a. But such cognates pointing to an IE *b* are not numerous. Both G. β and L. *b* are mostly from other sources, and seldom correspond.

137. IE *bh*. G. φέρω, L. *ferō*: Skt. *bharāmi*, NE *bear*.
G. φρᾱτηρ, L. *frāter*: Skt. *bhrātar-*, NE *brother*
G. ἔφῡ, L. *fuit*: Skt. *bhū-*, NE *be*
G. νέφος, L. *nebula*: Skt. *nabhas*
G. ἀλφός, L. *albus*, Umbr. *alfer*

L. *lubet, libet,* Osc. *loufir*:Skt. *lubh-,* NE *love*

    138. IE *t.* G. τρεῖς, L. *trēs*:Skt. *trayas,* NE *three.*

G. ταναός, L. *tenuis*:Skt. *tanus,* NE *thin*

    139. IE *d.* G. δέκα, L. *decem*:Skt. *daça,* NE *ten.*

G. ἔδω, L. *edō*:Skt. *admi,* NE *eat*

    140. IE *dh.* G. τίθημι, θήσω, L. *faciō*:Skt. *dhā-* 'place', NE *do.*

G. θῡμός, L. *fūmus*:Skt. *dhūmas* (**77**)

G. θύρᾱ, L. *foris*:NE *door* (but Skt. *dvar-* with *d* for *dh* under the influence of *dvāu* 'two'; cf. use of L. *forēs* for the two leaves of a door)

G. ἐρυθρός, L. *ruber* (*rūfus,* loanword from an *f*-dialect):Skt. *rudhiras,* NE *red*

L. *verbum*:Lith. *vardas,* NE *word,* from the root **wer-* (cf. G. ἐρῶ, ῥῆμα) and the suffix *-dho-*

L. *stabulum, stabilis* (cf. Umbr. *staflarem*) from the root of *stō* with suffix *-dhlo-, -dhli-*

L. *iubeō*:Skt. *yudh-* 'fight', Lith. *judinu* 'move, shake' (the semantic development assumed for Latin, 'stir up' to 'order', is credible; and *iussī, iussus* show that the *b* of *iubeō* must be from a dental)

G. αἴθω, L. *aedēs*:Skt. *edhas*

G. μέσος from **μέθιος*(**183**), *medius,* Osc. m e f i a í : Skt. *madhyas,* Goth. *midjis*

L. *vidua*:Skt. *vidhavā,* NE *widow*

    141. τ>σ *in Greek.*—The assibilation of τ before ι is seen in large classes of words. But τ may also remain unchanged before ι, and the precise conditions governing this difference of treatment cannot be satisfactorily formulated. The facts may be grouped as follows:

    1. τ remains: initially, as in τίς, τῑμή, etc.; when preceded by σ, as in ἐστί, πίστις, etc.; also in many other cases, as in ἔτι, ἀντί, feminines like πολῖτις, adjectives like πολιτικός, verbs like πλουτίζω etc.

    2. τ becomes σ: in most of the nouns formed with the suffix *-ti-,* as βάσις (Skt. *gatis*), στάσις (Skt. *sthitis*), λύσις, θέσις, λέξις, ποίησις, etc. (but πίστις, πύστις, also μάντις, μῆτις and some

others); in most adjectives in -ιος and nouns in -ία derived from stems containing τ, as πλούσιος (πλοῦτος), ἀμβρόσιος, ἀμβροσία (ἄμβροτος), ἐργασία (ἐργάτης), etc.

3. τ becomes σ in Attic-Ionic, Lesbian, and Arcadian-Cyprian, but remains unchanged in the other dialects (Doric, etc.):

3 sg. Att. τίθησι, δίδωσι, etc.:Dor. τίθητι, δίδωτι, etc.

3 pl. Att. φέρουσι, τιθέασι, εἰσί, etc.:Dor. φέροντι, τίθεντι, ἐντί, etc. Att. εἴκοσι, διᾱκόσιοι, τριᾱκόσιοι, etc.:Dor. Ϝίκατι, διᾱκάτιοι, etc.

a. A similar dialectic variation is seen in a few other forms, e.g. Ἀρτεμίσιος, Ἀρταμίτιος, Ἀφροδίσιος, Ἀφροδίτιος, etc. Att.-Ion. ἔπεσον=Dor. ἔπετον, aor. of πίπτω, is not satisfactorily explained.

b. A similar change of τ before υ is also to be recognized, though under still more limited and indefinable conditions than that before ι. Thus δουλόσυνος, δικαιοσύνη, etc., probably from -τυνος, with a suffix related to Skt. -tvana- (**464.**8); with dialectic variation, as in 3, Att. ἥμισυς, Dor. ἥμιτυς (suffix -tu- as in τρικτύς, etc.); Att. σύ, Dor. τύ (L. tū).

142. d > l in Latin.—Original *d* is replaced by *l* in several words. Possibly these were adopted from some local dialect in which there was a regular change of *d* to *l*, although there is no positive evidence of such a change in Sabine or any other known dialect.

lacrima from *dacrima*:G. δάκρυ, NE *tear*

lingua from *dingua*:NE *tongue*, OE *tung* (**79**)

oleō beside *odor*:G. ὄζω, ὄδωδα

lēvir for **laever*, **daiwēr*:G. δαήρ, Skt. *devar-*

But for *Ulixēs* the *l* is attested in Greek variant forms of Ὀδυσσεύς, as Ὀλυσσεύς, Ὠλίξης.

a. In early Latin also *r* for *d* in *arfuise, arvorsu, apur finem,* etc. Possibly a regular change of *d* before *f* or *v*, with some extension to other cases, but later elimination in favor of the usual *ad*, etc.

THE GUTTURAL STOPS

143. In considering the relations of the gutturals, using this as a convenient (though far from appropriate) general term for all kinds of *k*-sounds, it is necessary to distinguish two main series of gutturals, and, as regards their representation, to divide the IE languages into two groups.

One series, known as the "palatals" and denoted here by $\hat{k}, \hat{g}, \hat{g}h$

(some use k' or simple k), is represented by simple gutturals in the western or "centum" group (so called from L. *centum*), which includes the Greek, Italic, Celtic, and Germanic branches, but by sibilants (see **144***b*) in the eastern or "satem" group (so called from Av. *satəm* = L. *centum*), which includes Indo-Iranian, Balto-Slavic, Armenian, and Albanian. These palatals were presumably forward k-sounds in the parent speech, whence arose the sibilants of the satem group by a prehistoric development similar to that which took place even in parts of the centum group in later periods and under special conditions, e.g. the change of L. *c* before a front vowel in the Romance languages (L. *centum*, It. *cento*, Fr. *cent*).

The other series, known as "labiovelars" and denoted here by q^w (some use k^w), g^w, $g^w h$, is represented in the centum group by k^w sounds (e.g. L. *qu*) or sounds resulting therefrom (e.g. Osc. *p*, G. *π, τ*), but in the satem group by simple gutturals or in part by palatals derived therefrom. The name labiovelar and the designation by q^w, etc., are intended to indicate two distinct characteristics of these sounds, by which they differed from the palatals: (1) the term velar and the use of q that they were back gutturals, (2) the term labio- and the use of ^{w} that they were accompanied by rounding of the lips. It is only the first characteristic which is important for the satem group, in which the second characteristic plays no rôle (that is the ^{w} disappears), and the different development of the IE palatals and labiovelars depends wholly upon the difference in their guttural positions (front or back). Conversely for the centum group it is only the second characteristic which is important, and the difference between palatals and labiovelars resolves itself into one between simple k-sounds and k^w-sounds.

144. Still a third series of gutturals, known as "plain velars" and denoted by q, g, gh, is assumed to cover the correspondence in certain groups of cognates which show a plain guttural throughout, thus agreeing with the palatals in the centum languages, but with the labiovelars in the satem languages.

G. κρέας, L. *cruor*:Skt. *kravis*   G. στέγος, L. *tegō*:Lith. *stogas*
G. στείχω, Goth. *steiga*:Skt. *stigh-*

a. From a labiovelar one would expect, in the first example, G. πρέας (cf. πρίαμαι: Skt. *krīṇāmi*), while from a palatal one would expect Skt. *çravis* (cf. *çrātas*: G. ἄκρᾱτος). Hence the dilemma which leads to the assumption of this third series, at least as a convenient formula (see **128***a*).

There are also cases in which words with plain gutturals in the centum group are without cognates in the satem group, so that they might belong with the palatals or plain velars. In all cases of ambiguity with regard to the particular guttural series one may use the indifferent *k*, etc., in the reconstructed IE forms. The matter of the plain velars and other complications will be disregarded hereafter.

b. The development of palatals to sibilants was complete for the entire satem group only in the case of the voiceless $\hat{k}$. The $\hat{g}$ and $\hat{g}h$ also became sibilants in Iranian and Balto-Slavic, but in Sanskrit remained on an intermediate stage of development and are represented by *j* and *h*.

c. The sounds classed as palatals in Sanskrit grammar must not be confused with the IE palatals. Thus Sanskrit palatal *c* is not from IE palatal $\hat{k}$, which gives the "palatal sibilant" *ç*, but is the result of a secondary palatalization of *k* (IE q^w) before a front vowel, e.g. before *i* in *cid* (=L. *quid*) beside *kas* or before an *a* which comes from IE *e*, as in *ca* (=L. *que*). That is, in a case like *ca* the palatalization must have begun when the vowel was still a front vowel, and this constitutes one of the most striking proofs of the priority of the Greek and Latin vowel system with *a, e, o* compared to Skt. *a* (**73**.4). The corresponding secondary palatalization of *g* and *gh* (IE g^w and g^wh) resulted in *j* and *h*, respectively, but these, as noted in *b*, may also represent IE $\hat{g}$ and $\hat{g}h$. Hence Skt. *j* and *h* are each of double origin, though the difference in origin discloses itself even in Sanskrit in certain combinations.

d. The author now prefers k^w for the voiceless labiovelar (q^w, above), the indication of back guttural being unnecessary and in case of the corresponding voiced sounds not shown without the use of a special *g*-letter. Furthermore, *k, g, gh* are best used to cover all cases not definitely attributable to either the labiovelar or the palatal series, that is, to the "plain velars" and to such cases as are referred to in the second paragraph of this page.

145. The normal representation of the palatals and the labiovelars may be surveyed in the accompanying table.

IE	CENTUM LANGUAGES									SATEM LANGUAGES			
	G.			L.				Osc.-Umbr.	NE	Skt.	Av.	Lith.	ChSl.
k̂	κ			c				k	h	ç	s	š	s
ĝ	γ			g				g	k	j	z	ž	z
ĝh	χ			h	g	f		h	g	h	z	ž	z
q, g, gh	as above									as below			
qʷ	π	τ	κ	qu			c	p	wh, f	k, c	k, c	k	k, č, c
gʷ	β	δ	γ	v	gu		g	b	qu, c	g, j	g, j	g	g, ž, z
gʷh	φ	θ	χ	f	v	gu	g	f	w, g	gh, h	g, j	g	g, ž, z

G. sub-columns: Before α, ο, or cons. | Before ε(ει, ευ), η, ι | Before or after υ
L. notes: (before or after cons.) | (bef. u) | Initial | Intervocalic | After n | Before cons. or u

PALATALS

146. IE k̂. G. ἑκατόν, L. *centum*, Goth. *hund*: Skt. *çatam*, Av. *satəm*, Lith. *šimtas*, ChSl. *sŭto*.

G. δέκα, L. *decem*, Goth. *taíhun*: Skt. *daça*, Av. *dasa*, Lith. *dešimt*, ChSl. *desętŭ*

G. οἶκος, L. *vīcus*, Goth. *weihs*: Skt. *viç-*, Av. *vis-*, Lith. *vieš-patis*

G. δείκνῡμι, L. *dīcō*: Skt. *diç-*

147. IE ĝ. G. γένος, L. *genus*, NE *kin*: Skt. *janas*, Av. *zana-*

G. γιγνώσκω, L. *(g)nōscō*, NE *know*: Skt. *jñā-*, Lith. *žinoti*, ChSl. *znati*

G. γεύω, L. *gustus*, Goth. *kiusan* 'test' (NE *choose*): Skt. *juš-* 'enjoy', Av. *zaoša-* 'pleasure'

148. IE *ĝh*. G. χαμαί, L. *humus*:Av. *zəmō* (gen. sg.), Lith. *žemė*, ChSl. *zemlja*.

G. χήν, L. *ānser* (for *hānser*), NE *goose*:Skt. *haṅsas*, Lith. *žąsis*

G. ὄχος, L. *vehō*, OE *wegan* (NE *weigh*):Skt. *vah-*, Av. *vaz-*, Lith. *vežu*, ChSl. *vezǫ*

G. λείχω, L. *lingō*:Skt. *lih-*, Lith. *liežiu*, ChSl. *ližǫ*

G. τεῖχος, Osc. f e í h ú s s 'muros', L. *fingō*, *figmentum* (also *figūra* with *g* by analogy of *fingō*), Goth. *deigan* 'mold' (cf. NE *dough*):Skt. *dih-* 'smear', Av. *pairi-daēza-* 'surrounding wall, garden' (whence was borrowed παράδεισος)

G. χέω, L. *fundō*, Goth. *giutan*:Skt. *hu-* 'pour, offer libation', Av. *zaotar-* 'priest'. Cf. also L. *f* from IE *ĝhw* (**150**)

149. L. *h* was faintly sounded, and probably quite silent in colloquial speech, as is shown by the fact that its presence does not interfere with (1) elision, (2) shortening of vowels before another vowel (**103**), cf. *pre-hendō*), (3) change of intervocalic *s* to *r* (**164**, cf. *diribeō*), or (4) contraction of like vowels (**105**, cf. *nīl* from *nihil*). In consequence, there was confusion of spelling in many words, as *humerus* beside correct *umerus*, and the grammarians were at great pains to give detailed instructions in this matter. Generally the approved spelling, which we follow, was the etymologically correct one, but not always, e.g. *ānser* (**148**).

The letter *h* was sometimes used as a sign of hiatus, as in AHENVS beside AENVS (*aēnus*), thus distinguishing *aē* from the diphthong *ae*.

a. After classical Latin had become a book language and *h* had wholly disappeared from the vulgar tongue, the effort to bring it out in the reading of Latin texts led to an exaggerated guttural pronunciation which is reflected in such MS spellings as *michi*, *nichil* for *mihi*, *nihil*.

150. Palatals+*w*. The combinations IE *k̂w*, etc., show a development in Greek and Latin closely parallel to that of IE *qʷ*, etc. That is, as is natural, the guttural is similarly affected by the full *w* which follows it in the case of *k̂w*, as by the *w*- element which accompanies it in the case of *qʷ*. The only difference is that in Greek the two distinct sounds *k̂w* give a double consonant, while the single q^w gives a single consonant. Even this difference of course disappears in the case of initial k̑w, etc.

k̑w. G. ἵππος, L. *equus*—Skt. *açvas*

(q^w: G. ἕπομαι, L. *sequor*—Skt. *sacāmi*)

ĝhw. G. θήρ (Lesb. φήρ, cf. **154**.2), L. *ferus*—Lith. *žvéris*

(g^wh. G. θερμός, L. *formus*)

LABIOVELARS

151. IE q^w G. ποῦ, πόθεν, τίς, τε, L. *quī, quod, quis, quid*, Osc. *pod, pid*, Goth. *hwas*, OE *hwā, hwæt* (NE *who, what*):Skt. *kas, cid, ca*, Lith. *kas*, ChSl. *kŭto, čĭto*.

G. πέντε, πεμπάς, πέμπτος, L. *quīnque* (from *penque, **40**.8), *quīn(c)-tus, quincu-plex*:Skt. *pañca*, Lith. *penki*

G. τέσσερες, τέτταρες, L. *quattuor*:Skt. *catvāras*, Lith. *keturi*

G. λείπω, L. *relinquō, relictus*, Goth. *leihwan* 'lend':Skt. *ric-*, Lith. *lieku* 'leave'

G. ἕπομαι, L. *sequor, secūtus, secundus* (from *sequondos, **170**), *socius* (from dissyllabic **soq^wyos*, **180**):Skt. *sac-*, Lith. *seku*

G. πέσσω (from **peq^wyō*, **182**), πέψω, πεπτός, L. *coquō* (from *pequō, **40**.8, **80**.3), *coctus*:Skt. *pac-* 'cook', Lith. *peku* 'bake'

G. τίνω, τῑμή, ποινή:Skt. *ci-* 'requite', Av. *kaēnā* 'penalty', ChSl. *cěna* 'reward' (cf. **51**, 9–10)

G. κύκλος, OE *hwēol* (NE *wheel*):Skt. *cakram* 'circle'

G. λύκος (L. *lupus*, **155**.6) from IE **luq^wos* beside **wļq^wos* in Goth. *wulfs*, Skt. *vṛkas*, Lith. *vilkas*

152. IE g^w. G. βαίνω, L. *veniō*, Osc.-Umbr. *ben-*, Goth. *qiman*, OE *cuman* (NE *come*):Skt. *gam-*.

G. βιβρώσκω, L. *vorō*:Skt. *girāmi* 'devour', Lith. *geriu* 'drink'

G. βοῦς (L. *bōs*, **155**.6), OE *cū* (NE *cow*):Skt. *gāus*

G. βαρύς, L. *gravis*:Skt. *gurus*

G. ἀδελφός from *ἀ-δελφός (**161***a*):Skt. *sa-garbhyas* 'full brother', lit. 'of the same womb' (*garbha-* 'womb')

G. βίος (**154**.4), L. *vīvus*, Osc. b i v u s (nom. pl.), OE *cwic* 'living' (NE *quick*):Skt. *jīvas*, Lith. *gyvas*

L. *unguen*:Skt. *añjis*

G. γυνή, Boeot. βανά, OE *cwēn* 'woman, wife' (NE *queen*):Skt. *janī*, ChSl. *žena*

In G. βάλλω beside Arc. δέλλω and in G. βούλομαι beside Locr. δείλομαι, regardless of outside connections, the interchange of β and δ points to IE g^w.

153. IE g^wh. G. θερμός, L. *formus*, OE *wearm* (NE *warm*): Skt. *gharmas*.

G. θείνω, ἔπεφνον, πέφαται, φόνος (**119**.6), L. *dē-fendō*:Skt. *han-* 'smite, slay' (3 sg. *hanti*, 3 pl. *ghnanti*), Lith. *genu* 'drive'

G. νίφα L. *nix, nivis, ninguit*, Goth. *snaiws*, OE *snāw* (NE *snow*), Lith. *sniegas*

G. ὄφις (**154**.4):Skt. *ahis*

G. ἐλαχύς, ἐλαφρός, L. *levis*:Skt. *laghus* 'light, swift, small', Lith. *lengvas* 'light' (IE *$leng^wh$, *lng^wh-, and leg^wh- without nasal)

L. *cōnīveō* (**207**.4):Goth. *hneiwan* 'bow'

154. *Remarks on the representation in Greek.*—The general rule given in the table in **145**, with which most of the examples in **151–53** comply, namely labials before *a, o* and consonants, dentals before front vowels, gutturals before or after *v*, is subject to certain reservations.

1. There is much analogical leveling in favor of the labial. Thus the π of λείπω, ἕπομαι, ἕπος (:Skt. *vacas*) is generalized, regardless of the following vowel, as λείπει, ἕπεται, ἕπεος. Interchange within an inflectional paradigm (as λείπω, *λείτει) is unknown, and the Greeks were unconscious of the actual relation in groups like ποῦ:τίς, τιμή:ποινή, θείνω:ἔπεφνε.

The same leveling sometimes occurs in groups of cognates, as βέλος (the regular δ before ε only in Arc. δέλλω) after the analogy of βάλλω.

2. It is a notable characteristic of the Aeolic dialects that even before a front vowel the labial is usual in most words (not in all, e.g. τίς, τε, etc.), as Lesb., Thess. πέμπε=πέντε, Lesb. πέσσυρες, Hom. πίσυρες, Boeot. πέτταρες=τέσσερες, Lesb. πήλυι=τῆλε.

3. There are some dialect forms with κ instead of usual π or τ in the pronouns, as Ion. (Hdt.) κῶς=πῶς, Thess. κίς=τίς.

4. Even in Attic-Ionic we find β and φ before ι in βίος (but Heracl. ἐνδεδι-ωκότα=ἐμβεβιωκότα) and ὄφις. There is no satisfactory explanation of this divergence from the development of q^w to τ before ι in τίς, τιμή, etc.

5. For the development in connection with a following *y*, see **182.**

155. *Remarks on the representation in Latin.*

1. Beside *qu* from q^w, we should expect *gu* (with consonantal *u*) from g^w, corresponding to the parallelism in Osc.-Umbr. *p:b*, or G. π:β. But this *gu* remains only after a nasal, as in *unguen*, otherwise the *g* is lost, hence *veniō*, etc. Similarly for intervocalic g^wh, *ninguit* but *nivis*.

2. Whereas in Greek we have labials before another consonant, in Latin the *w*-element was lost. So *quīn(c)tus, relictus* in contrast to G. πέμπτος. The simple guttural arising in this position was sometimes generalized. So from *vōx* also *vōcis, vōcem*, etc., and the verb *vocō, vocāre*, with no trace anywhere in Latin of a form with *qu*, in contrast to G. ἔπος, etc.

3. Before *r* the *w*-element was lost in the case of IE *g^w*, as *gravis, grātus* (Osc. gen. sg. *brateis*), but prior to such loss *g^wh* seems to have become *f* (as initially before a vowel), the combination *g^whr* yielding initial *fr*, medial *br*. So probably *frendō*:OE *grindan* 'grind'; *nebrundines* (Lanuvium; *nefrones* Praeneste):G. νεφρός; *febris* from **dheg^wh-ris*:Skt. *dah-* 'burn'.

4. The *w*-element was lost not only before *u*, but also, like the full IE *w*, before *o*, though here restored by analogy except in some isolated forms (see 170).

5. Initial *q^w* is lost before *u*, according to the most probable view regarding the pronominal adverbs *ubi, ut*, etc. (Osc. p u f , p u z ; cf. Skt. *kutas, kutra*, etc.), formed from stem **q^wu-* beside **q^wo-, q^wi-*, 308). Others explain as due to an analysis of *ne-cubi* as *nec-ubi*, etc. A similar loss of init. *q^w* before consonantal *u* is seen in *vapor*:Lith. *kvapas* 'breath, odor' (G. καπνός with κ by dissimilation), although this and some other similar equations are disputed.

6. Some forms are plainly loanwords from the outlying *p*-dialects (cf. Osc. *pod, ben-*, etc.). So *popīna* 'cookshop' beside *coquō*, and *bōs* and *lupus*.

LIQUIDS, NASALS AND s, w, AND y

156. Table of correspondences.

IE	G.	L.	Skt.	NE
r............	ρ	*r*	*r(l)*	*r*
l............	λ	*l*	*r, l*	*l*
n............	ν	*n*	*n*	*n*
m............	μ	*m*	*m*	*m*
s............	σ ' init. before vowel lost between vowels	*s* *r* between vowels	*s(ṣ, ḥ)*	*s* *r* between vowels in part
w............	ϝ, later lost	*v*	*v*	*w*
y............	' init. lost between vowels	*i*-cons. lost between vowels	*y*	*y*

157. IE *r* and *l*.

G. ἐρυθρός, L. *ruber*:Skt. *rudhiras*, NE *red*

G. φέρω, L. *ferō*:Skt. *bharāmi*, NE *bear*

G. κλυτός, L. *inclutus*:Skt. *çrutas*, NE *loud*

G. πλέω, L. *pluō*:Skt. *plu-*, NE *flow*

a. IE *r* and *l* are partially merged in Sanskrit, but are kept distinct in all the European languages. They interchange only in special cases of assimilation or dissimilation (40.9).

158. IE *n* and *m*.

G. νέ(ϝ)ος, L. *novus*:Skt. *navyas*, NE *new*

G. μήτηρ, L. *māter*:Skt. *mātar-*, NE *mother*

G. ὄνομα, L. *nōmen*:Skt. *nāma*, NE *name*

But final *m* becomes *ν* in Greek (211.2), and in Latin was weak (212).

Nasals other than *n* and *m* occur only by assimilation to a stop of a different series (194).

s

159. IE *s* remains unchanged, in both Greek and Latin, before or after a voiceless stop and when final.

G. ἐστί, L. *est*:Skt. *asti*   G. ἔδειξα, L. *dīxī*:Skt. *adikṣi*

G. γένος, L. *genus*:Skt. *janas*

160. G. κτ, etc.=Skt. *kṣ*. While Greek has regularly ξ from IE *k̂s*, as in δείξω, and ψ from IE *qʷs*, as in πέψω (151) there are some words in which Greek has τ or θ answering to the sibilant of cognates in other languages.

τέκτων:Skt. *takṣan-* 'carpenter', L. *texō*   κτίζω:Skt. *kṣi-* 'dwell'

χθών:Skt. *kṣās* 'earth' (beside forms pointing to simple *ĝh*, as G. χαμαί, L. *humus* 148)

ἄρκτος: Skt. *ṛkṣas*, Lat. *ursus*, Ir. *art*

φθίνω:Skt. *kṣi-* 'destroy', Ir. *tinaim* 'vanish'

a. The guttural was followed by some element (not an independent phoneme) resulting in a dental in Greek and Celtic, but a sibilant elsewhere. One may indicate this by *k̂ᴾ*, etc. or by *k̂ˢ*, etc.

There are also a few forms with κτ, χθ in which the dental answers to a Skt. *y*.

ἰκτῖνος; Skt. *çyenas* 'eagle, hawk' (beside Av. *saēna-* 'bird of prey', pointing to simple *k̂*)

χθές; Skt. *hyas* 'yesterday' (beside forms pointing to simple *ĝh*, as L. *heri*, OE *geostra*, NE *yester-day*).

Here may be mentioned also πτόλις, πτόλεμος in Homer and some dialects, for usual πόλις (Skt. *pūr* 'stronghold'), πόλεμος.

In all these cases the explanation of the Greek dental is doubtful.

161. Initial *s* before vowels remains in Latin, but in Greek becomes *h*, that is the 'spiritus asper' or 'rough breathing' commonly written ' (but orig. H = *h*, **68**).

G. ἑπτά, L. *septem*: Skt. *sapta*   G. ἵστημι, L. *sistō*

G. ἡμι-, L. *sēmi*-   G. ὁ, ἡ ; Skt. *sa, sā*

G. ἕπομαι, L. *sequor*: Skt. *sac*-

   a. The ' may be lost by dissimilation similar to that in τίθημι, etc. (**132**); ἔχω from *ἔχω (*σέχω, cf. ἔσχον; ἔχω: fut. ἕξω = τριχός: θρίξ) ἀδελφός (**155**), ἀθρόος from copulative ἀ- = Skt. *sa*-

162. The same change of *s* to *h* in Greek took place in the case of initial *sw, sr, sl, sm, sn* (for their history medially and in Latin, see **203**.2, **202**.1), which are sometimes represented in very early inscriptions by ϝh, ρh, λh, etc. (as if aspirated ϝ, etc.; cf. NE *which* in American pronunciation), and finally result in ', ῥ, but λ, μ, ν. Compounds and augmented or reduplicated forms of words with initial *sr, sl,* etc., show ρρ, and in Homer frequently λλ, μμ, νν, later λ, μ, ν.

ἡδύς, Dor. ἁδύς (inscr. ϝαδύς ; ϝhαδύς is not quotable, but cf. ϝhεκα-) : L. *suāvis*, Skt. *svādus*, NE *sweet*

ῥέω (insc. ρhοϝαῖσι) : Skt. *sru*-, NE *stream* (*str* from *sr*). Cf. κατα-ρρέω, ἔρρεον, etc.

λαμβάνω (insc. λhαβών), Hom. ἔλλαβε, later ἔλαβε

μειδάω Hom. φιλο-μμειδής: L. *mīror*, Skt. *smi*-, NE *smile*

νίφα Hom. ἀγά-ννιφος: L. *nix*, NE *snow*

163. In contrast to the development stated in **161** and **162**, there are some Greek forms with initial σ, as σῦς beside ὗς (L. *sūs*, NE *sow*), σμικρός beside μικρός, etc. The difference probably depended originally on different conditions of external combination (**213**), but just which is uncertain.

164. Intervocalic *s* is lost in Greek and becomes *r* in Latin.

Gen. sg. of *s*-stems, G. γένεος (Att. γένους), L. *generis*, from *ĝeneses/os (Skt. *janasas*)

gen. pl. of ā-stems, Hom. -άων (Att. -ῶν), L. -*ārum*, from *-āsōm (Skt. pron. ending -*āsām*) pres. subj. ἕω (Att. ὥ), L. fut. *erō*, from **esō* (cf. ἐστί, *est*)

L. *gerō* from **gesō* (cf. *gestus*)

L. *cūra* from **koisā* (cf. Pael. *coisatens* 'curaverunt')

165. In Greek the change was first to *h*, as initially (**161**). But this intervocalic *h* was lost in prehistoric times, leaving only indirect evidence of its existence in certain words in which it was anticipated initially, as εὕω (**167**).

Intervocalic σ was sometimes retained or restored by analogical influence. So in the aorists ἔλυσα, ἐφίλησα, etc., after the analogy of forms like ἔδειξα in which the σ was not subject to loss; in dat. pl. -οισι, etc., after the analogy of -σι in consonant stems; in forms like τίθεσαι, ἐτίθεσο (in contrast to φέρεαι, ἐφέρεο; see **344.**2) after the analogy of those like γέγραψαι, ἐγέγραψο.

In most cases intervocalic σ represents an earlier group of consonants, as σσ, τσ, etc.

166. The Latin "rhotacism", as the change of *s* to *r* is often called, was doubtless through the medium of a voiced *s*, that is, *z* (in Oscan the change did not go beyond this stage, cf. gen. pl. *egmazum*). But the evidence of early Latin transitional spelling with *z* is meager. The change to *r* was complete in the 4th cent. B.C. (cf. Cic. Fam. 9. 21. 2), but the grammarians quote many old forms with *s*, as *lases, arbosem*. Rhotacism occurs in many languages, and is seen in NE *were* beside *was*.

Final *s* was not affected in Latin (*domus, genus*, etc.), except by analogy, as in *honor*, for *honōs*, under the influence of *honōris*, etc.

a. There are a few apparent exceptions to rhotacism, mostly to be explained as loanwords. In general an intervocalic *s* of the literary period is from earlier *ss*, as in *causa* from *caussa*, which was still the spelling in Cicero's time, *clausī, clausus* from *claussī, claussus*.

167. *Remarks on the Greek spiritus asper.*—The regular sources of ' are either IE *s* (**161**) or IE *y* (**177**). But it occurs also in many words which began originally with a vowel, or with ϝ, where it is equally anomalous, since the loss of ϝ in itself left no such result (ϝέτος, ἔτος; ϝιδεῖν, ἰδεῖν, etc., **169**). So, for example, in ἵππος (but Ἀλκ-ιππος, etc., without aspiration):L. *equus*, Skt. *açvas*;

or in ἑσπέρα:L. *vesper*. The explanation is often doubtful, but the following points may be noted.

Initial υ- is always ὑ-, even when it represents IE initial *u-*.
ὕδωρ:Skt. *udan-* ὕστερος:Skt. *uttaras*
ὑπό, ὑπέρ:Skt. *upa, upari*, NE *up, over* (L. *sub, super* stand apart, with unorig. *s*, perhaps a relic of a prefixed *eks*)

Possibly υ- first became ιυ- (cf. NE *unit*, etc.), whence ὑ- as in the case of initial *y* (**177**).

' may result from the anticipation of an intervocalic *h* from *s* (**165**).
εὕω from *εὔhω, *euso:L. *ūrō*
ἱερός from *ἱhερός, *iseros* probably:Skt. *iṣiras* 'vigorous, fresh'
Cf. φρουρά from *πρo-hopá, φροῦδος from *πρo-hóδos

In ἵστωρ (ϝιδ-), ἑσπέρα (L. *vesper*), ἑστία (L. *Vesta*), ἕννῡμι, ἕσται, etc. (L. *vestis*), it has been suggested that the initial ϝ may have become ϝh, whence ' (**162**), by anticipation of a certain aspirate element in the σ (see **191**b and **206**.2b). But this is a very doubtful matter.

The ' is often due to analogy, as in ἡμεῖς after ὑμεῖς, dial. ὀκτώ after ἑπτά, late ἕτος, for ἔτος, after ἡμέρα.

168. *Psilosis.*—The spiritus asper ceased to be pronounced at an early period in East Ionic (thus leaving the letter H free for use as a vowel, **68**), Lesbian, and some other dialects. Eventually this happened everywhere. In Modern Greek the distinction of ' and ' is only a matter of spelling.

w

169. IE *w* remained in Latin as the consonant *u* (*v*); and in Greek as ϝ, which was lost at an early period in Attic-Ionic.
L. *video*, G. ϝιδεῖν, ἰδεῖν ; Skt. *vid-*, NE *wit*
L. *vōx*, G. ϝέπος, ἔπος:Skt. *vacas*
L. *vīcus*, G. ϝοῖκος, οἶκος:Skt. *viç-*, Goth. *weihs* (OE *wīc* loanword from Latin; cf. NE *War-wick, Green-wich*, etc.)
L. *novus*, G. νέϝος, νέος:Skt. *navas, navyas*, OE *nēowe*, NE *new*
L. *ovis*, G. ὄϝις, ὄϊς, οἶς:Skt. *avis*, OE *ēowu*, NE *ewe*

LATIN V

170. Loss of *v* (*w*), including the *w*-element of the IE q^w, occurred in prehistoric times before *o*.
deus from *dēos (**89**.2a), *deiwos:Skt. *devas*, Lith. *dievas*, OPr. *deiws*
deorsum, seorsum from *dē-vorsum, sē-vorsum*
*secundus, *secondos*, from *sequondos 'following' (*sequor*)

cottīdiē from **quotitei diē* (*quot*)   *colō* from **quolō, *quelō* (80.6)

so- from ***swo- *swe-** in *somnus*, etc. (80.2)

coquō from **quoquō, *quequō* (80.3)

iecur, *iecor from **iequor*: G. ἧπαρ, Skt. *yakṛt*, IE **yeqʷṛ(t)*

But this change is observed in relatively few words. In the great majority the *v* or *qu* was restored by the analogy of closely connected forms in which the *v* or *qu* was followed by a different vowel and so retained. Cf. NE *swore*, once pronounced like *sore* (cf. *sword*), but now with *w* restored after the analogy of *swear*. Thus *servos* (not *seros*) after *servī*, etc., whence later *servus* (82.5), *quod* (not *cod*) after *quī*, etc.; similarly *equos, sequontor*, whence later *ecus, secuntur*, and still later, by another analogical restoration of *qu, equus, sequuntur* (82.6).

    a. The distinction of *deus, dei* and *dīvus, dīvī*, both from the same source, is the result of leveling in opposite directions from **dẹos, *dẹvī*. Cf. NE *staff*, pl. *staffs* and *stave*, pl. *staves*, from earlier *staff*, pl. *staves*, like *shelf, shelves*.

    171. Loss of IE *w* also occurs:

Initially before *r, l*, or *u*.

rādīx from **wrādīx*: G. ῥίζα, ῥάδιξ (from ϝρ-), OE *wyrt*, NE *wort* in *figwort*, etc. (NE *root* is a Scandinavian loanword, hence *r* from *wr*, while in *write, wring*, etc., *w* is still preserved in the spelling though no longer pronounced)

lāna from **wlānā* (cf. **116**), beside *vellus*: NE *wool*

urgeō from **wurg-*(IE **wṛĝ-, *wᵘṛĝ-*, cf. **114b**): G. εἴργω (**ἐ-ϝεργω*, **106**), Lith. *veržiu* 'draw tight', OE *wrecan* 'drive, press, punish', NE *wreck, wreak*

After the labials *p* or *f*, whether the latter is from IE *bh* or *dh*.

aperiō from **ap-weriō*: Lith. *at-veriu* 'open'

fīō from **bhwiō*: *fuit*

forum from **dhworom*: ChSl. *dvorŭ* 'court'

    In *mollis* from **moldwis*: Skt. *mṛdus*, fem. *mṛdvī*.

    Sometimes between like vowels.

aetās from **aivitās*: *aevum*

lātrīna beside *lavātrīna*   *dīs, dītis* beside *dīves, dīvitis*

sīs in early Latin for *sī vīs*

172. Postconsonantal IE *w* in Latin.

Initial *dw* becomes *b*.

bis (early *duis*, Festus) from **dwis*: G. δίς (from **δϝίς*), Skt. *dvis*

bonus in early inscriptions *duonus* (i.e. *dwonus*)

bellum, early *duellum* (i.e. *dwellum* in early inscriptions and in
  Plautus; but as an archaic form employed by later poets, who
  probably associated it with *duo*, it is trisyllabic)

Intervocalic *dw* loses the *d*.

suāvis from **suādwis*: G. ἡδύς, Skt. *svādus*, fem. *svādvī*

Intervocalic *tw* becomes *tu* with vowel *u*.

quattuor (for *tt*, see **209**): Skt. *catvāras*

For the loss after *p* or *f*, see **171**.

a. The assumption that initial *tw* becomes *p* (like *dw > b*) rests on a few
doubtful etymologies. Assimilation of *lw* to *ll*, assumed by some, is also
doubtful.

173. Pronunciation of *v*. Latin *v* was simply a consonantal *u*,
not distinguished in spelling from the vowel *u*, and having substantially the value of English *w*. But in the early centuries A.D.
it came to be pronounced with more friction, first as a bilabial
fricative like Spanish *b*, then as a labiodental fricative like English
v. Intervocalic *b* also became a fricative. Hence the frequent
confusion of spelling between *v* and *b* in late inscriptions and in
manuscripts.

The change did not take place after *q* or *s*. Hence at the time
when the differentiation in spelling of *u* and *v* was introduced
(p. 75), the *v* was not employed in words like *quī*, *equus*, *suādeō*,
etc.

GREEK ϝ

174. The ϝ is of frequent occurrence in inscriptions of most dialects, except Attic-Ionic and Lesbian. Generally speaking, it disappeared first in the position before or after a consonant, where
it is preserved only in the earliest inscriptions of a few dialects,
next between vowels, and lastly initially before a vowel, where it survived in some dialects as late as the 2d cent. B.C., and even to the
present day in the isolated relic of Laconian known as Tsaconian.

The sound of ϝ was like that of English *w*. But probably it had become a fricative like English *v* in late times and is to be so understood when it is represented by β, as often in late inscriptions and glosses, e.g. βοικίαρ = Ϝοικίας, βεκάτεροι = Ϝεκάτεροι.

175. In Attic-Ionic Ϝ was lost at a very early date, so that there are but scant traces of it even in the earliest inscriptions. But Homeric prosody furnishes ample evidence of its former existence. Words which originally began with Ϝ frequently (1) make position, (2) prevent elision, (3) prevent shortening of a preceding long vowel or diphthong. On the other hand, such words often fail to have this effect, and, conversely, the absence of elision or of vowel shortening is not confined to cases where a Ϝ followed. It is especially in the prevention of elision where this is otherwise to be expected (as 'Ατρείδης τε ἄραξ, for which Ϝάναξ is widely attested in dialect inscriptions) that the proportion of effectiveness is overwhelming.

The Ϝ had no doubt disappeared from the spoken Ionic at the time of the final constitution of our text, hence the discrepancies. But the text still reflects in very large measure the habits of prosody which belong to a period when the Ϝ was still pronounced.

176. Examples of initial and intervocalic Ϝ have been given in **169.** The treatment of Ϝ in consonant groups is as follows:

1. Intervocalic νϝ, ρϝ, λϝ are preserved in the earliest inscriptions of some dialects. Otherwise the Ϝ is lost, (1) with lengthening of the preceding vowel in one group of dialects including Ionic, (2) without such lengthening in another group including Attic.

Early Dialect Forms	Ionic (Homeric)	Attic
ξένϝος......................	ξεῖνος	ξένος
κόρϝα.......................	κούρη	κόρη
ὅρϝος.......................	οὖρος	ὅρος
καλϝός......................	κᾱλός	καλός

There are many other cases in which the forms with νϝ, etc., are not quotable but are to be inferred from the corresponding relation between the Ionic and Attic forms, e.g. Ion. μοῦνος, Att. μόνος from *μόνϝος; Ion. οὖλος, Att. ὅλος from *ὅλϝος (cf. Skt. *sarvas*), etc.

2. A similar relation is seen in Ion. ἶσος, Att. ἴσος, from ϝίσϝος, attested in several dialects; Ion. νοῦσος, Att. νόσος from *νόσϝος. In these σϝ is of secondary origin (ϝίσϝος probably from *ϝίδ-σ-ϝος, related to εἶδος). The history of original intervocalic σϝ is parallel to that of original intervocalic σμ (**203.**2). *νασϝος (cf. ναίω, ἔνασσα) became in Lesbian first *ναϝϝος (like ἄμμε), whence *ναυϝος, ναῦος, elsewhere ναϝός (like ἁμέ), whence ναός, νηός, νεώς. For initial σϝ, see **162.**

3. δϝ is preserved in Corinth. Δϝενία = Δεινίου, and is indirectly attested by Hom. δείδια from *δεδϝια, and ἔδεισε with first syllable long (so written ἔδδεισε in some MSS), from *ἔδϝεισε.

4. τϝ appears initially as σ, medially as σσ or ττ with the same dialectic distribution as for κι etc. (**182**).
σός from *τϝός, beside τεός from *τεϝός:L. *tuus*, Skt. *tvas*
σείω:Skt. *tviṣ-* 'be stirred up'
Ion. τέσσερες, Att. τέτταρες:L. *quattuor*, Skt. *catvāras*

5. ϝρ is preserved in some dialect forms, as El. ϝρᾱτρᾱ = ῥήτρᾱ, Arg. ϝεϝρε̄μένα = εἰρημένα (cf. also βρήτωρ in texts of the Lesbian poets), from ϝρη- beside ϝερ- in ἐρέω:L. *verbum*. The spiritus asper in ῥήτρᾱ is probably only a graphic convention, due to the more numerous cases of ῥ from *sr*, as ῥέω (**162**).

In compounds and augmented or reduplicated forms of words with initial ϝρ, the ϝ unites with the preceding vowel to form a diphthong in Hom. ταλαύρινος from *ταλα-ϝρινος, Lesb. εὐράγη from* ἐ-ϝραγη (Att. ἐρράγη), and some others. But generally the result is ρρ, as in Att. ἐρρήθην (εἴρηκα is formed after the analogy of εἴληφα, **203**a), ἐρράγην, ἀναρρήγνῡμι, etc.

y

177. Initial *y* remains in Latin as consonantal *i*, and in Greek becomes regularly the spiritus asper, but in some words is represented by ζ, the special cause of this different development being obscure.

G. ἧπαρ, L. *iecur*:Skt. *yakṛt*   G. ὅς (rel. pron.):Skt. *yas*
G. ἅγιος, ἁγνός:Skt. *yaj-* 'worship'   L. *iuvenis*:Skt. *yuvan-*, NE *young*
G. ζυγόν, L. *iugum*:Skt. *yugam*, NE *yoke*

G. ζώννῡμι, ζωστός: Av. *yāsta-*, Lith. *juostas* 'girded'

G. ζέω, ζεστός: Skt. *yas-* 'be hot', NE *yeast*

178. Intervocalic *y* was lost in prehistoric Greek and Latin (Italic).

G. τρεῖς (dial. τρῆς, τρέες), L. *trēs*, from **treyes* (Skt. *trayas*) denominatives formed from vowel stems by the suffix -*yo*- (Skt. -*ya*-), as those in -εω, -εō, from -*eyō* (Skt. -*ayāmi*), etc. (**356**)

179. 1. In Greek an exception is that the *y* united with a preceding *υ* to form a diphthong *υι*, as in Lesb. φυίω, Att. υἱός and υἱύς. In other cases of an *i*-diphthong before a vowel, as in words in -αιω, -αιος, -ειος, etc., the *ι* does not represent an original intervocalic *y*, but rather a *y* which was left from some group as *sy*, *wy*, etc.

Thus ἡδεῖα from **ἡδεϝια*, ποιέω from ποιϝέω (cf. Boeot. ἐποί-ϝησε), ναίω from **νασιω*(cf. ἔνασσα), εἴην from **ἐσιην* (Skt. *syām*), ἀλήθεια from ἀληθεσια (ἀληθής), Hom. τελείω from **τελεσιω* (τέλος), Hom. gen. sg. ἐμεῖο from **ἐμεσιο*, gen. sg. -οιο from **-οσιο* (Skt. -*asya*).

For the last-named forms we have also, with loss of *ι* in the historical period, Hom. τελέω, Att. τελῶ, Hom. ἐμέο, ἐμεῦ, Att. ἐμοῦ, and gen. sg. Hom. -οο, -ου, Att. -ου. Cf. also Att. 'Ἀθηναία, later 'Ἀθηνάα, 'Ἀθηνᾶ; υἱός and ὑός; ποιῶ and ποῶ (so in inscriptions of many dialects); αἰεί (from αἰϝεί) and ἀεί; καίω (from **καϝιω*, cf. καύσω), κλαίω (from **κλαϝιω*), and κάω, κλάω (here perhaps regularly κάει, κλάει, but καίω, κλαίω, then with confusion). The special conditions that govern the loss of *ι* in some cases and its persistence in others are complex and partly obscure.

2. In Latin in forms like *eius, cuius, maior, peior* the *i* does not represent an original intervocalic *y*, but stands for two *i*'s (partly from *gy, dy*, **180**) of which the first formed a diphthong with the preceding vowel, while the second was consonantal. That is, the forms are really *eiius* (pronounced *eiyus*), etc., and are in fact frequently so written in MSS and inscriptions. The first syllable is long because it contains a diphthong (not *ēius*, etc.).

180. Postconsonantal *y* in Latin becomes vowel *i*.

medius from **medhyos*: Skt. *madhyas*, Goth. *midjis*

alius from **alyos*: G. ἄλλος   *veniō* from **gʷm̥yō*: G. βαίνω.

But initial and medial *dy* and medial *gy* become consonant *i*.
Iuppiter, *Iovis*, early L. *Diovis*: G. Ζεύς, Skt. *dyāus*
peior from **pedyōs* (cf. *pessimus* from **ped-temo-* or **ped-semo-*)
maior from **magyōs* (*magnus*)

   a. In words like *medius, alius*, etc., the *i* became again consonantal in
colloquial speech, e.g. *medyus*, whence It. *mezzo*.

181. Postconsonantal *y* in Greek combines with the preceding
consonant, yielding various results according to the character of
this preceding consonant. There are three large classes of forms in
which these changes are most widely observed.
Presents of the iota or *yo*-class (**360**)
Nouns of the first declension with nom. sg. in -ă, orig. -ιᾰ (**237**)
Comparatives in -ων, orig. -ιων (**293**)

182. With a voiceless guttural, whether the plain voiceless
stop or the aspirate, and whether of the palatal or labiovelar
series, the result is σσ or ττ, according to the dialect. In the three
categories named above (**181**) the same result appears in derivatives of stems ending in τ or θ, but this is due to the analogy of the
type established by the guttural derivatives, since the normal
phonetic treatment of τι and θι, as shown in more isolated words,
is different (**183**).

φυλάσσω, -ττω from **φυλακιω: φύλαξ*
πέσσω, -ττω from **peqʷyō*: fut. πέψω, L. *coquō* (**151**)
γλῶσσα, -ττα from **γλωχια: γλωχίς*
θάσσων, -ττων from **θαχιων* (or **θαγχιων*, **293a**): ταχύς
ἐρέσσω, -ττω from **ἐρετιω: ἐρέτης*
μέλισσα, -ττα from **μελιτια: μέλι, μέλιτος*
κρέσσων, κρείττων (**293a**) from **κρετιων: κρατύς*

   a. In words like the above, and likewise in the case of σσ, ττ from τϝ
(**176**.4), the σσ belongs to Ionic and the majority of dialects, while ττ is the
genuine Attic form as shown by Attic inscriptions from the earliest times.
The σσ of the tragedians and Thucydides is due to the literary influence of
the earlier established Ionic prose. From Aristophanes on, ττ prevails also
in literary Attic. There is fluctuation in the κοινή, with the non-Attic σσ
generally prevailing.

   b. The σσ (in some early Ionic inscriptions denoted by a special sign, beside the usual σσ), ττ represent a dialectic differentiation of some double

fricative which was the immediate result of κι, etc. Just what this was (for example, šš or fricative θθ?) must remain obscure, but its fricative character is indicated by the fact that before it a nasal was lost with lengthening of the preceding vowel, just as it was before σ from τι, τσ etc. (πᾶσα from πάνσα, *παντια, **183, 204**.2). So ἆσσον from *ἀγχιον (ἄγχι).

c. Initially the σσ, ττ were simplified to σ, τ.

Ion. σήμερον, Dor. σάμερον, Att. τήμερον, from *κι-άμερον (from *κι-:L. *cis, citra*)

σεύω from *qyewō (Skt. *cyavāmi* 'move, shake'), a poetical word, always keeping the σ- form

183. τι and θι give Att. σ not ττ, and Ion. σσ, σ (σσ beside σ in Homer, only σ in inscriptions; whereas σσ in φυλάσσω etc., **182**, does not become σ).

Att. ὅσος, Hom. ὅσσος, ὅσος, from *ὅτιος (similarly τόσος, πόσος, etc.)

Att. μέσος, Hom. μέσσος, μέσος (Boeot. μέττος), from *μέθιος: Skt. *madhyas*, L. *medius*

After a consonant or long vowel or diphthong, τι gives σ in all dialects.

πᾶσα, πάνσα from *πάντια, φέρουσα from *φέροντια, etc.

αἶσα from *αἰτια: Osc. *aiteis* 'partis'

a. The development was perhaps through τσ, which at any rate gives precisely the same results (**193a**).

184. A voiced guttural (whether IE palatal or labiovelar) or dental + ι gives ζ in Attic and Ionic alike (δδ in some dialects).

ἄζομαι from *ἄγιομαι (ἄγιος)

νίζω from *nigʷyō (cf. fut. νίψω and χέρ-νιβα etc.)

πεζός from *πεδιός (πούς, ποδός)

ἐλπίζω from *ἐλπιδιω (ἐλπίς, ἐλπίδος)

Ζεύς from IE *dyēus (Skt. *dyāus*)

185. Greek ζ has its main origin in these combinations γι and δι. Other sources are IE initial y as in ζυγόν (**177**), IE zd as in ὄζος from *ozdos (**203**.1) or a Greek combination of σ and δ as in Ἀθήναζε from -ασ-δε (**203**.1).

ζ had the value of zd in the best period of Attic-Ionic, but in late times became simple z. Evidence for the pronunciation zd is as follows:

1) Statements of the ancient grammarians that the three double consonants, ξ, ψ, and ζ, were composed respectively of κ and σ, of π and σ, and of σ and δ.

2) Transcriptions like 'Ωρομάζης = OPers. *Auramazda*

3) Loss of a nasal before ζ precisely as before στ, e.g. σύ-ζυγος like σύ-στασις (204.3).

But the pronunciation *dz* must have been current in some parts, and it was with this value that the letter I was carried to Italy where it was used to represent *ts* as in Osc. h ú r z 'hortus' from *hort(o)s*.

186. πι becomes ππ.

πτύω from *spyu- (beside *spu- in L. *spuō*, *speiw- in OE *spīwan* 'spew')

κόπτω, κλέπτω from *κοπιω, *κλεπιω (**359**)

187. λι becomes λλ.

ἄλλος from *ἄλιος : L. *alius*   στέλλω from *στέλιω

188. νι, ρι give

1. ν, ρ with diphthongization of the preceding vowel, if this is α or ο.

φαίνω from *φανιω   χαίρω from *χαριω   μοῖρα from *μορια
(cf. μόρος)

2. ν, ρ with lengthening of the preceding vowel, if this is other than α or ο (but νν, ρρ, in Lesbian and Thessalian).

κρίνω from *κρινιω   γέφῡρα from *γεφυρια
τείνω from *τενιω   φθείρω from *φθεριω

a. Note that τείνω, etc., have "spurious" ει, that is, a lengthened ε, and are co-ordinate with κρίνω, not with φαίνω. So Lesbian has φαίνω, but κτέννω (Att. κτείνω) like κρίννω.

Changes in Groups of Consonants[1]

189. The majority of changes in groups of consonants fall under the head of assimilation (**40.**8). The assimilation may be of the first consonant to the second (anticipatory, also called regressive, cf. **40.**8), as in L. *accipiō* from *adcipiō*, or conversely (called progressive), as in L. *ferre* from *ferse*. It may be in order

[1] The groups containing *y* and *w* have already been discussed.

only, as in L. *scrīptus* from **scrībtos*, or also in series as in L.
accipiō. Assimilation in order is far more general than that in
series, and, again, anticipatory assimilation is far more general
than the opposite. Thus in Greek and Latin groups of two stops
the assimilation is always of the first to the second, and it is universal in the matter of order, only partial in series. But in certain
combinations one consonant may dominate the other regardless
of their relative positions. Thus in Latin both *dl* and *ld*, likewise
both *nl* and *ln*, give *ll*.

In groups of consonants which have been brought into conjunction by composition the development does not always conform to
that which is observed in the corresponding inherited groups. The
phonetic law which affected the latter in prehistoric times may
have no force in the later period of composition, hence e.g. L.
sessum from **sed-tum* (**190**), but *at-tribuō*. Or again, and this is
the most frequent cause of the disparity, the consciousness of the
uncompounded forms may react against the tendency to assimilation or other phonetic change, as in L. *adsum, conlocō*, G. ἑυράπτω,
etc. In some cases the unassimilated form is only a pedantic
spelling, as probably in L. *adcipiō* beside usual *accipiō*. In others
it is probably the usual form of careful speech in contrast to the
colloquial, as in L. *adsum* and *conlocō*, which are uniformly so
spelled in inscriptions and MSS until a very late period, though
colloquial *assum* and *collocō* are attested by puns in Plautus.
In the conflict between the purely phonetic tendency and the
influence of the uncompounded forms, parallel compounds may
differ in the forms preferred, e.g. L. *conlocō* but *colligō*.

In a few cases assimilation in compounds is extended to groups
of consonants which normally are not assimilated, e.g. L. *arripiō,
surripiō* (*ad-r, sub-r-*).

STOP+STOP

190. A stop is regularly assimilated to the order of the following
stop. As regards series, the labials and gutturals remain such
before dentals, while dentals are assimilated to gutturals or
labials, and labials to gutturals. Dental+dental becomes σ+

dental in Greek, in Latin also *st* before *r*, otherwise *ss*, which becomes *s* after a consonant, long vowel, or diphthong (208.2).

The groups in which the second stop is a dental are the most important, since derivative suffixes and endings beginning with a dental are the most common. The other groups are mostly confined to compounds, and in Greek to a few Homeric and dialectic compounds of apocopated prepositions.

β, φ+τ..	ππ	τέτριπται (τρίβω) γέγραπται (γράφω)	b+t	pt	scrīptus (scrībō)
π, β+θ..	φθ	ἐπέμφθην (πέμπω) ἐρτίφθην (τρίβω)			
π, φ+δ..	βδ	κλέβδην (κλέπτω) γράβδην (γράφω)			
γ, χ+τ..	κτ	λέλεκται (λέγω) βέβρεκται (βρέχω)	g, h+t	ct	āctus (agō) vectus (vehō)
κ, γ+θ..	χθ	ἐπλέχθην (πλέκω) ἐλέχθην (λέγω)	qu, gu+t (see 155.2)	ct	coctus (coquō) ūnctus (unguō)
κ, χ+δ..	γδ	πλέγδην (πλέκω)			
τ, δ, θ+τ	στ	ἀνυστός (ἀνύτω) ἴστε (οἶδα) πέπεισται (πείθω)	t, d+t	ss s st	sessum (sedeō) clausus (claudō) dēfēnsus (dēfendō) rōstrum (rōdō)
τ, δ, θ+θ.	σθ	οἶσθα (οἶδα) ἐπείσθην (πείθω)			
τ+κ....	κκ	Hom. κακκείοντες (κατ-κ)	t, d+c, qu t, d+g	cc, cqu gg	accipiō (ad-cipiō) aggerō (ad-gerō)
τ+π....	ππ	Hom. κάππεσε (κατ-π)	t, d+p p, b+c p, b+g	pp cc gg	quippe (*quid-pe) occipiō (ob-cipiō) suggerō (sub-gerō)

STOP+S

191. A labial stop+*s* gives G. ψ, L. *ps.*

G. γράψω (γράφω), τρίψω (τρίβω), φλέψ (gen. φλεβός)

L. *scrīpsī (scrībō), nūpsī (nūbō)*

a. Words like *urbs, abs, observō* were pronounced, and in early inscriptions usually written, with *ps.* The spelling with *b* was introduced to conform to that of the other cases, *urbis,* etc., and the uncombined *ab, ob.*

b. Here, and likewise for **192, 193,** the general rule holds that before *s* a voiced stop becomes voiceless and a Greek aspirate becomes unaspirated. But in early Attic inscriptions, before the introduction of the Ionic alphabet, ψ and ξ were denoted, not by πσ, κσ, but by φσ, χσ, as φσέφισμα, ἔδοχσεν, as if the σ had some secondary aspirating effect on the preceding stop. Cf. also τέχνη from *τεκσνᾱ (206.2b).

192. A guttural stop+*s* gives G. ξ, L. *x*.

G. λέξω (λέγω), βρέξω (βρέχω), θρίξ (gen. τριχός)

L. *rēxī* (*regō*), *vexī* (*vehō*), *rēx* (gen. *rēgis*)

a. Under guttural stops are included of course the IE *g̑h* which gives L. *h* between vowels (**148**), and IE *g^wh* which gives L. *v* between vowels (**153**). Hence such relations as L. *vexī* to *vehō*, *nix* to gen. *nivis*, etc. In Greek, where the labiovelars become labials before a consonant, the result of combination with σ is of course ψ, as in πέψω (πέσσω, L. *coquō*, **151**).

193. A dental stop+*s* is assimilated to *ss*, which is further simplified to *s* after a consonant, long vowel, or diphthong, and when final, in both Greek and Latin (see **208**). After a short vowel we have *ss* in Latin, and also in Greek σσ in many dialects, but regularly σ in Attic and later Ionic (Homer having both σσ and σ).

G. dat. pl. φέρουσι from φέρονσι from *φεροντ-σι

G. κνῖσα, Hom. κνίση, from *κνῖδ-σ-ᾱ (cf. L. *nīdor*)

G. πούς (ου anomalous), Dor. πώς from *πωδ-s

Hom. ποσσί, ποσί, Att. ποσί, from *ποδ-σι

Hom. ἐκόμισσα, -ισα, Att. -ισα, from *ἐκομιδ-σα

L. *messuī* from *met-suī* (*metō*)

L. *clausī* from *claud-sī* (*claudō*)

L. *pēs* from *pēd-s*

a. In Latin and in most Greek dialects the result of the assimilation is identical with orig. *ss*, and its subsequent simplification to *s* the same. But in proethnic Greek the result of assimilation after a short vowel could not have yet reached the point of identity with orig. σσ. For two dialects, Boeotian and Cretan, which show orig. σσ unchanged, have ττ from τσ, as aor. ἐκόμιττα, and also from τι̯, θι̯ as μέττος (**183**). The merging of τσ and τι̯, θι̯ is complete, but of these with orig. σσ only partial.

NASAL+STOP (ALSO ms, my)

194. A nasal is assimilated to the series of a following stop. The guttural nasal (as in NE *sing*), for which there was no special letter, since the sound existed only in combination, was indicated in Latin by *n*, in Greek by γ. Thus in IE *peŋq^we, L. *quinque*, G. πέντε, dial. πέμπε, Skt. *pañca*, the various changes of the *q^w* are attended by corresponding changes of the preceding nasal.

G. συμβαίνω, συγγενής, συγχέω from συν-

L. *eundem* from **eum-dem* L. *prīnceps* from **prīm(o)-ceps*

195. In L. *ēmptus, sūmptus* the *m* was kept by the analogy of *emō, sūmō,* and *p* was inserted. The same analogical retention of *m* and insertion of *p* is seen in *sūmpsī* (cf. **40.**11). The normal development of *ms* would be *ns* in Latin.

G. μσ becomes νς. εἶς from ἔνς (**204.**4), from **ἕμς* (cf. L. *semel*), and this ἔνς together with ἕν, in which ν comes from final *m* (**211.**2), led to the generalization of the ν (ἑνός, etc.).

196. A change of *my* to *ny* is common to Greek and Latin. IE **gʷm̥yō* (Skt. *gam-,* NE *come*) becomes G. **βανιω,* βαίνω, L. *veniō* (with consonantal *i,* later vocalic, **180**). In Latin the *n,* which was regular in *ventum* also, was generalized, so that all forms of the verb have *n.*

STOP+NASAL

197. *Labial stop+nasal.*—The labial stop becomes a nasal of its own class, that is, *m,* in Latin, and also in Greek except that πν and φν remain unchanged.

L. *summus* from **sup-mos* (*sub,* ὑπό)

L. *Samnium* from **Sabh-niom* (Osc. *Safinim,* cf. L. *Sabīnī*)

L. *somnus* from **swep-nos* : Skt. *svapnas* (**80.**2), G. ὕπνος (**119.**3)

G. λέλειμμαι, τέτριμμαι, γέγραμμαι from **λέλειπμαι, *τέτριβμαι, *γέγραφμαι*

G. σεμνός from **σεβνός* (σέβομαι) But ὕπνος, καπνός, ἀφνειός, etc.

198. *Guttural stop+nasal.*—G. κμ, γμ, χμ, κν, etc., normally remain unchanged, as in ἀκμή, δραχμή, τέκνον, τέχνη, etc. But κμ and χμ are regularly replaced by γμ in the perfect middle forms like πέπλεγμαι, πεπλεγμένος (πλέκω), βέβρεγμαι (βρέχω), which follow the analogy of λέλεγμαι, λελεγμένος (λέγω).

L. *kn, km* become *gn, gm.* Initial *gn,* whether original or from *kn,* occurs in early Latin, but becomes *n* (cf. NE *knight, gnat*). *dignus* from **dec-nos* (*decet*) *segmentum* from **sec-mentom* (*secō*) *nōscō,* early *gnōscō* (cf. G. γιγνώσκω) *nātus,* early *gnātus* (cf. *gignō*) *nīxus,* early *gnīxus* (Festus) from **knīxos* (: Goth. *hneiwan* 'bow') *a.* L. *nōmen*, though unrelated to (*g*)*nōscō* (cf. G. ὄνομα, Skt. *nāma*, NE *name*), was popularly associated with it. Hence *cognōmen* formed on the analogy of *cognōscō* beside *nōscō*.

b. There are important indications that L. *gn* was once pronounced ŋ*n*, with a change of *g* to the guttural nasal, parallel to that of *p* to *m* in *somnus* (**197**). Such are: (1) the omission of *n* in *ignōscō, cognōscō*, etc.; (2) spellings like *sinnu = signum*, or *singnifer;* (3) the change of *e* to *i* before *gn*, just as before *n*+guttural (*dignus* like *lingua*, **79**.1), that is, in both cases before a guttural nasal.

On the other hand, the complete silence of the Latin grammarians and of writers like Cicero and Quintilian regarding any such pronunciation makes it most unlikely that this was usual in their time. The probable explanation is that the retention of *g* in the spelling reacted on the pronunciation, and that the "spelling pronunciation" (**46**) wholly prevailed in cultivated speech.

199. *Dental stop+nasal.*—G. τμ, δμ, θμ, τν, etc., normally remain unchanged, as in πότμος, ἀριθμός, ἔθνος, etc. So also in early ἴδμεν (Hom.), κεκορυθμένος (Hom.), πεφραδμένος (Hes.), κεκαδμένος (Pind.). But later such forms have σμ by analogy, as πέπεισμαι, πεπεισμένος (πείθω), after πέπεισται, ἐπείσθην, etc. (**190**), ἴσμεν after ἴστε; so sometimes in nouns, as ὀσμή from earlier ὀδμή, θεσμός beside dial. τεθμός.

In Latin the stop is assimilated to the nasal, and *mm* is further simplified to *m* if preceded by a long vowel or diphthong.
annus from **atnos* (Goth. *aþn* 'year')
rāmus from **rādmos* (*rādīx*)

GROUPS CONTAINING A LIQUID

LATIN

200. 1. *dl, ld, nl, ln, rl, ls* become *ll.*
sella from **sed-lā* (*sedeō*)　　　*sallō* from **saldō* (NE *salt*)
corōlla from **corōn-lā* (*corōna*)　　　*collis* from **colnis* (Lith. *kalnas*)
agellus from **ager-los* (*ager*)　　　*velle* from **vel-se* (cf. *es-se*)

a. So *colligō* from **con-legō*. But in most compounds the unassimilated forms, as *con-locō, in-lūstris*, etc., prevail until a late period (cf. **189**).

2. *rs* becomes *rr*, as final simplified to *r* (**212**.6).
ferre from **fer-se* (cf. *es-se*)
torreō from **torseō* (G. τέρσομαι, Skt. *tṛs-*)
far, farris from **fars, *farses* (Umbr. *farsio* 'farrea')

a. For actual *rs* from *rss, rtt*, cf. **190, 207**.3*a*.

3. Medial *tl* became *cl*, followed by the development of an anaptyctic vowel (107), e.g. *pōculum*, early *pōcolom*, from **pōclom*, this from **pō-tlom* (suffix *-tlo-*). Initial *tl* loses its *t*, e.g. *lātus* from **tlātos* (*tollō*).

4. Medial *mr* becomes *br* (cf. 201.1), e.g. *hībernus* from **heibri-nos*, **heimrinos* (cf. *hiems* and G. χειμερινός). Cf. *br* from *sr* (202.2). So also (though once disputed) initially, as *brevis*: G. βραχύς (βρ from μρ, 201.1), Av. *mərəzu-* 'short'.

5. *nr* and *dr* become *rr* in many compounds, while in others the unassimilated forms prevail, e.g. *cor-rumpō*, but *in-rumpō; ar-ripiō*, but *ad-rogō*.

GREEK

201. 1. μρ, μλ, νρ become μβρ, μβλ, νδρ (cf. 40.11), whence initially βρ, βλ, δρ.

ἄμβροτος, βροτός from **μροτός*: Skt. *mr̥tas*, L. *mortuus*

μέμβλωκα, βλώσκω from **μλω-* (cf. aor. ἔμολον)

ἀνδρός (also δρ-ώψ in Hesych.) from **ἀνρός* (ἀνήρ)

a. But in compounds νρ becomes ρρ, as συρρέω from **συν-ρέω*, παρρησίᾱ from **παν-ρησίᾱ*. So ἔρρυθμος beside ἔνρυθμος, but most compounds of ἐν remain unassimilated, as ἐνράπτω.

The difference in the treatment of συν- and ἐν- is observed also in other combinations (σύ-στασις, but ἔν-στασις, 204.3). There was a tendency to keep the ἐν- intact as thus more obviously distinguished from the ἐκ-.

b. From inherited νλ we should expect νδλ, parallel to μβλ from μλ or νδρ from νρ, but there are no examples. The assimilation in compounds, as σύλλογος, from **σύν-λογος* is parallel to that in συρρέω.

2. δλ, νλ in compounds, and sometimes λν, become λλ.

ἑλλᾱ́ from **ἑδ-λᾱ́* (like L. *sella*, 200.1) beside ἔδ-ρᾱ

σύλλογος from **σύν-λογος*

ὄλλῡμι from **ὀλ-νῡμι* (cf. δείκνῡμι)

a. In πίλναμαι, λν is restored by the analogy of δύναμαι, etc. Even ὄλλῡμι represents a secondary assimilation of a restored **ὄλνῡμι* (cf. Att. ἔννῡμι contrasted with Ion. εἵνῡμι, 203.2c), if the normal treatment of inherited λν is that indicated in 3.

3. The normal result of inherited λν appears to be λλ in Lesbian and Thessalian, elsewhere λ with lengthening of the preceding vowel, that is, with the same distribution as in the case of in-

herited σλ, σν, νσ, etc. (**203**.2). For a considerable group of words which show this result are most reasonably explained as coming from forms with λν. The only other possibility is λσ (**205**.2), which some scholars prefer to assume, but from the point of view of word formation this is much less probable in most cases.

Lesb. στάλλᾱ, Dor. στάλᾱ, Att.-Ion. στήλη, from *σταλ-νᾱ

Att.-Ion. εἴλω, εἰλέω (aor. ἔλσα), Heracl. ἐγ-ϝηληθίωντι, Lesb. ἀπ-έλλω, from *ϝελ-νω, *ϝελ-νέω

But βούλομαι rather from *βολσομαι (based on an aorist or desiderative σ-formation of the root *gʷel- in βάλλω) and so the dialect forms Thess. βέλλομαι, Locr. δείλομαι, etc., with βουλή, Dor. βωλά, Lesb. βόλλᾱ.

GROUPS CONTAINING S

LATIN

202. 1. An _s_ is lost before most voiced consonants (in compounds before all such), and a preceding vowel, if short, is lengthened (see also **207**.1).

īdem from *_is-dem_   _iūdex_ from *_ious-dex_ (_iūs_+_dic_-, **111**)
prīmus from *_prīsmos_ (Pael. _prismu_, cf. L. _prĭscus_)
bīnī from *_dwisnoi_ (_bis_)
aēnus from *_a(y)esnos_ (_aes_, cf. Umbr. a h e s n e s)

_a._ In _dī-gerō_, _dī-rigō_, etc., the _dī_- is due to the analogy of _dī-dō_, _dī-moveō_, etc. For the result of inherited _sg_ (_zg_) is _rg_ (_mergō_:Skt. _majj_- 'duck', Lith. _mazgóti_ 'wash'), and that of _sr_ is _br_ (below, 2).

_b._ The combination _sd_ doubtless became _zd_ in the parent speech, so that strictly one should speak of the loss of _z_ in an inherited word like _nīdus_ (NE _nest_, Skt. _nĭḍas_) from *_nizdos_, *_ni-sdos_ (_sd_ weak grade of _sed_- 'sit', with the prefix seen in Skt. _ni_- 'down').

_c._ Initial _sn_, _sm_, _sl_ likewise become _n_, _m_, _l_ (see **162**).
nix:NE _snow_, G. νίφα
_nō_, _nāre_:Umbr. _snata_ 'moist', Skt. _snā_- 'bathe', G. νάω

2. Medial _sr_ becomes _br_.
fūnebris from *_fūnes-ris_ (cf. _fūnestus_)
cōnsobrīnus from *-_swesr-īnos_ (cf. _soror_ from *_swesōr_)

_a._ Initial _sr_ probably gives _fr_, though there are no such undisputed examples (the best is _frīgus_: G. ῥῖγος) as for the medial _br_ from _sr_. The development was presumably from _sr_ through θr (fricative θ=NE _th_ in _thin_) to Italic _fr_, whence L. initial _fr_, medial _br_, as from IE _dhr_ (**140**).

3. In final *ns* the *n* was lost, with lengthening of the preceding vowel, in prehistoric times, as acc. pl. *-ās, -ōs, -īs, -ēs, -ūs* from *-ans, -ons*, etc. (G. dial. *-avs, -ovs* etc.; **234.**4, etc.).

In the case of medial *ns* and secondary final *ns* (from *nts*, etc.) the *n* lasted into the period of written records and so remained in the normal spelling. But here too its frequent omission in inscriptions (as the very common *cosul*, etc.) and lengthening of the preceding vowel (**99.**2) indicate that it was weakly sounded or probably wholly lost in common speech at an early period, as it certainly was eventually. The spelling without *n* was particularly common and more or less accepted in certain categories, notably the adverbs *totiē(n)s, deciē(n)s*, etc., derivatives in *-ē(n)sis*, etc. (also *-ōsus*, if from *-ōnsus*, **480**).

The fluctuation of spelling in such cases led to the false introduction of *n* in some words as *thēnsaurus* for *thēsaurus*, from G. θησαυρός.

a. It is often stated that words with *ns* were pronounced with nasalized vowel, but there is no evidence from the Roman grammarians, or otherwise, to this effect. It is probable that nothing more subtle is involved than a conflict between total omission of the *n* in common speech and its plain pronunciation (as before any other consonant) in careful refined speech, in which case it would be an example of spelling pronunciation (**46**).

GREEK

203. 1. σδ (or IE *zd*, cf. **202.**1*b*) is represented by ζ, pronounced *zd*, in Attic-Ionic.

᾿Αθήναζε from *᾿Αθηνας-δε (cf. οἶκόν-δε, etc.)

ὄζος from *ozdos: Goth. *asts* 'branch'

2. Intervocalic σρ, σλ, σμ, σν, and likewise νσ, lose σ, with lengthening of the preceding vowel. But in Aeolic (Lesbian, Thessalian, and often in Homer) there is assimilation to λλ, μμ, νν.

τρήρων from *τράσρων (cf. τρέω from *τρεσω)

Att. χίλιοι (**96***d*), Ion. χείλιοι, Lesb. χέλλιοι, from *χεσλιοι (Skt. *sa-hasra-*)

εἰμί, Lesb. ἔμμι (cf. Hom. ἔμμεναι), from *ἐσμι (Skt. *asmi*)

σελήνη, Dor. σελάνā, Lesb. σελάννā, from *σελασ-νā (σέλας)

ἔκρῑνα, Lesb. ἔκριννα, from *ἔκριν-σα

ἔφηνα, Dor. ἔφᾱνα, from *ἔφαν-σα

a. But compounds and augmented or reduplicated forms of words with initial ῥ, λ, etc., from original *sr*, *sl*, etc. (162), only rarely show this normal development of intervocalic σρ, σλ, etc., namely in Att. εἴληφα from *σέσλᾱφα (λαμβάνω), εἵμαρται from *σεσμαρται (μείρομαι). Usually the development was that stated in 162.

b. In Att. ἐσμέν the σ was restored under the influence of ἐστί, ἐστέ (Hom. εἰμέν shows the normal development); similarly in τετέλεσμαι after τετέλεσται (as πέπεισμαι after πέπεισται, 190), etc.

c. An σν which arose by composition in the historical period or by analogical restoration of σ became νν, as in Πελοπόννησος from Πέλοπος νῆσος, or Att. ἕννῡμι from *ἕσνῡμι with σ restored from ἕσσα, etc. (Ion. εἵνῡμι shows the normal development).

204. νσ. 1. Original intervocalic νσ gives the same result as σν (203.2).

2. Secondary intervocalic νσ, in which σ comes from τι (183), dental+σ (193), or τ before ι (141), remains unchanged in some dialects, but in most the ν is lost, with lengthening of the preceding vowel in Attic-Ionic, etc., with diphthongization to αι, οι, etc., in Lesbian.

*παντ-ια, πάνσα, πᾶσα, Lesb. παῖσα

dat. pl. *φεροντσι, φέρονσι, φέρουσι, Lesb. φέροισι

3 pl. φέροντι, φέρονσι, φέρουσι, Lesb. φέροισι

a. Att. ὕφανσις (ὑφαίνω), etc., were formed later and retained ν.

3. νσ+consonant (similarly ν+ζ = zd) loses ν without lengthening of the preceding vowel.

κεστός from *κενστός, *κεντ-τος (κεντέω)

σύστασις from *συν-στασις

σύζυγος from *συν-ζυγος (i.e. *συν-zdυγος)

Ἀθήναζε from *Ἀθηνας-δε (203.1), *Ἀθηνανς-δε

a. But ν is restored by analogy in compounds of ἐν, as ἔνστασις.

4. Final νσ in close combination with a word beginning with a consonant was subject to the loss of ν without vowel lengthening (above, 3). Otherwise it had the same history as the secondary intervocalic νσ (above, 2). In Cretan we find such doublets as

acc. pl. τὸνς ἐλευθέρονς but τὸς καδεστάνς. But in most dialects one type or the other was generalized, without regard to the initial of the following word, usually the τόνς, τάνς, or the resulting τούς or τώς, τᾱς (Lesb. τοίς, ταίς).

5. The different results of νσ may be surveyed in the accompanying table.

*ἐφανσα..........	*παντια, φέροντι	*κενστός	τόνς	
Lesb. ἔφαννα......	Arc. πάνσα, φέρονσι	κεστός	τόνς	τός
Dor. ἐφᾱνα........	....	....	↓	
Att. ἔφηνα........	Att. πᾶσα, φέρουσι	....	τούς τώς τοίς	

205. λσ, ρσ show a double treatment, which perhaps depended originally upon the position of the accent, e.g. κόρση, Att. κόρρη, but κουρεύς.

1. λσ remains. Likewise ρσ in most dialects, but this becomes ρρ in Attic and some others.

ἄλσος, τέλσον, ἔκελσα, ὦρσα

ἄρσην, Att. ἄρρην   θάρσος, Att. θάρρος

a. The earliest Attic inscriptions have θάρρος, etc., and θάρσος, etc., of early Attic writers are, like πράσσω, etc. **(182a)**, due to Ionic influence.

In Att. θηρσί, κάθαρσις, etc., σ is retained by analogy.

2. λσ, ρσ become λ, ρ with lengthening of the preceding vowel. In Lesbian and Thessalian there is assimilation to λλ, ρρ. The development here is parallel to that of σλ, σν, νσ **(203.2)**.

ἔστειλα, Lesb., Thess. ἔστελλα, from *ἔστελ-σα

ἔφθειρα, Lesb. *ἔφθερρα (cf. τέρραι = τεῖραι), from *ἔφθερ-σα

GROUPS OF THREE OR MORE CONSONANTS

GREEK

206. Many groups which are simplified in Latin remain unchanged in Greek, as ρκτ, λκτ, ρξ, λξ (L. *rct* > *rt*, etc., **207.2**). The more important changes are in groups containing σ.

1. Dental + σ becomes σ before or after another consonant.

πάσχω, with transfer of aspiration, from *παθ-σκω (cf. ἔπαθον) dat. pl. φέρουσι from φέρονσι (**204**.2) from *φεροντ-σι

νύξ, dat. pl. νυξί, from *νυκτ-ς, *νυκτ-σι (gen. sg. νυκτός)

2. σ is lost between two consonants in most groups.

γεγράφθαι from *γεγραφ-σθαι   ἐστάλθαι from *ἐσταλ-σθαι

λελέχθαι from *λελεχ-σθαι   ἐσπάρθαι from *ἐσπαρ-σθαι

a. So also πεφάνθαι with ν restored by analogy of πέφανται, etc. In the normal development of νσ+cons. the ν is lost (**204**.3).

b. In the groups κσν, κσμ, κσλ the σ caused aspiration of the preceding κ (cf. early Att. ἔδοχσε, **191***b*) and was then lost.

λύχνος from *λυκσνος (cf. L. *lūna* from *loucsnā*)

τέχνη from *τεκσνᾱ (cf. τέκτων, Skt. *takṣan-*, **160**)

πλοχμός from *πλοκσμος (cf. πλέκω)

3. But when σ stands between stops of the same class, the first stop is lost by dissimilation.

λάσκω from *λακ-σκω (cf. aor. ἔλακον)

διδάσκω from *διδακ-σκω (cf. διδαχή, L. *doceō*, *discō* from *di-dc-scō*)

βλάσφημος from *βλαπσ-φᾱμος (cf. βλάβος)

a. The preposition ἐξ would normally become ἐκ before most consonants (by 2), and ἐς before a guttural (by 3). But ἐκ was generalized in Attic-Ionic, and ἐς in some of the other dialects.

LATIN

207. Out of the great variety of changes the more important may be grouped as follows:

1. Stop+*s* becomes *s* before another consonant, and if this is voiced the *s* (which in this case may also come from *ns*) is lost (**202**.1).

inlūstris from *in-loucstris*   *lūna* from *loucsnā*

suspendō, suscipiō, sustineō from *subs-pendō*, etc.

sūmō from *subs-(e)mō*

ēdūcō from *ex-dūcō*   *trādūcō* beside *trāns-dūcō*

asportō from *abs-portō*   *ostendō* from *obs-tendō*

ēveniō from *ex-veniō*   *sēvirī* from *sex-viroi*

a. But in prepositional compounds recomposition is very frequent. So *subscrībō, abstineō, abscīdō, obstō, extendō, exclūdō, expōnō* (so regularly *ex* restored before voiceless stop in contrast to *ē* before voiced stop), etc.

Also *xt* in *dexter* (from *dexiter*, but even here Osc.-Umbr. *destr-*), *mixtus* (from *mixitos?) for which *mistus* also occurs, *textus* (prob. from *texitos* beside *texuī*, like *molitus* beside *moluī*, etc.; but could be simply by analogy of *texō*), *sextus* (by analogy of *sex*), *Sextius* but also *Sestius*.

2. A stop is lost between *r* or *l* and another consonant in most such groups. So in *rct, rtc, lct* (but *rpt, lpt* remain), *rdn, rcn, rcm, rpm, rbm, lcm, lgm, lpm*, also *rcs, lcs* (but these remain, when final, *rx, lx*); apparently also in *rts, lts*, but here the change belongs under **193**.

tortus, torsī, tormentum from **torctus, *torcsī, *torcmentom* (*torqueō*)

ultus from **ulctos* (*ulcīscor*)   *mulsī* from **mulcsī* (*mulceō*)

fulmen, fulsī from **fulgmen, *fulgsī* (*fulgeō*)

pulmentum from **pelpmentom* (*pulpa* from **pelpa* by **80**.6; cf. Umbr. *pelmner* 'pulmenti')

3. In the group *rst, rsc*, and *rsn* from *rtsn*, the *r* is lost; in *rsd* and inherited *rsn* (really *rzd, rzn*) the sibilant was lost.

tostus from **torstos* (*torreō* from **torseō*, **200**.2)

poscō from **porscō*: Skt. *pṛcchāmi* (**114**)

cēna from **cesnā, *cersnā, *certsnā* (Osc. k e r s s n u)

hordeum from **horsdeom*: NHG *Gerste*

perna from **persnā*: Skt. *pārṣṇis*, NHG *Ferse*

a. As in *rst, rsc*, so also in *rss* (from *rtt*, **190**) the *r* was lost. In most words the *r* was restored by analogy, and *rss* became *rs*, e.g. *vorsus* and compounds. But some forms with the loss of *r* survived, e.g. *dossum* beside *dorsum, rūsus* beside *rūrsus*, and notably *prōsa*, in specialized use *prōsa ōrātiō*, beside *prōrsus*.

4. *nct, ncn, ngn.*—*quīntus* from *quīnctus*. But *sānctus, iūnctus*, etc., with analogical restoration (*santus*, etc., only late).

quīnī from **quīncnoi* (*quīnque*), with vowel lengthening as before *nct, nx* (**99**.2)   Similarly

cōnīveō from **cōn-cnīveō*: Goth. *hneiwan* 'bow'

ignōscō, cognōscō from *in-, con-gnōscō* (see **198***b*)

SIMPLIFICATION OF DOUBLE CONSONANTS

208. 1. Greek σσ, whether original or from dental+σ or from τι, θι, was simplified after a consonant, a long vowel or diphthong, and when final. Between vowels σσ remains in many dialects, but becomes σ in Attic and later Ionic, Homer having both σσ and σ. See **183, 193,** and for original σσ, cf. dat. pl. γένεσ-σι, etc., Hóm. -εσσι and -εσι, Att. -εσι.

2. Latin *ss,* whether original or from dental+*s* or from dental +dental, is simplified after another consonant, a long vowel or diphthong, and when final. See **190, 193** and for original *ss* cf. *hausī* from *haus-sī* (*hauriō* from **hausiō*) in contrast to *gessī* (*gerō* from **gesō*).

But the simplification after a long vowel or diphthong was relatively late, the *ss* surviving down into the Augustan period. Quintilian states that *caussa, cāssus,* etc., were the spellings of Cicero's time, and the Monumentum Ancyranum of Augustus has *caussa, claussum* beside *clausum.*

a. The *ss* persisted in the perf. act. infin. *-āsse,* etc., under the supporting influence of the fuller forms in *-āvisse,* etc.

3. A late simplification of L. *ll* occurs in *mīlia* from *mīllia* (which is still the spelling of the Mon. Ancyr.), and *paulum* from *paullum.* Cf. also *vīlicus* beside *vīlla.* But in general *ll* remains even after a long vowel, as *mīlle, nūllus,* etc.

a. The simplification of *ll* in *mīlia,* as contrasted with *mīlle,* perhaps originated in the colloquial pronunciation *mīllya* (like *medyus,* **180***a*), whence *mīlya.*

4. For the simplification of L. *mm* from *dm* after a long vowel or diphthong, see **199.**

5. Some examples of simplification in Latin are apparently due to the position before the (historical) accent (though this view is also disputed), as *mamilla* beside *mamma, ofella* beside *offa, curūlis* beside *currus, omittō* from **om-mittō,* **ob-mittō* (but *summittō,* etc.).

DOUBLING OF CONSONANTS

209. Certain Latin words show doubling of a consonant, with shortening of the preceding vowel if long.

Iuppiter (this the approved spelling) from *Iūpiter* (**272.**2)
quattuor from **quatuor*:Skt. *catvāras*

a. In the case of *Iuppiter*, and also certain abusive epithets like *cuppes* (*cupiō*), *lippus*, *gibber*, one may compare the expressive doubling which is often observed in the hypocoristic form of proper names (petnames, nick-names), e.g. Boeot. Μέννει (Μένης), Ἀγαθθώ (ἀγαθός), L. *Acca*, *Appius*. Cf. also Dor. μικκός from the μικ- of μικρός.

ASSIMILATION AND DISSIMILATION OF NON-CONTIGUOUS CONSONANTS. METATHESIS. HAPLOLOGY

210. Most changes falling under these heads occur only spo-radically, under conditions too complex to admit of precise formu-lation. They are often observed in current speech as individual and momentary "slips of the tongue" (and corresponding "slips of the pen" are even more frequent). In some cases they recur with sufficient frequency to effect a permanent change. Special circumstances favoring such permanency are now and then ap-parent, e.g. in τίκτω from *τίτκω (reduplicated present, like πίπτω), with weak grade of the root seen in aor. ἔτεκον), where the trans-position resulted in the substitution of a familiar consonant se-quence (κτ) for an unfamiliar one (τκ) and in a form which fell within a familiar class (presents in -τω) and was further favored by the resemblance of τικ- to the τεκ- of ἔτεκον. For examples, see **40.**8, 9, 10, 13.

FINAL CONSONANTS

GREEK

211. 1. A final stop is lost.

voc. sg. παῖ from *παιδ (gen. παιδός), γύναι from *γύναικ (gen. γυναικός), ἄνα from *ἄνακτ (gen. ἄνακτος)

nom.-acc. sg. neuter of pronouns, τό (Skt. *tad*), τί (L. *quid*, Skt. *cid*), ἄλλο (L. *aliud*)

3 sg. and 3 pl. forms like ἔφερε, ἔφερον, from IE *ebheret, *ebheront (**337, 340**)

a. A final stop occurs only in ἐκ from ἐξ, οὐκ from οὐκί and in dialectic forms like κατ from κατά, ἀπ from ἀπό, etc.

2. Final μ becomes ν. Acc. sg. ending -ν = L. -*m*, Skt. -*m*. First singular secondary ending -ν = L. -*m*, Skt. -*m*, as ἔφερον (Skt. *abharam*).

LATIN

212. 1. Final *m* was weakly sounded or in part wholly lost, as shown by its frequent omission in early inscriptions and by the fact that it does not interfere with the elision of the preceding vowel when the next word begins with a vowel. On the other hand, it "makes position", like any other consonant, when the next word begins with a consonant.

a. Complete loss of *m* with elision of the preceding vowel is clear in cases like *animadvertō* (*animum advertō*), *vēneō* (*vēnum eō*), etc. But for cases like *multum ille* the precise practice is impossible to determine. Some of the grammarians state that the *m* was only obscured, while others speak of it as lost. They never allude to any nasalization of the vowel, such as is assumed by many modern scholars. Probably in common speech, in a closely connected group of words, the treatment was actually the same as in *animadvertō*. But in oratory and poetry there was apparently an attempt, probably more or less artificial, to retain some indication of the *m* (an approximation of the lips, a sort of *w*-glide ?), as well as of the preceding vowel.

2. Final *s* after a short vowel was weakened in early Latin, as shown by its frequent omission in early inscriptions and by the fact that it often fails to make position in early poetry. But it had regained its full value by the time of Cicero, who remarks that the omission of final *s* (when not followed by a vowel) was formerly good usage, but no longer so ("quod iam subrusticum videtur", Orator 48. 161).

3. IE final *t* became *d* in the Italic period, as in the 3 sg. secondary ending, e.g. Praenestine *fhefhaked*, early L. *feced, sied*, Osc. d e d e d , k ú m b e n e d . But in Latin except in the earliest inscriptions, the *t* from the primary ending -*ti* was generalized.

a. Hence the final *d* of early L. abl. sg. -*ōd*, etc., and of nom.-acc. sg. neut. *id, quod*, etc., may represent either IE *t* or *d*, the corresponding Skt. forms being equally ambiguous.

4. Final *d* after a long vowel was lost toward the end of the 3d cent. B.C., as in the ablative singular in -*ā*, -*ō*, etc., and the imperative in -*tō*, which in early inscriptions (and in Oscan) appear as -*ād*, -*ōd*, -*īd*, -*ūd*, and -*tōd*. The monosyllabic *mēd, tēd* survived somewhat longer and occur before vowels in Plautus.

a. The SC de Bacch. (**29**) has *sententiād, preivātōd, facilumēd, magistrātūd,* etc., consistently in the text of the decree, but this is due to the conservation characteristic of legal style. The subjoined instructions for publishing the decree read *in agro Teurano,* showing that the *d* was already lost in current speech.

5. The final consonant of certain groups was lost, as in *cor* from **cord* (gen. *cordis*), *lac* from **lact* (gen. *lactis*), etc. Certain other groups were first assimilated and then simplified (see the following).

6. Double consonants were simplified, as in

2 sg. *es* from *ess*   *mīles* from *mīless, *mīlets* (gen. *mīlitis*)

ter from *terr, *ters, *tris* (**109, 200.**2)

ager from **agerr, *agers, *agros* (**109, 200.**2)

far from **farr, *fars* (gen. *farris* from **farses,* **200.**2)

nom.-acc. sg. *hoc* from *hocc, *hod-c(e)*

a. In Plautus *es* regularly, and sometimes *ter* and the last syllable of *mīles,* have the value of long syllables, which means the survival of *ess, mīless, terr,* before vowels. In the case of *hoc,* which is regularly a long syllable even in the later period, it is expressly stated by the grammarians that the pronunciation was *hocc* before a vowel, e.g. *hocc erat.* By analogy there arose also in the nominative singular masculine, beside *hic,* a *hic* with long syllable, that is *hicc.*

b. L. *sāl* is probably for **sall* from **sals* = G. ἅλς, though there are other possibilities; so perhaps *pār* for **parr* from **pars.*

CHANGES IN EXTERNAL COMBINATION

213. Changes in external combination, that is, those depending upon the relation of a word to the rest of the sentence, are common in actual speech, but generally only a small part of such changes is reflected in the written form of a literary language. Cf. **40.**14.

In Greek certain changes belonging under this head, as the familiar elision, etc., are observed in our literary texts, but many others common in inscriptions are disregarded. In the Latin literary texts there is still less of such matters.

But in both languages there are some recognized sentence doublets, parallel to NE *a* and *an,* as G. ἐξ, ἐκ, L. *ex, ē, ab, abs, ā,* etc.

Several matters that involve the subject of external combination have been mentioned in connection with particular initial or final sounds, as, for example, the history of final $\nu\sigma$ (**204.**4), and other finals (**211, 212**). But there remain others.

GREEK

214. 1. Elision of a final short vowel (also $\alpha\iota$ of verbal endings, sometimes $o\iota$) before a word beginning with a vowel, subject to certain well-known exceptions, is more consistently noted in our current texts than in MSS and inscriptions, where there is great fluctuation in the writing even in metrical texts.

a. The absence of elision (hiatus) in Homer is partly due to the earlier presence of initial ϝ in the following word, but is by no means confined to such cases.

b. In the case of $\alpha\iota$ or $o\iota$, the way for elision was prepared by the change of ι to ι̯ and its loss between vowels (**178**).

2. Shortening of a final long vowel or diphthong before a word beginning with a vowel, like that in the interior of a word (**98.**3), is observed in Homer, and there are occasional inscriptional examples in which this is indicated in the spelling.

3. Aphaeresis, or inverse elision, mostly after $\mu\dot{\eta}$ or $\ddot{\eta}$, as $\ddot{\eta}$ 'μέ, occurs in poetry and occasionally in inscriptions. Though called by a different name, this is probably the same as crasis, in reality simple contraction.

4. Crasis, in a closely connected group of words, most frequently forms of the article or $\kappa\alpha\dot{\iota}$ with the following, occurs in poetry and prose, and examples occur in early inscriptions of all dialects.

Crasis is simply a special name for vowel contraction, and generally follows the rules of internal contraction. But in Attic the vowel of the second or principal word determines the quality of the contracted vowel, as $\dot{\alpha}\nu\dot{\eta}\rho=\dot{o}$ $\dot{\alpha}\nu\dot{\eta}\rho$, in contrast to Ion. $\dot{\omega}\nu\dot{\eta}\rho$ with the normal contraction of $o+a$ to ω as in Att.-Ion. $\tau\bar{\iota}\mu\hat{\omega}\mu\epsilon\nu$ from $\tau\bar{\iota}\mu\dot{\alpha}o\mu\epsilon\nu$.

5. Apocope, the loss of the final short vowel of prepositions before a consonant, is common in Homer and in many dialects. In

some dialects it is more extensive than in Homer, so in Thessalian even ἀπ, ἐπ, ὑπ. But in Attic-Ionic it is almost unknown.

6. Assimilation of the final consonant to the initial consonant of the following word is seen in Homer and in many dialects in the case of apocopated prepositions, as ἂμ πεδίον, κὰπ πεδίον, κὰρ ῥόον, etc. A vast deal more of such assimilation, especially in forms of the article, that does not appear in our current texts, is very common in inscriptions, including Attic, more in the earlier than in the later. Cases like τὸμ πόλεμον, τὴμ βουλήν, τὸγ κήρυκα are common even in late Attic inscriptions and in papyri, and have persisted in actual speech down to the present day. The more radical assimilations, as in τὸλ λόγον, τοὺν νόμους, etc., are found only in the earlier inscriptions.

215. The ν movable in forms like λέγουσι(ν), εἶπε(ν), etc., is an added element which, except for a few examples of dat. pl. -σιν in other dialects, is peculiar to Attic-Ionic. Here it appears from the earliest inscriptions on with increasing frequency and before both vowels and consonants. In Attic it came ultimately to be used more commonly before a vowel or before a pause, though never with any absolute consistency. It cannot be a purely phonetic addition, but must have come in by analogical extension from certain forms in which the ν was inherited. Thus from pronominal datives like Att. ἡμῖν (cf. Lesb. ἄμμιν and ἄμμι) it passed to dat. pl. -σι, as φύλαξι(ν), thence to 3 pl. λέγουσι(ν), thence to 3 ps. τίθησι(ν); and again from 3 sg. ἦεν, ἦν (orig. 3 pl., **340.**2) to οἶδε(ν), ἔθηκε(ν), etc.

LATIN

216. Latin literary texts show still less of such matters, since even the elision was not noted in writing, and aphaeresis (e.g. *copiast = copia est*) only occasionally. It is only in the more carelessly written inscriptions that one finds frequent examples of assimilation, e.g., *im (in) balneum, cun (cum) suis, cun coniugi, quan (quam) nunc.*

Elision was doubtless common in actual speech in the case of groups of closely attached words. So clearly in *magnopere, animadverto (animum adverto)*, etc. But the Roman poets extended the use of elision far beyond its probable practice in ordinary speech. Certain statements of some writers imply that they read Latin poetry with slurring of the vowel rather than with elision. If this was usual in poetry and oratory, it was probably only an artificial compromise between the elided and the full form, an attempt to retain something of the vowel without giving it the value of a syllable. For words ending in *m*, see also **212.1a.**

ACCENT

217. Under accent one understands variations of either intensity or intonation, and speaks of a stress accent or a pitch accent according as one or the other element is the more conspicuous. In English the word accent is one of stress, while variation in pitch is mainly a matter of sentence accent, as in the rising tone of interrogation. The accent of Sanskrit and Greek, the two earliest-known IE languages, was a pitch accent, and it is a fair inference that this was the character of the IE accent in the last period of the parent speech. But no doubt the element of stress was also present, and at an earlier period of the parent speech, when the reduction of unaccented vowels took place, stress seems to have been the effective factor (**122**).

A distinction of simple and compound accent, or of acute and circumflex, to adopt the familiar terms applied to Greek accent, existed in the parent speech, at least in final syllables. Compare G. τῑμή, τῑμῆς with Lith. nom. *mergà*, gen. *mergõs*, or καλοί, καλῶν, καλοῖς with Lith. *gerì, gerū̃, geraĩs*. The IE circumflex appears to have arisen in connection with certain Proto-IE processes of contraction and compensative lengthening, much as the Greek circumflex in part is connected with contraction in Greek (τρεῖς from τρέες).

The circumflexed long vowels and diphthongs were longer than those with acute accent, say as three morae to two, if we adopt the quantity of a short vowel as a convenient unit or "mora". This quantitative difference shows itself, for example, in the treatment of final vowels in Lithuanian, and also in Greek in the different values of final -οι or -αι in determining the word accent. These final diphthongs were shortened—from three to two morae, so that they still count as long, in categories in which when accented they show the circumflex—from two morae to one, so that they count as short, in categories in which if accented they have the acute. Thus nom. pl. οἶκοι (cf. θεοί), but loc. sing. οἴκοι (cf. Ἰσθμοῖ), and 3 sg. opt. λείποι where related Lithuanian forms show the circumflex on the ending.

As regards position, the IE accent was a "free accent", as opposed to a "fixed accent", either absolutely fixed, as, for example, in languages with constant initial accent, or relatively fixed, as in Greek and Latin, where it is restricted to the last three syllables. Thus in Sanskrit the accent may stand on the first, last, or any intermediate syllable, regardless of the number of syllables or quantity of the vowels (e.g. ápratīta-, tigmámūrdhan-, parivatsará-, bubódha, bubudhé, bubudhimáhe). And the Sanskrit accent, which agrees with that to be inferred from certain consonant changes in Germanic (Verner's Law), is in the main the inherited IE accent. Several of the Slavic languages, as Russian and Serbo-Croatian, still have a free accent in this sense.

GREEK

218. The Greek accent was one of pitch, as is clear from its description by Greek writers and from the terminology employed, e.g. τόνος, προσῳδία, ὀξεῖα, βαρεῖα. The term βαρεῖα (τάσις) was appropriately used for the 'low' pitch of the unaccented syllable, whereas, had the accent been one of stress, it could only have been employed for the 'heavy' stress of the accented syllable. The absence of vowel syncope and other phenomena which commonly result from a stress accent, and the independence of word accent and verse ictus, all point in the same direction. In Modern Greek, on the other hand, the accent, while retaining its old position, is one of stress. The change, which was no doubt a gradual one, was established by the 4th cent. A.D., when accentual verse begins. There are much earlier indications of stress in colloquial and dialectic speech.

The acute accent was one of high pitch, the grave one of low pitch, and the circumflex a combination of the two (´ `, whence

^ ^). That is, the circumflex, occurring only with diphthongs or long vowels, consisted of high pitch on the first mora of the diphthong or long vowel, followed by low pitch on the second mora, e.g. παῖς = πάἰς or πῦρ = πύὐρ.

a. All syllables not having the acute or the circumflex, that is, what we call the unaccented syllables, were regarded as having the grave, and were sometimes so marked, e.g. Μἐνἐλἀὸς. Sometimes all the syllables preceding the one with the acute were marked as grave, e.g. ἐπἐϳϲεὐοντο, or again the one immediately preceding, e.g. κρατἐρος.

The only use of the grave accent sign in our current texts, namely in place of the acute on the final before another word, reflects (as do some other peculiarities in the use of the accent signs) a Byzantine convention, at variance with the practice of the Alexandrian period as observed in the papyri. In certain cases the sign may be understood as a survival of its original use in the so-called unaccented syllables. Thus in τὸν πόλεμον the τὸν was really proclitic just as much as the ὁ of ὁ πόλεμος; and so in ἀνὰ λόγον, ἀπὸ δείπνου the prepositions were proclitic like ἐν, εἰς, ἐκ, ἐξ (sometimes ἐν, ἐκ in papyri, but in the practice finally established the ` was not written in these prepositions which had also a breathing sign; similarly in the case of ὁ, ἡ).

Except in such cases of close combination, the use of the grave on final syllables in place of the acute is a convention which had no basis in actual speech.

After the pitch accent had become one of stress, all distinction between the acute (including the grave on final syllables) and the circumflex disappeared. The use of the three signs in Modern Greek is only a historical convention.

219. In the matter of position the IE system of free accent was replaced by one in which the accent must fall within the last three syllables, and if the ultima was long within the last two. Or expressed in terms of morae, the accent could stand on the fourth mora from the end in a case like ἄνθρωπος, otherwise not farther back than the third mora from the end. Hence the circumflex (= ´ `) was excluded from the antepenult, and from the penult when the ultima was long.

If the IE accent had been farther back it was brought forward sufficiently to fall within the required limits. Thus Skt. *bhára-māṇas, bháramāṇasya*, but G. φερόμενος, φερομένου. In such cases the accent was as far back as was allowable in the Greek system, that is, it was what from the Greek point of view is known as the recessive accent.

If on the other hand the IE accent stood anywhere within the limits which came to be prescribed in Greek, it might and generally did remain unchanged. Thus G. πούς, ποδός, ποδί, πόδα like Skt. *pắt, padás, padí, pắdam;* πατήρ, πατέρας, πατράσι like Skt. *pitá, pitáras, pitṛ́ṣu;* ὕστερος like Skt. *úttaras.*

But within the last three syllables there have also been changes of accent, due to various and often obscure causes, in particular words and in certain classes of words. One that is of wide scope, though there are also many exceptions, is the shift of the accent from ultima to penult in forms of dactylic ending, e.g. ποικίλος, ἡδύλος, στωμύλος in contrast to τυφλός, παχυλός, ὑψηλός, etc.

a. The accentual treatment of enclitics and of the word preceding an enclitic, the details of which need not be repeated here, is in general accord with the Greek avoidance of more than two unaccented syllables.

220. The accent of the Greek verb is regularly recessive, that is, in the finite forms, with the exception of some imperatives like ἰδέ, ἐλθέ, etc. (Only apparent exceptions are forms of the contract verbs, like τιμᾷ from τιμάει.) This is in notable contrast to the accent of the noun, which may stand on any one of the last three syllables. Thus we have εἶμι, ἴμεν although the original accentuation was that of Skt. *émi, imás;* or δέδορκα, δεδόρκαμεν in contrast to Skt. *dadárça, dadṛçimá.* The explanation is as follows:

In the parent speech the verb was sometimes accented and sometimes unaccented, that is enclitic, as in Sanskrit where it was regularly unaccented in independent clauses unless standing at the beginning. In Greek, where no more than two syllables could be left unaccented at the end of a word and enclitics of more than two syllables were impossible, the enclitic forms of the verb (except the few which would fall within the limits possible for enclitics) would have to receive an accent; and this accent would be in the earliest possible position, just as in the case of all words whose accent was originally farther back and was moved forward to come within the required limits. Just as *φέρομενος became φερόμενος, so ˊ δεδορκα became δέδορκα, which then answers to the Sanskrit unaccented *dadarça* and not to the accented *dadárça*.

Furthermore, all the accented forms whose accent either preceded or fell just within the limits of the Greek system would also have the recessive accent. Thus πεύθεται, πευθόμεθα may answer to the Sanskrit *bódhate*, *bódhāmahe* as well as to the unaccented forms. This would be the case throughout the present system in the commonest present classes.

Since nearly all the unaccented forms and the majority of the accented forms came regularly to have the recessive accent in Greek, this was generalized and extended to those forms which might have retained an accent nearer the end of the word, e.g. ἴμεν (Skt. *imás*), ἴδμεν, ἴσμεν (Skt. *vidmá*), augmentless forms of aorists like ἔλιπον, ἔφυγον, as λίπον, λίπε, λίποιμι, λίποι, where the accent was originally on the thematic vowel and was so preserved in the infinitive and participle, λιπεῖν, λιπών.

LATIN

221. Between the IE system of free accent and the historical Latin accent there intervened, it is believed, a period of initial stress accent, in which all words were stressed on the first syllable. It was under this older accentual system that most of the syncope and weakening of vowels, described in **108, 110**, took place. For in the numerous cases like *dexter* from **dexiteros* or *perfectus* from **perfactos* the vowels affected stood in what under the historical system were the accented syllables. The older system must have prevailed when such Greek words were borrowed as τάλαντον and ἐλαίϝα which became *talentum* and *olīva*, or when the name Ἀκράγας, Ἀκράγαντος yielded *Agrigentum*. Even in Plautus and Terence there seems to be a last survival of it in words of the *facilius* type (˘ ˘ ˘ ˊ) which are generally so placed that the verse ictus falls on the first syllable.

222. The historical Latin accent resembled the Greek in that it could not stand farther back than the third syllable from the end of the word. Hence one speaks of the "three-syllable law" governing both. But beyond this general restriction the resemblance ceases. In Latin it was the quantity of the penult which determined the position within these limits. The Latin accent was regularly recessive, while in Greek it was recessive in the verb but not necessarily so in other forms. This would naturally result from a preceding system of initial accent replacing an IE accent on the ultima, which might otherwise have survived within the three-syllable law and did survive in Greek (ποδός, πατήρ, etc.)

Exceptions are only apparent, due to the loss of a final syllable by syncope or contraction, as *illīc* from *illīce*, *audīt* from *audīvit*, *Vergīlī* from *Vergīliī*.

a. If the late Roman grammarians were right in their statement that words ending with the enclitics *-que, -ve, -ne, -ce* were always accented on the syllable preceding the enclitic, even when this was short, e.g. *bonáque*, *līmināque*, this might readily be explained as a generalization, since the majority of forms in *-que*, etc., would necessarily be so accented, as *bonúm-que*, *bonṓque*, *bonī́que*, etc. But the relation to the ictus observed in poetry and the metrical clausulae make it probable that down through the Augustan period the accent was in accordance with the general system, *bónaque*, etc.

223. Whether the Latin accent of the classical period was one of stress or of pitch is a question upon which the evidence is apparently conflicting and modern scholars disagree. It was unquestionably a stress accent in late Latin, as shown by the treatment of unaccented vowels in the Romance languages.

The Roman grammarians, down to the 4th cent. A.D., describe accent in terms that are appropriate only to a pitch accent. This is far from conclusive, for in general not only was their whole terminology a literal translation of the Greek, but their statements are often mere reflections of their Greek models, in some cases forced or even absurd as applied to Latin. Even in the passage of Cicero (Or. 56–58) where he identifies accent and melody and speaks of its use in oratory, his reference to the technique of Greek oratory suggests the inspiration of his ideas.

Still, it may be said, he would hardly have so identified Greek and Latin accent had there not been an appreciable element of pitch in the latter. In favor of a pitch accent is further urged the

Roman adoption of the Greek quantitative meter, it being held that under a system of stress accent the strict observance of quantity in the unaccented syllables would have been remarkable if not impossible, and the frequent conflict between accent and verse ictus intolerable.

On the other hand, it has been proved that the correspondence between accent and ictus in Plautus and Terence, and also, for the last two feet, in the writers of hexameter, is greater than could be accidental and implies a conscious attention of the poets to the matter. Furthermore, certain phonetic processes point to an accent of stress, such as the iambic shortening (**102**), which was operative in the time of Plautus, and the persistent tendency to syncope (**108**). To be sure, the most extensive syncope occurred under the older system of initial accent and so proves nothing for the historical accent. But there are also cases in which the syncopated forms either first arose or became more generally current within the historical period, indicating that the tendency persisted in all periods of the language. Several other changes, as that of *ov* to *av* (**83**.2) or the simplification of double consonants in *ofella* beside *offa* (**208**.5), have been attributed to the influence of the following accent, but may depend upon other factors and are inconclusive.

We may conclude that the historical Latin accent comprised both pitch and stress and that the dominance of one element was not nearly so marked as was that of pitch in ancient Greek or that of stress in present English.

But the probability is still, as we see the situation, that stress was the more effective element in the phonetic development of the language, was in reality the more important characteristic of the accent in ordinary speech—while, on the other hand, the element of pitch was made more of stylistically, owing to Greek influence. The familiarity of educated Romans with Greek accent and technique, while it certainly could not have caused them to adopt an element of accent wholly foreign to their natural speech, might well have made them more conscious of an existing element of pitch and even led them to a studied enhancement of it in actual practice, for example in oratory.

INFLECTION

THE PARTS OF SPEECH

224. The familiar classification of the parts of speech is, with some modifications, that which was gradually evolved by the Greek philosophers and grammarians, from whom it was borrowed by the Roman grammarians. But when it is said that the Greeks "discovered the parts of speech", it is not to be thought that they discovered some great fundamental truth. They simply worked out a particular classification, among many that are possible, which we follow in the main. It was not based upon any single logical principle, but upon a variety of criteria, a word's inner content, its form (e.g. presence of case forms as part of the definition of a noun), relation to other words, position (preposition, though we may ignore this now and speak of a postpositive preposition). It involves difficulties of precise definition, especially if applied to a language of different structure from that for which it was devised. But with all its defects it remains a fairly workable system, and attempts to substitute other classifications have never succeeded.

225. The Greek and Roman classification and the later modification are shown in the accompanying table

Greek	Roman	Modern
ὄνομα	*nōmen*	{noun {adjective
ῥῆμα	*verbum*	verb
μετοχή	*participium*	
ἄρθρον		article
ἀντωνυμία	*prōnōmen*	pronoun
πρόθεσις	*praepositiō*	preposition
ἐπίρρημα	*adverbium*	adverb
σύνδεσμος	*coniūnctiō*	conjunction
	interiectiō	interjection

a. The Roman grammarians made up for the lack of an article in Latin by adding the interjection. Both the Greeks and Romans included under ὄνομα, *nōmen* what we now distinguish as noun (or substantive) and adjective. They

168

made numerous subdivisions of their noun, and among other terms Priscian uses *adiectīva* of words added to other appellatives. The participle has been rightfully demoted.

Under pronouns the Greeks included only the personal pronouns and possessives. So some of the Romans, while others included forms like *ūnus*, *ūllus*, *alius*, etc., or were in doubt about them. The difficulty of a precise delimitation still persists. We observe that words meaning *any*, *all*, *other*, etc., have in a measure the feeling of pronouns and may or may not show pronominal inflection (so L. *tōtus*, but not *omnis*).

DECLENSION

GENDER

226. The distinction of three genders, masculine, feminine, and neuter, is characteristic of Greek and Latin, together with most of the other IE languages. This grammatical gender, except as it agrees with natural gender (male, female, sexless), is a purely formal distinction, observed in part in the forms of the nouns but more fully in the forms of the adjectives and pronouns.

The neuter has a distinctive form only for the nominative-accusative. Otherwise it agrees with the masculine.

Masculine and feminine have the same form in many classes of nouns, some adjectives, and the interrogative-indefinite pronoun. The *o*-stem nouns with nom. sg. *-os* are mostly masculine, but some are feminine in both Greek and Latin. The *ā*-stem nouns are mostly feminine, but a few are masculine in Latin, and in Greek a new and productive type of masculine *ā*-stems, with distinctive forms for the nominative and genitive singular, grew up.

This distinction of masculine *o*-stems and feminine *ā*-stems, which among nouns was prevailing but not universal, was an absolute one in the case of certain pronouns and in the commonest type of adjectives, namely that represented by G. *-os*, *-η*, *-ον*, L. *-us*, *-a*, *-um*. It is such adjective and pronominal forms that most consistently carry the marks of gender. They determine for us the gender of a noun where this is not shown by the form of the noun itself.

Besides the *ā*-stem, there was another distinctively feminine type, the *yā*-stem with gradation, nom. sg. *-ī* in Sanskrit, etc., but -ια or ͺα in Greek (237). This furnished the feminine of adjective *u*-stems and consonant stems, e.g. Skt. *svādvī*, G. ἡδεῖα, Skt. *bharantī*, G. φέρουσα from *φέροντͺα. This type has disappeared in Latin, where adjectives of the third declension have the same form for masculine and feminine, except in a few *i*-stems like *ācer, ācris* (and here the distinction is secondary, 283).

a. The neuter has disappeared as a distinct category, that is, it is merged with the masculine, in the Romance languages; likewise in Lithuanian. In present English the only relics of formal gender distinction are a few pronominal forms, as *he, she, it* (also masc.-fem. *who*, neut. *which, what*), and here it is virtually always one of natural gender.

b. The origin of grammatical gender, and its relation to natural gender, has been much disputed. It was once thought to rest on a widespread personification of material objects, with metaphorical extension of natural gender. This has no doubt been a factor in some cases, but on such a wholesale scale seems unlikely. There is some reason to believe that formal gender distinction had its beginning in certain pronouns, such as IE **so, *sā, *tod* (Skt. *sa, sā, tad*, G. ὁ, ἡ, τό), and that **sā* (the ancestor of NE *she*) was a prime factor in establishing the relation between forms in *ā* and feminine gender. After certain sets of forms became associated with male or female creatures respectively, the same forms when they happened to be used in connection with inanimate objects are called by analogy masculine or feminine, without any real feeling of sex being involved.

However, there are difficulties in pursuing this view in detail. Gender is a phenomenon that was already fully developed in the parent speech, its evolution wrapped in the obscurity of a remote past. Apart from certain general probabilities, we must simply take it as we find it.

NUMBER

227. Besides the singular and plural, the parent speech possessed a dual, denoting 'two' or 'a pair'. The dual occurs in the earliest stages of most of the IE languages, but in the historical period its use has been constantly on the wane, until it has disappeared from nearly all (it is still in use in Lithuanian, Slovenian, and Wendish).

In Greek it occurs in the literature from Homer down through the classical period, and in the inscriptions of many dialects. It does not occur in Hellenistic Greek, for example, in the New Testament.

In the case of Latin and the Italic dialects it had disappeared as a distinct category in prehistoric times, though certain Latin forms are of dual origin, as *duo*, and *ambō* = G. ἀμφώ.

a. Some scholars have thought to recognize a survival of the dual in the form of the gentile following two praenomina in a few early inscriptions, as *M. C. Pomplio*. But this is merely the nom. sg. (with final *s* omitted as often, **212.**2), in formal agreement with the second praenomen, though belonging to both.

CASE

228. The parent speech had eight cases, the six that are known in Latin, together with the locative and instrumental, whose names and uses are also familiar to students of Latin syntax.

The dative and ablative plural had the same form, likewise the genitive and ablative singular except in *o*-stems. The vocative plural had the same form as the nominative except that the accent was sometimes different.

In Latin the old ablative, locative, and instrumental are merged in the ablative. The locative survives as a regular case in Oscan-Umbrian (e.g. e í s e í   t e r e í 'in eo territorio'), but in Latin only in isolated forms like *humī*, etc.

In Greek the old genitive and ablative are merged in the genitive; the dative, locative, and instrumental in the dative.

a. Eight cases are preserved in Indo-Iranian; seven in Balto-Slavic (where genitive and ablative are merged); seven in Oscan-Umbrian; six in Latin; five in Greek (four in Modern Greek, where the dative is obsolete in the spoken language); four in Celtic and Germanic (as still in German); two (for the noun) in present English; one (for the noun) in French, Italian, Spanish.

The merging of two or more cases in one, which has already taken place to some extent in Greek and Latin, but has gone much farther in most of the modern European languages, is known as case syncretism. It is due to a variety of factors, such as:

The overlapping of areas of usage.—Thus one may drink from, in, or by means of a cup. One may carry something in the hand or with the hand.

Phonetic changes resulting in loss of formal difference.—In vulgar Latin the loss of final *m* and of difference in vowel quantity led to formal identity of accusative and ablative in the singular (not in the plural; the formal identity in the singular was only a contributory factor).

Increasing use of prepositional phrases which expressed all that the case forms expressed and more precisely, making the latter dispensable.—Even in Latin and Greek the prepositional phrases had encroached largely on the pure case uses, and in later times this went much farther.

Fixed word order.—This goes hand in hand with loss of formal case distinctions.

DECLENSION OF NOUNS

229. Table of IE case endings.

	Cons. Stems	*ā*-Stems	*o*-Stems	*i*-Stems	*u*-Stems
			Singular		
Nom.	*s*, O	*ā*	*os*	*is*	*us*
Voc.	O	*a, ai*	*e*	*i, ei*	*u, eu*
Acc.	*m̥*	*ām*	*om*	*im*	*um*
Nom.-acc. n.	O		*om*	*i*	*u*
Gen.	*es, os, s*	*ās*	*osyo, oso, ī* (?)	*eis, ois, yes, yos*	*eus, ous, wes, wos*
Dat.	*ei, ai*	*āi*	*ōi*	*eyei (eyai)*	*ewei (ewai)*
Abl.	=Gen.	=Gen.	*ōd, ēd*	=Gen.	=Gen.
Instr.	*bhi, mi*	*ābhi*, etc.	*obhi*, etc.	*ibhi*, etc.	*ubhi*, etc.
		ā	*ō, ē*	*ī*	*ū*
Loc.	*i*, O	*āi*	*oi, ei*	*eyi, ē(i)*	*ewi, ēu*
			Plural		
Nom.-voc. pron.	*es*	*ās*	*ōs* / *oi*	*eyes*	*ewes*
Acc.	*n̥s*	*ās, āns*(?)	*ons*	*ins*	*uns*
Nom.-acc. n.	*ə*		*ā*	*ī*	*ū*
Gen. pron.	*ōm*	? / *āsōm*	*ōm* / *oisōm, eisōm*	*iōm, yōm*	*uōm, wōm*
Dat.-abl.	*bhos, mos*	*ābhos*, etc.	*obhos*, etc.	*ibhos*, etc.	*ubhos*, etc.
Instr.	*bhis, mis*	*ābhis*, etc.	*ōis*	*ibhis*, etc.	*ubhis*, etc.
Loc.	*su*	*āsu*	*oisu*	*isu*	*usu*

230. Notes on the preceding table.

1. The table gives a survey of the case endings that are indicated for the parent speech by the combined evidence. The dual is omitted, since the IE forms can be only partially determined, and only one (the nom.-acc. of *o*-stems) is certainly reflected in Greek. Some pronominal endings that bear on Greek and Latin noun inflection are included.

2. Under vowel stems the stem vowel is included, while under cons. stems only the endings proper are given, or if there is no ending added to the stem this is indicated by O = zero. In some cases it would be feasible to follow the latter system for vowel stems also, giving, for example, -*m* as the acc. sg. ending, or -*s* as the nom. sg. ending of *o*-, *i*-, and *u*-stems, with O for *ā*-stems.

But often the stem vowel and case ending were united by contraction or otherwise, so that we cannot separate them except by resort to speculation on their Proto-IE form. Thus the nom. pl. of *o*-stems was probably formed from the stem vowel *o*+the ending *-es*, Proto-IE *-o-es*, but the historical evidence takes us back only to an IE *-ōs*.

3. The *o*-stems are more exactly stems in *e/o*, parallel to the verbal "thematic vowel" *e/o*. For the stem vowel, while *o* in the majority of cases, has the *e*-grade in the voc. sg. and in alternative forms of several other cases.

Similarly the *i*- and *u*-stems are stems in *i/ei* and *u/eu*, with gradation, but with a totally different distribution of the grades from that in cons. stems (**243**). Strong grades appear in the gen. sg. and voc. sg., and in the antevocalic form *ey* or *ew* in the dat. sg., loc. sg., and nom. pl., and a lengthened grade in the loc. sg. *-ēi* (whence *-ē*, **94**), *-ēu*.

Pedantic consistency with the practice of quoting verbal roots in the *e*-grade would require us to speak of *e-*, *ei-*, and *eu*-stems.

4. Besides the *i*- and *u*-stems there were also *ī*-stems and *ū*-stems, not included in the table. In these there is an interchange of *ī* and *ū* with *i(y)* and *u(w)* followed by the cons. stem endings. Thus Skt. *dhīs*, gen. sg. *dhiyás*, nom. pl. *dhíyas*, *bhrūs*, gen. sg. *bhruvás*, nom. pl. *bhrúvas*, G. ὀφρῦς, gen. sg. ὀφρύος, nom. pl. ὀφρύες.

There were also *ī/yā*-stems, not included in the table, for which see **237**.

5. In the gen. sg. the common element is *s*. In cons. stems usually *-es* or *-os*, rarely *-s*. In *i*- and *u*-stems the normal type, as indicated by the usual forms of most IE languages (except Greek and Latin where only L. *-ūs* shows it) was that in *-eis*, *-ois* (Skt. *-es*, Goth. *-ais*, Lith. *-ies*, Osc. *-eis*) and *-eus*, *-ous* (Skt. *-os*, Goth. *-aus*, Lith. *-aus*, Osc. *-ous*, L. *-ūs*), that is, *-ei-s*, etc., with strong grade of the stem vowel and weak grade of the case ending. But there are also some forms pointing to an alternative type *-yes*, *-yos* (Ved. *avyas*, Hom. ὄιος, Att. οἰός) and *-wes*, *-wos* (Ved. *paçvas*, *madhvas*, Hom. γουνός from *γουϝος, etc.), that is, *-y-es*, etc., with weak grade of the stem and strong grade of the ending.

6. For the dat. sg. of cons. stems Sanskrit (*pade*, etc.) points to a diphthong which might be IE *ei*, *oi*, or *ai*. The Greek dat., being of loc. origin (ποδί=Skt. loc. *padí*), does not help. The infin. in *-μεναι*=Skt. *-mane* appears to be a dat. in origin, and thus points to IE *-ai*. But certain Greek dialect forms as Διεί and the Oscan forms m e d í k e í, etc., point to IE *-ei*. Hence both *ai* and *ei* are given in the table as alternative IE endings.

7. In the instr. sg. and pl. and in the dat.-abl. pl. there are two parallel sets of endings, beginning with *bh* in most of the IE languages, but with *m* in Germanic and Balto-Slavic. So far as these are represented in Greek or Latin they belong to the *bh*-type, namely G. -φι, L. *-bus*. L. dat.-abl. pl. *-bus* is from *-bhos*, as are certain Celtic forms, while Skt. *-bhyas*, as if from *-bhyos*, has *y* perhaps by mixture with the ending *-bhi*. G. -φι in Homer serves in a

variety of case functions and is indifferent to number, as βίη-φι 'by might', θύρη-φι 'at the door', ὄρεσ-φι 'on the mountains', ἀπὸ ναῦ-φι 'from the ships'.

8. In Greek and Latin the instr. sg. is not represented in any of the regular case forms, but only in some adverbs (511.7); and the instr. pl. only in the *o*-stem form.

9. In the loc. sg. of consonant stems, besides the usual type with ending -*i*, there were also simple stem forms without ending. Thus from *n*-stems Vedic forms in -*man* beside -*mani*, to which correspond the G. infinitives in -μέν, like δόμεν.

10. In the loc. pl. the Sanskrit and Slavic forms point to IE -*su*. The G. dat. pl. -σι may reflect an alternative IE -*si*, but more probably is a Greek modification of -*su* under the influence of the loc. sg. (G. dat. sg.) ending -*i*. The *o*-stem form -*oisu*, Skt. -*eṣu*, ChSl. -*ěchŭ*, G. -οισι, is ultimately of pronominal origin (see 303.3–7).

11. For the acc. pl. of *ā*-stems the Sanskrit and Gothic forms point to IE -*ās*, in which the *n* of the original -*ns* had been lost. But the Greek, Latin, and Balto-Slavic forms come from -*ans*, which may represent IE -*āns*, this being a sentence doublet of -*ās*, or may be due to a later restoration of *n* after the analogy of -*ons*, etc.

12. For the gen. pl. the Sanskrit, Greek, and Gothic forms point to IE -ōm, the Celtic and Slavic to -*om*. The Latin (and Italic) may be derived from either -ōm or -*om*, but are assumed in this book to be from -ōm, like the Greek, etc. Perhaps the earliest form was -*om* (in ultimate origin nom.-acc. sg. of an adjective *o*-stem, like gen. pl. L. *nostrum*, Skt. *asmākam?*), then combined (or recombined) with *o*-stems to form -ōm, which then spread widely to other stems, with subsequent local redistribution of -*om* and -ōm, regardless of the stem.

For *ā*-stems the IE ending was presumably a contracted form of -ăŏm, but this is not reflected by the actual forms of the several languages, which are either of pronominal origin, like the Greek and Italic, or after the analogy of other stems (as Skt. -ānām, OHG -ōno from *n*-stems).

ā-STEMS. THE GREEK AND LATIN FIRST DECLENSION

231. The Greek and Latin first declension represents the IE *ā*-stems, except that the Greek type with nominative in short *a*, like θάλασσα, is of different origin, which will be discussed later.

For the change of *ā* to η in Ionic, and in Attic except after ε, ι, ρ, and for apparent exceptions to the rule, like Att. κόρη, see 88.

232. Table of *ā*-stem declension.

	GREEK				LATIN	OSCAN (OR UMBRIAN)	OTHER LANGUAGES, SELECTED FORMS
	Doric, etc.	Attic		Ionic			

Singular

Nom.	τιμά̄	χώρᾱ	τιμή	χώρη	via	*touto*	Skt. *senā̆*
Gen.	τιμᾶς	χώρᾱς	τιμῆς	χώρης	*familiās*	*eituas*[1]	Goth. *gibōs*, Lith. *mergōs*
					viāī		
					viae		
Dat.	τιμᾱͅ	χώρᾳ	τιμῇ	χώῃ	*viae*	d e i v a i	Goth. *gibai*, Lith. *mergai*
Acc.	τιμά̄ν	χώρᾱν	τιμήν	χώρην	*viam*	v í a m	Skt. *senām*
Voc.	τιμά̆	χώρᾱ	τιμή	χώρη			
					via		
	Hom. *νύμφα*, Lesb. *Δίκα*					U. *Tursa*	
Abl.					*viā*	*toutad*[1]	

Plural

Nom.	All dialects τιμαί				*viae*	*scriftas*	Skt. *senās*, Goth. *gibōs*
Gen.	Dor., etc. τιμά̄ων, -ᾶν　Att. τιμῶν Ion. τιμέων, -ῶν				*viārum*	*egmazum*	Skt. pron. *tāsām*
Dat.[2]	Most dialects τιμαῖς　Ion. τι-μῇσι Lesb. φόβαισι　Early Att. δί-κησι				*viīs*	D i u m p a i s	Skt. loc. *senāsu*
Acc.	Dor. τιμάνς, -ᾱς, -ας　Att.-Ion. τιμά̄ς Lesb. δίκαις				*viās*	v í a s s	OPruss. *rankans* Skt. *senās*, Goth. *gibōs*

---

[1] Really *eituās*, *toutād*, etc. See p. 25 ftn.

[2] In this and the subsequent tables, Dat. in the plural stands for the dative in Greek, the dative-ablative in Latin.

233. 1. *Nom. sg.*—IE -*ā*, G. -*ā*, -*η*. The long vowel was retained in Oscan-Umbrian, but with a rounding (cf. NE *call*) which is represented by Osc. -ú, *o*, Umbr. -u, -*o*, beside -a. In Latin the shortening probably started in iambic words (**102**), and with the support of the regular shortening in the acc. -*am* was generalized.

2. *Gen. sg.*—IE -*ās*, G. -*ās*, -*ης*. This was retained in Oscan-Umbrian, but in Latin only in a few forms in early authors, like

viās in Ennius, and later in the phrases *pater familiās*, etc. It was replaced by *-āī*, with *ī* taken over from the gen. of the second declension (cf. G. *-āo* in place of *-ās*, in masculines, and the resulting *-αυ* in Arcadian extended to feminines). This *-āī* occurs beside *-ae* in Plautus and occasionally in later poets. By shortening of the vowels it became *-ai*, whence the usual *-ae*.

a. The form *-aes* in some late epitaphs is only an imitation of the G. *-ης*, with *ae* in its later pronunciation for the open *η*.

3. *Dat. sg.*—IE *-āi*, G. *-ą̄*, *η* (really *-āι*, *-ηι*, **95**), in Latin shortened to *-ai* (**94**), whence the usual *-ae*.

a. In early Latin inscriptions there are a few examples of a dative in *-ā*, which may represent the alternative development of a long diphthong (**94**), parallel to that which prevailed in the *-ō* from *ōi* in the second declension.

4. *Acc. sg.*—IE *-ām*, G. *-āν*, *-ην* with the regular change of final *m* (**211.**2), L. *-am* with shortening of the vowel before final *m* (**101**). Oscan has the long vowel in p a a m = *quam*, but perhaps only in monosyllables.

5. *Voc. sg.*—The usual Greek form is the nom. The true voc., IE *-a*, is seen in Hom. *νύμφα*, also Δίκᾰ in Sappho. It was also preserved in Oscan-Umbrian (Umbr. *Tursa* with *-a*, not *-o* as in the nom.). In Latin after the shortening of *ā* in the nom. the two cases would be identical, so that the Latin voc. may be either the old voc., or the nom. used as voc. as in Greek.

6. *Abl. sg. in Latin.*—The Latin *-ā* is from *-ād*, frequent in early inscriptions (*sententiād*, etc.), also in Oscan, and this was formed after the analogy of *-ōd* in the second declension. Whereas in the parent speech the abl. and gen. sg. had the same form, except in *o*-stems where there was a distinct abl. form in *-ōd* or *-ēd*, there developed in the Italic period a whole set of ablatives modeled after the inherited *-ōd*, namely *-ād*, *-īd*, *-ūd*, whence with the loss of final *d* after a long vowel (**212.**4) the usual *-ā*, *-ō*, *-ī*, *-ū*.

7. *Loc. sg.*—IE *-āi*, whence L. *-ai*, *-ae* in *Rōmai*, *Rōmae*, etc. Cf. Osc. m e f í a í v í a í 'in media via'. In Greek there are some loc. forms in *-αι* formed after the analogy of *-οι*, as in Θηβαι-γενής, πάλαι, etc.

234. 1. *Nom. pl.*—IE *-ās* was replaced in Greek by *-αι* formed after the analogy of *-οι*. Similarly in Latin, at a time when the nom. pl. of *o*-stems was still *-oi* (later *-ī*), only that here the *-ās* first became *-āi* (with *i* from the *-oi*, but *ā* retained; *-ai* after *-oi*, as in Greek, would have given later *-ī*), whence, just as in the dat. sg., *-ai*, *-ae*. In Oscan-Umbrian the *-ās* remained.

2. *Gen. pl.*—The IE pronominal ending *-āsōm* (Skt. *-āsām*) was extended to nouns in prehistoric Greek and Italic. Hence in Greek, with loss of intervocalic σ (**164**), *-āων*, the earliest actual Greek form and the source of all the others, occurring in Homer (where it must be Aeolic, beside the Ion. *-εων*), Thessalian, and Boeotian, contracted to *-ᾱν* in most dialects, but Att.-Ion. *-ήων*, Ion. *-έων*, *-ῶν*, Att. *-ῶν* (**88, 98.**3, **104.**5); Osc.*-azum*, L. *-ārum* (**164, 101, 82.**2).

a. L. *-um* occurs in some Greek proper names as *Aeneadum* (cf. G. *-ων*); in *amphorum, drachmum* and in masc. forms like *agricolum, Troiugenum*, which follow the analogy of the old *o*-stem forms (see **240.**2).

3. *Dat. (-abl.) pl.*—G. *-αις* is formed after the analogy of *-οις*, likewise in Italic *-ais* after *-ois* (cf. Osc. *-ais, -ois*), whence L. *-eis, -īs* (**91**). An original loc. in *-ᾱσι* (cf. Skt. *-āsu*; intervocalic σ retained by analogy of *-σι* in cons. stems) serves as the dat. in early Attic inscriptions, as δίκησι (δικΕσι), ταμίᾱσι, and persists in locative adverbs like 'Αθήνησι, θύρᾱσι. From this with ι after the analogy of *-οισι* comes early Att. *-ησι, -ᾱσι* (in a few inscriptions), Ion. *-ησι*. Lesb. *-αισι* is directly after *-οισι*.

a. In Attic inscriptions *-αις* is the latest form in chronological sequence, prevailing after about 420 B.C. But most dialects have it from the earliest times. L. *deābus, fīliābus*, etc., are not inherited (as if :Skt. *-ābhyas*), but formed with *-bus* of 3.decl., etc., to distinguish fem. from masc. forms.

4. *Acc. pl.*—All forms of Greek and Italic go back to *-ans* (**230.**11). G. *-ανς*, preserved in Cretan and Argive, whence usual *-ᾱς*, Lesb. *-αις*, in some dialects *-ας* (**204.**4). Osc. -a s s , Umbr. *-af* (in which *-ss* and *-f* represent the *-ns*), L. *-ās*, like *-ōs* from *-ons*, etc. (**202.**3).

235. *The dual.*—The Greek dual forms are special Greek formations on the analogy of those of the second declension, namely *-ᾱ* (kept thus in Att.-Ion.) after -ω, and -αιιν, -αιν after -οιιν, -οιν. In the article and some of the other pronouns the *o*-stem forms are regularly used for the feminine, as τώ, τοῖν (rarely τά, ταῖν).

GREEK MASCULINE ā-STEMS

236. 1. The Greek masculine ā-stems form a distinctive and productive type, differing from the feminines in the nom., gen., and (in part) the voc. sg. Yet there are scattered dialectic examples of masculines with unchanged inflection, nom. sg. -ā, gen. sg. -ās.

2. *Nom. sg.*—-ās, -ης, with -*s* added after the analogy of -*os*.

a. The Homeric forms in -τᾰ, as ἱππότα, μητίετα, etc. (cf. also εὐρύοπα), occurring as epithets with another noun, are probably stereotyped vocatives used also in apposition with nominatives. Cf. L. *Iuppiter* which is a vocative in origin (**272.**2). According to another view they represent an (otherwise unsubstantiated) IE nom. in -*tə* from stems in -*t*, so that ἱππότα would belong to the stem seen in L. *eques, equitis*.

3. *Gen. sg.*—-ās was replaced by -āo with *o* taken over from the final of the *o*-stem gen., -οιο, -οο. This -āo occurs in Homer (Aeolic, beside Ion. -εω) and in several dialects, contracted to -ā in Doric, etc., Ion. -ηο, -εω, -ω (**88, 98.**3, **104.**5). Attic -ου, however, is not from this form (which would give -ω), but is the *o*-stem form taken over complete.

4. *Voc. sg.*—Words in -τᾱς, -της and some others (national names like Πέρσης and compounds like παιδοτρίβης) have -ᾰ, the original voc. which is rare in feminines. Otherwise the original nom. form in -ā, -η is employed, as in the feminines, only here differentiated from the nom. with its added -*s*.

THE GREEK TYPE WITH NOM. SG. IN -ᾰ

237. The Greek feminine forms with nom. sg. in -ᾰ, though differing from the regular ā-stems only in the nom.-voc. and acc. sg. and classed with them under the first declension, represent a quite distinct type historically—one that in other languages remains more obviously distinct and is classed as a different declension, owing to the fact that the nom. sg. ends in -ῑ (or -*i* from -ῑ). This type is a *yā*-stem with gradation, ῑ/yā in Sanskrit (nom.

devī, acc. *devīm*, gen. *devyās*, dat. *devyāi*, etc.) and elsewhere, but
ῐ̯ă/ῐ̯ā in Greek. The Greek *ῐ̯ă* has been variously explained, but
it probably represents an uncontracted weak grade, IE *y̆ə*, in
contrast to the more usual contracted *ī* (cf. πρίαμαι, Skt. *krī-*, etc.,
124). However this may be, the historical equivalence of the
Greek type with the *ī/yā* stems elsewhere is obvious from their
correspondence in specific categories, as the feminine of participles
and other cons. stems and of *u*-stems. Thus:

> φέρουσα from *φεροντῐ̯α =Skt. *bharantī*, cf. also Lith. *vežanti*,
> Goth. *frijondi*, etc.
> φέρουσαν from *φεροντῐ̯αν =Skt. *bharantīm*
> φερούσης from *φεροντῐ̯ᾱς =Skt. *bharantyās*
> ἡδεῖα from *ἁδεϝῐ̯α   =Skt. *svādvī*

It is in such categories that this is the normal type of feminine.
While in "adjectives of the first and second declension" the "first
declension" means the regular *ā*-stems, in "adjectives of the first
and third declension" it means the type with nom. in -*ă*.

But this type was also employed in feminine nouns formed from
stems or roots ending in a consonant. Such nouns in Greek form
an apparently miscellaneous group within the first declension, for
which the grammars give certain mechanical rules. Their disguised unity is brought out only when one extracts from these
rules the fact that, with but few exceptions, the -*ă* is preceded by
an actual *ι* or by a group of sounds which comes regularly from
some combination with *ι̯*, e.g. λλ, from λῐ̯ (**187**), σσ, ττ from κῐ̯,
etc. (**182**), σ from ντῐ̯ etc. (**183**), ζ from δῐ̯, etc. (**184**), αιν from
ανῐ̯ (**188**), -ῡρ from υρῐ̯ (**188**), etc.

That is, as a class and most of them in actual fact come from
early forms in *ῐ̯α*. But some words which never had *ῐ̯α* have been
drawn into this type, as τόλμα, μέριμνα, δίαιτα, etc.

a. All words derived from -*ῐ̯α* had inevitably a long penult, hence the
analogical extension was most natural in other words with long penult. In
some cases this was Attic only, or even late Attic, as κνῖσα (Hom. κνίση),
πεῖνα (earlier πείνη), etc.

The type is perhaps also secondary in abstracts like ἀλήθεια 'truth', where
Ionic has ἀληθείη, etc.

O-STEMS. THE GREEK AND LATIN SECOND DECLENSION

238. Table of *o*-stem declension.

	Greek	Latin	Oscan	Sanskrit	Other Languages, Selected Forms
			Singular		
Nom.	λύκος	*lupus*	h ú r z	*vŗkas*	Lith.*vilkas*,Goth. *wulfs*
Gen.	λύκου, -οιο	*lupī*	s a k a r a k l e í s	*vŗkasya*	OIr. *maqi*
Dat.	λύκῳ	*lupō*	h ú r t ú í	*vŗkāya*	Av. *haomāi*, Lith. *vilkui*
Acc.	λύκον	*lupum*	*dolom*	*vŗkam*	Lith. *vilką*
N.A.N.	ζυγόν	*iugum*	s a k a r a k l ú m	*yugam*	
Voc.	λύκε	*lupe*	U. *Tefre*	*vŗka*	Lith. *vilke*
Abl.		*lupō*	*dolud*	*vŗkād*	Lith. gen. *vilkō*
Loc.	οῖκοι, ἐκεῖ	*humī*	t e r e í	*vŗke*	
			Plural		
Nom.	λύκοι	*lupī*		pron. *te*	Goth. pron. *þai*, Lith. *vilkai*
Gen.	λύκων	*deum* *lupōrum*	N ú v l a n ú s *zicolom*	*vŗkās* *vŗkānām*	Goth. *wulfōs*
Dat.	λύκοις, λύκοισι	*lupīs*	*zicolois*	inst. *vŗkāis* loc. *vŗkeṣu*	Lith. inst. *vilkais* ChSl. loc.*vlйcěchǔ*
Acc.	λύκους, Cret. λύκονς	*lupōs*	f e í h ú s s	*vŗkān*	Goth. *wulfans*, OPruss. *deiwans*
N.A.N.	ζυγά	*iuga*	*comono*	*yugā* (Ved.)	
			Dual		
N.A.V.	λύκω	*ambō*		*vŗkā* (**Ved.**)	Lith. *vilku*, ChSl. *vlйka*
G.D.	λύκοιν			*vŗkāu*	Goth. *ahtau*

239. 1. *Nom. sg.* IE—*os*, G. -*os*, early L. -*os*, whence usual -*us* (**82.**2). For L. *puer*, *vir*, *ager*, etc., see **109.** Regular syncope of the *o* in Oscan-Umbrian, as Osc. h ú r z (*z = ts*), *Bantins*.

2. *Gen. sg.*—IE -*osyo*, earliest Greek, with loss of intervocalic *s* (**164**), -*oιo*, preserved in Homer and Thessalian, whence Thess. -*oι* with apocope, elsewhere, with loss of *ι* (**179.**1), -*oo*, contracted to -*ου* or -*ω* (**96**).

The L. -*ī*, which is an inherited -*ī*, as shown by the uniform spelling in the early inscriptions in which there is no confusion of *ī* and *ei* (89.2), has no connection with the preceding. Only in Celtic is there a corresponding regular gen. formation.

In nouns in -*ius* and -*ium* the -*iī* was regularly contracted to -*ī*, as *consilī*, *imperī*, etc., with position of accent retained. This was the normal form down through the Augustan period, but later was replaced by -*iī*, with *i* restored after the analogy of the other cases. In proper names the older form was more persistent, as *Vergilī*, etc.

a. The Latin-Celtic -*ī* may represent a collateral IE ending originally employed only in special uses, and possibly to be recognized in some Sanskrit forms in -*ī* appearing in the first part of certain compounds, as *stambhī-bhū-* 'become a post', from *stambha-*.

3. *Dat. sg.*—IE -*ōi*, G. -*ῳ* (really -*ωι*, **95**); in Italic with twofold development (**94**), -*oi* in Oscan-Umbrian and in *Numasioi* of the Praenestine fibula (**29**), but -*ō* in Latin.

4. *Acc. sing.*—IE -*om*, G. -*ον* (211.2), early L. -*om*, whence the usual -*um* (82.2).

5. *Nom.-acc. sg. neut.*—IE -*om*, with the same history as the preceding.

6. *Voc. sg.*—IE -*e*, G. -*ε*, L. -*e*. But L. *puer* (yet *puere* in Plautus), *vir*, etc., whether with loss of the final *e* or nom. forms. From words in -*ius* a few early forms in -*ie* are quoted, as *fīlie*, but regularly *fīlī* and so in proper names, *Valerī*, etc.

7. *Abl. sg.*—IE -*ōd*, Osc. -*ud* from -*ōd*, early L. -*ōd*, whence the usual -*ō* (212.4). It survives in Greek in the Doric adverbs like ὄπω 'whence', Delph. ϝοίκω 'from the house' (Att. ὁπόθεν, οἰκόθεν). The IE -*ēd* appears in adverbs, early L. *facilumēd*, usual -*ē*.

8. *Loc. sg.*—IE -*ei* and -*oi*, both seen in Greek adverbs, as οἴκοι, ἐκεῖ, Dor. ὄπει, etc. In Italic -*ei*, Osc. e í s e í t e r e í 'in eo territorio', whence L. -*ī* in *domī*, etc.

a. That in Latin "the loc. sg. has the same form as the gen. sg." is a convenient practical statement for school grammars, especially as it serves for both the first and the second declensions. But it has no historical basis and would not hold for early Latin (gen. -*ī*, loc. -*ei*).

240. 1. *Nom. pl.*—IE *-ōs* in nouns, *-oi* in pronouns, with the distribution shown in Sanskrit and Germanic, as Skt. *te vṛkās* as if G. *τοὶ *λύκως*. In Greek and Latin the pronominal form was generalized, in Oscan-Umbrian conversely the noun form (Osc. N ú v l a n ú s 'Nolani', *ius-c* 'ii'). L. *poploe* quoted (with later spelling for *oi*) from the Carmen Saliare, otherwise early *-ei*, usual *-ī*.

a. Inscriptions, mostly of the 2d cent. B.C., show some forms in *-eis*, *-īs*, as *magistreis*, *eeis* (in pronouns also in Plautus, as *hīsce*), in which *s* has been added after the analogy of the nom. pl. of the third, fourth, and fifth declensions.

b. From *deus* the normal form was *dī*, likewise dat.-abl. pl. *dīs*, resulting from contraction that took place at an intermediate stage in the development of the diphthongs. That is, **dei(w)oi*, **dei(w)ois* (170) became **dēẹ̄*, **dēẹ̄s* (89.2, 90), contracted to **dē̦*, **dē̦s*, whence *dī*, *dīs*. The spelling in inscriptions is usually *di*, *dis*, while *dii*, *diis*, more frequent in MSS, is an artificial compromise. Real dissyllabic *deī*, *deīs*, with analogical restoration of *e* from the other cases, occur in later poets.

2. *Gen. pl.*—IE *-ōm*, G. *-ων* (211.2), Osc.-Umbr. *-um*, *-om*, early L. *-om* (101), later *-um* (82.2), retained usually in words for coins or measures, etc. (hence by analogy also *amphorum*, *drachmum* from *ā*-stems, and *passum* from *u*-stem); in stereotyped phrases as *duumvirum*, *praefectus fabrum*, *socium* 'allies', frequently *līberum*, *deum;* occasionally in poetry *virum* and others.

The usual L. *-ōrum* is a specifically Latin formation, after the analogy of *-ārum*.

3. *Dat. (-abl.) pl.*—G. *-οις* from IE instr. *-ōis* (Skt. *-āis*) with shortening of the long diphthong (94); likewise Italic *-ois*, Osc. *-ois*, L. *poploes* quoted from the Carmen Saliare, otherwise early *-eis*, usual *-īs*.

Ion., Lesb., and early Att. *-οισι* is the loc. form (cf. Skt. *-eṣu;* intervocalic *σ* retained by analogy of *-σι* in cons. stems).

a. Attic inscriptions have both *-οισι* and *-οις* down to about 440 B.C., then *-οις*. Most of the dialects have *-οις* from the earliest times.

4. *Acc. pl.*—IE *-ons*, G. *-ονς* preserved in Cretan and Argive, whence, according to dialect, *-ως*, *-ος*, *-οις*, *-ους* (204.4), Osc. - ú s s , L. *-ōs* (202.3).

5. *Nom.-acc. pl. neut.*—IE -*ā*, identical in form with the nom. sg. of *ā*-stems, and probably in origin a feminine collective. In Italic it has the same history as the nom. sg. in -*ā*, namely Osc. -*o*, etc. (**233.**1), but shortened in Latin. G. -*a* may be due to one or both of two factors: (1) shortening before a word beginning with a vowel (**214.**2), (2) influence of the ending of cons. stems (**246.**6).

241. 1. *Nom.-acc.-voc. dual.*—For masculine, IE -*ōu* and -*ō*, sentence doublets, both represented in Sanskrit (-*ā* more common in Vedic, only -*āu* in later Sanskrit). G. -*ω* corresponds to the Vedic and Balto-Slavic forms, also L. *ambō, octō* (the numeral for 'eight' being an old dual, Skt. *aṣṭā, aṣṭāu*, Goth. *ahtau*), and *duo* (with iambic shortening). It was extended to neuters, as *ζυγώ*, etc., which originally had a different form.

2. *Gen.-dat. dual.*—Hom. -*οιιν*, usual -*οιν*. This cannot be fully identified with dual forms elsewhere, and its history is obscure. It was extended to cons. stems and all others of the third declension. Arcadian has -*οιυν*, also -*αιυν* from *ā*-stems.

a. Skt. gen.-loc. -*ayos* points to IE -*oy-ous*, and ChSl. -*oju* in pronouns similarly to -*oyous* or -*oyou*. The *oy*, doubtless pronominal in origin (cf. **303.**3–6), agrees with the first syllable of the Greek forms, and there is some ·elation between the *ou* of the second syllable and the Arc. forms in -*υν*.

CONSONANT STEMS

242. The case endings proper are virtually the same for all kinds of cons. stems. But there are other characteristics of the declension that are dependent upon the form of the stem, and one distinguishes different classes according as the stem ends in a stop, in a liquid or a nasal (mostly *r*-stems and *n*-stems), or in *s*. For the partial fusion of cons. stems with *i*-stems in Latin, see **262.**

The history of the case endings proper, applying to cons. stems in general, will be given in connection with the stems in stops, leaving for other classes only some special peculiarities.

243. *Accent and gradation.*—There was once a system of accentual shift between stem and ending, with accompanying vowel gradation. This was partly obscured by leveling even in the parent speech (as in the *s*-stems), but was maintained in many monosyllabic stop stems and in the *r*- and *n*-stems, as shown most clearly in Sanskrit.

The "strong cases" were (for masc. or fem. forms): nom. sg. with the lengthened ($\bar{e}$ or $\bar{o}$) grade of the stem; the acc. sg., voc. sg. (loc. sg. in part), nom.-acc.-voc. dual, and nom. pl., all with the strong (*e* or *o*) grade.

The others were the "weak cases", with accent on the ending and weak grade of the stem, though the latter for obvious reasons does not appear in stems like **ped-*.

The loc. sg. goes with the weak cases in the accent of monosyllabic stop stems, as Skt. *padí*, G. ποδί. But in the gradation of *n*- and *r*-stems it shows both strong and weak forms, as Skt. *pitári*, but G. πατρί, Skt. *mūrdháni* and *mūrdhní*.

Of all this, the one feature that has most generally persisted in Greek and Latin is the lengthened grade in the nom. sg. masc. or fem., as G. Dor. πώς, L. *pēs;* in *n*-stems, G. *-ην, -ων,* L. *-ō;* in *r*-stems, G. *-ηρ, -ωρ,* L. *-er, -or* (from *-ēr, -ōr,* **101**); in *s*-stems, G. *-ως* (αἰδώς) and *-ης* (εὐμενής), L. *-ōs* (*flōs, honōs;* later *-or,* **255**).

Beyond this, Greek has the accent shift, with or without gradation, in forms like πούς, ποδός, θρίξ, τριχός, and both accent shift and gradation in the type πατήρ, πατρός, and a few *n*-stems, as ἀρήν, ἀρνός, κύων, κυνός.

The accent shift in G. πούς, ποδός, etc., is the same as in Sanskrit except in the acc. pl. πόδας in contrast to Skt. *padás.* In the gradation of πατήρ, etc., the strong grade of the nom. pl. πατέρες (like Skt. *pitáras*) has extended to the acc. pl. πατέρας and even to the gen. pl. πατέρων (but also Hom. πατρῶν).

In the majority of *r*- and *n*-stems the old gradation has been still further reduced by analogical leveling, either generalization of the lengthened grade of the nom. sg. (as *-ων, -ωνος*), or in the other cases of the *e*-, *o*-, or weak grade (see **249**).

244. Table.

	Greek	Latin	Sanskrit
Singular			
N.V.	Dor. πώς[1]	*pēs*	*pāt*
Gen.	ποδός	*pedis*	*padás*
Dat.		*pedī*	*padé*
	ποδί		*padí* loc.
Acc.	πόδα	*pedem*	*pádam*
Abl.		*pede*	*padí* loc.
Plural			
N.V.	πόδες	*pedēs*	*pádas*
Gen.	ποδῶν	*pedum*	*padắm*
Dat.		*pedibus*	*padbhyás*
	ποσί		*patsú* loc.
Acc.	πόδας	*pedēs*	*padás*

[1] For Att. πούς, see p. 109 ftn.

245. 1. *Nom. sg.*—IE -*s*. For its union with the final stop of the stem (and similarly that of the -σι in the G. dat.-pl.), see **191-93**.

2. *Gen. sg.*—IE -*es* and -*os* with vowel gradation. The former prevails in Latin, -*es* in a few old inscriptions (*Salutes, Veneres, Apolones*), whence the usual -*is* (**112**). The -*os* gives the regular G. -*os* and the occasional L. -*os*, -*us* in inscriptions, as *Diovos, rēgus, nōminus*, etc.

3. *Dat. sg.*—IE -*ei* (**230**.6), Osc. -*ei*, early L. -*ei*, -*ẹ̄* (*Hercolei, Hercole, Martei, Iunone*), whence the usual -*ī* (**89**.2).

The Greek dat. sg. in -ι is in origin the IE loc.

4. *Acc. sg.*—IE -*m̥*, whence regularly (**115**) G. -*a*, L. -*em*.

a. Skt. -*am* in *pādam*, etc., has the *m* added after the analogy of vowel stems. Similarly G. -*αν* occasionally in the dialects and frequently in late inscriptions.

5. *Nom.-acc. sg. neut.*—IE stem form without ending. So L. *cor* (from **cord*, cf. Skt. *hṛd*), *lac* (from **lact*), G. γάλα (from **γαλακτ*), etc.

6. *Voc. sg.*—Generally in stop stems the nom. sg. serves also as

the vocative. But Greek has some distinct vocatives, stem forms with regular loss of the final stop, as παῖ (stem παιδ-), γύναι (γυναικ-), ἄνα (ἀνακ-, ἀνακτ-), and so regularly from stems in -ιδ- or -ντ-, as ἐλπί, γέρον.

In some of the other classes of cons. stems the voc. is distinguished from the nom. in gradation and accent, as πάτερ, Σώκρατες.

7. *Abl. sg. in Latin.*—The L. abl. sg. in -*e* is best explained as the IE loc. with regular change of final *i* to *e* (74*b*).

The same form occurs in locative expressions like *rūre, Carthāgine*, beside others in -*ī*, like *rūrī* which follow the analogy of *o*-stem forms like *domī*.

In early Latin occur forms with the *i*-stem ending (260.7), as *conventionīd, airīd, bovīd*.

246. 1. *Nom. pl.*—IE -*es*, G. -ες, Osc. -*s* with syncope (m e d - d í s s from **meddikes;* so h u m u n s from **homōnes*). In Latin this ending, which would have yielded -*is* as in the gen. sg., was replaced by the -*ēs* of *i*-stems (261.1).

2. *Gen. pl.*—IE -*ōm*, G. -ων (211.2), Osc.-Umbr. -*um, -om,* early L. -*om* (101), usual -*um* (82.2).

3. *Dat.-abl. pl.*—IE -*bhos*, Italic -*fos* (with syncope, Osc. - f s , - s s , - s , Umbr. -*s*), early L. -*bos* (137), usual -*bus* (82.2). Originally added directly to the stem, as if L. **pedbus* (cf. Skt. *padbhyas*), but this replaced by the *i*-stem form (261.3) in Latin, hence *pedibus*, etc. (so also in Oscan, as *ligis* 'legibus', but in Umbrian by the *u*-stem form, as *fratrus* 'fratribus').

4. G. dat. pl. -σι is in origin the loc. pl. answering to Skt. -*su* (see 230.10). For -σιν see 215.

   a. Besides the usual forms like φύλαξι, ποσσί, ποσί (from **ποδ-σι, 193), forms in -εσσι are characteristic of the Aeolic dialects and are frequent in Homer, as πόδεσσι, κύνεσσι, ἄνδρεσσι, βόεσσι (or with simplification of the σσ, as αἴγεσι). The probable explanation is that this spread from the regular -εσ-σι of σ-stems, as in βέλεσσι, ἔπεσσι. After its spread to other stems it even reacted on the σ-stems in Hom. ἐπέεσσι.

5. *Acc. pl.*—IE -*ns*, whence regularly (115) G. -*as*, It. -*ens*, whence L. -*ēs* (202.3).

6. *Nom.-acc. pl. neut.*—IE -*ə*, Skt. -*i*, G. -*α* (85). This would

give also the L. -*a*, but there is reason to believe that the latter is from -*ā*, the *o*-stem form (**240.**5), this having been extended to all neuters in the Italic period, as appears from the Oscan-Umbrian forms. A survival of this -*ā* is seen in the numerals *trīgintā*, etc.

247. *Dual. Nom.-acc.-voc.*—Greek has -ε for all genders and for all classes of the third declension, including ι- and ν-stems. This possibly represents the IE ending of masc. and fem. cons. stems, but there is no clear evidence from the other IE languages (Sanskrit has -*āu*, the *o*-stem form, in masc. and fem., and -*ī* in neuters; Slavic has the *i*-stem form in masc. and fem., and the *o*-stem form in neuters).

Gen.-dat.—Greek has -οιν, Hom. -οιιν, the form of *o*-stems.

r-STEMS AND n-STEMS

248. *Nom. sg. masc. fem.*—The IE form ended in the lengthened grade of the stem, without *s* (that is, the *s* which was probably once present as in other cons. stems was already lost in the parent speech). Furthermore the final *r* or *n* was lost under certain conditions, so that there were sentence doublets such as -*ōr* and -*ō*, or -*ōn* and -*ō*, of which one type or the other might come to prevail in a given language. Greek reflects the forms with final *r* or *n*, Sanskrit those without, while Latin agrees with Greek for the *r*-stems, but with Sanskrit for the *n*-stems. Thus:

G. πατήρ, ῥήτωρ | L. *pater, victor* (**101**) ‖ Skt. *pitā, dātā*
G. ποιμήν, ἀγών ‖ L. *sermō, homō* | Skt. *rājā*

a. Such is the situation in the typical classes. There are some few words with stems ending in *r* or *n*, but without gradation and with nom. sg. in -*s*. Thus G. μάρτυς from *μαρτυρς (cf. Cret. μαίτυρς), Dor. μάκαρς; μέλας, τάλας, from *μελανς, *ταλανς, κτείς from *κτενς, δελφίς (also late δελφίν), and others in -*īs*, -*īνος*. So L. *sanguīs* from *sanguins, formed to gen. *sanguinis*, etc. (also early L. neut. *sanguen, sanguinis*).

249. *Gradation of the stem.*—The IE system of gradation (see **243**) has been modified by analogical leveling, resulting in a variety of types.

1. G. πατήρ, μήτηρ, θυγάτηρ, γαστήρ, with weak grade in gen. sg., dat. sg., dat. pl., otherwise the *e*-grade. Thus πατρός, πατρί,

πατράσι (cf. Skt. dat. sg. *pitré*, loc. pl. *pitṛ́ṣu*), but πατέρα, πάτερ, πατέρες (cf. Skt. *pitáram, pítar, pitáras*), πατέρων, πατέρας. In Homer the distribution is less fixed, e.g. πατέρος beside πατρός, πατρῶν beside πατέρων, θυγάτρες beside θυγατέρες, etc.

2. G. ἀνήρ, with e-grade only in the voc. sg. ἄνερ, otherwise the weak grade generalized, as ἀνδρός (from *ἀνρός, 201.1), ἀνδρί, ἀνδράσι, also ἄνδρα, ἄνδρες, etc. (in Homer fluctuation between these forms and ἀνέρος, ἀνέρες, etc.)

L. *pater, māter, frāter* show the same generalization of the weak grade outside of the nom. sg. and voc. sg., e.g. not only *patris* like πατρός, but also *patrem* like ἄνδρα and in contrast to πατέρα, Skt. *pitáram*.

3. G. αἰθήρ, αἰθέρος, similarly ἀήρ, δαήρ, etc., with generalization of the e-grade. So ἀστήρ, ἀστέρος, etc., but ἀστράσι with weak grade.

4. G. agent nouns like σωτήρ, σωτῆρος, with generalization of the lengthened grade of the nom. sg., except in the voc. sg. σῶτερ.

5. G. agent nouns like ῥήτωρ, ῥήτορος, with generalization of the o-grade.

6. L. agent nouns like *victor, victōris*, likewise *soror, sorōris* (Skt. *svasar-*), with generalization of the lengthened grade of the nom. sg. before the shortening of *-ōr* to *-or*. Hence parallel to G. σωτήρ, σωτῆρος, but in contrast to ῥήτωρ, ῥήτορος.

7. G. κύων, voc. sg. κύον, otherwise with the weak grade generalized, as κυνός (cf. Skt. *çunás*), κυνί, κύνα, κύνες, etc., parallel to ἀνήρ, ἀνδρός. So ἀρήν, ἀρνός, ἀρνί, ἄρνα, ἄρνες, etc. L. *carō, carnis* (Umbr. k a r u , dat. sg. k a r n e).

8. Type of G. ἀγών, ἀγῶνος, L. *sermō, sermōnis*, also G. Ἕλλην, Ἕλληνος, with generalization of the lengthened grade of the nom. sg.

9. Type of G. δαίμων, δαίμονος, ποιμήν, ποιμένος, L. *homō, hominis*, with generalization of the e- or o-grade. An indirect trace of the weak grade is seen in dat. pl. δαίμοσι, ποιμέσι, which represent *δαίμασι, *ποιμάσι (a = IE n̥), with the vowel changed to conform to that of the other cases (not with substitution of the full μον or μεν which would have resulted in *δαίμουσι, *ποιμεῖσι).

An actual form similar to the assumed *ποιμᾶσι is φρασί beside usual φρεσί from φρήν.

In L. *homō, hominis,* and likewise in neuters like *nōmen, nō-minis,* the *in* may represent either *en* or *on,* with regular weakening in medial syllables (**110**.2, 3).

a. There is no Latin type corresponding to the Greek type in -ην. Only the rare word *liēn, liēnis* answers in inflection, as in meaning, to G. σπλήν, σπληνός, and was probably influenced by it; *flāmen* and *pecten* are probably neuters in origin; *oscen, tibīcen,* etc., are compounds from the root of *canō* with the regular weakening (**112**).

250. *Neuter n-stems.*—The IE neuter *n*-stems are only apparently lacking in Greek. They are represented by the neuter τ-stems, as ὄνομα, ὀνόματος = L. *nōmen, nōminis* = Skt. *nāma, nām-nas.*

The original *ν*-stem shows itself in the derivatives, as ὀνομαίνω (*-αν-ιω), σημαίνω, etc. So also in dat. pl. -ασι (cf. Skt. -*asu*), for if this were from *-ατ-σι, one would expect traces of -ασσι (as in Hom. ποσσί from *ποδ-σί). The nom.-acc. sg. has the weak grade of the stem, IE -ṇ, G. -α, L. -en, Skt. a.

a. The precise source of the G. τ- inflection is uncertain. There are several possible factors. (1) a *t*-element which is sometimes added in the nom.-acc. sg. of *r/n* stems (**251**), as Skt. *yakṛt,* gen. *yaknas, çakṛt,* gen. *çaknas.* This might have extended to the other cases at the expense of the *n*-stem form, as -ατος in place of -ανος. (2) IE adverbial -*tos,* Skt. -*tas* with ablatival force and often used co-ordinately with the regular ablative form. Hence ὀνόμα-τος might answer to Skt. *nāma-tas.* (3) Parallel suffixes -*men-* (nom.-acc. sg. -*mṇ*) and -*mṇto-,* as in L. *fragmen* and *fragmentum.* The latter would give rise to nom.-acc. pl. -μάτα.

251. *Neuter r/n stems.*—A peculiar mixed type, with nom.-acc. sg. ending in -*r,* the other cases from an *n*-stem, occurs in several of the IE languages and is evidently inherited from the parent speech. In Greek the *n*-stem forms are represented by -ατος, etc. (**250**).

L. *femur, feminis* (beside *femoris* with generalized *r*)

G. ἧπαρ, ἥπατος like Skt. *yakṛt, yaknas,* L. *iecur* (*iocur*), once **iecinis* beside *iecoris* (like *feminis, femoris*), whence the blend *iocineris* (similarly *iter, itineris*)

G. οὖθαρ, οὖθατος, Skt. *ūdhar, ūdhnas,* L. *über,* but *überis* with generalized *r.*

G. ὕδωρ, ὕδατος, like Umbr. u t u r , abl. u n e from **udne* (Skt. has nom.-acc. *uda-ka-m,* gen. *udnás;* cf. also Goth. *watō, watins,* with *n*-stem, OE *wæter,* etc., with *r*-stem generalized)

For the nom.-acc. form there is variation between:

IE -ŗ, as G. ἧπαρ, L. *iecur* (from *-or*), Skt. *yakŗt*

IE -*er*, as L. *über,* Skt. *ūdhar*

IE -*ōr*, as G. ὕδωρ, Umbr. u t u r

252. *Greek τ-stem forms in other neuters.*—A few of these possibly reflect occasional IE combinations of *n*-stems with others, parallel to the well-defined *r/n* type (**251**). But most of them are due to the analogical spread in Greek of *τ*-forms from the great mass of neuters belonging under **250, 251**. This took place especially in Attic and spread further in the later κοινή.

Homer has οὖς, οὔατος (Att. ὠτός), κάρη, κράατος, κρᾶτός, etc., and from the *u*-stems γόνυ, δόρυ, besides γουνός, δουρός from **γονϝος, *δορϝος* (**176.**1, **266.**2), also γούνατος, δούρατος from **γονϝατος, *δορϝατος,* whence likewise Att. γόνατος, δόρατος (**176.**1).

Att. πέρας, πέρατος belongs in origin with the type ἧπαρ, ἧπατος, as shown by Hom. πεῖραρ, πείρατος, pointing to **περϝαρ, *πέρϝατος,* which would give Att. **πέραρ,* πέρατος (**176.**1), of which **πέραρ* was replaced by πέρας after the analogy of other neuters in *-ας.*

Conversely τέρας, κέρας, which have only *σ*-stem inflection in Homer (τέραα, κέραος), have Att. τέρατος, κέρᾱτος (except in the military phrase ἐπὶ κέρως), the latter from **κερα-ατος,* a blend of κέραος and **κέρατος* (cf. **γονϝατος* above). Similarly Att. φῶς, φωτός (Hom. φάος, φάει), Att. κρέας, κρέως, but later κρέατος.

a. Apart from the neuters, the *τ*-stem inflection is secondary in several others as γέλως, ἔρως (orig. *σ*-stems like αἰδώς, **255**), cf. γελαστός, ἐραστός), χρώς, ἱδρώς, where Homer has no *τ*-forms except from χρώς (χρωτός, χρωτ' beside usual χροός, χρόα).

253. There are no productive types of stems ending in *m* or in *l.*

There is only one *m*-stem in Latin, namely *hiems, hiemis,* and none in Greek. Originally *m*-stems were χιών, χιόνος (cf. L. *hiems,* Av. gen. sg. *zimō,* etc.) and χθών, χθονός (cf. χαμαί, L. *humus,* Av.

zemō, etc.), but the *ν* which arose regularly from final *m* in the nom. sg. was, under the further influence of the inherited *n*-stems, generalized. Similarly in the numeral εἷς, ἑνός (cf. ὁμός, L. *semel*), the *ν* which arose regularly in ἕνς (from *ἕμ-ς) and ἕν (from *ἕμ) was generalized.

There is only one λ-stem in Greek, namely ἅλς, ἁλός, cognate with L. *sāl* (**212.**6*b*), *salis*. Latin has also *sōl*, *sōlis* (from *sāwel*, cf. ἥλιος, ἀέλιος, etc.), *vigil* (probably an *i*-stem form originally), and some compounds of verbal stems, as *exsul*, *cōnsul*, etc.

S-STEMS

254. The most important type of *s*-stems is that of the neuters in *-os*. The stem has vowel gradation, the *o*-grade in the nom.-acc. sg., the *e*-grade in all other cases, IE nom.-acc. sg. *-os*, gen. sg. *-eses/os*, etc.

G.	L.	Skt.	ChSl.
γένος	*genus*	*janas*	*slovo*
γένεος, Att. γένους	*generis*	*janasas*	*slovese*

For the loss of intervocalic *s* in Greek, and its change to *r* in Latin, see **164.** In Greek the uncontracted forms occur in Homer and elsewhere, as Hom. βέλεος, βέλεϊ, βέλεα, βελέων, while Attic has only the contracted forms, as γένους, γένει, γένη, γενῶν. Dat. pl. Hom. βέλεσσιν (also βελέεσσιν, **246.**4) and βέλεσιν, Att. γένεσι(ν) (see **208.**1).

In Latin, beside the type *genus*, *generis*, with the original gradation preserved, there is the type *corpus*, *corporis* in which the *o*-grade of the stem was generalized by extension from the old nom.-acc. sg. in *-os*. The *e*-grade may still appear in adverbs or derivatives, as in *temperī*, *tempestas* beside *tempus*, *temporis*.

a. There are also a few neuters in which the *-s* of the nom.-acc. sg. has been replaced by *r* after the analogy of the other cases, as *rōbur* (early *rōbus*, cf. *rōbustus*), *fulgur*, gen. *fulguris*, *aequor*. Cf. *honor*, *honōris*, etc. (**255**).

b. Greek neuters in *-as*, as γέρας, gen. γέραος, Att. γέρως, correspond to some Sanskrit neuters in *-is*, like *kravis*=κρέας, and reflect IE stems in *-əs-*, of which the vowel originally belonged to a dissyllabic verb stem (**127**).

Hom. acc. pl. γέρᾰ, κρέᾰ etc., beside regular τέραα, are of doubtful explanation.

Some neuters in -*as* have gen. -*eos*, etc., like the neuters in -*os*, instead of normal -*aos*, etc., e.g. Hom. οὖδας, οὔδεος.

For the secondary τ-inflection of Att. τέρας, etc., see **252**.

255. *Masculines and feminines in -ōs.*—This is a rare type in Greek, but productive in Latin.

Hom. ἠώς, Att. ἕως, Lesb. αὔως, from IE **āusōs* (L. *aurōra*, from **āusōs-ā;* cf. *Flōra* beside *flōs*) beside IE **usōs*, Skt. *uṣās*, gen. *uṣasas*. The nom. sg. had the lengthened grade -*ōs*, the other cases -*os*-, hence, with loss of intervocalic *s* and vowel contraction, Hom. gen. sg. ἠοῦς, acc. sg. ἠῶ. Att. ἕως has been drawn into the analogy of νεώς etc., but still has acc. sg. ἕω. In Attic only αἰδώς follows the original type.

In Latin the lengthened grade of the nom. sg. has been generalized. So *flōs*, *flōris*, etc., with rhotacism of the intervocalic *s*. Likewise *honōs*, *honōris*, but here the *r* of the oblique cases was carried over to the nom. sg. and the vowel shortened (**101**), hence the usual *honor*, *honōris*, and similarly the whole large class of masculine verbal abstracts like *amor*, *labor*, *timor*, etc.

So *arbor* from *arbōs*, but gen. *arboris* without the generalization of the lengthened grade.

a. The -*ōs* persists in the monosyllables *flōs, rōs, mōs*. In general the nom. sg. -*or* is usual from Plautus on, but the older forms in -*ōs* appear occasionally even in later writers, especially *honōs*.

256. *Masculines and feminines in -ēs.*—There is the closest agreement between the Greek and Sanskrit *s*-stem adjectives, which are formed from (in Greek, mostly with composition) the neuter nouns in -*os*. The stem had the lengthened grade *ēs* in the nom. sg. masc.-fem., the *e*-grade *es* in all the other forms, including the nom.-acc. sg. neut. (here in contrast to the -*os* of nouns).

	Greek	Sanskrit
Nom. sg. m. f.	εὐμενής	*sumanās*
Nom.-acc. sg. n.	εὐμενές	*sumanas*
Gen. sg.	εὐμενέος, Att. -οῦς	*sumanasas*
Acc. sg.	εὐμενέα, Att. -ῆ	*sumanasam*

Greek nouns in -ης are all of this adjective type in origin. So ἡ τριήρης (ναῦς) 'the triply fitted (ship), trireme', and the numerous proper names like Σωκράτης (cf. κράτος), Δημοσθένης (cf. σθένος), etc. These proper names may have acc. sg. in -ην after the analogy of names in -ης of the first declension, as Σωκράτην like Θουκυδίδην.

a. Isolated relics of this type in Latin are perhaps *Cerēs, Cereris, pūbēs, pūberis, mulier* (cf. *muliebris* from **mulies-ris* by **202**.2), *degener*.

257. *Miscellaneous s-stems.*—G. μῦς, μυός (thus agreeing with the type ὀφρῦς, -ύος, and so acc. sg. μῦν), L. *mūs, mūris, glīs, glīris, mās, maris*.

L. *vīs* and *spēs* have pl. *vīrēs, spērēs*, as if from *s*-stems, which may be inherited (cf. Skt. *vayas* 'strength') or analogical. The nom. sg. *vīs* may be from an *s*-stem, or from an *ī*-stem (G. ἴς), while the other cases of the singular are from simple *vi*-.

The neuters *iūs, iūris* and *rūs, rūris* belong in origin to the type *genus, generis*, coming from **yewos, *rewos*, with syncope of *o*.

i-STEMS

258. Table of *i*-stem declension.

	Greek			LATIN	SANSKRIT	OTHER LANGUAGES, SELECTED FORMS
	I Most Dial.	II Homer also	III Attic			
Singular						
Nom.	πόλις		πόλις	*turris*	*agnis*	
Gen.	πόλιος	πόληος	πόλεως	*turris*	*agnes*	Osc. *aeteis*, Lith. *naktíes*
Dat.				*turrī*	*agnaye*	
	πόλιι, πόλῑ	πόληϊ	πόλει		loc. *agnā*	
Acc.	πόλιν		πόλιν	*turrim, -em*	*agnim*	Osc. s l a g í m
N.A.N.	-πολι (adj.)			*mare*	*vāri*	
Voc.	πόλι		πόλι	=nom.	*agne*	
Abl.				*turrī, -e*		Osc. s l a a g i d
Plural						
Nom.	πόλιες	πόληες	πόλεις	*turrēs*	*agnayas*	Osc. t r í s
Gen.	πολίων		πόλεων	*turrium*	*agnīnām*	Osc. a í t t í ú m
Dat.	πόλισι		πόλεσι	*turribus*	*agnibhyas* loc. *agniṣu*	Osc. l u i s a - r i f s
Acc.	πόλινς, -ις Hom. πόλιας	πόληας	πόλεις	*turrīs, -ēs*	*agnīn*	Umbr. *trif*, Goth. *þrins*
N.A.N.	τρία			*maria*	*vārīṇi*	

259. 1. In Greek there was a redistribution of the vowels reflecting the original gradation (IE *i* and *ei, ey,* also *ēi,* 230.3), resulting in two main dialectic types (258, cols. I and III) and the partial development of a third type (258, col. II).

The original distribution in the plural is seen in the forms of the numeral τρεῖς, as nom. pl. Cret. τρέες, Ther. τρῆς, Att. τρεῖς, all from IE *treyes* (cf. Skt. *trayas,* L. *trēs*), but gen. pl. τριῶν (cf. L. *trium*) even in Attic, dat. pl. τρισί (cf. Skt. *triṣu*) even in Attic, acc. pl. *τρίνς (Cret. τρίινς with ι introduced anew from τριῶν, etc.), τρῖς (but here Att. τρεῖς).

2. The type πόλις, πόλιος, etc., with ι throughout is common to all dialects except Attic, and is also Attic in the isolated οἶς 'sheep', gen. οἰός (accent after the analogy of other monosyllabic stems like βοῦς, βοός), from ὄϝις (cf. L. *ovis,* Skt. *avis*), ὄϝιος (cf. Skt. gen. *avyas*). The acc. pl. had regularly -ινς (cf. Arg. ὄϝινς) or the resulting -ῑς. Hom. πόλεις probably for πόλῑς, but also πόλιας with the cons. stem ending.

This type may be explained simply as a generalization of the ι which was inherited in most of the forms, at the expense of the ε (from the strong grade IE *ey*) which belonged to others, for example, nom. pl. πόλιες in place of *πολεες after the analogy of πολίων, πόλισι, etc. (that is, just the opposite of what happened in Attic; see below).

a. Another possible factor is the influence of an IE type which has otherwise disappeared from Greek, namely that of Skt. (Ved.) *nadīs,* gen. sg. *nadias,* nóm. pl. *nadias,* loc. pl. *nadīṣu,* as if G. *πολῑς, πόλιος, πόλιες, *πόλῑσι.

3. The type of Hom. πόληος, etc., may be explained as follows. An IE loc. sg. in -ē (from -ēi, the lengthened grade of the stem, without case ending, see 230.9) is indicated by Ved. *agnā,* and this would give G. *πόλη. Hence, with -i added after the analogy of the other Greek datives, πόληϊ, from which η spread to πόληος, πόληες, πόληας.

From πόληος comes Att. πόλεως with quantitative metathesis (98.3); and from πόληϊ an Att. πόλη in some inscriptions.

4. *Attic.*—Gen. sg. πόλεως from πόληος (see above, 3). In poetry also πόλεος, with ε from dat. sg. and the usual gen. sg. ending. Dat. sg. πόλει, also Hom. πόλεϊ, πτόλεϊ, from IE *-eyi*. Voc. sg. πόλι, IE *-i*.

The plural forms result from an early extension of ε from the nom. -ε-ες (IE *-eyes*), -εις, to the other cases at the expense of the orig. ι, so gen. πόλεων, dat. πόλεσι (contrast τριῶν, τρισί), acc. *πόλενς, whence πόλεις.

The same substitution of ε for ι extends to the dual forms πόλει from *πόλεε, and πολέοιν. Hom. ὄσσε is from *οκϳε.

5. The acc. pl. neut., as τρία, is generally taken as having α from the other stems, orig. the cons. stem ending. But it is also possible that it reflects an IE uncontracted *iə*, so that τρία is related to Ved. *trī* just as πρίαμαι to Skt. *krī-* (**124**).

LATIN

260. 1. *Nom. sg.*—IE *-is*, L. *-is* unchanged in most words. Syncope and vowel development in *imber* from **imbris*, like *ager* from **agros* (**109**), likewise in adjectives like *ācer*. Syncope also in *gēns*, *mōns*, *pars*, etc. (**108**).

The forms in *-ēs*, like *sēdēs* (gen. pl. *sēdum*), *aedēs*, *caedēs*, etc., cannot belong originally to *i*-stems, unless they are nom. pl. forms which came to be construed as singular collectives, this being one of several possible explanations. They may reflect a rare type of stems in *-ē-*, nom. *-ēs*.

2. *Gen. sg.*—IE *-eis* (**230**.5), Osc. *-eis* (extended to cons. stems and even to the *o*-stems), which would have given L. *-īs*, was completely displaced by the *-is* of cons. stems (**245**.2).

3. *Dat. sg.*—IE *-eyei* (cf. Skt. *agnaye*) would yield the L. *-ī* (through *-eei*, *-ēi*, *-ei*), but this may equally well represent the cons. stem ending (**245**.3).

4. *Acc. sg.*—IE *-im*, L. *-im* retained in a few words, but in most replaced by the *-em* of cons. stems (**245**.4).

5. *Nom.-acc. sg. neut.*—IE *-i*, L. *-e* (**74***b*) in *mare*, etc. Forms like *animal*, *exemplar* are from *-āli*, *-āri*, with loss of the final vowel (**108**) and subsequent shortening of *ā* before the final *l* or *r* (**101**).

6. *Voc. sg.*—There is no distinct voc. form like G. πόλι. The nom. was used, just as in cons. stems.

7. *Abl. sg.*—Italic *-īd*, formed after the analogy of *-ōd* (see **233.**6), Osc. - i d (=*-īd* in contrast to - í m =*-im*), early L. *-īd*, whence *-ī*. This was much more persistent than the acc. *-im*, being usual or frequent in many nouns, including most neuters, and regular in adjectives. But in the majority of nouns the *-e* of cons. stems is more usual.

261. 1. *Nom. pl.*—IE *-eyes* (Skt. *-ayas*, G. -εες, -εῖς), L. *-ēs* (**178**).

2. *Gen. pl.*—IE *-iōm*, L. *-ium* (**101, 82.**2).

3. *Dat. abl. pl.*—IE *-ibhos*, whence Italic *-ifos*, Osc. (with syncope) - í f s , - í s s , - i s , early L. *-ibos*, usual *-ibus*.

4. *Acc. pl.*—IE *-ins* (G. dial. -ινς), L. *-īs* (**202.**3). This remained the usual form down to the Augustan period, when the *-ēs* of cons. stems became increasingly frequent and eventually prevailed.

5. *Nom-acc. pl. neut.*—L. *-ia* probably from *-iā* (cf. Umbr. *trio* with *o* from *ā*) with *-ā* from *o*-stems (**240.**5). L. *trī* in *trīgintā* (**315**) like Ved. *trī*.

262. The partial fusion of cons. stems and *i*-stems in Latin may be summarized as follows:

The cons. stems furnished the gen. sg. *-is*.

The *i*-stems furnished the nom. pl. *-ēs* and the dat.-abl. pl. *-ibus*.

The cons. stem endings encroached upon those of the *i*-stems in the following order of time and frequency:

1) acc. sg. *-em* upon *-im*
2) abl. sg. *-e* upon *-ī*
3) acc. pl. *-ēs* upon *-īs*

The dat. sg. *-ī* may be from either class or both.

The two classes are usually kept distinct in the nom. sg., and most consistently in the gen. pl. and nom.-acc. pl. neut. It is upon this basis that we still call forms like *pēs*, *rēx*, etc., cons. stems, and forms like *turris*, *fīnis*, etc., *i*-stems.

But there are also nouns which do not conform to either of

these types, and which are "mixed stems" in a peculiar sense That is, they are mixed stems, not in the sense that all nouns of the third declension are such historically, but from the point of view of the usual Latin types (see **263**).

The fusion of cons. stems and *i*-stems had begun in the Italic period, but was carried farther in Latin than in Oscan-Umbrian (cf. e.g. the nom. pl., **246**.1).

263. *Latin "mixed stems".*—The most important type is that in which the singular agrees with that of stop stems like *pēs, rēx,* but the plural with that of *i*-stems (gen. pl.-*ium*), as *gēns, mōns, pars, nox, urbs,* etc. The majority of these are orig. *i*-stems, formed with the suffix -*ti*- (Skt. -*tis*, G. -σις), with syncope of the *i* in the nom. sg., e.g. *mors* from **mortis* (Skt. *mṛtis*). A few may have been cons. stems, as probably *dēns* (cf. Skt. *dant-*, G. ὀδούς, ὀδόντος), with *i*-stem plural (but also *dentum,* Varro) after the analogy of *gēns,* etc. Some are words whose cognates show an interchange of *t-* and *ti*-stems, as *nox* (cf. G. νύξ, νυκτός, but Lith. *naktis;* Skt. usually *nakti-*) and especially words like *cīvitās* with gen. pl. -*um* or -*ium* (cf. G. -της, -τητος, but Skt. -*tāt-* and -*tāti-*).

A few orig. *s*-stems have gen. pl. -*ium*, as *mūs, mās, glīs.* So also *as, assium, os, ossium.* But for some of these, and in fact for a number of words, the evidence as tó the usual gen. pl. form is insufficient.

The opposite relation to that noted in forms like *gēns,* gen. pl. *gentium* is seen in *canis,* gen. pl. *canum* and a few others. Some are original cons. stems, as *canis* (cf. G. κύων, Skt. *çvan-*), *iuvenis* (cf. Skt. *yuvan-*), *mēnsis* (cf. G. μήν, gen. μηνός, Lesb. μῆννος from stem **μηνς-*), so that in these the gen. pl. -*um* is regular and the nom. sg. -*is* secondary (cf. the complete transition to an *i*-stem in *nāvis* = G. ναῦς). From *senex* (with a guttural suffix, cf. Skt. *sanaka-* beside *sana-*, IE **seno-*) the rest of the declension follows that of its opposite *iuvenis,* and so gen. pl. *senum* after *iuvenum.* From *volucris* the gen. pl. *volucrum* is perhaps due to the analogy of *celerum.* Several other nouns in -*is* or -*ēs* have gen. pl. -*um* beside -*ium*, most frequently *sēdēs.*

u-STEMS AND ū-STEMS

264. Table of *u*-stem and *ū*-stem declension.

	I			II		
	Greek	Latin	Sanskrit	Latin	Greek	Sanskrit
			Singular			
Nom.	πῆχυς	ἡδύς	*tribus*	*sūnus*	*sūs*	σῦς	*bhrūs*
						ὀφρῦς βότρυς	
Gen.	πήχεως	ἡδέος	*tribūs*	*sūnos*	*suis*	συός	ὀφρύος	*bhruvas*
	υἱέος						
Dat.			*tribuī,*	*sūnave*	*suī*		*bhruve*
	πήχει	ἡδεῖ	*tribū*	loc. *sūnāu,*		συΐ	ὀφρύι	loc.
				-avi			*bhruvi*
Acc.	πῆχυν	ἡδύν	*tribum*	*sūnum*	*suem*	σῦν	ὀφρῦν	*bhruvam*
							βότρυν	
N.A.N.	ἄστυ	ἡδύ	*genu(ū?)*	*madhu*			δάκρυ	
Voc.	πῆχυ	ἡδύ	Nom.	*sūno*	Nom.	σῦ	ὀφρῦ βότρυ	Nom.
Abl.			*tribū*		*sue*			
			Plural				
Nom.	πήχεις dial. -εες	ἡδεῖς	*tribūs*	*sūnavas*	*suēs*	σύες	ὀφρύες	*bhruvas*
Gen.	πήχεων	ἡδέων	*tribuum*	*sūnūnām*	*suum*	συῶν	ὀφρύων	*bhruvām*
Dat.			*tribubus,*	*sūnubhyas*	*suibus,*			*bhrūbhyas*
	πήχεσι	ἡδέσι	*ibus*	loc. *sū-*	*sūbus*			
				nuṣu		συσί	ὀφρύσι	loc. *bhrū-* *ṣu*
Acc.	πήχεις dial. -υνς, -έας	ἡδεῖς	*tribūs*	*sūnūn*		σῦς, σύας	ὀφρῦς ὀφρύας	*bhruvas*
					suēs			
N.A.N.	ἄστη dial. -εα	ἡδέα	*genua*	*madhūni*			δάκρυα	

265. The IE *u*-stem declension is represented in Latin by the fourth declension; in Greek by the masculine and neuter of adjectives like ἡδύς, but in only a few nouns, namely πῆχυς, πέλεκυς, πρέσβυς (orig. an adjective), the neut. ἄστυ, also υἱύς (=usual υἱός) in Attic inscriptions, Homer, and several dialects.

The majority of Greek nouns follow type II (gen. sg. -υος), which is based upon the IE *ū*-stems but has spread at the expense of the *u*-stems so as to include most of the nouns in -υς and the neuters like δάκρυ, μέθυ. Fluctuation between the two types is seen in the Attic inflection of ἔγχελυς, gen. sg. -εως or -υος, etc.

u-STEMS

266. 1. *Nom. sg.*—IE -*us*, G. -*υς*, L. -*us*.

2. *Gen. sg.*—IE -*eus*, -*ous* (cf. Skt. *sūnos*, Goth. *sunaus*, Lith. *sūnaus*, Osc. *castrous*), early L. -*ous* (once *senātous*), L. -*ūs*. Early L. *senātuos*, *fructuis*, etc., represent a different formation, either an inherited parallel type in -*u-os*, -*u-es* (see **230**.5), or more probably formed anew in Latin from dat. sg. -*uī*. G. -*εος*, as regularly in adjectives (*ἡδέος*, etc.) and also, except in Attic, in the few nouns left in this type (Hom. *υἱέος*, *ἄστεος*, Cret. *υἱέος*, Boeot. *ἄστιος*), is from -*εϝος* with *εϝ* after the analogy of other cases, as dat. sg. -*εϝι*, nom. pl. -*εϝες*.

Att. *ἄστεως* follows the analogy of *πόλεως* (**259**.4) likewise *πήχεως*, *πρέσβεως*.

The neuters *γόνυ*, *δόρυ* have Hom. *γουνός*, *δουρός* from **γονϝος*, **δορϝος* (like Ved. *paçvas*, *madhvas*, **230**.5), and similarly the other cases, as *δουρί* from **δορϝι*, *δοῦρα* from **δορϝα* (for the *τ*-stem forms, as *γούνατος*, Att. *γόνατος*, see **252**). Of the same type is Hom. *υἷος* from **υἱϝος*, whence also dat. sg. *υἷι*, acc. sg. *υἷα*.

3. *Dat. sg.*—IE -*ewei* (cf. Skt. *sūnave*, ChSl. *synovi*), whence regularly (cf. **newos* to *novus*, **80**.1; **dē-novō* to *denuō*, **110**.5) L. -*uī*. The form in -*ū* is from -*ou* (cf. Umbr. dat. sg. *trifo*), this probably an old loc. sg. (cf. Umbr. m a n u v - e 'in the hand') from IE -*ēu*, -*ou* (cf. Skt. *sūnāu*). G. *ει* from -*εϝι* is the loc. sg. IE -*ewi* as in Ved. *sūnavi*.

4. *Acc. sg.*—IE -*um*, G. -*υν*, L. -*um*.

5. *Nom.-acc. sg. neut.*—IE -*u*, G. -*υ*, L. *u* or *ū*(?). L. -*ū* in the few forms quotable from poetry (*genū*, *cornū*, etc.) might be explained as an old neut. pl. form or as an old dual form. But one doubts whether this was actually the normal form, and not rather the -*u* to be expected.

6. *Voc. sg.*—IE -*u* (beside -*eu*, Skt. -*o*), G. -*υ*. In Latin the nom. form is used.

7. *Abl. sg.*—Italic -*ūd*, formed after the analogy of -*ōd* (see **233**.6), early L. -*ūd* (*magistrātūd*), whence -*ū*.

267. 1. *Nom. pl.*—IE -*ewes* (cf Skt. *sūnavas*, ChSl. *synove*), G. -*εϝες* (not yet quotable), -*εες* uncontracted in most dialects, Att. -*εις*.

It is a question whether L. -ūs is also to be derived from -ewes by assuming early syncope of the e in the final syllable (-ewes, -owes, -ous, -ūs; otherwise the result would be -uis, like -uī in dat. sg., 266.3), or is the acc. pl. form used as nom. pl. under the influence of the identity of the two cases in the -ēs of cons. stems. An occurrence of the form in Oscan, or in an early Latin inscription, showing whether the spelling was -OVS or -VS, would settle the matter.

2. *Gen. pl.*—IE -uōm, early L. -uom (om being kept much longer than in the other declensions because of the preceding u, 82.5), later -uum. The form -um occurs long before the change of -uom to -uum and therefore cannot be a contraction of the latter. It started in *passum*, formed after the analogy of other words denoting measures and coins, as *iugerum, amphorum, nummum*, etc. (240.2), and passed to others, as *currum*.

G. -νων retained in words which follow type II, as δακρύων, but in type I replaced by -εων with ε from the nom., as ἡδέων, Att. πήχεων (with accent after gen. sg. πήχεως).

3. *Dat. pl.*—IE -ubhos, L. -ubus retained in certain words, but generally -ibus. Here there is a complication of phonetic factors (cf. *optumus, optimus*, etc., 110.4 with a) and others, and insufficient evidence as to the actual facts in normal speech. The -ubus was favored in *artubus, arcubus, partubus* to distinguish them from the corresponding forms of *ars, arx, pars;* also in *tribubus*, which is prescribed by the grammarians as the only correct form and is uniform in our literary texts, though an early inscription has *trebibos;* it occurs in *specubus* beside *specibus, lacubus* beside *lacibus*, and occasionally in several other words.

G. νσι representing the IE loc. (cf. Skt. -uṣu) was retained in the words which passed over to type II, as δακρύσι, but in type I was replaced by -εσι with ε from the nom., as ἡδέσι, πήχεσι.

Hom. υἱάσι (also Cretan) has α from the analogy of πατράσι, etc.

4. *Acc. pl.*—IE -uns, G. -υνς, -ῡς, L. -ūs (202.3). G. -υνς occurs in Cret., Arg. υἱύνς, and from it comes the -ῡς of words that follow type II. Otherwise it was replaced, at least in Attic-Ionic, by a form with ε from the nom., either -ενς, whence Att. -εις, or -εϝας, Hom. -εας ·(πελέκεας, πολέας).

5. *Nom.-acc. pl. neut.*—L. *-ua* probably from *-uā* (cf. Umbr. *castruo* with *o* from *ā*), with *-ā* from *o*-stems **240**.5). G. *-va* in δάκρυα, etc., of type II, but in type I replaced by *-εϝa*, after the analogy of *-εϝες*, whence Hom. ἄστεα, Att. ἄστη, Att.-Ion. ἡδέα regularly uncontracted (late ἡμίση, etc.).

a. The spread of ε from the strong grade at the expense of υ throughout the plural (and also the dual, as in πήχει, πηχέοιν), is parallel to the spread of ε at the expense of ι in Att. πόλεων, πόλεσι, πόλεις, etc. (**259**.4), only that the latter is specifically Attic, whereas forms like πήχεων, πήχεσι, etc., are at least Attic-Ionic. The situation in the other dialects is imperfectly known.

ū-STEMS

268. The Greek inflection given under type II, that is, with gen. sg. *-νος*, is based upon that of IE *ū*-stems, which are directly represented by σῦς, ὀφρῦς, and some others. The majority of the orig. *u*-stem nouns also follow this type. If barytone they retain the short υ in the nom., acc., and voc. sg. (βότρυς, στάχυς, δάκρυ, etc.), while if accented on the last syllable, they usually have *-ῦς*, etc. (Hom. βρωτῦς, etc., IE suffix *-tu-*), though with some fluctuation.

The inflection of ὀφρῦς agrees very closely with that of Skt. *bhrūs*. But acc. sg. ὀφρῦν, not ὀφρύα (which is rare and probably due to the analogy of acc. pl. ὀφρύας) like Skt. *bhruvam;* acc. pl. ὀφρύας like Skt. *bhruvas* sometimes in Homer, but regularly ὀφρῦς from *-υνς* the *u*-stem form; dat. pl. ὀφρύσι with the *u*-stem form, not *-ῦσι* like Skt. *-ūṣu.*

In Latin the *ū*-stem type is represented by the isolated *sūs* and *grūs*, while *socrus*, which originally belonged to it (cf. Skt. *çvaçrūs*, gen. sg. *çvaçruvas*, ChSl. *svekry*, gen. sg. *svekrŭve*), has become a *u*-stem. The acc. sg. *suem* shows the original formation in contrast to Umbr. *sim* (from *sūm*, like G. σῦν). The dat.-abl. pl. is regularly *suibus* with the usual *i*-stem form, but rarely *sūbus* (cf. Skt. *-ūbhyas*) or *subus* (with *u* from *suēs*, etc.)

DIPHTHONGAL STEMS

269. *Greek nouns like* βασιλεύς, φορεύς, φονεύς, *etc.*—This very productive type of agent nouns is peculiar to Greek. It has no equivalent in the other IE languages, and while it is doubtless connected in some way with IE *u*-stems or words formed with the suffix -*wo*-, its precise relation to these is obscure. But its history within Greek is clear. The stem was -ηυ- or -ηϝ- throughout, parallel to the generalized -ων- in ἀγών, ἀγῶνος. The ηυ became ευ in prehistoric times (94), while antevocalic ηϝ remained intact (as in Cyprian) or, with loss of ϝ, in Homer and various dialects.

Nom. sg........*βασιληύς to βασιλεύς (94)
Gen. sg.........βασιλῆϝος, Hom. -ῆος, Ion. -έος, Att. -έως (98.3)
Dat. sg.........βασιλῆϝι, Hom. -ῆϊ, Ion. -έϊ, Att. -εῖ
Acc. sg.........βασιλῆϝα, Hom. -ῆα, Ion. -έα, Att. -έᾱ (98.3)
Voc. sg.........*βασιληῦ to βασιλεῦ

Nom. pl.........βασιλῆϝες, Hom. -ῆες, Ion. -έες, Att. -ῆες, -ῆς, -εῖς
Gen. pl.........βασιλήϝων, Hom. -ήων, Ion. -έων, Att. -έων
Dat. pl.........*βασιληῦσι to βασιλεῦσι (94)
Acc. pl.........βασιλῆϝας, Hom. -ῆας, Ion. -έας, Att. -έᾱς, -εῖς

a. In Attic the nom. pl. -ῆς (from -ῆες) is the prevailing form till about 350 B.C. The later -εῖς is from -έες with ε from -έων, etc. The nom. pl. forms were also used for the acc. pl., after the analogy of the agreement in πόλεις, πήχεις, etc. So occasionally -ῆς, and regularly -εῖς from about the end of the 4th cent.

The acc. sg. -ῆ from -ῆα is early in some dialects, and occurs in the κοινή.

b. A nom. sg. -ης, probably re-formed from gen. sg. -ηος, etc., is regular in Arcadian (φονής, etc.), and in proper names occurs elsewhere. Such a variant form of Ὀδυσσεύς was Ὠλίξης, L. *Ulixēs* (142).

c. The proper names in -ευς sometimes show forms differing from those given above, as Hom. Τυδεύς, Τυδέος, Τυδέϊ, Τυδέα, and Τυδῆ. Such forms point to a grade -εϝ- in contrast to the usual generalized -ηϝ-.

270. *Greek nouns like* ἥρως, πάτρως, *etc.*—In this small class the stem is -ωυ-, -ωϝ, parallel to -ηυ, -ηϝ- in βασιλεύς (269). Nom. sg. -ως from -ωυς (cf. βῶς beside βοῦς, 94) or possibly re-formed from the other cases. Gen. sg. -ωος, dat. sg. -ωϊ and -ῳ, acc. sg. -ωα and -ω (also -ων after vowel stems), all from -ωϝος, etc., though forms with ϝ are not yet quotable. For πάτρως, μήτρως cf. the *u*-element in πατρυιός, μητρυιά, L. *patruus*, Skt. *pitṛvyas* 'father's brother'.

271. *Greek nouns like* πειθώ, Σαπφώ, *etc.*—The stem is -οι-, seen in the voc. sg. -οῖ, but with loss of intervocalic ι in gen. sg. -όος, -οῦς, dat. sg. -όϊ, -οῖ, acc. sg. -όα, -ω. Nom. sg. with lengthened grade -ωι (attested by early inscriptions and the grammarians) and -ω. A close parallel is the isolated Skt. *sakhā* 'friend', acc. sg. *sakhāyam*.

272. *Monosyllabic diphthongal stems.*—

1. G. βοῦς, L. *bōs* (loanword, **155**.6).

Nom. sg. with lengthened grade, IE **gʷōus* (Skt. *gāus*), whence (**94**) G. βοῦς, Dor. βῶς, L. *bōs*. Acc. sg. βοῦν, formed from βοῦς after the analogy of vowel stems. So also Att. acc. pl. βοῦς in contrast to Hom. βόας.

The other cases are from **gʷow-*, as G. βο(ϝ)ός, βο(ϝ)ί, L. *bovis*, *bove* (Skt. *gave*), *bovem*, or from **gʷou-*, as G. βουσί (Skt. *goṣu*), L. *būbus* (Skt. *gobhyas*). The rare L. *bōbus* has *ō* from nom. sg.

a. Att. χοῦς, in origin a contracted o-stem (**χοϝos*), is inflected like βοῦς, as gen. sg. χοός, etc. In Hellenistic Greek there are similar forms of νοῦς, πλοῦς, etc.

2. G. Ζεύς, L. *Iuppiter*, *Iovis*. The IE stem is **dyeu-* with gradation.

Nom. sg. with lengthened grade, IE **d(i)yēus* (Skt. *dyāus* 'sky'), whence (**94**) G. Ζεύς, also L. *diēs* from which a full *ē*-stem inflection is developed (**273**).

Voc. sg. **dyeu*, G. Ζεῦ, in Italic combined with *pater*, like G. Ζεῦ πάτερ, in Umbr. I u p a t e r (so also dat. sg. I u v e　p a t r e), L. *Iūpiter* with regular weakening of medial vowel (**110**.1), then *Iuppiter* (**209**), this vocative form serving also for the nominative.

The other Latin cases are from **dyew-*, whence (**80**.1, **180**) early L. *Diovis*, usual *Iovis*, *Iovī* (so Osc. D i ú v e í, I u v e í, Umbr. I u v e , Skt. *dyave*), *Iovem*.

The other Greek cases are from **diw-*, the weak grade, as Δι(ϝ)ός (Skt. *divás*), Δι(ϝ)ί, Δι(ϝ)α.

The extension of the weak grade to Δία is parallel to that in ἄνδρα, κύνα (**249**.2, 7).

In Homer and various dialects also Ζηνός, Ζηνί, Ζῆνα, built up from an acc. sg. **Ζῆν* (or actual Ζῆν in Hom. Il. 8. 206, etc.?) = Skt. *dyām*.

3. G. ναῦς. The IE stem is *nāu-* without gradation.

Nom. sg. IE **nāus* (Skt. *nāus*), whence ναῦς. In Hom. νηῦς, also dat. pl. νηυσί, the η is restored from the other cases.

Gen. sg. IE *nāwós (Skt. nāvás), whence Dor. vāós, Hom. vηós, Att. vεώs (98.3). So in the other cases, stem vā(ϝ)-, Hom. vη-, Att. vη- in vηï, vῆες or shortened in vεῶν. Att. acc. sg. vαῦν and acc. pl. vαῦs are formed from nom. sg. vαῦs after the analogy of vowel stems, in contrast to Hom. vῆα, vῆας (so Skt. nằvam, nằvas). In Latin the word has become an i-stem, nāvis.

THE LATIN FIFTH DECLENSION

273. The history of the Latin fifth declension has been much disputed, and is in some respects still a problem. There is nothing similar in the other IE languages except the Lith. iē-stems (žemė, gen. sg. žemẹ̃s, etc.), and, apart from their not agreeing in the nom. sg., they have been shown to be largely, if not wholly, yā-stems in origin. Elsewhere there are a few isolated nouns in -ē (probably verb stems used substantively), like G. χρή 'need, necessity', Skt. çraddhā- 'faith' (cpd. of dhā-, IE *dhē). But there is no evidence of any productive type of ē-stems.

The Latin fifth declension represents then a special Latin development (or partly Italic, since there are some traces of it in Oscan-Umbrian). It is an ē-declension built up from some few forms containing an inherited ē, on the analogy of the ā-declension.

The two words that are the commonest, and whose history is best known, are diphthongal stems in origin, namely:

diēs from *dieus (Skt. dyāus, etc., **94**)

rēs from *rēis (Skt. rās, gen. sg. rāyas)

The ē which arose from a long diphthong (**94**) in the nom. sg. and acc. sg. (cf. Skt. acc. sg. dyām beside divam, but rāyam) was the foundation of an apparent ē-stem, from which the other cases were formed, mostly parallel to those of ā-stems. Possibly fidēs and spēs are to be reckoned as inherited ē-stems, analogous to G. χρή.

Words of the type faciēs, speciēs, etc., appear to be transfers from yā-stems, with which some of them interchange in the historical period, as māteriēs, māteria, dūritiēs, dūritia, etc. This cannot be ascribed to any known phonetic change, but rests on an analogical spread, for which the comprehensive *rēs* may be chiefly responsible.

274. 1. *Gen. sg.*—The occasional *-ēs* of early poetry (*diēs*, *rabiēs*) is formed after the analogy of the old *-ās* (**233.**2); the *-ēī* after the analogy of the early *-āī* (**233.**2). Plautus has *rēī*, *reī*, and monosyllabic *rei*. This last represents a phonetic development parallel to that of the *-āī* to *-ai*, *-ae*. It may be further represented by forms that occur with the spellings *-ī*, and *-ē* (as *famī*, *diē*), but their authenticity and significance are uncertain. In general the older forms, which kept the stem vowel and ending distinct, were those approved in the classical period, namely *-ēī*, usually retained after a vowel (*diēī*, etc.), otherwise shortened to *-eī* (*reī*, *fideī*, etc.).

2. *Dat. sg.*—The early monosyllabic *-ei* (*rei*, *diei*) may be from an *-ēī* formed after the analogy of *-āī* before the shortening, or directly after *-ai*, *-ae*. The identity with the gen. sg. *rei*, etc., led to further confusion, and the gen. forms in *-ēī*, *-eī* came to be the approved dat. forms also.

3. *Acc. sg.*— *-em* from *-ēm*, with *ē* in part from a long diphthong (**273**).

4. *Abl. sg.*— *-ē* from *-ēd* (though not quotable), formed after the analogy of *-ād*, etc.

5. *Nom. pl.*— *-ēs* may have started in *rēs* from **rēyes* (Skt. *rāyas*), or be formed after the analogy of the old nom. pl. *-ās* before its displacement (**234.**1).

6. *Gen. pl.*— *-ērum* after *-ārum*.

7. *Dat. abl. pl.*— *-ēbus* after *-ibus*, etc.

8. *Acc. pl.*— *-ēs* after *-ās* (or earlier *-ens* after *-ans*).

NOUNS OF VARIABLE DECLENSION: HETEROCLITES

275. Nouns of variable declension, or heteroclites (ἑτερόκλιτα "differently declined"), may represent a mixture of two inherited parallel stems, as L. *domus* which has partly *u*-stem declension corresponding to that of ChSl. *domŭ*, and partly *o*-stem declension corresponding to that of G. δόμος, Skt. *damas*.

Or they may represent a mixed type already established in the parent speech, such as the IE *r/n* neuters reflected in L. *femur*, *feminis*, etc. (**251**); or, again, a later but still prehistoric type of mixture, such as the Latin third declension.

Most commonly they are due to analogical formations favored by certain case forms that are common to different stems, as G. Σωκράτην (see **256**) after Θουκυδίδην etc., favored by the common nom. sg. -ης, or, as some Latin interchanges between *o*- and *u*-stem or between *o*- and neut. *s*-stem forms, favored by the common nom. sg. -*us* (*hortus, tribus, genus*).

276. Among the many examples of heteroclitic forms the following may be noticed here:

1. Interchange between *o*- and *u*-stem forms in Latin. Besides *domus*, which stands by itself (**275**), several names of trees show some fluctuation, as *fāgus, laurus*, *o*-stems, but also nom.-acc. pl. -*ūs*, conversely *quercus*, *u*-stem but also gen. pl. *quercōrum*.

Nouns in -*tus* have in early Latin a gen. sg. -*ī*, as *senātī* (also Osc. *senateis*, not -*ous*), *quaestī, exercitī*, etc.

In late vulgar Latin the *u*-stems were completely fused with the *o*-stems and disappeared as a distinct class.

2. Interchange between *o*-stems and neut. *s*-stems. G. σκότος, gen. sg. σκότου or σκότους, and so in the other cases. L. nom.-acc. sg. *vulgus, pelagus* (G. loanword, πέλαγος, neut. *s*-stem), *vīrus* (cognate with G. ἰός, *o*-stem), like *genus*, but gen. sg. -*ī*, etc.

3. Further interchange between *o*-stems and cons. stems. Mainly in neuters, where the nom.-acc. pl. form was the same. L. *vās, vāsis*, but pl. *vāsa, vāsōrum*. L. *iūgerum, iūgerī*, but pl. *iūgera, iūgerum* (which may be the *o*-stem form like *nummum*), *iūgeribus*. There are several examples of -*ibus* in place of -*īs*.

4. For Latin, cf. also the interchange between the first and fifth declension in *māteria, māteriēs*, etc. (**273***a*); between the third and fifth in some of the nouns in -*ēs*, as *famēs*, gen. sg. *famis*, abl. sg. *famē*; between *i*-stems and cons. stems in *canis*, gen. pl. *canum*, etc. (**263**).

5. For Greek, cf. also the mixture of τ-stem forms with others in neuters (**252**), also in γέλως, etc. (**252***a*); the *o*- and *v*-stem forms in υἱός, υἱύς (**265**); the diphthongal inflection of Att. χοῦς, etc. (**272.1***a*).

NOUNS OF VARIABLE GENDER

277. Many nouns have a different gender in singular and plural, frequently with a distinction in sense. G. ὁ σῖτος, pl. τὰ σῖτα; ὁ δεσμός, pl. τὰ δεσμά and οἱ δεσμοί; τὸ στάδιον, pl. τὰ στάδια and οἱ στάδιοι. L. *locus* masc., pl. *loca* 'places' and *locī* 'passages in authors'; *iocus*, pl. *ioca* and *iocī; frēnum*, pl. *frēna* and *frēnī*.

Some of these reflect an association between the neuter plural and a collective. In late vulgar Latin many neuter plurals came to be felt as singular collectives and were declined as feminines of the first declension, e.g. *gaudia*, whence It. *gioia*, Fr. *joie*, NE *joy*.

INDECLINABLE AND DEFEÇTIVE NOUNS

278. Among the indeclinable nouns are the names of the letters in both Greek and Latin, as G. ἄλφα, βῆτα (only late forms with τ-inflection, as gen. sg. σίγματος, after the type of ὄνομα), L. *a, be,* etc. G. χρεών (mostly nom.-acc., but also τοῦ χρεών) is from χρεὼ ὄν, parallel to ἄδηλον ὄν, etc. Hom. nom.-acc. δῶ = δῶμα (in Hesiod, pl. = δώματα), κρῖ = κριθή, look like abbreviated forms (and as such were imitated by later writers), but their actual source is uncertain. The majority of indeclinable nouns are words of foreign origin, or onomatopoeic syllables like G. μῦ, L. *mu*.

Among the so-called defective nouns are many in which the lack of a quotable example of a particular case form may well be accidental. Thus, until recent times the proper nom. sg. ἀρήν (usually replaced by ἀμνός) to gen. ἀρνός, etc., was unknown, but it has turned up in a 5th-cent. Attic inscription, and the older ϝαρήν in Cretan. Nouns that occur only in a single case form are merely isolated survivals of words that had otherwise become obsolete, or in part had from the outset been used only in what was equivalent to an adverbial phrase. Thus G. acc. sg. νίφα in Hesiod is the sole relic of a *νίψ, *νιφός, the inherited word for 'snow' corresponding to L. *nix, nivis*, Goth. *snaiws*, OE *snāw*, NE *snow*, etc., but displaced (apart from the deriv. νιφάδες 'snow-flakes') by χιών, χιόνος. The isolation of L. *nātū* 'by birth', *sponte* 'of free will', *forte* 'by chance', etc., of which other case forms are unknown or rare, is similar to the restriction of NE *sake* (in contrast to OE *sacu* and the cognate NHG *Sache*) to the phrases *for the sake of*, *for one's sake*. The matter belongs mainly to the history of the vocabulary.

DECLENSION OF ADJECTIVES AND PARTICIPLES

279. Greek and Latin have the same principal type of adjectives (**280**), but otherwise little in common in their adjective types. Greek has *u*-stem adjectives, which are unknown in Latin. Conversely Latin has *i*-stem adjectives, which are rare in Greek. The cons. stem adjectives are of different types in each.

O- AND ā-STEM ADJECTIVES

280. The commonest type of adjectives is that in which the masculine and neuter are formed from an *o*-stem, the feminine from an *ā*-stem, as G. σοφός, σοφή, σοφόν, L. *bonus, bona, bonum*.

The declension is that which has been discussed for nouns. L. *ruber*, *līber*, like *ager*, *puer* (**109**). But Latin adjectives in *-ius* have gen. sg. *-iī* and voc. sg. *-ie* (for nouns, see **239**.2, 6). Greek adjectives like ἄξιος have nom. pl. fem. and gen. pl. fem. with the accent of the corresponding masculine forms, as ἄξιαι, ἀξίων, in contrast to the regular οἰκίαι, οἰκιῶν.

a. The declension of G. μέγας is built up from an inherited nom.-acc. sg. neut. μέγα=Skt. *mahi* (IE *meĝ(h)ə, cf. **85**). To this was formed nom. sg. masc. μέγας, acc. sg. masc. μέγαν, while all the other forms are from μεγα-λο-, μεγα-λᾱ- with added suffix.

281. Greek adjectives of two endings, as masc. fem. ἄλογος, neut. ἄλογον. This type is especially characteristic of compounds, and there it has its origin. For example, ἄ-λογος 'one without reason' retained the original λόγος whether used in apposition to a masculine or to a feminine, without shifting in the latter case to a more distinctively feminine form. Since Greek has many feminine nouns in -ος, there was no serious discordance in this retention of the -ος in the feminine (as there would be in Sanskrit, where there are no feminine *a*-stems, and where a compound of an *a*-stem if used as feminine must pass over to the *ā*-stem form). Only a special neuter form was developed, as ἄλογον.

From the very numerous compounds of o-stems, like ἄλογος, the type spread to other compounds, like ἄδικος from δίκη, and further to many simple adjectives, as φρόνιμος, ἥσυχος, ἵλεως (from -ηος, like νεώς, **98**.3).

a. There are several adjectives, especially among those in -ιος, -αιος, etc., which fluctuate between the declension with two endings and that with three.

GREEK U-STEM ADJECTIVES

282. The Greek adjectives like ἡδύς, γλυκύς, etc., represent an inherited type of adjectives which is common in Indo-Iranian, Lithuanian, and Germanic, but is unknown in Latin. In Latin the original *u*-stem adjectives have mostly become *i*-stem adjectives, by the addition of *i*, which perhaps started from a lost nom. sg. fem. in -ī (like Skt. svādvī). Thus L. *suāvis* from * *suādvis* (Skt. svādus, fem. svādvī, G. ἡδύς), *gravis* (Skt. gurus, G. βαρύς), *tenuis* (Skt. tanus).

The Greek declension of the masculine and neuter has been discussed in connection with the noun (**266, 267**). The feminine is formed, like that of consonant stems, with the suffix ιă/ιā, as in Sanskrit with the corresponding ī/yā (**237**). But in Greek this is added to the strong grade of the *u*-stem, in Sanskrit to the weak grade (in the parent speech there was probably an accentual shift with gradation between different case forms). Thus G. ἡδεῖα from -εϝια but Skt. svādvī.

a. The declension of πολύς is built up from an inherited nom.-acc. sg. neut. πολύ=Skt. *puru*, Goth. *filu*. To this was formed nom. sg. masc. πολύς, acc. sg. masc. πολύν, while all the other forms are from πολλο-, πολλᾱ-. These are perhaps from *πολυ-λο-, like μεγα-λο- beside μεγα- (**250***a*), though this attractive explanation involves a serious difficulty (vowel syncope would be anomalous in Greek, and by haplology one would expect *πολυ-λο- > *πολο-).

LATIN I-STEM ADJECTIVES

283. In Latin the *i*-stem adjectives are numerous, while in Greek they are rare. Often the Latin forms correspond to o-stem adjectives elsewhere, as *similis*, *humilis* to G. ὁμαλός, χθαμαλός, or to *u*-stem adjectives, as *suāvis*, etc. (**282**).

The normal type is that of two endings, like masc.-fem. *gravis*, neut. *grave*. The declension is that of the *i*-stem nouns, only that here the abl. sg. is regularly *-ī*.

The type with three endings is a special development of the preceding. For example, masc.-fem. *ācris* became *ācer* (like *ager*, **109**), also masc. or fem. as actually in early Latin (cf. also Umbr. *pacer* masc. or fem.). Beside this there was a restored *ācris* like *inlūstris* or early L. *alacris*, etc. From the two forms *ācer*, *ācris*, both used for masc. or fem., the *ācer* came to be used as masc. only, after the analogy of *o*-stem forms like *ruber*, fem. *rubra*, and *ācris* was left for the feminine.

a. In Greek, simple ι-stem adjectives are very rare, as ἴδρις, τρόφις. Adjective compounds of ι-stems, as ἄπολις, keep the ι-stem inflection in most dialects, but in Attic follow the type ἔρις, ἔριδος.

CONSONANT STEM ADJECTIVES

284. *s-stem adjectives.*—Greek type εὐμενής, εὐμενές mostly compounds (see **256**). Latin comparatives, like *melior*, *melius* (see **292**).

L. *vetus* 'old' is an old neuter noun (cf. G. Ϝέτος 'year'), first used in apposition to another neuter (e.g. *vīnum vetus*) and then generally as an adjective. Similarly L. *über* 'abundant' is the neuter *r*-stem *über* 'udder' used without change as an adjective.

285. *n-stem adjectives in Greek.*—Type σώφρων. The only difference from the noun declension (**249.**9) is in the neut. -ον (pl. -ονα), which was supplied to -ων, after the analogy of εὐμενής, εὐμενές and the like, in place of the original neuter represented by ὄνομα, etc. (**250**). A similar replacement of the original neuter form by the form of the stem appearing in the oblique cases occurs in the other ν-stem adjectives and the ντ-stem adjectives and participles, e.g. neut. τέρεν, μέλαν, χαρίεν, λέγον, etc.

Beside this common type in -ων, there are a few other ν-stem adjectives, in which there is a separate feminine form. Thus:

τέρην, (cf. ποιμήν), τέρεινα (*τερενϳα), τέρεν

μέλᾱς (from *μελαν-s), μέλαινα (*μελανϳα), μέλαν

τάλᾱς (*ταλαν-s), τάλαινα (*ταλανϳα), τάλαν

Like τέρην, except that there is naturally no feminine form, ἄρρην, ἄρρεν

286. *The Greek type* χαρίεις, χαρίεσσα, χαρίεν.—Formed from noun stems with the suffix -ϝεντ- = Skt. -vant- in rūpa-vant- 'beautiful', etc., IE -went-, weak grade -wṇt-. The strong grade -ϝεντ- is generalized in the masculine and neuter, as gen. sg. -εντος, nom. sg. -εις from -ϝεντς, nom.-acc. sg. neut. -εν from -ϝεντ. The feminine is not from -ϝεντ-ι̯α which would give -εῖσα (as in part. τιθεῖσα), but from -ϝετ-ι̯α (**182**), this from -ϝατ-ι̯α (-ϝατ- = IE -wṇt-, cf. Skt. fem. rūpa-vatī), with the vowel changed to ε under the influence of the -ϝεντ- forms (cf. ποιμέσι for -άσι, 249.9). A few forms with ϝ are quotable from inscriptions, as Boeot. χαρί-ϝετταν, Corcyr. στονόϝεσσαν.

This class of adjectives is almost wholly poetical, very few of them occurring in Attic prose. Hence they commonly appear with the non-Attic σσ in the feminine, and in uncontracted forms like μελιτόεις, τῑμήεις, etc. But some gave rise to nouns in common use which appear in their proper Attic form, as names of cakes like πλακοῦς, μελιττοῦττα, οἰνοῦττα, or place names like Ῥαμνοῦς.

287. *The Greek ντ-participles.*—These have the regular cons. stem declension in the masculine and neuter, while the feminine is formed with the ι̯α/ι̯ᾱ suffix, as nom. sg. φέρουσα from *φεροντι̯α = Skt. bharantī (**237**).

The nom. sg. masc. had -ντ-ς, whence -ς with lengthening of the preceding vowel (**204.4**), as διδούς from *διδόντς, λύσᾱς from *λύσαντς, τιθείς from *τιθεντς, λυθείς from *λυθεντς.

But from thematic stems, where according to the evidence of other languages we should also expect -οντς, yielding -ους as in διδούς, we have rather φέρων, λιπών, etc. These are apparently formed after the analogy of the regular -ων of ν-stems. Cf. the occasional shift of ν-stems to ντ-stems, as in λέων, λέοντος, originally an ν-stem as shown by the fem. λέαινα and by L. leō, leōnis, likewise in δράκων, θεράπων.

288. *The Greek perfect active participle.*—For the formation, see **435**. The old s-stem forms survive in nom. sg. masc. -ως, parallel to αἰδώς (255), nom.-acc. sg. neut. -os, parallel to γένος, while the other masc. and neut. forms are from a τ-stem. Fem. -υια from -υσια = Skt. -uṣī.

289. *The Latin nt-participles and adjectives like duplex, audāx, etc.*—The absence of a distinct feminine form of the participle, in contrast to Greek, Sanskrit, etc., is connected with the general fusion of *i*- and cons. stems in Latin. An old nom. sg. fem. **ferentī* = Skt. *bharantī* would be drawn into the common *i*-stem class, becoming **ferentis*, whence *ferēns*, like *mors* from **mortis*, etc. (**108**). The subsequent distribution of *i*- and cons. stem forms has nothing to do with gender. The *i*-stem forms, favored by the adjective type *gravis*, prevailed in the gen. pl. *-ium* (in early Latin still sometimes *-um*, as *amantum*, Plautus), nom.-acc. pl. neut. *-ia*, while in the abl. sg. there was fluctuation between *-e* and *-ī*, with a tendency to prefer the latter in adjectival use, as regularly in the adjectives proper.

The most remarkable feature of the Latin type is the nom.-acc. sg. neut. in *-s*, as *amāns*, *duplex*, for which there is no wholly convincing explanation. A phonetic change of final *nt* to *ns*, which would explain the participial form (as coming from the original neuter form in *-nt*), is assumed by some scholars, but is very doubtful. For the compound adjectives, a form like *duplex* (Umbr. t u p l a k , without *s*) may be taken as the masculine form retained even in apposition with the neuter, for which there are some parallels (as Ved. *dvipāt* 'bipes', masc. form used also as neuter).

290. *Other cons. stem adjectives in Greek.*—Adjectivally used compounds may be formed from any type of cons. stem, as ἀπάτωρ, nom.-acc. pl. neut. ἀπάτορα beside πατήρ, with gradation as in σώφρων beside φρήν (**120**), εὔελπις, neut. εὔελπι, gen. sg. εὐέλπιδος; ἄχαρις, neut. ἄχαρι, gen. sg. ἀχάριτος, etc. Compounds of *i*-stems, as ἄπολις, ἄπολι, have partly -ιδος, etc., in Attic.

Other adjectives have only a masc.-fem. form, with no neuter. as ἅρπαξ, etc.

COMPARISON OF ADJECTIVES

291. The IE suffixes of comparison were as follows:

COMPARATIVE: -*yes*-, with gradation
SUPERLATIVE: -*isto*-

These were originally primary suffixes, added to the root rather than to the stem of the adjective. The addition of -*yes*- to certain forms ending in *ĭ* gave rise to a productive -*ĭ-yes*-. In Sanskrit -*īyas*- is the usual form, as in *svādīyas*-, comp. of *svādu*- 'sweet', while the simple -*yas*- occurs only in a few words, as *sanyas*- (cf. L. *senior*) comparative of *sana*- 'old'. But in Avestan it is always -*yah*- = Skt. -*yas*-. The superlative suffix -*isto*- is obviously -*is-to*-, the weak grade of -*yes*-, with suffix -*to*-.

G. ἥδιστος, Skt. *svādiṣṭhas*, Goth. **sutists* (cf. *smalists*), NE *sweetest*

292. The Latin comparatives have the nom.-acc. sg. neut. from the grade -*yos*-, as *melius* from **melyos* (**180**), like *genus*. All the other forms are from the grade -*yōs*, which belonged to the nom. sg. masc.-fem. and was extended to the other cases, with subsequent change of the intervocalic *s* to *r* and the analogical substitution of *r* for *s* in the nom. sg. and resulting shortening to -*or*. That is, *melior, meliōris* has the same history as *honor, honōris* (**255**), and the forms *meliōris*, etc., were used for the neuter also.

a. L. *minor, minus* are not formed with the comparative suffix. An adj. **minu-s* 'less', from the stem seen in *minuō* 'lessen' and so having comparative force from the meaning of the root itself, was naturally associated with the regular comparatives, especially its opposite *maior, maius*, and by their analogy became *minor, minus*.

b. L. *plūs* has a complicated and disputed history, but the most probable view is as follows: An orig. **plē-yos* (from the root of **plē*- 'fill' seen in L. *plē-nus*, G. πλήρης, etc., as is likewise G. πλείων, πλεῖστος ; precisely reflected in Skt. *prāyas*-, Av. *frāyō*) became **plēos*, **pleos*, then **pleus* under the influence of *minus* (see above, *a*), whence regularly (**92**) *plous* (SC de Bacch.), *plūs*. Cicero's *ploera* must then be a false archaism. The plural *pleōrēs* (so to be read in the Carmen Saliare) would be regular, from **plē-yōs-ēs*, while *plūrēs* is formed anew from *plūs*. Likewise the superlative *plūrimus* would be formed anew from *plous, plūs*, in place of the regular formation from **plēis*- which appears in the *plisima* 'plurima' quoted from the Carmen Saliare. The spelling *ploirume* in the early Scipio epitaph, which is earlier than the *plouruma* of another inscription and which seems to support *ploera*, is an admitted difficulty for the view expressed. But much greater difficulties are involved in starting from a form *plō-is-*, especially as there is no support for *plō-* beside *plē-* in any of the cognate formations.

293. In the Greek comparatives of the type ἐλάσσων, ἡδίων the shorter forms of certain cases are from -*yos*- or -*ĭ-yos*- (cf. Skt. -*īyas*-, **291**), as acc. sg. masc.-fem. and nom.-acc. pl. neut. ἐλάσσω, ἡδίω from *ἐλαγχ-ιοσα, *ἀδ-ῐ-ιοσα, nom. and acc. pl. masc.-fem. ἐλάσσους, ἡδίους from nom. pl. *ἐλαγχ-ιοσες, *ἀδ-ῑιοσες.

The usual forms in -ων, -ονος have their origin in an *n*-stem extension of the weak grade -*is*- such as is seen also in the Germanic comparatives, as Goth. *sut-izan-* (Eng. -*er* in *sweeter* is of the same origin) and in the Lithuanian comparatives as *saldesnis* 'sweeter', (from -*yes-ni-s*). From -*is-ōn* would come -ιων (ἡδίων) and then by mixture with the forms coming from -*yos*- or -*ĭ-yos*- (above) also -ιων (ἐλάσσων, etc.) and -ῑων (ἡδίων). The fluctuation in the quantity of the ι (usually ῑ in Attic poetry, ῐ in Homer and Doric poetry) is the same for ἡδίων etc., as for ἡδίω, etc.

a. The lengthened vowel of the root syllable in ἐλάσσων, θάσσων, Att. ἐλάττων, θάττων (ᾱ shown by the accent of the neuter, as Att. θᾶττον), is explained by deriving these from ἐλαγχιων, etc. (like ἆσσον from *ἀγχιον to ἄγχι, **182***b*).

But in μᾶλλον from *μαλιον to μάλα it must be due to some analogy. Likewise the ει of Att. μείζων, κρείττων (also ὀλείζων after μείζων) in contrast to the regular Ion. μέζων, κρέσσων from *μέγιων, *κρέτιων, must be due to the analogy of some words in which the ει is regular, as perhaps χείρων, which may come from *χεριων, and ἀμείνων, which has orig. ει.

b. Hom. πλέες, πλέας (also Cret. πλίες etc.), are from an *s*-stem form, probably *plē-is-*, beside *plē-yos-* (cf. **292***b*).

294. Another type of comparison is more common in Greek and in Sanskrit, namely that in G. -τερος, -τατος, Skt. -*tara-*, *tama-*.

The comparative represents a specialized use of the suffix -*tero-* (also -*ero-*) that appears in words of contrasted relation like G. δεξιτερός, ἀριστερός, L. *dexter, sinister*, G. ἡμέτερος, L. *noster*, G. πότερος, Skt. *kataras*.

The superlative reflects the suffix seen also in L. *ultimus*, Goth.

aftuma, etc., which with Skt. *-tama-* point to an IE *-ṭṃo-*, and for which the Greek equivalent would be *-ταμο-*. This was replaced by *-τατο-* under the influence of the other superlative suffix *-ιστο-*, just as the *-mo*-suffix was replaced by *-το-* in certain ordinals, as δέκατος contrasted with L. *decimus*, Skt. *daçamas* (**318**).

These suffixes (in contrast to those of **291**) were regularly added to the stem of the positive. Thus δηλό-τερος, δηλό-τατος ; γλυκύ-τερος, γλυκύ-τατος ; μελάν-τερος, μελάν-τατος ; ἀληθέσ-τερος, ἀληθέσ-τατος ; χαριέσ-τερος, χαριέσ-τατος (from *χαριέτ-τερος, etc., **190**, **286**).

a. But from *o*-stem adjectives with short penult we find regularly -ω-τερος, etc., as σοφώ-τερος, σοφώ-τατος; νεώ-τερος, νεώ-τατος. This type probably started in certain words in which the suffixes were added to adverbs in -ω like ἀνώ-τερος, ἀνώ-τατος from ἄνω. It was favored because of the resulting avoidance of a long succession of short syllables.

Only apparent exceptions are στενό-τερος, κενό-τερος since these are from earlier *στενϝο-τερος, *κενϝο-τερος. For combination of stop and liquid the earlier syllabic value prevails, hence πικρό-τερος, πικρό-τατος. In poetry there are occasional variants from the general rule.

b. From the regular forms like ἀληθέσ-τερος, χαριέσ-τερος (above), etc., -έστερος, -έστατος were extended to adjectives in -ων and to some in -οος (-ους), including all in -νοος (-νους), also to some others. Thus εὐδαιμον-έστερος, εὐδαιμον-έστατος ; (ἁπλο-έστερος) ἁπλούστερος, ἁπλούστατος ; εὐνούστερος, εὐνούστατος ; poet. ἀφθονέστερος, ἀφθονέστατος.

c. From several adjectives in -αιος and some others we have -αιτερος, etc., as γεραίτερος from γεραιός; μεσαίτερος, μεσαίτατος from μέσος. This type started in certain forms in which the suffixes were added to adverbs in -αι like παλαί-τερος, παλαί-τατος from πάλαι.

d. Another analogical extension is that of -ιστερος, -ιστατος from regular forms like ἀχαρίσ-τερος (*ἀχαρίτ-τερος, **190**) to some others of derogatory meaning, as κλεπτίστερος, κλεπτίστατος ; λαλίστερος, λαλίστατος.

295. The Latin superlative is based upon that of the type mentioned in the preceding paragraph (Skt. *-tama-*, etc.). But much of the history is obscure, especially as regards the commonest form, *-issimus*.

The clearest forms historically are those that are irregular from the Latin point of view, such as *ultimus, intimus, infimus, plūrimus, summus* (from *sup-mo-*), which directly reflect the suffix

-ṭṃo-, -ṃo-, or -mo. Furthermore *pessimus* is regular from **ped-ṭṃo-* (cf. *peior* from **ped-yōs*, 180), and *maximus, proximus* are perhaps formed with -ṃo- from adverbs ending in *s*.

The commoner types of superlative point to an element -sṃo- in place of -ṭṃo-, but the precise analysis and source of the *s* is uncertain. Thus *ācerrimus* comes from **ācersemos*, this from **ācrisṃos;* similarly *facillimus* from **facilsemos*, this from **faclisṃos*. These may be further analyzed as **ācri-sṃos, *facli-sṃos*, or as **ācr-is-ṃos, *facl-is-ṃos* with -*is*- representing the weak grade of the comparative suffix (cf. *mag-is* and *mag-is-ter*) or taken over from the old -*is-to*-. The most usual type, as in *clārissimus, gravissimus*, is also the most difficult. Apparently to be analyzed as -*is-sṃo*, it is possibly a blend of the old -*isto*- and -*sṃo*-.

296. *Composite comparison.*—Several of the commonest adjectives have their comparative and superlative formed from other, formally unrelated, words, just as in NE *good, better, best*, or *bad, worse, worst*. Thus:

G. ἀγαθός, ἀμείνων, ἄριστος (or βελτίων, βέλτιστος)

G. κακός, χείρων, χείριστος (beside κακίων, κάκιστος)

L. *bonus, melior, optimus*

L. *malus, peior, pessimus*

L. *multus, plūs, plūrimus*

a. This is a phase of the same phenomenon that shows itself also in some of the commonest verbs, as in NE *be, am, was*, or *go, went*. So L. *est, fuit; ferō, tulī*; G. ἔρχομαι, ἦλθον ; φέρω, οἴσω, ἤνεγκα, etc. Words of different formal origin and originally of somewhat different meaning became associated in usage, and supplemented each other. The term "defective" (comparison, etc.) is less appropriate than "composite" or "supplementary".

PRONOUNS

PERSONAL PRONOUNS

297. The personal pronouns in the various IE languages, in spite of obvious relationship, show a bewildering variety of forms from which it would be idle to attempt to reconstruct precise paradigms for the parent speech. So far as reconstructed IE forms are employed here, it is only as the proper theoretical bases for certain limited sets of correspondences. Thus G. ἐγώ, L. *ego*, and Goth. *ik* may be combined on the base of an IE **eĝō*, while Skt. *aham*, Av. *azəm*, OPers. *adam* are as if from an IE **eĝhom*, and there are still other variations.

The pronoun of the first person was made up of four distinct formal groups, all represented in English, namely by *I, me, we, us.* The Greek and Latin forms belong with *I, me,* and (less obviously) with *us.*

The pronoun of the second person was made up in the singular of a group of forms to which NE *thou, thee* belong, containing **tŭ, **tewe-, **twe-, **te-;* in the plural, of two formal groups, one to which NE *ye* belongs (but not *you,* which has a different history), and another containing **wes* in various grades, to which all the Greek and Latin plural forms belong.

The reflexive pronoun, which was originally a reflexive of all persons, was made up of an element **sewe-, **swe-, **se-.* The Greek forms of this stem partly retain their reflexive force in Homer, but are generally used for simple reference to the third person.

298. 1. *Nom. sg.*—G. ἐγώ, L. *ego* with iambic shortening (**102**). Cf. Goth. *ik*, OE *ic* (and *īc*), NE *I*.

G. σύ (so in most dialects), Dor. τύ, L. *tū.* Cf. Goth. *þu*, OE *þū*, NE *thou.* IE **tu* and **tū.* The σ of σύ is after the analogy of that in the other cases where it comes regularly from **tw-* (**176.**4).

2. *Gen. sg.*—Hom. ἐμεῖο, σεῖο, εἷο, from **eme-syo, **twe-syo, **swe-syo,* parallel to τοῖο from **to-syo.* Hence ἐμέο, ἐμεῦ, Att. ἐμοῦ, with enclitic from stem *me-*, **μειο, **μεο, μευ, Att. μου ; σέο, σεῦ, Att. σοῦ, enclitic σεο, σευ, Att. σου ; ἕο, εὗ, Att. οὗ, enclitic ἑο, ἑυ, Att. οὑ.

Also ἐμέθεν, σέθεν, ἕθεν, with the same adverbial ending as in ἄλλο-θεν, etc.

Also, after the analogy of the cons. stem ending, Dor. ἐμέος, ἐμεῦς ; τέος, τεῦς ; Locr. ϝέος.

L. *meī, tuī, suī* are in origin gen. sg. of the possessives *meus, tuus, suus.* Early Latin also *mīs, tīs,* perhaps from enclitic **moi, **toi* (Skt. gen.-dat. *te, me,* G. μοι, σοι) with gen. sg. ending *-s.*

3. *Dat. sg.*—G. ἐμοί, μοι, the latter = Skt. enclitic gen.-dat. sg. *me;* σοί, σοι from **twoi,* Dor. τοί, τοι, Hom. τοι, from **toi* = Skt. enclitic gen.-dat. *te;* οἷ, οι, in many dialects ϝοι, from **swoi,* Hom. also ἑοῖ from **sewoi.*

Doric also ἐμίν, τίν, ϝίν, with the same ending as in the dat. pl. Hom. ἄμμιν, etc. (**299.**3).

L. *mihi, tibi, sibi* with iambic shortening (**102**) from *mihī, tibī, sibī,* these, with weakening of *e* to *i* (**79.**2), from **meĝhei, *tebhei, *sebhei.* Cf. Umbr. *mehe, tefe,* Osc. t f e i , s í f e í , OPruss. *tebbei, sebbei,* ChSl. *tebě, sebě,* and for the consonants of the ending also Skt. *mahyam, tubhyam.* Beside *mihi* also *mī,* like *nīl* from *nihil.*

4. *Acc. sg.*—G. ἐμέ, με ; σέ, σε, Dor. τέ (Dor. also τύ, nom. used as acc.); ἕ, ἑ (in dialects ϝε), Hom. also ἑέ. These point to *(e)*me,* **twe,* etc., without case ending, as do Goth. *mi-k, si-k* (cf. NHG *mich, dich, sich*) with an added particle, and as Skt. enclitic *mā, tvā* (beside emphatic *mām, tvām*) point to **mē, *twē.* L. *mē, tē, sē,* though they seemingly agree with Skt. enclitic *mā, tvā,* are from the earlier attested *mēd, tēd, sēd,* in which the *d* presumably represents an added particle.

5. *Abl. sg.*—L. *mē, tē, sē* are from early L. *mēd, tēd, sēd,* with the same ablative ending *d* as in nouns and other pronouns. Cf. Skt. *mad, tvad* from **med, *twed* with short vowel in contrast to the Latin.

299. 1. The plural of the pronouns of the first and second person contain respectively **nes* and **wes* with gradation. Thus:

*nes, *nos and **wes, *wos*   Skt. enclitic acc.-gen.-dat. *nas, vas;*
   also in the Latin possessives *noster* and *vester,* early *voster*
*nēs, *nōs and **wēs, *wōs*   L. *nōs, vōs*
*n̥s and **us.* The former in Goth. *uns,* NHG *uns,* OE *ūs,* NE *us;* both, with an added element in Greek and Sanskrit forms (see below, 3)

2. *Latin.*—Nom.-acc. *nōs, vōs* are inherited forms differing only in gradation from Skt. *nas, vas.* Their use as nominatives is secondary, replacing that of forms allied to NE *we, ye.*

Gen. pl. *nostrum, vestrum* (early L. *vostrum,* **83.**1) are in origin gen. pl. forms of the possessives *noster, vester;* as *nostrī, vestrī* used for the objective genitive are gen. sg. forms of the same, and analogous to gen. sg. *meī, tuī*. Dat. pl. *nōbīs, vōbīs*, early L. *nōbeis, vōbeis*, contain *nō-, vō-*, abstracted from *nōs, vōs*, and a blend of an old *bh*-ending (like *-bhos*, L. *bus*, **230.**7) with that of *o*-stems in *illīs*, early *illeis*.

3. The Greek and most of the Sanskrit plural forms are made up of the weak grades **n̥s* and **us* with the addition of a particle *-sme*, allied to the *sm*-element in other pronominal forms like Skt. *tasmāi, tasmin*, etc. (**303.**7).

Acc. **n̥s-sme, *us-sme*. Skt. *asmān, yuṣmān* (init. *y* from *yūyam*, like NE *ye*), with adoption of the acc. pl. ending from other pronouns as *tān*; G. **ἀσμε, *ὑσ-με*, whence regularly (**203.**2) Lesb. ἄμμε, ὔμμε, Dor. ἀμέ, ὑμέ. The ' in ἀμέ, is due to the analogy of ὑμέ, where it is regular before init. *v* (**167**). Hence again in Attic-Ionic, with η from ᾱ and with added case ending, Hom. ἡμέας, ὑμέας (-εας as in σ-stems and *v*-stems), Att. ἡμᾶς, ὑμᾶς (with unusual contraction of εα to ᾱ instead of η, perhaps belonging with the instances mentioned in **104.**6), enclitic ἧμας, ὗμας.

The other cases are from forms like the above, with adoption of case endings:

Nom. Lesb. ἄμμες, ὔμμες, Dor. ἀμές, ὑμές, by the addition of *s* to ἄμμε, etc., giving -ες as in cons. stems; but Att.-Ion. ἡμεῖς, ὑμεῖς, formed to ἡμέας, etc., after the analogy of -εῖς to -έας in σ- and *v*-stems.

Gen. Lesb. ἀμμέων, Dor. ἀμέων, Ion. ἡμέων, ὑμέων, Att. ἡμῶν, ὑμῶν, enclitic ἧμων, ὗμων.

Dat. Lesb. ἄμμιν, ἄμμι, ὔμμιν, ὔμμι, Dor. ἀμίν, ὑμίν, Att.-Ion. ἡμῖν, ὑμῖν, enclitic ἧμιν, ὗμιν. The ending seems to be the same that appears in Sanskrit in the loc. sg. masc. of impersonal pronouns, as *ta-smin*, etc. (**303.**8), beside which Avestan has forms without the final *n* (cf. ἄμμιν, ἄμμι). There is no clear explanation of the *ī* in Att.-Ion. ἡμῖν, ὑμῖν.

4. The dual of the first person, νώ, agrees with Skt. *nāu*, Av. *nā*. Hom. νῶϊ, from **νω-φι*, probably a blend of νώ and a form related to ChSl. *vě*, Goth. *wit* 'we two'.

The σφ-forms of the dual of the second person and dual and

plural of the third or reflexive are of obscure origin. The latter are possibly built up from a weak form of the reflexive *se and the case ending -φι (230.7), that is, starting from σφι, σφιν.

300. *Possessive pronouns.*—The possessives are adjectives formed from the stems of the personal pronouns by the addition of -o- (fem. -ā-), or in some with the suffix -tero- serving here as in other words of contrasting relations (like G. δεξιτερός, L. *dexter*, etc. **294**).

1. G. ἐμός. L. *meus* from *meyos*, like ChSl. *mojĭ* from *moyos*, probably formed from the gen.-dat.-loc. *mei, moi (Skt. *me*, G. μοι).

2. G. σός from *twos, and τεός from *tewos. From *tewos also Italic *towos (cf. Umbr. *touer* 'tui'), early L. *tovos* (rare), whence usual *tuus* with the weakening (**110.**5) in proclitic use.

3. G. ὅς from *swos, and ἑός from *sewos. From *sewos also Italic *sowos (cf. Osc. s ú v a d 'sua'), early L. *sovos* (rare), whence the usual *suus* with weakening as in *tuus*.

a. This stem (like the corresponding substantive pronoun) was originally a reflexive with reference to all persons and numbers, as in Sanskrit and in the Balto-Slavic languages. There are traces of this wider use in Homer, where ὅς sometimes means 'my own' or 'your own' (Λ 142, ι 28, etc.).

b. The rare early L. *sīs, sās*, etc. (to be distinguished from the similar forms of a demonstrative pronoun so-, **306.**7), may come from *swo- with loss of *w* before *o* (**170**), or may reflect a by-form of the stem without *w*, as in L. *sibi*.

4. G. ἡμέτερος and ἁμός. L. *noster*, from *nos beside *nōs* (**299.**1).

5. G. ὑμέτερος and ὑμός. L. *vester*, early L. *voster*, from *wos beside *vōs* (**299.**1).

6. G. σφέτερος from σφεῖς, etc., after the analogy of ἡμέτερος.

301. *The Greek reflexive pronouns.*—The usual Greek reflexive pronouns are combinations of the personal pronouns with the intensive αὐτός. In Homer they are still uncompounded, as ἐμοὶ αὐτῷ, σοὶ αὐτῷ, ἑοῖ αὐτῷ. The later Ionic forms in Herodotus, ἐμεωυτοῦ, etc., started with the dat. sg. ἑωυτῷ from ἑοῖ αὐτῷ.

The Attic forms, ἐμαυτοῦ, σεαυτοῦ or σαυτοῦ, ἑαυτοῦ or αὑτοῦ, would seem to be most simply explained as starting from the acc. sg. forms ἐμ' αὐτόν, σὲ αὐτόν, ἓ αὐτόν. But if they are properly ἐμαυτοῦ, etc., to which some late forms like ἑᾱτοῦ point, they will rather have started with the dat. sg. ἑοῖ αὐτῷ, like the Ionic forms, corresponding to the latter in the same phonetic relation as Att. ἀνήρ to Ion. ὡνήρ.

a. The dialects have various expressions for the reflexive, as (1) the personal pronouns with αὐτός, as in Homer; (2) αὐτός alone as sometimes in Homer; (3) αὐτὸς αὐτός, αὐτοσαυτός, αὐσαυτός, etc.

302. *The Greek reciprocal pronoun.*—The stem ἀλλᾱλο-, Att.-Ion. ἀλληλο-, occurring only in oblique cases of the dual and plural, originated in phrases like *ἄλλος ἄλλον, *ἄλλοι ἄλλους, etc., parallel to L. *alter alterum, alii alios,* etc. Dissimilation accounts for the simplification of the second λλ. The ᾱ is surprising, for it could arise phonetically only from certain feminine and neuter forms, such as ἄλλᾱ ἄλλᾱν, whence *ἀλλάλᾱν, then with plural ending ἀλλάλᾱs (ἀλλήλᾱs), or *ἄλλα ἄλλα, whence ἄλλᾱλα (ἄλληλα). Its generalization may have been favored by the numerous stem compounds like στρατᾱγός (στρατηγός).

DEMONSTRATIVE, INTERROGATIVE, INDEFINITE, AND RELATIVE PRONOUNS

PECULIARITIES OF DECLENSION

303. The declension of the various classes of pronouns other than personal agrees much more nearly with that of nouns and adjectives. But it presents a number of characteristic peculiarities.

1. *Nom.-acc. sg. neut.*—The IE ending was *-d,* in *o*-stems *-od* in contrast to *-om* of nouns, in *i*-stems *-id* in contrast to *-i* of nouns. In Greek, where a final dental was lost, the difference persisted in *-o* contrasted to *-ov* of nouns. L. *id, illud* (from *-od*), *hoc* from **hod-ce, quod, quid.* G. τό, αὐτό, τοῦτο, ἐκεῖνο, τί. Cf. Skt. *tad, yad, kad,* with the particles *id, cid* (or *tat, cit,* etc., the final *t* and *d* being interchangeable); also, with added particle, Skt. *idam* (:L. *idem*), Goth. *ita, þata* (with Gmc. *t* from *d*).

2. *Nom. sg. masc. in -o.*—G. ὁ, Skt. *sa,* Goth. *sa,* all pointing to an IE **so* without the usual case ending. L. *hic* from **ho-ce* (**306.**₃).

3. *Nom. sg. masc. in -oi.*—L. *quī* from *quoi* (*qoi* in the Duenos inscription; cf. also Osc. p u i). The relative was frequently unaccented, hence the same phonetic development (*quoi, quei, quī*) as in final syllables (**90**).

4. *Nom. sg. fem. in -ai.*—L. *hae-c, quae.* Cf. Osc. p a i , OPruss. *quai, stai,* Av. possessive forms *xᵛaē, θwōi* (from *swai, *twai).

5. *Nom.-acc. pl. neut. in -ai.*—L. *hae-c, quae.* Cf. Osc. p a i , OPruss. *kai* 'what'.

6. *Nom. pl. masc. in -oi.*—In Greek and Latin no longer distinctively pronominal, since it was extended to nouns (**240.**1).

7. The same *i*-element as in 3–6 appears also in the gen. pl. masc. *toisōm (Skt. *teṣām*), which is not represented in Greek or Latin; further in the loc. pl. masc. *toisu (Skt. *teṣu*), but here it had extended to nouns even in the parent speech (**230.**10).

8. A series of forms containing an *sm*-element, such as Skt. dat. sg. *tasmāi,* loc. sg. *tasmin,* is represented in the Italic dialects (Umbr. *esmei* 'huic', p u s m e 'cui'), but not in Latin; in Greek by Cret. ὅτῑμι = ὅτινι and less directly by forms of the personal pronouns ἄμμιν, etc. (**299.**3).

304. 1. *The Latin genitive singular.*—The origin of *eius, huius, cuius* (really, *eiius* etc., **179.**2) and *illīus, istīus, ipsīus* is much disputed. The view preferred here is as follows: The form *cuius*, earlier *quoius*, is a stereotyped nom. sg. masc. of the possessive adjective *cuius, -a, -um*, earlier *quoius, quoiius*, which is most frequently used in early Latin, is attested for the Italic dialects (Osc. p u i i u 'cuia'), and which may further be identified in form with G. ποῖος. That is, from a phrase like *quoiios servos, in which the adjective form might refer to a man or a woman, this form came to serve as the gen. sg. of *quī* and *quis,* receiving some formal support from the still existing genitive forms in *-os* (**245.**2).

After *quoiios were formed **eiios, eius* and **hoiios, hoius, huius*.

The forms like *illīus* may be regarded as old genitives in *-ī* made over into *-ios* after the analogy of **quoiios,* *eiios.

a. In early poetry *quoius, eius, huius* must sometimes be read either as two short syllables or one long. There are grounds for believing the latter reading correct, that is, monosyllabic *quois, eis, huis,* just as *illīus* must sometimes be read *illīs.* All these arose from the fuller forms standing in close combination with a following word and unaccented, by syncope of the vowel of the final syllable.

From *illī(u)s modī, istī(u)s modī* arose further *illīmodī, istīmodī,* with loss of *s* before *m* (**202.**1), and from these again some other forms in *-ī,* as *istī formae.*

2. *The Latin dative singular.*—The ending is the same as the loc. sg. *-ei* of *o*-stems. This served for the masc. and neut. dat. sg. of pronouns in Italic (Osc. dat. sg. *altrei,* cf. also Umbr. *esmei*), and in Latin was further extended to cover the dat. sg. fem., though some examples of a distinct feminine form, as *eae, istae,* occur in early Latin. So *illī, istī, ipsī.*

The datives of *is, hic, quī* go back to *eiiei, *hoiiei, quoiiei,* formed with the same ending to the genitives **eiios (eius),* etc.

The *eiiei* is represented by *eiei* of an inscription and by what is read as *ēī* in early poetry, where, however, monosyllabic *ei* is more common. This latter is perhaps the regular form of the classical period, parallel to the monosyllabic *huic, cui.* For *eī* (with *ī* restored after the analogy of *illī,* etc.) is not attested before Ovid.

The **hoiiei, quoiiei (quoiei* in early inscriptions) are represented by the forms read as *hūic, quōī* in early poetry, beside more usual monosyllabic *huic* (also *hoic, hoice* in inscriptions) and *quoi* (the regular spelling of inscriptions till after 50 B.C.), later *cui.* Dissyllabic *hŭĭc, cŭĭ* occur only in late poetry (Juvenal, Martial).

THE GREEK DEMONSTRATIVE PRONOUNS

305. 1. The definite article, ὁ, ἡ (ἁ), τό, is in origin a demonstrative pronoun. In Homer it still has demonstrative force to a large extent, and if also used as an article it is not an obligatory complement of a noun with definite reference as in Attic (except with proper names). It corresponds to Skt. *sa, sā, tad* and Goth. *sa, so, þata (þat-a),* all from IE **so, *sā, *tod.* The stem was *so-, sā-* in the nom. sg. masc. and fem., but *to-, tā-* in all other cases. So nom. pl. τοί, ταί (cf. Skt. *te, tās*) in most of the West Greek dialects and often in Homer, but replaced by οἱ, αἱ after the analogy of the singular ὁ, ἡ, in Attic-Ionic, etc.

2. ὅδε, ἥδε, τόδε is formed from the preceding by the addition of the particle -δε. The dialects have parallel forms with other particles, as Thess. ὄνε, Arc. ὀνί, Arc.-Cypr. ὀνύ.

3. οὗτος, αὕτη, τοῦτο is also built up from ὁ, ἁ, τό, with the addition of a particle υ (cf. Skt. nom. sg. masc. fem. asāu) and the further addition of what was at first perhaps the nom.-acc. sg. neut. τό repeated (e.g. το-ῦ-το) or used as a particle (e.g. also *ο-ῦ-το). The combination then took on declension based on this final element, with variation of the first syllable only as between οὐ-, του- and αὐ-, ταυ- according to gender. Some dialects have οὐ or του- throughout, as οὗτα, τοῦτα = ταῦτα. Att.-Ion. nom. pl. οὗτοι, αὗται in place of τοῦτοι, ταῦται are like οἱ, αἱ in place of τοί, ταί (see above, 1).

4. ἐκεῖνος is ἐ-κεῖνος with a prefixed pronominal particle like that in L. e-quidem, Osc. e-tanto 'tanta'. κεῖνος, in dialects also κῆνος, is from *κε-ενος, in which the first part is also a pronominal particle like that in L. ce-do, huius-ce, while the second is probably from a demonstrative stem *ἐνο- akin to Skt. ana- (instr. anena) and ChSl. onŭ. Dor. τῆνος corresponds in use, but is of different origin, derived from an adverb seen in Hom. τῇ 'there'.

5. ὁ δεῖνα is of disputed origin. Possibly it started from an acc. sg. τόνδε ἕνα, whence τονδεῖνα, felt as τὸν δεῖνα, with resulting ὁ δεῖνα, etc.

THE LATIN DEMONSTRATIVE PRONOUNS

306. 1. *is, ea, id.*—The forms *is, id,* and an early acc. sg. masc. *im,* are from a stem *i-,* seen also in Osc. *iz-ic,* i d - i k , Goth. *is* 'he', Skt. nom.-acc. sg. neut. *id-am,* acc. sg. masc. *im-am.* The other forms (but for the gen. sg. and dat. sg. see **304**) are from *eo-, eā-,* these from **eyo-, *eyā-,* which perhaps started from some particular case forms (cf. Skt. nom. sg. masc. *ay-am,* Vedic instr. sg. fem. *ayā*).

a. The nom. pl. masc. and dat.-abl. pl. are *eī, eīs* in early Latin, but in the classical period are contracted to *ī, īs,* often spelled *iī, iīs.* In later poets appear again *eī, eīs* restored by analogy. Cf. the corresponding forms of *deus* (**240.**1*b*).

2. *īdem, eadem, idem.*—Formed from the preceding with the addition of a particle *-dem.* Nom. sg. masc. *īdem* from **is-dem* (202.1). But nom.-acc. sg. neut. *idem* is *id-em* with a particle *-em,* like Skt. *id-am.* The abl. sg. forms may also be analyzed as *eōd-em, eād-em,* with the old abl. ending preserved by its medial position. It is possible that these gave rise to the *-dem* of the other forms. But there is also no objection to assuming here (and likewise in forms like *tan-dem, prī-dem*) another particle *-dem,* related to others beginning with *d* as in *quam-de, quī-dam.*

3. *hic, haec, hoc.*—The stem is *ho-, hā-,* as if from an IE **g̑ho-,* but there are no cognates in the other languages except possibly certain enclitic particles of emphasis. The particle *-c(e),* which is optionally added in many forms, as *huius-ce, hōs-ce, hīs-ce,* etc., beside usual *huius,* etc. (in early Latin also *hōrunc, hārunc*), is permanently attached in the singular forms except the genitive and in the nom.-acc. pl. neut. *haec.*

Nom. sg. masc. *hic,* early *hec,* probably with weakening in proclitic use from **ho-ce* (or perhaps first **ho > *he* by 83.3), in which **ho* is an old nom. sg. without *s,* like IE **so,* G. ὁ (303.2). In early poetry the form is always a short syllable before a word beginning with a vowel, but later is more often a long syllable, in which case it is to be understood as *hicc* (as correctly stated by the grammarians and sometimes so written), due to the analogy of nom.-acc. sg. neut. *hoc* which is regularly a long syllable, that is, *hocc* from **hod-ce.*

Acc. sg. masc. *hunc,* early *honc,* from **hom-ce,* as acc. sg. fem. *hanc* from **ham-ce.* Abl. sg. *hōc, hāc* from **hōd-ce, *hād-ce.* For *huius, huic,* see 304.1, 2; for *haec,* see 303.4, 5.

4. *ille, illa, illud.*—The etymology is doubtful. An archaic *olle* or *ollus* is quoted by the grammarians from ancient laws, and some forms of this are used by later writers, as *ollī, olla,* etc. This is perhaps from a stem **ol-no-,* which is the source of certain Slavic forms and of which the first part would be seen in L. *ultra* (from **ol-trād*) and *ōlim.* The usual *ille* might be from *olle,* with the vowel changed under the influence of *is* and *iste.* The *e* of *olle, ille* would be from the analogy of *iste* or others with *e* from the pro-

nominal nom. sg. in -*o* (**303**.2). But there are other possible ways of analyzing these forms and the whole matter is quite uncertain.

5. *iste, ista, istud*.—Probably from *esto- (so Umbr. *esto*, etc.), with change to *isto*- under the influence of *is*. It may contain the stem *to- (Skt. *ta*-, G. το-, **305**.1), but even this analysis is uncertain.

6. *ipse, ipsa, ipsum*.—From *is-pse, that is, *is* with added particle -*pse*, as indicated by early L. *ea-pse, eum-pse, eam-pse, eā-pse* (also in *reāpse* from *rē eāpse*), beside which there are some probable readings with both parts declined, as *eumpsum*. The usual forms are from *ipse* declined after the analogy of *ille, iste*, but with nom.-acc. sg. neut. -*um*, not -*ud* (early Latin also nom. sg. masc. *ipsus*).

7. The rare early L. *sum, sam, sōs, sapsa* (quoted from Ennius), *sumpse* (Plautus) are from the stem IE *so-, *sā-, seen in G. ὁ, ἡ, Skt. *sa, sā* (**305**.1).

THE INTERROGATIVE, INDEFINITE, AND RELATIVE PRONOUNS

307. The Greek interrogative-indefinite, τίς, τί, τὶς, τὶ, the Latin interrogative-indefinite, *quis, quid*, and the Latin relative, *quī, quae, quod*, represent an IE interrogative-indefinite pronoun which is found in all the IE languages. Its use in Latin as a relative is secondary, one that developed in Italic, it being Oscan-Umbrian as well as Latin. The same relative use developed elsewhere, but mostly in the historical period, as in the case of NE *who, which*, which were not used as relatives until the end of the 12th cent. or later.

a. But there is some reason to believe that the indefinite relative use ('whoever', etc.) had already developed in part in the parent speech. This is also the most probable connecting link in the evolution of the Latin definite relative use.

308. The stem was *qʷo- (with fem. *qʷā-) or *qʷi- in the declined forms, also *qʷu- in adverbs. For the phonetic changes of the initial consonant, see **154, 155.5**).

1. *Stem* *qʷo-.—G. πο- in adverbs and derivatives, as ποῦ, πόθεν,

πότερος, ποῖος, etc., L. *quī* (from *quoi*, **303.**3), *quod*. Cf. Osc.
p ú i , p ú d , Skt. *kas*, Goth. *hwas*, Lith. *kas*, ChSl. *kŭ-to*.

2. *Stem* **qʷi-*.—G. τίς, τί, L. *quis, quid*. Cf. Osc. p í s , p í d ,
Av. *ciš*, Skt. particle *cid*, Goth. *hwi-leiks*, OE *hwilc*, NE *which*,
ChSl. *či-to*.

3. *Stem* **qʷu-*, *in adverbs*.—Cf. Skt. *ku-tra* 'where?', *ku-tas*
'whence?', etc. G. ὅπυι in some dialects for usual ὅποι. Osc. p u f
'ubi', p u z 'ut', L. *ubi, ut, unde*. So. L. *uter* with *u* from an adverbial form like Skt. *ku-tra*, in place of *quoter: G. πότερος, Skt.
kataras. Cf. Osc. p ú t e r e í - p í d 'utroque', etc., from **potero-*.

309. G. τίς, τί.—Most of the case forms are from a secondary
stem τιν-, as τίνος, τίνι, τίνα, τίνες, etc. This probably started
from an acc. sg. *τί-ν, this becoming τίνα after the analogy of ἕνα
(acc. sg. of εἷς) through the association in the indefinite use of the
pronoun.

To the original *i*-stem belong τίς, τί, dat. pl. τίσι, and the peculiar Hom. ἄσσα, Att. ἄττα = τινά, which are abstracted from
phrases like πολλά ττα and so are really σσα, ττα from *τια. So
also ἄσσα, ἄττα = ἄτινα are from *ἄτια.

The gen. sg. Hom. τέο, τεῦ, Att. τοῦ = τίνος is from an IE
*qʷesyo with the *e*-grade of the *o*-stem (so Av. *cahyā* in contrast to
Skt. *kasya*). To this gen. sg. τέο were formed dat. sg. τέῳ, τῷ and
Hom. τέων, Hdt. τέοισι.

a. That no τεῖο is attested in Homer, like τοῖο or like ἐμεῖο beside ἐμέο,
may well be accidental. But some scholars believe otherwise and derive τέο
from an IE *qʷeso, attested by OHG *hwes*, ChSl. *česo*.

310. *The declension of L. quī and quis.*—The differentiation
between relative *quī, quae, quod* and interrogative (-indefinite)
quis, quid, while it is by no means an absolute one, is observed
also in the corresponding Oscan-Umbrian forms, and so has its
beginnings in the Italic period. Early L. *quēs* is also indefinite in
contrast to relative *quei*, e.g. *sei ques esent quei sibei deicerent*
in SC de Bacch., *siques homines sunt quos* in Cato.

But in the other case forms there is no trace of such differentiation in the distribution of *o*-stem and *i*-stem forms, which is the
same for all uses.

The fem. *quae* goes normally with masc. *quī*, *quis* being masc. or fem. like other *i*-stems and like G. τίς. But *quae* is sometimes used for the interrogative, and for the indefinite use the usual form is *qua* or sometimes *quae*. So nom. acc. pl. neut. indef. *qua* or *quae*.

The formal distribution of the stems is then as follows, with inclusion in parentheses of the less usual forms or related adverbs, etc.

o-Stem		*ā*-Stem	*i*-Stem	
quī	*quod*	*quae, qua*	*quis*	*quid*
	cuius (304.1)			
	cui (304.2)			
(conj. *quom*)	*quod*	*quam*	*quem*	*quid*
	quō	*quā*		(*quī-cum*, adv. *quī*)
quī	*quae, qua*	*quae*	(*quēs*)	
	quōrum	*quārum*		
	(*quīs*)			*quibus*
quos	*quae, qua*	*quās*		(conj. *quia*)

311. *The Greek relative and indefinite relative pronouns.*

1. ὅς, ἥ (ἄ), ὅ corresponds exactly to the Sanskrit relative *yas*, *yā*, *yad*, stem *ya*-, representing an IE **yo*-, found also in other languages with partly relative, partly demonstrative force.

   a. In Homer and in many dialects the forms of the article are used as relatives.

2. ὅστις, ἥτις, ὅτι is a combination of ὅς and the indefinite, with declension of both parts, as gen. sg. οὖτινος, ἧστινος, etc. There is another set of forms in which only the second part is declined and usually with the shorter forms of τίς in the oblique cases. Thus Hom. ὅτις, ὅττεο, ὅτεω, ὅτινα, ὅτεων, ὀτέοισι, ὅτινας ; Att. ὅτου, ὅτῳ and rarely ὅτων, ὅτοις. The first part is that which belongs to the nom.-acc. sg. neut. ὅτι, Hom. ὅττι (from **ὅδ-τι*, combined before the loss of the final dental), whence ττ in Hom. ὅττεο, Lesb. ὅττινες, etc.

   a. The derivation of ὅτι from a **σϝοδ-τι*, given by some, rests on a single occurrence of ϝότι, which is at variance with all other evidence and probably an error.

NUMERALS

CARDINALS

312. The parent speech had words for 1–10 (though different forms for the colorless 1), with combinations for 11–19; for 20, 30, etc., and 100, 200, etc., with combinations for the intervening numbers; perhaps also for 1,000, though here there is no general agreement.

The system is obviously the decimal, based originally on the counting of the fingers. But there are some traces of the intrusion of a sexagesimal system with its grouping by sixties or the subordinate dozens or scores. Of the digits the first four were declined, the rest indeclinable.

313. 1–10.—1. IE *oi- with various suffixes, as *oi-no-, *oi-wo, *oi-qʷo-. L. ūnus, early oinos, oenus, Goth. ains, OE ān. Cf. Av. aēva- from *oi-wo-, Skt. eka- from *oi-qʷo-. This group is represented in Greek by οἴνη 'ace on the dice', and οἶος 'alone', Cypr. οἶϝος, but not as a numeral.

G. εἷς, Cret. ἕνς, from *sem-s, neut. ἕν from *sem, with extension of ν to ἑνός, etc., fem. μία from *σμια, all related to L. semel, simul, G. ἅμα, ὁμός.

Hom. ἴα (Aeol.), once also ἰός, is from a pronominal stem ι (cf. Cret. ἰός = ἐκεῖνος).

2. IE *duō(u) and *dwō(u), with dual inflection. Skt. dvāu, Vedic dvāu, dvā as one or two syllables, fem. and neut. dve, Goth. twai, OE twā (= Skt. dve).

Hom. δύω (= Vedic dvā in 2 syll.), but δώδεκα from *δϝω (= Vedic dvā in 1 syll.), Hom. also δύο, as regularly in other dialects, probably from δύω by shortening before a word beginning with a vowel (**214.**2). Used indeclinably in Homer and often in Attic, but also Att. gen.-dat. δυοῖν, late δυεῖν; plural forms δυῶν, δυοῖς, δύας, etc., in various dialects and in late Attic.

L. nom. (acc.) masc., nom.-acc. neut. duo, from *duō by iambic shortening, otherwise plural forms as nom. fem. duae, gen. duōrum (also duom, duum), duārum, dat. duōbus, duābus, acc. duōs, duās.

In compounds IE *dwi-, Skt. dvi-pad-, OE twi-fēte, L. bi-pēs, G. δί-πους (for this last some assume a parallel *di-). In Italic also du-, L. du-plex, du-centī, Umbr. du-pla, t u - p l a k , du-pursus 'bipedibus'.

3. IE *tri-, nom. pl. *treyes. Skt. trayas, G. τρεῖς, L. trēs. For declension in Greek see 259.

4. IE *qʷetwer- with gradation, *qʷetwor-, *qʷetur-, *qʷetwr̥-, also *qʷe̥twor-, *qʷtur-, etc.

Skt. nom. pl. catvāras, acc. pl. caturas, Hom. τέσσαρες, Hom. πίσυρες (121, 154.2), Ion. τέσσερες, Att. τέτταρες, Boeot. πέτταρες, Dor. τέτορες (τ instead of σσ, ττ, after τετρα- in dat. pl. τέτρασι from *τετϝρασι, in τέτρατος and in compounds), L. quattuor (121, 209).

In compounds IE *qʷetur-, Skt. catur-, *qʷetwr̥-, G. τετρα- ; *qetru-, Av. čaθru-, L. quadru- (d unexplained, see 315a).

5. IE *peŋqʷe. Skt. pañca, G. πέντε, Lesb., Thess. πέμπε (154.2), L. quīnque (40.8, 79).

In compounds G. πεντε-, but mostly πεντα-, after τετρα-, ἑπτα-, δεκα-.

6. IE *s(w)eks. With w, G. ἕξ, dial. ϝέξ, Av. xšvaš, W. chwech; without w, L. sex, Skt. ṣaṣ, Goth. saíhs, Lith. šeši.

In compounds G. ἑξ- (ἑκ-, ἑσ-), and ἑξα- after ἑπτα- etc.

7. IE *septm̥. Skt. sapta, Goth. sibun, OE seofon, G. ἑπτά, L. septem.

8. IE *oḱtō(u), a dual form. Skt. aṣṭā(u), Goth. ahtau, G. ὀκτώ, L. octō.

In compounds G. ὀκτω-, and ὀκτα- after ἑπτα-, etc.

9. IE *newn̥, *enwn̥. Skt. nava, Goth. niun, L. novem (m from septem, decem). G. *ἐνϝα in ordinal Hom. εἴνατος, Att. ἔνατος (176.1). G. ἐννέα difficult, but probably a blend of *ἐνϝα and *νεϝα.

10. IE *dekm̥. Skt. daça, Goth. taíhun, G. δέκα, L. decem.

314. 11-19.—Compounds or compound phrases. Skt. ekādaça, dvādaça, etc.

G. ἕνδεκα, δώδεκα, dial. also δυώδεκα, δυόδεκα, δέκα δύο, τρεῖς καὶ δέκα or (especially when the subject precedes) δέκα τρεῖς, etc.

L. *ūndecim* (from **oinc-decem* formed after stem compounds like *ūniversus*), *duodecim, trēdecim* (**trēs-decem*, **202.**1), *quattuordecim, quīndecim, sēdecim* (**sex-decem*, **207.**1), *septendecim*, all with *-decim* for which we should expect rather *-dicem*. Also *octōdecim, novendecim*, but usually *duodēvīgintī, ūndēvīgintī*. Also *decem duo* (cf. Umbr. *desen-duf*), *decem et duo*, etc.

315. 20–90.—Compounds of **k̑m̥t-, *k̑omto-*, etc., probably from **dk̑m̥t-*, etc., from **dek̑m̥*. Skt. *viṅçati-, triṅçat-*, etc.

Dor. ϝίκατι, Att. εἴκοσι (**ε-ϝικοσι*, with prothetic ε; ο after -κοντα; East G. -σι from -τι), L. *vīgintī*, from an IE dual form **wi-k̑m̥tī*, this probably by dissimilation from **dwi-k̑m̥tī*.

G. τριάκοντα, τετταράκοντα (but Dor. τετρώκοντα), πεντήκοντα, ἑξήκοντα, but from ordinal forms ἑβδομήκοντα, ὀγδοήκοντα, ἐνενήκοντα.

L. *trīgintā, quadrāgintā, quīnquāgintā, sexāgintā, septuāgintā* (*septu-* unexplained), *octōgintā, nōnāgintā* (from ordinal).

a. The second part of these numerals for 30–90 is a neuter plural of **k̑omto-, *k̑m̥to-* (or *k̑m̥t-*), with final *ā* in Latin in contrast to the usual neuters (**240.**5, **246.**6). The first part is likewise a neuter plural in L. *trīgintā* (with *trī* like Vedic neut. pl. *trī*, in contrast to usual *tria* from **triā* with *o*-stem ending, **261.**5), G. τριάκοντα (τριά with *o*-stem ending, whence usual τρία), τετταράκοντα; so perhaps, with *o*-stem ending, L. *quadrāgintā*, whence by analogy *quinquāgintā*, etc. The lengthening in πεντήκοντα, whence ἑξήκοντα, etc., and in Dor. τετρώκοντα, is possibly due to the analogy of τριάκοντα. But the explanation of these forms and of L. *quadrāgintā*, etc., is far from certain.

The L. *int* for *ent* is perhaps due to vowel assimilation in *vīgintī*, whence by analogy also *quadrāgintā*, etc. (in contrast to *quadringentī*, etc.).

There is no adequate explanation of the voiced in place of voiceless stop in several of the numeral forms, namely *d* for *t* in L. *quadru-, quadrāgintā, quadringentī*, *g* for *c* in L. *vīgintī, trīgintā*, etc., *quadringentī, quīngentī*, etc. (beside *ducentī, trecentī, sescentī*). Cf. also G. ἕβδομος, ὄγδοος (**318**).

316. 100, 200, etc.—IE **k̑m̥to-*, like the second part of the words for 20, 30, etc., but used alone for a decad of decads. Originally declined and construed as a neuter noun, as in Sanskrit, Germanic, Celtic, and Balto-Slavic, but an indeclinable adjective in Greek and Latin. Skt. *çata-*, nom.-acc. sg. *çatam*.

L. *centum*, G. ἑκατόν, that is, ἑ-κατόν 'one hundred', a blend of **ἕν κατόν* and **ἁ-κατόν*.

G. διᾱκόσιοι, τριᾱκόσιοι, etc., Arc. -κάσιοι, Dor. -κατιοι, from *-ḱṃtio-, with Att.-Ion. o for α (as in εἴκοσι) after the forms in -κοντα. διᾱκόσιοι (instead of *δικοσιοι) after τριᾱκόσιοι.

L. ducentī, etc. (rarely also ducentum, etc., as neuter nouns), from *-ḱṃto-. trecentī from *tricentī with vowel assimilation, sescentī from *sex-centī (207); with unexplained g for c (see also 315a, end) quīngentī from *quīnqu(e)centī, septingentī from *sep-tem-centī (79.1), nōngentī from *novemcentī (92.2c), and, after the analogy of these three, also quadringentī, octingentī.

317. 1,000.—Att. χῑ́λιοι (ῑ from ē, 96d), Ion. χείλιοι, Lac. χήλιοι Lesb. χέλλιοι, from *χεσλιοι (203.2), may be connected with Skt. sahasra-, this being analyzed as sa-hasra- 'one thousand'. L. mīlle has also been combined with these on the basis of a feminine abstract *smī ĝhslī (*smī = G. μία, ĝhslī with weak grade of *ĝheslo-), but this is quite uncertain.

ORDINALS

318. The ordinals, except those for 'first' and 'second', are de-rived from the cardinals with the suffixes -to- or -mo-, or some-times with simple -o-. Cf. Skt. caturthas 'fourth' but daçamas 'tenth', saptathas or saptamas 'seventh', L. quārtus, quīntus, sextus, but septimus (*septṃ-o-), decimus (*deḱṃ-o-), nōnus (*novenos, 92.2d). Greek has -mo- only in ἕβδομος, otherwise -to-, as πρῶτος, τρίτος, τέταρτος, etc.

G. πρῶτος from *prō-to-, Dor. πρᾶτος from a weak grade (as in Skt. pūrvas 'in front, former', Lith. pirmas 'first'), L. prīmus from *prīs-mo- (cf. prīscus). Cf. Umbr. promom, OE forma and fyrst, Skt. prathamas, etc., all from varieties of *pro 'before'.

G. δεύτερος from δεύω 'fail to reach', hence 'behindhand, second' (cf. δεύτατος 'last').

L. secundus, pple. (see 170, 439) of sequor, hence 'following'.

L. tertius from *tritio- (cf. 109) beside G. τρίτος from *tri-to-. Cf. Skt. tṛtīyas.

L. quārtus (for ā, see 99.2b), quartus, with a after quattuor, from *quortos (cf. Praen. Quorta), this from *qᵘtwṛto- (cf. G. τέτρατος from *τετϝρατος, Lith. *ketwirtas;* *quortos* instead of *tuortos by influence of *quattuor*).

G. ἕβδομος, Dor. ἕβδεμος from *ἕβδμος, *sebdmo- (cf. ChSl. sedmŭ), this by assimilation from *septmo-, *septṃo-, L. *septimus*.

G. ὄγδοος from ὄγδοϝος (now attested) and L. *octāvus* reflect some such form as *oktōwos from *oktōu (**313.**8), but the precise phonetic development is obscure.

MULTIPLICATIVES

319. The term "multiplicative" is commonly applied to forms like G. τριπλοῦς, L. *triplex*, NE *threefold* or *triple*. In their use they cover a variety of relations to the numeral, some of which may also be distinguished by distinctive formal types. In origin they are possessive compounds of words meaning 'fold' or the like, and their first extension from the literal meaning was to ('three' serving here as typical) 'having three parts', as in L. *triplex mundus*, the threefold world of sky, land, and sea.

Hence also 'of three kinds', a use shading off imperceptibly from the preceding, but one for which special types may develop, as late L. *trifārius*, NHG *dreierlei*.

Hence also (with less subordination of the parts to the whole) 'consisting of three in a group', as in L. *triplex mūrus* 'a triple wall', that is, a series of three walls, or NE *triple play, triple victory* (three together). This is the collective use, for which there may be also distinctive formal types called "collectives".

Hence also (a group of three being a given unit raised to the third power) 'three times as much or as many', as in L. *duplex centuriōnī, triplex equitī* 'double pay to the centurion, triple pay to the knight'. This is the proportional use, for which there may also be distinctive types sometimes called "proportionals". So Att. τριπλάσιος, though τριπλοῦς is used in the same sense in most dialects and sometimes in Attic; L. *triplus*, though *triplex* is also so used.

320. The common multiplicatives of Greek, Italic, and the Germanic languages are compounds the second part of which contains the root *pel- 'fold' or the same with a guttural (cf. G.

πλέκω, L. *plicō*) or dental extension (cf. Goth. *falþan*, OE *fealdan* 'fold').

G. τριπλόος, τριπλοῦς (dial. also διπλεῖος), L. *triplus*, Umbr. *tripler.*

L. *triplex*, Umbr. t u p l a k 'duplex', Hom. τρίπλαξ 'with three bands', δίπλαξ 'with two folds'.

Att. τριπλάσιος (proportional use) from a *τρί-πλα-τος (like ἀμβρόσιος from ἄμβροτος) beside poet. τρί-παλ-τος. Also τριπλασίων with comparative form favored by the meaning and frequent construction with following ἤ. Ion. τριπλήσιος (Hdt.), if genuine, is after the analogy of adjectives in -ησιος.

Cf. Goth. *ainfalþs*, OE *þrīfeald*, NE *threefold* (while NE *triple* is from L. *triplus*).

a. Other, less common, Greek types are:

τριφάσιος (Hdt.) 'of three kinds' or collective, from *τρι-φατος, probably to φαίνω.

τρίπτυχος, from πτύξ 'fold'.

τριφυής, τρίφυιος 'of three parts, kinds' and proportional, from φῠ- 'be' (cf. φύσις 'nature'). Cf. El. δίφυιος = Att. διπλάσιος ; δεκάφυια ζωάγρια 'tenfold rewards' in Callimachus.

τρισσός, Att. τριττός, from *τριχιος, from adv. τρίχα ; Ion. τριξός from *τριχθιος from adv. τριχθά. Mostly collective 'consisting of three', in Hellenistic times frequent for 'in three copies, in triplicate'.

b. The Latin adverbs *bifāriam*, *trifāriam* mean 'in two (three) parts', so *multifāriam* 'in many places'. The adjectives *trifārius*, etc., derived from them, do not occur till the 2d cent. A.D., and the specialized sense 'of three kinds', etc. (reflected in NE *multifarious*), belongs mainly to mediaeval Latin.

c. A distinctive type of numeral derivative, not a multiplicative, is G. τριταῖος 'on the third day', etc.

DISTRIBUTIVES

321. The Latin distributives *bīnī*, *ternī*, etc., are in origin collectives. That is, their "non-distributive" use in *bīnās litterās*, etc., is the earlier, and they gained their distributive force from the context, in which the distributive notion was already expressed, as it continued to be in large measure. Thus where Greek used the simple cardinals with a distributive word or phrase, as ἑκάστῳ δύο 'two for each', Latin used the collectives, as *ūnīcuique*

bīnī 'two together for each'. The collectives are particularly appropriate for such a context, and became fixed in Latin usage,
themselves absorbing distributive force.

They are related to certain collective forms in Germanic and
Balto-Slavic, and like them are formed with the suffix *-no-*. Thus
bīnī from **dwis-no-* (cf. *bis* from **dwis*), *trīnī* (preferred in the old
collective use) from **tris-no-*, while *ternī* is formed anew from *ter*
(this from **tris*), *quaternī* from *quater*, and, by analogy of *bīnī*,
trīnī, also *quīnī*, *sēnī* (**sex-noi*), *septēnī*, *octōnī*, *novēnī*, *dēnī*, etc.

Different of course is *singulī*, a derivative of **sem-* in *semel*, etc.

There is no series of distributive adjectives in Greek or in any
other IE language except Latin. Distribution is expressed in
Greek by the cardinals with some form of ἕκαστος or εἷς, or a
prepositional phrase. Thus πέντε ἑκάστῳ (or καθ' ἕκαστον, καθ' ἕνα)
or ἀνὰ πέντε 'five apiece'.

COLLECTIVES

322. As previously noted, the multiplicatives may have collective sense, and there are certain derivatives that are primarily
adjective collectives, as G. τρισσός, etc. (see **320a**), likewise Hom.
δοιοί, and in origin the Latin distributives.

The collective notion may also be expressed in prepositional
phrases, as G. ἀνὰ τρεῖς 'by threes'. Such phrases are commonly
called distributive, but where the meaning is simply 'by threes, in
groups of three', they should obviously be classed as collective.
In many languages the same phrase is used both for the collective
and for the true distributive sense. So G. ἀνὰ τρεῖς is, according
to the context, either 'by threes' or 'three apiece'.

Collective nouns, meaning 'group of three, triad', etc., occur in
the IE languages in considerable variety, partly in specialized
applications. Cf. NE *quartette, sextette* in music, but *foursome* in
golf, *decade* in time, etc. The principal series in Greek and Latin
are:

G. τριάς, -αδος, etc. These started in forms like ἑπτάς, δεκάς
with α from IE *ṃ*. Cf. Skt. *daçat-* 'decad', also *pañcad-* 'pentad',
etc. By analogy also μονάς 'unit' from μόνος.

L. *ternĭō*, etc., formed from *ternī*, etc., after the type *legiō*, *legiōnis*, etc.

Other, more specialized types are:

G. τριττύς 'sacrifice of three animals' and a division of the tribe, πεντηκοστύς, 'body of fifty men', χῑλιοστύς 'body of a thousand men'.

L. *decuria*, *centuria*, Umbr. *dequrier* 'decuriis'. Cf. Osc. p u m p e r i a s 'quincuriae', OIr. *cōicer* 'group of five', and others, pointing to an IE type of collectives with *r*, possibly starting from a *q^wetwer-yā-*, *q^wetur-yā* (cf. **313**.4).

NUMERAL ADVERBS

323. The most distinctive class and the one to which the term "numeral adverbs" is often applied specifically is that denoting how many times.[1]

G. ἅπαξ from ἁ-(IE *$s\underline{m}$-) and an adverbial form from the root of πήγνῡμι, ἐπάγην 'fix'

L. *semel*, likewise from *sem-* (cf. *simul*). Cf. Skt. *sa-kṛt* 'once'

IE *dwis*, Skt. *dvis*, G. δίς, L. *bis*

IE *tris*, Skt. *tris*, G. τρίς, L. *ter*

L. *quater* from *quatrus* = Av. *caθruš*.

G. τετράκις, πεντάκις, etc. (dial. also -ι and -ιν, cf. Att. πάλιν)

L. *quīnquiē(n)s*, *sexiē(n)s*, etc., like *totiē(n)s*, *quotiē(n)s*, formed with *-ient* (IE *-ṇt-*, cf. Skt. *kiyat* 'how much?')+adverbial *s* (as in *bis*, also *abs*, etc.)

a. In late times these adverbs came to be replaced by phrases analogous to NE *three times* (now usual for *thrice*, while *twice* persists), etc. So Hellenistic τρεῖς καιρούς (NG τρεῖς φορές ; cf. G. φορά 'movement', πίνειν κατὰ φοράν 'drink at one gulp') late L. *tribus vicibus* (Fr. *trois fois*).

b. Among other numeral adverbs are: G. τρίχα or τριχθά 'in three parts or ways', τετραχθά, πένταχα, etc., hence also τριχῇ, τριχοῦ, τριχῶς in same meaning; τριπλῇ, τριπλῶς, τρισσῶς, etc.

---

[1] These are also sometimes called multiplicative adverbs, but they are clearly not co-ordinate with the multiplicative adjectives. An adverb corresponding to an adjective like τριπλοῦς 'of three parts', etc., is one like τρίχα 'in three parts'; conversely an adjective corresponding to an adverb meaning 'three times' is one meaning 'occurring three times', like NHG *dreimalig*. Such an adjective type, where it exists, is derived from the adverbs, and there is no such type in Greek or Latin. The term multiplicative was originally and is still most commonly applied to adjectives like G. τριπλοῦς, L. *triplex*, and is best retained in this application.

PREPOSITIONS

324. The discussion of prepositions and their uses belongs properly to the dictionary, or under the head of syntax. But it may be noted here that about half of the Greek and Latin prepositions are formally related to each other, although in some cases their meanings have widely diverged.

Greek	Latin	Greek	Latin
ἀντί	ante	ἐπί	ob
ἀπό	ab, abs, ā	περί	per
ἐν	} in	πρό	prō
εἰς		ὑπέρ	super (**167**)
ἐξ, ἐκ	ex, ē	ὑπό	sub (**167**)

a. G. ἐν was originally used with acc. and dat., just as L. *in* with acc. and abl., and this double use of ἐν persisted in several dialects. But in others the ἐν with acc. was replaced by an extension ἐν-ς, whence (**204.**4) ἐς or εἰς.

VERBS

SURVEY OF THE VERB SYSTEM

325. *Voice.*—The parent speech had two voices, an active and a medio-passive. The latter is represented by the Greek and Sanskrit middle, a type common to Greek and Indo-Iranian, with relics in other branches; and also by the Latin deponent-passive, a different formal type, common to Italic and Celtic and now attested in Tocharian and Hittite. There was no specifically passive voice. Apart from the use of the middle in passive sense, the forms used to express the passive are different in the several languages and grew up independently.

a. The middle was used for actions in which the subject was intimately concerned (more than as the mere doer), what one did to oneself (reflexive middle), for oneself, with one's own possessions, what one felt oneself, etc. Its force is best observed from Greek usage. But even here the distinction from the active is often subtle, and sometimes wholly illusive. In Latin the passive use was the dominant one. The deponents show some agreement with the middle elsewhere, either in the individual word, as *sequitur* = G. ἕπεται, Skt. *sacate*, or in the type of words. But the distinction from the active had mostly vanished, and the deponents were felt simply as "passive forms with active meaning". In late Latin the deponents were more and more replaced by active forms, until they finally disappeared.

326. *Mood.*—The moods of the parent speech were the indicative, subjunctive, optative, and imperative, as in Greek and Indo-Iranian. The functions of the subjunctive and optative are best observed from Greek usage, which agrees in its main lines with that of the Veda. In Latin (likewise in the Italic dialects) the subjunctive and optative were merged, in both form and function, in the one mood known as the subjunctive. The same is true of the Germanic languages, and in present spoken English even the subjunctive is virtually obsolete. In classical Sanskrit the subjunctive disappears (except the forms of the first person serving as imperative), only the optative remaining in use. In Greek the use of the optative is on the wane in the Hellenistic period, being infrequent in the New Testament, and it eventually disappears.

a. In Vedic Sanskrit (and in the earliest Avestan) the augmentless past tenses of the indicative are often used with subjunctive force, especially in prohibitions introduced by *mā* (= G. *μή*). This doubtless reflects a usage of the parent speech, and the Italic and Celtic *ā*-subjunctive rests on such a use of certain indicative forms.

The term "injunctive" is often employed in this connection. But one must guard against supposing that this is a distinct formal category, co-ordinate with the other moods. It must be understood as a short expression for "past indicative forms with subjunctive force".

327. *Tense.*—The tenses of the parent speech served to denote differences in the "aspect" of the action, and to some extent also differences of time. It is the aspect of the action that was indicated by the different tense stems, while certain tenses of these tense stems denoted past time. Thus:

Present stem, action going on, situation

Present indicative, such action or situation in present (or sometimes future, or indefinite) time

Imperfect indicative, such action or situation in past time

Aorist stem, momentary action, the point of beginning (ingressive aorist) or end (resultative aorist), or more generally action viewed in summary without reference to duration

Aorist indicative, such action in past time

Perfect stem, action completed

Perfect indicative, action completed with present result. Present state of the subject, resulting from previous action or experience

There was probably no distinctive future tense, future time being expressed by the present indicative, by the subjunctive, or by certain *s*-formations with desiderative and future force (see **388**).

There were no tenses of relative time (i.e. relative to time other than that of the speaker) like the Latin pluperfect and future perfect; nor past and future forms of the true (present) perfect, like the Greek pluperfect and future perfect.

a. The tense values assumed for the parent speech are substantially those observed in Greek. In Latin the original perfect and aorist are merged in the perfect, and apart from the distinction in use between imperfect and perfect, which still survives in the Romance languages, the Latin tenses are purely temporal. In general the tendency in most of the IE languages has been to use the simple tenses for distinctions of time, leaving the aspect of the action either unexpressed or expressed by other means. In the Slavic languages there is an elaborate and subtle system of aspects, two parallel conjugations known as "imperfective" and "perfective", of which the latter has much in common with certain values (not all) of the old aorist.

b. In the perfect indicative the completed action from which comes the present result may be lost sight of, so that the form is in feeling a simple present. Thus IE **woida* 'I have seen' (cf. L. *vīdī*), hence simply 'I know', as in G. οἶδα, Skt. *véda*, Goth. *wait*.

In line with its original value of indicating the state of the subject is the fact that it may stand in contrast with a transitive present active and in agreement with a present middle, as G. πέποιθα 'am persuaded', in contrast to πείθω 'persuade', but like πείθομαι ; or again the fact that in many verbs only the perfect middle occurs, or is earlier than the perfect active.

In Homer (as also mostly in the Rigveda) the perfect still indicates the present state of the subject, as πέποιθα 'am persuaded', τέθνηκε 'is dead', ἕστηκε 'is standing', etc., and so also in the few cases where the verb is transitive, as μυρί' Ὀδυσσεὺς ἐσθλὰ ἔοργεν, describing Odysseus as one who has wrought countless brave deeds and so is of proved prowess. From cases like the last it is an easy transition to the situation where the result is not any particular state of the subject and the perfect denotes simply completed action as in τοῦτο δέδωκε 'has given this'. This wider use of the perfect is well established only from the 5th cent. B.C. on. The further step, the use of the perfect as a simple past tense, the "historical perfect", is sometimes observed in the Attic writers, and becomes common in the Hellenistic period. This confusion with the aorist eventually led to the disappearance of the perfect except for a few survivals in modern aorist forms. In its older value its place was taken by periphrastic expressions like ἔχω γράψας or ἔχω γε-γραμμένον.

Similar transitions in the use of the perfect took place at various periods in the other IE languages. In Latin the development of the historical perfect belongs to the prehistoric period.

c. The term "aspect", though first applied to the peculiar Slavic system, is used above in a broader sense. It is convenient, in its very vagueness, as covering certain disparate non-temporal distinctions which are difficult to define precisely and differ greatly in the several languages.

328. *Number.*—Like the noun, the verb had a dual as well as singular and plural. Dual forms of the second and third person were freely employed in Greek, but eventually disappeared, like the dual forms of the noun (**227**).

329. *Non-finite forms. Infinitives and participles.*

1. *Infinitives.*—The infinitive is in origin a case form of a noun which has become attached to the verb system, sharing in some of the characteristics of a verb, such as voice, tense, and construction with the direct object. The process had no doubt begun in the parent speech, but without stabilization of any particular set of forms as infinitives. This is indicated by the situation in Vedic Sanskrit with its multiplicity of forms serving as infinitives, and by the great diversity between the forms which became established as infinitives in the several IE languages.

2. *Participles.*—The parent speech had:

Active participles, formed with the suffix *-nt-*.

Perfect active participles, formed with the suffix *-wes-*.

Middle participles, formed with the suffix *-meno-*.

Verbal adjectives formed from the root or verb stem (not from a tense stem) with the suffixes *-to-* or *-no-*, having for the most part the force of a past passive participle (**437.**1) but also formed from intransitive verbs.

PERSONAL ENDINGS

330. The personal endings that are common to several tenses are for convenience discussed in advance of the treatment of tense formation. But certain endings that are peculiar to the perfect, and others that are peculiar to the imperative, are discussed later in connection with these formations.

The two sets of endings known as primary and secondary are so called from their distribution as it appears most clearly in Greek and Sanskrit, namely, primary endings in the present indicative, secondary endings in the imperfect and aorist and in the optative, with fluctuation in the subjunctive. There are relics of a similar distribution in other branches of IE, but in Celtic it is along entirely different lines.

For the difference between thematic and unthematic forms, which must be alluded to in discussing the endings, see **349.**1*a*.

PERSONAL ENDINGS OF THE ACTIVE

331. Table of the active personal endings.

IE		SANSKRIT		GREEK		LATIN	
Primary	Secondary	Primary	Secondary	Primary	Secondary	Primary	Secondary
Singular							
1 *-mi, -ō*	*-m, -m̥*	*-mi*	*-m, -am*	-μι, -ω	-ν, -α	*-ō*	*-m*
2 *-si*	*-s*	*-si*	*-s*	-σι	*-s*		*-s*
3 *-ti*	*-t*	*-ti*	*-t*	-τι	O	(Osc.-*t*) *-t*	(Osc., early L. *-d*)
Dual							
1 *-wes, -wos*	*-we*	*-vas*	*-va*				
2 *-tes* (?)	*-tom*	*-thas*	*-tam*	-τον	-τον		
3 *-tes*	*-tām*	*-tas*	*-tām*	-τον	-τᾱν, Att.-Ion. -την		
Plural							
1 *-mes, -mos*	*-me* (?)	*-mas*	*-ma*	Dor. -μες, Att. -μεν		*-mus*	
2 *-te* (?)	*-te*	*-tha*	*-ta*	-τε		*-tis*	
3 *-nti*	*-nt*	*-nti*	*-n*	-ντι	-ν	(Osc.-*nt*)-*nt*	(Osc.-*ns*)
-enti	*-ent*	*-anti*	*-an*	-εντι	-εν	(Osc. *-ent*)	(Osc. *-ens*)
-n̥ti	*-n̥t*	*-ati*		-ατι			
				-αντι	-αν		

332. Table of present and imperfect indicative active, thematic.

IE	Sanskrit	Greek	Latin	Gothic
		Present		
Sing.				
1 * *bhérō*	*bhárāmi*	φέρω	*legō*	*baíra*
2 * *bhéresi*	*bhárasi*	φέρεις	*legis*	*baíris*
3 * *bhéreti*	*bhárati*	φέρει	*legit*	*baíriþ*
Plur.				
1 * *bhéromes, -mos*	*bhárāmas*	Dor. φέρομες, Att. -μεν	*legimus*	*baíram*
2 * *bhérete*	*bháratha*	φέρετε	*legitis*	*baíriþ*
3 * *bhéronti*	*bháranti*	Dor. φέροντι, Att. φέρουσι	*legunt*	*baírand*
		Imperfect		
Sing.				
1 * *ébherom*	*ábharam*	ἔφερον	[*legēbam*	
2 * *ébheres*	*ábharas*	ἔφερες	*legēbās*	
3 * *ébheret*	*ábharat*	ἔφερε	*legēbat*	
Plur.				
1 * *ébherome*	*ábharāma*	Dor. ἐφέρομες, Att. -μεν	*legēbāmus*	
2 * *ébherete*	*ábharata*	ἐφέρετε	*legēbātis*	
3 * *ébheront*	*ábharan*	ἔφερον	*legēbant*]	
Dual				
2 * *ébheretom*	*ábharatam*	ἐφέρετον		
3 * *ébheretām*	*ábharatām*	ἐφερέτην, Dor. -τᾱν		

333. Table of present and imperfect indicative active, unthematic.

IE	Sanskrit	Greek	Latin	Old Lithuanian
		Present		
Sing.				
1 * *ésmi*	*ásmi*	εἰμί, Lesb. ἔμμι	*sum*	*esmi*
2 * *éssi, ési*	*ási*	εἶ, εἶς, ἐσσί	*es*	*esi*
3 * *ésti*	*ásti*	ἐστί	*est*	*esti*
Plur.				
1 * *smés, smós*	*smás*	ἐσμέν, εἰμέν	*sumus*	*esme*
2 *stḗ	*sthá*	ἐστέ	*estis*	*este*
3 *sénti	*sánti*	Dor. ἐντί, Att. εἰσί	*sunt*, O.-U. *sent*	Goth. *sind*
		Imperfect		
Sing.				
1 * *ésm̥*	*ásam*	ἦα, ἦ, ἦν	[*eram*	
2 * *éss*	*ā́s, ā́sīs*	ἦσθα	*erās*	
3 * *ést*	*ā́s, ā́sīt*	Dor. ἦς, Att. ἦν	*erat*	
Plur.				
1 * *ésme*	*ā́sma*	ἦμεν	*erāmus*	
2 * *éste*	*ásta*	ἦστε, ἦτε	*erātis*	
3 * *ésent*	*ásan*	Dor. ἦν, Att. ἦσαν	*erant*]	

334. Other examples of unthematic present and imperfect indicative active.

Sanskrit	Greek	Latin	Sanskrit	Greek	Sanskrit	Greek
			Present			
Sing.						
1 *émi*	εἶμι	*eō*	*dádhāmi*	τίθημι	*sunómi*	δείκνῡμι
2 *éṣi*	εἶ	*īs*	*dádhāsi*	τίθης	*sunóṣi*	δείκνῡς
3 *éti*	εἶσι	*it*	*dádhāti*	Dor. τίθητι, Att. -σι	*sunóti*	δείκνῡσι
Plur.						
1 *imás*	ἴμεν	*īmus*	*dadhmás*	τίθεμεν	*sunumás*	δείκνυμεν
2 *ithá*	ἴτε	*ītis*	*dhatthá*	τίθετε	*sunuthá*	δείκνυτε
3 *yánti*	ἴᾱσι	*eunt*	*dádhati*	Dor. τίθεντι Att. τιθέᾱσι	*sunvánti*	Dor. *δείκν- υντι, Att. δεικνύᾱσι
			Imperfect			
Sing.						
1 *áyam*	ἦα, ἦειν	[*ībam* etc.]	*ádadhām*	ἐτίθην	*ásunavam*	ἐδείκνῡν
2 *áis*	ἦεισθα, ἦεις		*ádadhās*	ἐτίθεις	*ásunos*	ἐδείκνῡς
3 *áit*	Hom. ἦε, Att. ἦει(ν)		*ádadhāt*	ἐτίθει	*ásunot*	ἐδείκνῡ
Plur.						
1 *áima*	ἦμεν		*ádadhma*	ἐτίθεμεν	*ásunuma*	ἐδείκνυμεν
2 *áita*	ἦτε		*ádhatta*	ἐτίθετε	*ásunuta*	ἐδείκνυτε
3 *áyan*	ἦεσαν, ἦσαν, etc.		*ádadhus*	Dor. ἐτί- θεν, Att. ἐτίθεσαν	*ásunvan*	Dor. ἐδείκ- νυν, Att. ἐδείκνυσαν

335. *First singular.*—Primary ending -*mi* in unthematic forms, -*ō* in thematic (the thematic vowel being included in the -*ō*), as in G. εἰμί, τίθημι, etc., but φέρω, λέγω, etc. In Sanskrit the -*mi* was extended to thematic verbs. In Latin the -*mi* is not represented, the -*m* of *sum, inquam* being the secondary ending. For iambic shortening in *volo, nescio*, and eventually short *o* in all forms except monosyllables, see **102.**

Secondary -*m* after vowels, L. -*m*, G. -*ν*. Secondary -*m̥* after consonants, G. -*a* in Hom. ἦα and in the aorist, as ἔλῡσα. (In Skt. *āsam*, etc., the *m* is added after the analogy of the thematic forms.)

336. *Second singular.*—Primary -*si* in Hom. ἐσσί from *es-si, and in εῖ from *esi (Skt. *asi*), whence also Hom. εῖs with s added after the analogy of φέρεις, etc.; εῖ (to εἶμι) from *ei-si (Skt. *eṣi*). Other μι-verbs have the secondary ending, as τίθης, ἵστης, δίδως, δείκνῡς. But a Dor. τίθησι occurs, perhaps formed anew after ἐσσί or with -ι from 3 sg. τίθητι.

The thematic form, as φέρεις, is best explained as coming from *φερει, representing IE *bheresi (according to another view it would represent an original form in -*ei*), with addition of the secondary ending -*s* after the analogy of ἔφερες.

The -σθα in Hom. ἦσθα, τίθησθα, etc. spread from perfect forms like οἶσ-θα in which the ending is -θα (**402.**1), ἦσθα itself being perhaps in origin such a perfect form, that is, ἦσ-θα.

L. -*s* may represent either the primary -*si* with loss of the final *i* (as in 3 sg., 3 pl., **337**, **340**), or the secondary -*s*, or both.

337. *Third singular.*—The primary -*ti* appears in Greek only in unthematic forms, as ἐστί, Dor. τίθητι, δίδωτι, Att. τίθησι, δίδωσι.

The thematic form, as φέρει, cannot possibly come from IE *bhereti, which would give a Dor. *φερετι, Att. *φερεσι. It seems to be formed to 2 sg. φέρεις after the analogy of the relation between 2 sg. ἔφερες and 3 sg. ἔφερε.

The secondary -*t* was regularly lost in Greek (**211.**1), hence ἔφερε, and ἦs from *ἦσ-τ, the regular form preserved in most dialects, but in Attic-Ionic replaced by the originally 3 pl. ἦν (**340.**2).

In Italic the endings -*ti* and -*t* became respectively -*t* and -*d*, the difference between primary and secondary endings being thus still maintained. Cf. Osc. 3 sg. pres. indic. f a a m a t , k a s i t but 3 sg. perf. indic. k ú m b e n e d , 3 sg. pres. subj. f a k i i a d . In early Latin too, inscriptions have *fhefhaked, feced, sied*, but usually -*t* in all tenses, as later.

338. *First plural.*—The primary -*mes*, -*mos* is represented by Dor. -μες (common to most of the West Greek dialects) and by L. -*mus*. The -μεν of Attic-Ionic, etc., agrees with Skt. secondary -*ma* except for the final ν (of uncertain source) and is doubtless in origin the secondary ending. But the actual distribution of -μες and -μεν, is not one of primary and secondary ending, one or the other being generalized according to the dialect.

339. *Second plural.*—The Sanskrit distinction between primary -*tha* and secondary -*ta* is perhaps not original. At any rate other languages point only to -*te*. So G. -τε, and L. -*te* in the imperative. L. -*tis* is from -*te-s*, with *s* added after the analogy of the 2 sg. ending -*s*.

340. *Third plural.* 1. *Thematic.*—Primary -*onti* in Dor. φέρουτι, Arc. φέρουσι, Lesb. φέροισι, Att.-Ion. φέρουσι (204.2), L. *ferunt*, -*ont* in early inscriptions. (The reading *tremonti* in a quotation from the Carmen Saliare is open to doubt. All other evidence indicates that -*nti* became -*nt* in the Italic period.) Secondary -*ont*, whence with loss of the final dental G. ἔφερον.

2. *Unthematic -enti, -ent.*—IE **sénti*, Skt. *sánti*, Goth. *sind*, Osc.-Umbr. *sent*, G. **εντί*, whence, with substitution of ' after the analogy of all the other present forms, Dor. ἐντί, Att.-Ion. εἰσί. For Hom. ἔασι beside εἰσί, see below, 5. IE **ésent*, Skt. *ásan*, G. ἦεν, ἦν used as 3 sg. in Attic-Ionic, but originally 3 pl. as is ἦν regularly in the Doric dialects. Att.-Ion. ἦσαν has -σαν from the σ-aorist.

This is the only Greek present which shows this form of the endings, which originally, if we judge by the situation in Sanskrit, belonged to all the unthematic present classes except the reduplicating.

3. *Unthematic -n̥ti, -n̥t.*—This form was regular after a consonant when the ending was unaccented, in contrast to the accented -*énti*. In Sanskrit it belongs to the reduplicating class, as *júhvati*, *dádati*, *dádhati*, etc., with accent on the syllable of reduplication. To Skt *dádhati* would correspond a G. **τίθατι*, which does not exist, any more than a **τίθμεν* like Skt. *dadhmás*. Since in Greek the weak form of the present stem is τιθε- (τίθε-μεν, τίθε-τε), it takes the form of the ending which is normal after a vowel, namely -ντι as seen in Dor. τίθεντι. So also Dor. δίδοντι in contrast to Skt. *dádati*. But the -n̥ti form of the ending, though not

reflected in any Greek present, is represented by the -ατι, -ασι (not
-ᾱσι) of scattered perfect forms, as Dor. ἀνατεθήκατι, Arc. ἐσλε-
λοίπασι, Hom. πεφύκασι.

The secondary -n̥t is indirectly represented by -αν (-σαν) of the
aorist (see below, 5).

4. In Greek all the active unthematic presents except εἰμί are
from roots or present stems ending in a vowel, and their earliest
3 pl. forms had the regular endings -ντι, -ν, like the thematic
forms. So Dor. φαντί, τίθεντι, δίδοντι, also, though not yet
quotable, δείκνυντι and probably ἴντι. Hence Att.-Ion. φᾱσί, and,
with a shift of accent (if correctly recorded) due to the influence
of the contract verbs, Ion. τιθεῖσι, διδοῦσι, δεικνῦσι, also the
rare ἴσι. But Att. τιθέᾱσι, etc., for which see below, 5.

The corresponding secondary ἔτιθεν, ἔδιδον, ἔθεν, ἔδον, etc.,
are the regular forms of most dialects outside of Attic-Ionic, and
some such occur in Homer, as ἔσταν, ἔφαν, ἔβαν. In Attic-Ionic
these were replaced by ἐτίθεσαν, ἔθεσαν, etc., with -σαν taken over
from the aorist.

In late Greek -σαν spread even to thematic forms as ἐλάβοσαν,
ἐλέγοσαν, and to the optative as ἔχοισαν.

5. G. -αντι (-ᾱσι), -αν.—These cannot directly represent any
of the IE varieties of the endings, but have grown up and become
productive in Greek.

The most easily explained is the secondary -αν (-σαν) of the
aorist (εἶπαν, ἔλῡσαν) which is -α (from -ατ) representing IE -n̥t
(see above, 3) with ν added after the analogy of all the other types
with ν from -nt. After the spread of the a to most of the forms,
so that the aorist stem was apparently -α-, -σα- (see 396), the -αν
would be felt as -α-ν with the usual -ν ending. In several dialects
this -αν spread to other aorist types at the expense of -ν, e.g.
Boeot. Locr. ἀνέθεαν, Arc. συνέθεαν—just as in Attic-Ionic the
full -σαν spread to ἔθεσαν, etc.

In the perfect the old -ατι (see above, 3) was generally replaced
by -αντι (whence Att.-Ion. -ᾱσι) after the analogy of the more
common ending -ντι.

The spread of -ᾱσι to present forms occurs only in Attic-Ionic and is mostly Attic only. Thus Hom. ἔᾱσι (beside εἰσί) and ἴᾱσι (to εἶμι), in Attic not only ἴᾱσι, but also τιθέᾱσι, διδόᾱσι, ἱστᾶσι (from *ἱστά-ᾱσι), δεικνύᾱσι, etc.

a. The precise stages in the evolution of this -αντι, -ᾱσι are variously stated. The view taken here is that it first displaced -ατι in the perfect, and from there spread to the present. Att. τιθέᾱσι is then analogous to Ion. 3 pl. mid. τιθέαται with -αται from the perfect (344.6).

341. *Dual.*—The Greek secondary endings -τον, -τᾱν (Att.-Ion. -την) correspond exactly to the Sanskrit secondary endings -tam, -tām, on the basis of IE -tom, -tām. In the primary tenses there is no trace of the original primary endings. Instead, the secondary -τον is used, and serving here for the third as well as the second person. Even in the secondary tenses the distribution of -τον, -την is not fully maintained, e.g. sometimes 3 pers. -τον in Homer, or 2 pers. -την in Attic.

PERSONAL ENDINGS OF THE MIDDLE

342. Table of middle personal endings.

IE		Sanskrit		Greek	
Primary	Secondary	Primary	Secondary	Primary	Secondary
			Singular		
1 -ai (?)	-i (?)	-e	-i	-μαι	-μᾱν, Att.-Ion. -μην
2 -sai	-so, -thēs (?)	-se	(Av. -ṇha) -thās	-σαι	-σο
3 -tai	-to	-te	-ta	-ται	-το
			Plural		
1 -medhai	-medhə	-mahe	-mahi	-μεθα	
2 ?	?	-dhve	-dhvam	-σθε	
3 -ntai	-nto	-nte	-nta	-νται	-ντο
-ṇtai	-ṇto	-ate	-ata	-αται	-ατο

343. Table of the present and imperfect indicative middle.

Sanskrit	Greek	Sanskrit	Greek
Present	Thematic	Imperfect	
Sing.: 1 *bháre*	φέρομαι	*ábhare*	ἐφερόμην
2 *bhárase*	φέρεαι, -ῃ	*ábharathās*	ἐφέρεο, -ου
3 *bhárate*	φέρεται	*ábharata*	ἐφέρετο
Plur.: 1 *bhárāmahe*	φερόμεθα	*ábharāmahi*	ἐφερόμεθα
2 *bháradhve*	φέρεσθε	*ábharadhvam*	ἐφέρεσθε
3 *bhárante*	φέρονται	*ábharanta*	ἐφέροντο
Unthematic			
Sing.: 1 *áse*	ἧμαι	*ási*	ἤμην
2 *ásse*	ἧσαι	*ásthās*	ἧσο
3 *áste*	ἧσται	*ásta*	ἧστο
Plur.: 1 *ásmahe*	ἤμεθα	*ásmahi*	ἤμεθα
2 *áddhve*	ἧσθε	*áddhvam*	ἧσθε
3 *ásate*	Hom. εἵαται	*ásata*	Hom. εἵατο

344. 1. *First singular.*—G. -μαι, in contrast to Skt. -e from -*ai*, may owe its μ to the influence of the active -μι. But it is also possible that the parent speech had -*mai* in unthematic presents, -*ai* in thematic, the Greek and Sanskrit forms resulting from leveling in opposite directions. The secondary -μᾱν, Att.-Ion. -μην, is without parallel and nothing can be said as to its origin.

2. *Second singular.*—G. -σαι, -σο represent the IE endings as do the corresponding pairs 3 sg. -ται, -το and 3 pl. -νται, -ντο. Only in this case Sanskrit has a different secondary ending, -*thās*, instead of -*sa*, for which, however, we have the Iranian equivalent in the Av. -*ηha*.

a. Under normal phonetic development the -σαι, -σο, would remain unchanged after a consonant (γέγραψαι, ἐγέγραψο), while after a vowel, with the regular loss of intervocalic σ (164) they would appear as -αι, -ο. This distribution is more nearly maintained in Homer than in Attic, where there is an extensive analogical restoration of -σαι, -σο, of which only the beginnings are seen in Homer. Thus Attic has -σαι, -σο, regularly in the present and imperfect indicative and present imperative of unthematic verbs, as τίθεσαι, ἐτίθεσο, τίθεσο (but subj. τιθῇ, opt. τιθεῖο) ; likewise in the perfect and pluperfect, as δέδοσαι, ἐδέδοσο. Homer has such forms as δίζηαι, ἐμάρναο, βέβληαι, beside others like the Attic, as παρίστασαι, παρίστασο.

The forms resulting from the loss of intervocalic σ prevail in the present and imperfect of the thematic verbs and in the aorist. Thus, with uncontracted forms usually in Homer, contraction in Attic, φέρεαι, φέρῃ, ἐφέρεο, ἐφέρου, ἔθεο, ἔθου, ἐλύσαο, ἐλύσω.

In the 2 sg. pres. indic. the later Attic spelling -ει (95) persisted in the tradition in certain words, as βούλει, οἴει, ὄψει.

In Hellenistic Greek -σαι, -σο spread from the unthematic verbs to the contract verbs (cf. ἀκροᾶσαι NT) and eventually to all the thematic verbs. So Mod.G. φέρεσαι, κάθεσαι, etc.

3. *Third singular.*—G. -ται, -το represent the IE endings without change.

4. *First plural.*—G. -μεθα agrees with the Sanskrit secondary ending -mahi (Av. -maiᵈ̄ī) on the basis of an IE -medhə.

The -μεσθα of poetry is a convenient metrical variant, with σθ for θ after the analogy of 2 pl. -σθε.

5. *Second plural.*—G. -σθε is without parallel elsewhere and of obscure origin. According to one view it rests on the infinitive in -σθαι, this being used as an imperative and becoming -σθε after the analogy of the active -τε.

6. *Third plural.*—G. -νται, -ντο represent the IE endings in their postvocalic form; while -αται, -ατο, like Skt. -ate, -ata, represent the form taken after consonants, IE -n̥tai, -n̥to.

a. The forms -αται, -ατο occur in only a few present stems, as Hom. εἵαται, εἵατο (for ἧαται, ἧατο; cf. Skt. āsate, āsata), but regularly in Homer and Herodotus in the optative and in the perfect and pluperfect. Thus Hom. γενοίατο, τετεύχαται, ἐτετεύχατο, and, with extension to vowel stems, βεβλήαται, βεβλήατο. From forms like the last with vowel shortening come the later Ionic -εαται, -εατο in Herodotus, as κεκλέαται, etc., and with further extension to the present even τιθέαται, etc.

Similar perfect and pluperfect forms occur in other dialects, and in Attic inscriptions down to about the end of the 5th cent. B.C., when they are replaced by the periphrastic forms.

345. *Dual.*—The Greek dual endings are obviously formed after the analogy of the active endings, -σθον, -σθον after -τον, -τον, and -σθον, -σθᾱν (Att.-Ion. -σθην) after -τον, -τᾱν (Att.-Ion. -την). The σθ is the same element as in 2 pl. -σθε, 3 sg. imperat. -σθω, etc.

The 1 dual -μεθον, quotable only in three poetic forms, is formed from 1 pl. -μεθα with -ον from -σθον.

346. The Latin deponent-passive represents a type which is unknown in Greek, Sanskrit, and most of the IE languages, but is common to the Italic and Celtic branches and is now attested also in Tocharian and Hittite, with traces in Phrygian and Armenian. It is in origin a medio-passive of a different formal type from that discussed in **342** ff., though partly dependent upon the latter, and appears to have developed in part at least in the parent speech. It is characterized by an *r*-element, which was combined partly with active, partly with middle forms. Its history in detail is somewhat obscure. The following analysis is based upon the Latin forms, but is applicable to several of those in other languages.

The Latin 2 sg. and 2 pl. forms are not of the *r*-type seen in the other persons, and the same is true of the Celtic 2d pl. form.

347. 1. *First singular.* L. -*r* added to the active -*ō* or substituted for the active -*m*. Thus *legōr* (*morōr*, etc., in Plautus), whence regularly (**101**) *legor; legār* (*ūtār* in Plautus) beside act. **legām*, whence *legar* beside act. *legam;* similarly *legēbar, legerer,* etc.

2. *Second singular.*—L. -*re* from 2 sg. mid. -*so*, with rhotacism and change of final *o* to *e* (**83.**3). Hence also -*ris* from -*re-s* with -*s* after the analogy of the 2 sg. active. The imperative has only -*re*, as *legere* parallel to active *lege*. The -*ris* of other forms represents a differentiation after the analogy of pres. indic. *legis* to imperat. *lege*. But even in the non-imperative forms -*re* prevails in early Latin (Terence has only -*re*, Plautus has mostly -*re*, but occasionally -*ris*) and also in Cicero except in the present indicative of passives. In the Augustan period -*ris* is the more usual form.

a. Some inscriptional forms, as *ūtārus*, seem to reflect a similar but earlier extension of -*so* to -*so-s*.

3. *Third singular.*—L. -*tur* from -*to-r*, formed by the addition of *r* to the secondary middle ending -*to*. The imperat. -*tor* is

from *-tōr*, with substitution of *r* for the final of the active *-tōd* (**429**).

4. *First plural.*—L. *-mur* from *-mor*, with substitution of *r* for the final of the active *-mos*.

5. *Second plural.*—L. *-minī* is best regarded as nom. pl. of a middle participle = G. -μενοι, used with omission of the copula to supply the second plural lacking in the *r*-type. According to another view it is an infinitive = G. -μεναι, used first in the imperative.

6. *Third plural.*—L. *-ntur* from *-nto-r*, with the addition of *r* to the secondary ending *-nto*, the formation being parallel to that of the third singular. The imperat. *-ntor* is from *-ntōr*, parallel to the 3 sg. *-tor* (see above, 3).

348. In the Italic dialects only 3 sg. and 3 pl. forms are quotable. Umbrian has 3 pl. *-ntur*, like the Latin, in secondary tenses, 3 sg. *-ter* in primary tenses. Oscan has 3 sg. *-ter*, 3 pl. *-nter*, e.g. *uincter* 'convincitur', k a r a n t e r 'vescuntur'. So Marruc. *ferenter* 'feruntur'. The 3 pl. *-nter* is probably from *-ntro*, a blend of *-nto* and *-ro*.

There are also forms of a different type in which *r* alone appears as the ending, as Umbr. *ferar* 'feratur', Osc. 3 sg. perf. subj. s a k r a f í r 'one shall consecrate'. There are similar forms in Celtic, and also in Hittite.

These forms and the whole medio-passive *r*-type were formerly thought to have been built up in Italic and Celtic upon a series of 3 pl. *r*-endings which will be discussed in connection with L. 3 pl. perf. *-ēre* (**417.**6). The discovery of the *r*-type in Tocharian and Hittite, pointing to its development in the parent speech, alters the situation. But it does not make any less probable an ultimate connection between the medio-passive *r*-type and the 3 pl. *r*-endings. It merely sets it back to a remote period.

TREATMENT OF THE STEM BEFORE THE ENDINGS

349. Certain matters that pertain to the stem to which the endings are added and affect several of the various tense formations may be considered here.

1. In the forms known as thematic the endings are added to the thematic vowel, *e* or *o*. The distribution was that observed in Greek, namely *o* in the first singular, first and third plural, otherwise *e*.

In Latin, owing to the regular changes in medial and final syllables, the thematic vowel is represented by *i* or *u*. Thus *legis, legit* (**112**), *legimus, legitis, legitur* (**110**.2, 3), *legunt, leguntur* (**82**.2, 3). Only before *r* does *e* remain unchanged (**110**.3), as 2 sg. *legeris*. In the first plural the weakening of *-o-mos* would yield partly *-imus*, partly *-umus* (**110**.2, 4). But the former, supported by 2 pl. *-itis*, prevails except in a few verbs in which there is no 2 pl. *-itis*, as *sumus, possumus, volumus, nōlumus, mālumus, quaesumus*.

a. The term "thematic vowel" means strictly nothing more than stem vowel, but in practice it is applied to the *e/o* stem vowel, which plays the most significant rôle. Unthematic forms are those in which the endings are added directly to the root or to a suffix not containing the *e/o* vowel. The distinction corresponds to the familiar Greek classification of verbs in -ω and those in -μι. In Latin there are only relics of unthematic forms, mainly among the irregular verbs.

2. Most unthematic forms show gradation of either the root or the suffix in the same tense. The strong grade appears in the singular, the weak in the dual and plural.

Thus G. εἶμι but ἴμεν (cf. Skt. *émi* but *imás*), τίθημι but τίθεμεν, δίδωμι but δίδομεν, ἵστᾱμι (Att. ἵστημι) but ἵσταμεν, δάμνᾱμι (Att. δάμνημι) but δάμναμεϝ, δείκνῡμι but δείκνυμεν, etc. So in the optative (suffix *yē/ī*) εἴην but εἶμεν, τιθείην but τιθεῖμεν, etc.

So also originally in the perfect, only that here the singular had the *o*-grade, as οἶδα but Hom. ἴδμεν (cf. Skt. *véda* but *vidmá*).

In the present of εἰμί (**333**) the strong grade is extended to the first and second plural, as ἐσμέν, ἐστέ in contrast to Skt. *smás, sthá*.

a. But monosyllabic forms of dissyllabic stems (**126, 127**.2) commonly appear without gradation in the same tense. Thus Skt. 3 sg. *yā̆ti*, 1 pl. *yā̆mas*, 3 pl. *yā̆nti*, and similarly *prā̆ti, drā̆ti, snā̆ti*, etc. In Greek such forms are ἄημι (cf. Skt. *vāmi*), δίζημαι, and aorists like ἔδρᾱν, ἔβην, ἔβλην, ἔγνων, ἔφῡν, ἔδῡν, etc., which have the long vowel throughout, except for the regular shortening before ντ (**98**.2), as in the act. pple. (ἀέντες, γνόντες, etc.) and the old 3 pl. forms like ἔβαν, ἔγνον, ἔφυν, etc. After the analogy of such forms, also ἔστην, pl. ἔστημεν (instead of *ἔσταμεν) in contrast to ἔθεμεν, ἔδομεν.

In Latin some few forms of the first and second conjugations may belong here, as (*nō*) *nās, nat, nămus*, etc. (cf. Skt. *snā̆si, snā̆ti, snā̆mas*), or (*pleō*), *plēs, plet, plēmus* (cf. Skt. *prā̆ti, prā̆mas*).

3. In Latin, when the endings were added to a stem ending in a long vowel, this was regularly shortened before the endings -*m*, -*t*, -*nt*, and -*r* (**101**). Hence the contrast between long and short vowel in many of the tenses, e.g. imperf. indic. *legēbam*, -*bās*, -*bat*, -*bāmus*, -*bātis*, -*bant;* pass. -*bar*, -*bāris*, etc.; so in the pres. indic. of the first, second, and fourth conjugations, in the fut. indic. of the third and fourth conjugations, in the pluperfect, and in all the tenses of the subjunctive. In all of these the stem vowel was originally long throughout.

THE AUGMENT

350. The augment reflects an IE adverbial particle **e* which was frequently prefixed to a past tense of the indicative but was not a fixed and necessary part of the form. In Homeric Greek, as in Vedic Sanskrit, the past tenses appear with or without the augment. In classical Greek, as in classical Sanskrit, the augment has become fixed, and augmentless forms belong only to poetic usage. Its original independence is shown by the rule that the accent cannot precede it, just as it cannot precede the last of two prefixed prepositions, e.g., παρ-έσχε like παρ-έν-θες.

The augment is known only in Greek, Indo-Iranian, and Armenian (with Phrygian). In Latin, as in most of the IE languages, there is no trace of it.

In Greek it is the syllabic augment that reflects the original type, e.g. ἔφερε = Skt. *ábharat*. The temporal augment follows a new principle, which arose by analogical imitation of certain cases in which the augment *e* contracted with the initial vowel of the root to the corresponding long vowel. Thus from IE **es-* the form with the augment **e-es-*, contracted to **ēs-*, as in Skt. *āsam*, Hom. ἦα. From the relation observed in such inherited forms (η:ε), one of apparent lengthening, this was extended to all verbs beginning with a vowel, hence ᾱ (Att. η):α, ω:ο, ῑ:ι, ῡ:υ, etc.

351. 1. The syllabic augment is sometimes ἠ instead of ἐ. Most of the examples are from roots beginning with ϝ, and since in Vedic Sanskrit *ā* also occurs, especially before *v* (*āvar*, etc.), this may represent an inherited by-form, IE *ē̆- beside *e-. Thus Hom. ἤείδει from *ηϝειδ-, and with quantitative metathesis (98.3) Att. ἐάγην from *ηϝάγην, ἑώρων from *ἠϝόρων, ἑάλων from *ἠϝάλων.

But the later Attic ἠβουλόμην, ἤμελλον, ἠδυνάμην are probably due to the analogy of ἤθελον (from ἐθέλω) beside ἔθελον (from θέλω).

2. Verbs which originally began with s, y, w, sw had properly the syllabic augment, and if contraction took place this followed the rules of Greek contraction according to the dialect. Thus from ἔχω (*σεχω) imperf. *ἔσεχον, Att. εἶχον, in some dialects ἦχον (96b), in contrast to ἦν, etc., with η in all dialects representing an IE contraction. Similarly εἶρπον (ἔρπω, *σέρπω), εἰπόμην (ἔπομαι, *σέπομαι), ἐωνούμην (ὠνέομαι, *ϝωνέομαι), Cret. ἔϝαδε, Ion. ἔαδε(ἀνδάνω, *σϝανδάνω), etc. The ' in εἶρπον, etc., may be due to the analogy of the present, or have arisen like that of εὕω (167).

But some take the temporal augment after the analogy of those with original vowel initial. So ἷζον (ἵζω, *σισδω), ὥρκισα (ὀρκίζω), Att. ᾤκουν (οἰκέω, ϝοικέω), ἡλισκόμην (ἁλίσκομαι, ϝαλίσκομαι), aor. ἥλων beside ἑάλων (above, 1), etc.

3. In prepositional compounds the normal position of the augment is after the preposition, as συνέλεγον, ἐξέβαλλον, etc. But some compounds of which the uncompounded forms were not in common use were treated like simple verbs. So ἐκαθήμην from κάθημαι, ἠμφίεσα from ἀμφιέννυμι, ἠπιστά-μην from ἐπίσταμαι, etc.

REDUPLICATION

352. Reduplication is in origin the doubling of a form to indicate repetition or emphasis. A curtailed form of such doubling became a formative element in the parent speech. As a feature of tense formation it appears in certain presents and aorists, but has its chief importance in the perfect.

1. A fuller form of reduplication appears in the Sanskrit intensives, as *dar-dar-ti, car-kar-ti*, etc.; and in G. πορ-φύρω, παμ-φαίνω, L. *mur-murō*, etc. From this type comes the so-called Attic reduplication, as in ἀρ-αρ-ίσκω, perf. -ἄρ-ᾱρα, Hom. ἐδ-ηδώς, etc.

2. Present reduplication, usually with *i*-vowel. Skt. *pi-parti, ti-ṣṭhati* (but *da-dhāti, da-dāti*, with *e*-vowel reduplication, as in 3), G. ἵ-στημι, τί-θημι, δί-δωμι, γί-γνομαι, δι-δάσκω, L. *si-stō, gi-gnō*.

3. Perfect reduplication, usually with *e*-vowel. Skt. *da-darça, ta-tāna*, G. δέ-δορκα, λέ-λοιπα, L. *ce-cinī, pe-pulī*. In Sanskrit and in Latin (**411**) the vowel of the reduplication is partly replaced by that of the root syllable.

4. In the present and perfect reduplication, if the root begins with a single consonant this is repeated in the reduplication, as above. Skt. *da-darça*, G. δέ-δορκα, etc. The dissimilation of aspirates (**132**) accounts for Skt. *dadhāti*, G. τίθημι. If the root begins with two or more consonants, it is the first of these that is normally repeated, as in Skt. *pa-praccha*, G. γέ-γραφα, etc. So from a root beginning with *st* the normal is *s-st*, as in L. *si-stō*, G. ἵ-στημι, Av. *hi-štaiti*, but we find also *t-st* in Skt. *ti-ṣṭhati*, *st-st* in Goth. *stai-stald*, and *st-t*, doubtless by dissimilation from *st-st*, in L. *ste-tī* (so also *spo-pondī*, early L. *sci-cidī*).

5. But in Greek many perfects have only ε as reduplication. So regularly from roots beginning with στ, σπ, etc., ζ, ξ, ψ, πτ, γν and in part from those beginning with ρ (so always in Attic), γλ, βλ, γρ. This type started with perfects from roots beginning with σ+cons. (including ζ, and ρ from *sr*), e.g. ἔσταλμαι, ἔσπαρμαι, in which the init. *s* of the reduplication became ' (**162**) and ἑ became ἐ by association with the augment. From such the ἐ spread to words beginning with other combinations. There is fluctuation in several verbs (γλύφω, βλαστάνω, etc.) and sometimes a dialectic difference, as Ion. ἔκτημαι = usual κέκτημαι, Cret., El. ἔγραμμαι = usual γέγραμμαι.

6. The perfects εἴληφα (λαμβάνω) and εἵμαρται (μείρομαι) come regularly from *σέσλᾱφα, etc. (**203**.2). From these the ει spread to εἴρηκα, εἴληχα (λαγχάνω), and -εἴλοχα, -εἴλεγμαι (λέγω).

FORMATION OF THE PRESENT STEM

353. The parent speech had a great variety of present formations. It is probable that these originally had some special significance in relation to the kind of action expressed. But for the most part this is obscure, and we have to take them simply as so many formal types.

In the several IE languages some of these types remain productive, while others disappear or are represented only by a few relics. By phonetic changes or otherwise one type may give rise to several, or conversely two or more may be merged in one. New types arise and become productive. The final grouping is so diverse that different classifications impose themselves for the various branches of the IE family. This is markedly true in respect to Greek and Latin. The classification of Latin verbs under the four conjugations is the one best suited to the actual Latin grouping, but would be quite unsuitable for Greek.

Hence, after a brief survey of the important IE present classes, those of Greek and Latin will be considered separately. Since aorist stems, apart from the s-aorists, are of the same formal type as some of the present stems, they are included in the following survey.

SURVEY OF IE PRESENT CLASSES

354. Parallel unthematic and thematic classes.[1]

1. Root class. Present stem = root. Usually shift of accent between root and endings and corresponding gradation of root.

Skt. *ásti*, G. ἐστί, L. *est*

Skt. *éti*, G. εἶσι, L. *it*

Cf. paradigms in **333, 334**

a. From dissyllabic stems (**127**) there are forms with

1) Weak grade of second syllable. Skt. *svápi-ti*, *vámi-ti*. Cf. G. ἐμέω for *ϝέμεμι with transfer to thematic type; κρέμαμαι, δέαμαι.

2) Strong grade of second syllable. Skt. *yā-ti*, *snā-ti*. G. ἄημι (cf. Skt. *vā-ti*), aor. ἔδρᾶν, ἔβλην (see **349.**2a).

2. Simple thematic class. Present stem = root with thematic vowel. Two types:

A. Accent on root, strong grade of root.

Skt. *bhára-ti*, *séca-ti*, *bódha-ti*

G. φέρω, λείπω, φεύγω

L. *lego, dīco, dūco*

B. Accent on thematic vowel, weak grade of root.

Skt. *diçá-ti*, *iudá-ti*, aor. *ásica-t*

G. γράφω, aor. ἔλιπον, ἔφυγον, infin. λιπεῖν, φυγεῖν

L. *rudō* (cf. Skt. *ruda-ti*, beside *rodi-ti* of 1a)

The separation of these two original types has no importance for the classification of Greek and Latin presents. It is the prevalence of Type B in aorist forms that is significant for the Greek relations.

3. Reduplicating class.

Skt. *dá-dhā-ti*, *dá-dā-ti*, *bí-bhar-ti*

G. τί-θημι, δί-δω-μι, ἵσ-τη-μι

The prevailing form of the reduplicating syllable is that with the *i*-vowel.

4. Reduplicating thematic class.

Skt. *tí-ṣṭha-ti*, *pí-ba-ti*

G. γί-γνομαι, μί-μνω

L. *si-stō, gi-gnō*

---

[1] Sanskrit forms are here quoted in the third singular, as in some cases showing the stem more clearly than the first singular.

(Nasal Classes)

5. Nasal infix class. Occurs only in Indo-Iranian. Weak grade of root, with insertion of *na* in strong forms, *n* in weak.

Skt. *yu-ná-k-ti*, 1 pl. *yu-ñ-j-más*

6. Nasal infix class, thematic. Weak grade of root with inserted *n* and with thematic vowel.

Skt. *yu-ñ-játi*

L. *iu-n-gō, ru-m-pō*

G. *λα-μ-β-άνω*, *πυ-ν-θ-άνομαι*, with nasal suffix also

7. *nā-* class. Suffix *-nā-*, weak grade *-nə-* or, before a vowel, *-n-.*

Skt. *ji-nắ-ti*, 1 pl. *ji-nī-más*, 3 pl. *ji-n-ánti*

G. *δάμ-νᾱ-μι* (Att. *δάμνημι*), 1 pl. *δάμ-να-μεν*

G. *-να-* represents the proper weak grade *-nə-*, while Skt. *-nī-* instead of *-ni-* is secondary.

8. *no*-class. Suffix *-no-*[1] or *-ɟo-*.

Skt. *mr̥-ṇá-ti* (beside *mr̥-ṇắ-ti* of 7)

G. *κάμ-νω, δάκ-νω, ἁμαρτ-άνω*

L. *cer-nō, ster-nō*

9. *nu*-class. Suffix *-neu-*, weak grade *-nu-*.

Skt. *su-nó-ti*, 1 pl. *su-nu-más*

G. *δείκ-νῡ-μι*, 1 pl. *δείκ-νυ-μεν*

G. *-νῡ-* instead of *-νευ-* may be due to the analogy of *νᾱ/να* in 7.

10. *nu*-class, thematic. Suffix *-nwo-* or *-nuo-*.

Skt. *cí-nva-ti* (beside *ci-nó-mi*, 9)

G. *τίνω*, Hom. *τῑ́νω*, from **τί-νϝω* (176.1)

L. *mi-nuō, sternuō* (but *nu* extended to whole verb stem)

a. Not only 5, but also 7 and 9, were originally formed with a nasal infix, the *nā*-class from dissyllabic roots ending in a long vowel, the *nu*-class from roots ending in *-eu*, weak *-u*. Some of the forms may clearly be analyzed in this way. Thus Skt. *ji-n-ắ-nti* beside *jyā-* in fut. *jyā-syati*, G. *δάμ-ν-α-μεν* beside *δαμα-* in *ἐδάμασα*, Skt. *çr̥-n-ó-ti, çr̥-n-u-más* beside *çro-, çru-* in *çró-tum, çr̥u-tá-*. But from such forms were abstracted suffixes which became productive.

355. Other thematic classes.

1. *sko-* class. Suffix *-sko-*. Often called the inchoative class, from the prevailing force in Latin.

Skt. *gáccha-ti, icchá-ti, pr̥cchá-ti*

G. *βάσκω, ἀρέσκω, εὑρίσκω*   L. *crēscō, nōscō, poscō*

a. Same with reduplication.

G. *γιγνώσκω, διδάσκω*   L. *discō*.

2. *yo-* class. Suffix *-yo-*, in interchange with *-ye-* or in some languages with *-ĭ-*. Two types parallel to those of 354.2.

---

[1] Really *-nᵉ/o-* that is, *n*+thematic vowel. But for convenience we shall write *-no-* just as for the noun suffix *-no-* (which is also really *-nᵉ/o-*). Similarly *-yo-*, *sko-*, etc.

A. Accent on root, strong grade of root.

Skt. *páçya-ti, hárya-ti*

G. στέλλω from *στελ-ϳω, τείνω from *τεν-ϳω

L. *speciō (-spiciō), aperiō*

B. Accent on suffix, weak grade of root.

Skt. *mriyá-te, kriyá-te*

G. βάλλω from *βαλ-ϳω, βαίνω from *βαν-ϳω   L. *morior, veniō*

The separation of these two types is necessary in Sanskrit, where the forms of Type B always have intransitive or passive force and are inflected only in the middle. It has no importance for the classification of Greek or Latin presents.

In Greek a new classification is imposed by the variety of phonetic changes resulting from the combinations with *y* (**182-88**). Hence presents in -σσω or -ττω, in -ζω, in - λλω, etc.

In Latin the important distinction is that between presents of the type *capiō*, 1 pl. *capimus* and those of the type *veniō*, 1 pl. *venīmus*. Such inflection with -ĭ or -ī- in interchange with -yo-, instead of the usual -y ᵉ/o- indicated by the inflection in Greek, Sanskrit, and most of the IE languages, is characteristic of Italic and Balto-Slavic. Cf. Lith. *myliu*, 1 pl. *mylime* (with short *i*), ChSl. *gorją*, 1 pl. *gorimŭ* (*i* from *ī*). In Balto-Slavic there are also *yo*-presents with the -y ᵉ/o- inflection as in Greek, etc. Some scholars regard the -ĭ- of the Italic and Balto-Slavic forms as the result of contraction taking place independently in Italic and Balto-Slavic. But there are such serious obstacles to this view that the assumption of an inherited parallel -ĭ-/-yo- type is preferred here. See also **376a**.

356. *Denominative yo- class.*—The usual formation of denominatives is by the addition of the suffix -*yo*- to the stem of the noun. The formation is most transparent in Sanskrit, where the -*ya*- is everywhere preserved, while in Greek and Latin it is disguised by the loss of intervocalic *y*, contraction, and other phonetic changes.

Noun Stem	Denom. Stem	Skt.	G.	L.
ā	-*ā-yo*-	*pṛtanāyáti* (*pṛtanā-*)	τῑμάω (τῑμή)	*cūrō* (*cūra*)
o-	-*e-yo*-	*devayáti* (*devá-*)	φιλέω (φίλος)	*albeō* (*albus*)
i-	-*i-yo*-	Ved. *janiyáti* (*jáni-*)	μηνίω (μῆνις)	*fīniō* (*fīnis*)
u-	-*u-yo*-	Ved. *gātuyáti* (*gātú-*)	μεθύω (μέθυ)	*metuō* (*metus*)
s-	-*s-yo*-	*rajasyáti* (*rájas-*)	τελείω, -έω (τέλος)	*fulguriō* (*fulgur*)
n-	-*n-yo*-	*ukṣanyáti* (*ukṣán-*)	ὀνομαίνω (ὄνομα)	
d-	-*d-yo*-		ἐλπίζω,	*custōdiō*
etc. (any stop)	etc.	*bhiṣajyáti* (*bhiṣáj-*)	(ἐλπίς, -ίδος)	(*custōs, -ōdis*)

While this shows the original relation between noun stem and denominative stem, the various forms of the latter become independently productive and occur in derivatives of noun stems other than those to which they belong in origin. Especially -āyo- is freely used for denominatives of o-stems (the frequency of parallel ā-stem collectives is doubtless a factor in this) in most IE languages, and its Latin representative is by far the commonest denominative type, regardless of the noun stem (**370.**1).

357. *Causative -éyo- class.*—This is formally distinguished from the denominatives of o-stems by the difference of accent as shown in Sanskrit (caus. *-áya-*, denom. *-ayá-*). The root normally has the o-grade. The meaning is very commonly, though not exclusively, causative, hence the usual name. This type is most conspicuous in Sanskrit, important also in Germanic. In Greek and Latin, where the criterion of accent is no longer available, it is formally indistinguishable from denominatives in *-éω, -eō*, and only a few verbs are clearly to be reckoned here on account of their meaning.

Skt. *sādáyati* 'cause to sit, set' from *sad-* 'sit'

Goth. *satjan* 'set' (NE *set*) beside *sitan* 'sit'

G. φοβέω 'frighten' beside φέβομαι 'be afraid'

L. *moneō* 'remind, admonish' from *men-* of *meminī* 'remember'

THE PRESENT CLASSES IN GREEK

THE THEMATIC CLASSES, EXCLUSIVE OF THE CONTRACT VERBS

358. *Simple thematic class* (**354.**2).—The great majority are from roots of the e-series and in the e-grade. Thus φέρω, λέγω, μένω, ἔχω, λείπω, φεύγω, τρέπω, etc. So also ῥέω from *ῥέϝω, πλέω from *πλέϝω, etc.

With other grades or from roots of other series, γράφω, γλύφω, ἄγω, αἴθω, λήγω, etc.

a. With reduplication (**354.**4). So γί-γνομαι, μί-μνω, πῖ-πτω (ῖ due to the analogy of ῥῖπτω?), ἴσχω (from *σι-σχω, to ἔχω), τί-κτω from *τί-τκω, **210**).

359. *Tau-class. Presents in -πτω.*—These belong in origin to the yo-class, starting with forms like κόπτω from *κοπϳω (**186**). Hence by analogy similar forms from roots ending in any labial, as καλύπτω (cf. καλύβη), κρύπτω (cf. κρύφα), including some in which the labial comes from a labiovelar, as πέπτω beside normal πέσσω, πέττω (182). This was favored by their many common forms, as the aorists in -ψα.

This class is then properly co-ordinate with the subdivisions of the iota class, that is, presents in -πτω with those in -σσω, -ζω, -λλω, etc.

360. *Iota or yo- class* (355.2).—The different phonetic changes that attend the combination of *y* with a preceding consonant (182–88) result in a variety of distinct types.

1. *Presents in* -σσω, *Att.* -ττω.—From verb stems ending in a voiceless guttural or dental, namely κ, χ (or in some cases an IE labiovelar), τ, or θ; also from some ending in γ.

φυλάσσω, -ττω, from *φυλακ-ψω. Cf. φύλαξ, φύλακος

ὀρύσσω, -ττω, from *ὀρυχ-ψω. Cf. ὀρυχή

πέσσω, -ττω, from *peqʷ-yō. Cf. aor. ἔπεψα

ἐρέσσω, -ττω. Cf. ἐρέτης

κορύσσω (poetical; no Att. -ττω). Cf. κόρυς, κόρυθος

ἀλλάσσω, -ττω. Cf. ἀλλαγή

a. Only those from a stem ending in a voiceless guttural are the result of regular phonetic development. The others follow their analogy (see 182–84). Stems ending in γ by normal phonetic development of -γ-ψω give presents in -ζω, but since in the future, aorist, perfect middle, etc., they have the same forms (-ξω, -ξα, -κται, etc.) as those ending in κ or χ, their presents may follow the analogy of the latter. Hence ἀλλάσσω, -ττω, τάσσω, -ττω (cf. ταγή), etc., or only Att. σφάττω in contrast to the regular Ion. σφάζω from *σφαγ-ψω (cf. σφαγή).

2. *Presents in* -ζω.—From verb stems ending in a voiced guttural or dental, namely γ (or an IE labiovelar gʷ), or δ (see **184**).

ἁρπάζω from ἁρπαγ-ψω. Cf. ἁρπαγή

νίζω from *nigʷyō. Cf. fut. νίψω, and χέρ-νιβα

ἐλπίζω from ἐλπιδ-ψω. Cf. ἐλπίς, ἐλπίδος

The great majority are from stems ending in δ, or analogical extensions of such. Especially -άζω and -ίζω starting from -αδ-ψω and -ιδ-ψω, became widely productive, forming denominatives from stems of all kinds to the number of several thousands.

In general, -άζω is more common from ā-stems and neuter *n*-stems, -ίζω from other stems.

Thus δικάζω (δίκη), ἀγοράζω (ἀγορά), θαυμάζω (θαῦμα), ὑβρίζω (ὕβρις), νομίζω (νόμος), τειχίζω (τεῖχος), ἑλληνίζω (Ἕλλην).

a. In the future and aorist the difference between guttural and dental stem normally shows itself (ξ from guttural+σ, Att. σ from dental+σ), but owing to the common present there is sometimes confusion. Thus from ἁρπάζω the regular ἥρπαξα in Ionic, but ἥρπασα in Attic. The great mass of derivatives in -άζω and -ίζω follow the treatment of dental stems, as Att. ἐδίκασα, ἐνόμισα. But Homer has πτολεμίζω, and forms like ἐδίκαξα are the usual ones in Doric.

3. *Presents in -λλω.*—From verb stems ending in λ (see **187**).

στέλλω from *στελ-ι̯ω   ἀγγέλλω from ἀγγελ-ι̯ω

4. *Presents in -αίνω and -αίρω.*—From verb stems ending in αν and αρ (see **188.1**).

φαίνω from *φαν-ι̯ω   χαίρω from *χαρ-ι̯ω

From denominatives like μελαίνω (μέλας, μέλανος), ποιμαίνω (from the weak stem of ποιμήν), etc., the -αίνω spread and forms numerous denominatives from other stems, as λευκαίνω (λευκός), θερμαίνω (θερμός), etc.

5. *Presents in -είνω, -είρω, -ῑνω, -ῑρω, -ῡνω, -ῡρω.*—From verb stems ending in εν, ερ, ιν, ιρ, υν, υρ (see **188.2**).

τείνω from *τενι̯ω   φθείρω from *φθερ-ι̯ω
κρῑνω from *κρι-ν-ι̯ω   οἰκτίρω, from *οἰκτιρ-ι̯ω
πλῡνω from *πλυ-ν-ι̯ω   μαρτύρομαι from *μαρτυρ-ι̯ομαι

Forms like κρῑνω, κλῑνω, πλῡνω differ from the others in that their ν is not a part of the original verb stem, but an added element. They are from *κρι-ν-ι̯ω, *κλι-ν-ι̯ω, *πλυ-ν-ι̯ω, with a combination of two present suffixes, e.g. *κρι-νω then *κρι-ν-ι̯ω. From the latter the κριν-, as an apparent verb stem, spread in part to the other tenses. So aor. ἔκρῑνα from *ἔκρινσα, ἔκλῑνα, ἔπλῡνα, but perf. κέκρι-ται, κέκλι-ται, πέπλυ-ται, aor. pass. ἐκρίν-θην beside ἐκρί-θην, etc.

Like πλῡνω in origin is the productive -ῡνω in the numerous denominatives from υ-stems and from others by analogy, as βαρύνω from *βαρυ-ν-ι̯ω (βαρύς), ἡδύνω (ἡδύς), παχύνω (παχύς), λεπτύνω (λεπτός)

6. *Miscellaneous.*—To this class belong also in origin:

Some presents in -αιω, as καίω from *καϝ-ιω (cf. ἔκαυσα), κλαίω from *κλαϝ-ιω (cf. ἔκλαυσα). For Att. κάω, κλάω, see 179.1.

Those in -ευω, from -εϝ-ιω. The normal phonetic development would yield -ειω (cf. ἡδεῖα from ἡδεϝ-ια, and καίω above), and this is the actual form in the Elean dialect (φυγαδείω = φυγαδεύω), but elsewhere it was replaced by -ευω with ευ from the other tenses.

Denominatives in -ιω and -νω, as μηνίω (μῆνις), μεθύω (μέθυ). See 356. Also some of the primary verbs in -νω, as φύω, Lesb. φυίω. Whether λύω and others belonged originally to this or to the simple thematic class is impossible to determine. They generally show -ŭω in Homer, but -ῡω in Attic.

The great majority of the contract verbs in -αω, -εω, -ο[']ω (363).

361. *no-class* (354.8, 10).

Presents in -νω, as δάκ-νω, κάμ-νω, τέμ-νω, πῐ-νω.

But τίνω, φθάνω, φθίνω, Hom. τῑνω, φθᾱνω, φθῑνω, are from *τι-νϝω, etc. (176.1), thematic forms of the *nu*-class (354.10). Forms like δεικ-νύω are later transfers from δείκ-νῡ-μι, etc. Isolated and not certainly explained is ἐλαύνω (verb stem ἐλα-).

Presents in -ανω, as αὐξ-άνω, ἁμαρτ-άνω, αἰσθ-άνομαι. These have the suffix with syllabification of the *n*, that is, -ṇō, whence -ανω (115).

Presents in ανω with nasal infix in the verb stem, as λα-μ-β-άνω, λα-ν-θ-άνω, ἀ-ν-δ-άνω, πυ-ν-θ-άνομαι. This type is a combination of the preceding with the thematic nasal infix class (L. *rumpō*, 354.6). Cf. parallel presents like Lith. *bundu* and *budinu*, as if G. *πύνθω and *πυθάνω.

362. *sko-class* (355.1).

Presents in -σκω, as βά-σκω ἀρέ-σκω ; with reduplication γι-γνώ-σκω, βι-βρώ-σκω ; with consonant changes (206.1, 3) λάσκω from *λακ-σκω (ἔλακον), διδάσκω from *διδακ-σκω, πάσχω from *παθ-σκω, μίσγω from *μιγ-σκω(?).

a. As ἀρέ-σκω is from a dissyllabic stem (cf. ἤρεσα), so also, with reduplication ἀρ-αρί-σκω (cf. ἀρι-θμός). But -ισκω became productive, and in most cases there is no stem form ending in ι (some think of a relation between the ι and the η of some forms, e.g. εὑρί-σκω beside fut. εὑρή-σω, but even this is doubtful). Thus εὑρίσκω, ἁλίσκομαι, στερίσκω, or, with secondary addition to a stem ending in a long vowel, θνῇσκω, μιμνῇσκω, θρῴσκω.

A few have inchoative meaning, as γηράσκω 'grow old', ἡβάσκω 'grow young', but this force never became dominant as in the corresponding Latin presents in -scō.

An offshoot of this class, with a specialized use which must have started in some particular forms like φάσκον from φάσκω, is represented by the Ionic iterative imperfects and aorists like φεύγεσκον, φύγεσκον.

THE CONTRACT VERBS

363. The great mass of the contract verbs are denominatives (356).

1. -αω.—Those in -αω represent the IE -ā-yo- type, based on ā-stems. The shortening of the vowel in the present stem is due to the analogy of -εω. The great majority are derived from actual ā-stems, as τῑμάω (τῑμή), νῑκάω (νίκη), σῑγάω (σῑγή).

There are a few primary verbs in -αω, as δράω (verb stem δρᾱ-), and those like σπάω (ἔσπασα, ἔσπασμαι, verb stem σπα- or σπασ-), χαλάω, etc.

2. -εω.—Those in εω represent chiefly the IE -e-yo- type, based on o-stems. They are derived from o-stems, as φιλέω (φίλος), οἰκέω (οἶκος), but also frequently from others, as φωνέω (φωνή), μαρτυρέω (μάρτυς).

Some represent the IE -es-yo- type, from s-stems, as τελέω, Hom. τελείω, aor. ἐτέλεσσα. But most derivatives of σ-stems are completely merged with those from o-stems, as μῑσέω (μῖσος), ἀλγέω (ἄλγος), aor. -ησα.

Some represent the IE -ē-yo- type (357). But they were formally merged with the denominatives of o-stems, taking the same verb stem in η outside the present, and are mostly indistinguishable from them. Thus φοβέω, in origin a causative of φέβομαι, was felt as a denominative of φόβος, like φιλέω from φίλος. An isolated case, without verb stem in η, is δοκέω, aor. ἔδοξα.

There are also a few primary verbs in -εω, mostly presents of the simple thematic class in origin, as ῥέω from *ρεϝω, πλέω from *πλεϝω, ζέω from *ζεσω (cf. aor. ἔζεσα from *ἐζεσσα; Skt. yas-), τρέω from *τρεσω; but δέω 'bind' from *δε-μω.

3. -οω.—Those in -οω represent a special Greek type of de-

nominatives of *o*-stems, usually with factitive force, as δηλόω 'make clear' (δῆλος), δουλόω 'enslave' (δοῦλος) in contrast to δουλεύω 'be a slave'. Beside the inherited type in -εω, this new type grew up as an obvious parallel to that of -αω from ᾱ-stems. Some think it started in non-present forms like -ωσα, -ωθην, -ωθεις, -ωτος, which in Homer are more frequent than the present forms.

364. *Inflection of the contract verbs.*

1. There is great divergence among the dialects in the matter of contracted and uncontracted forms and in the results of contraction (see **104**).

In general, uncontracted forms are most frequent in Ionic, while Attic stands at the other extreme, with almost complete contraction.

As between the different classes, uncontracted forms are most frequent from verbs in -εω, less frequent from those in -αω, and least frequent from those in -οω.

Thus Hom. φιλέει and φιλεῖ, φιλέοντες and φιλεῦντες, always φιλέουσι, φιλέοι, φιλέωμεν, etc. (though these are sometimes to be read with synizesis), with a considerable preponderance of uncontracted forms; ὑλάει, ὕλαον, etc., or more frequently forms like ὁρόω, ὁράασθαι (with 'distraction'', **104**.₇), beside contracted ὁρᾷ, νῑκᾷ, ἐνῑκων, etc.

In Attic, contraction is the rule. Only a few dissyllabic presents in -εω like πλέω, δέω 'need', etc., have uncontracted forms, as πλέω, πλέομεν (but πλεῖ, πλεῖτε), πλέῃ, πλέοι.

2. In certain dialects, namely Lesbian, Thessalian, Arcadian, and Cyprian, the contract verbs have unthematic inflection. Thus in Alcaeus and Sappho κάλημι, ἐπαίνεντες (=Att. ἐπαινοῦντες), Thess. στραταγέντος (=Att. στρατηγοῦντος), Arc. ποίενσι (like τίθενσι). In Attic the optative shows a similar transfer (**422**).

There are also dialectic forms like ἀδικήω, στεφανώω, with the long-vowel stem of other tenses extended to the present.

3. There are a few contract verbs which differ from the usual type in that they come from -ηω, -αω, -ωω and consequently show different results of contraction. Thus Att. ζῶ, 3 sg. ζῇ, 3 pl. ζῶσι, infin. ζῆν, from *ζήω, *ζήει, etc. (*ζήω from *ζη-μω, parallel to Hom. ζώω from *ζω-μω). So χρῶ 'utter an oracle,' 3 sg. χρῇ, διψῶ, πεινῶ infin. διψῆν, πεινῆν (cf. Hom. διψάων, πεινάων), ψῶ, σμῶ, κνῶ infin. ψῆν, etc.; χρῶμαι 'use', 3 sg. χρῆται, infin. χρῆσθαι, from χρηέομαι; ῥῑγῶ, infin. ῥῑγῶν (also ῥῑγοῦν), ἱδρῶ, Hom. ἱδρώω, from stems ῥῑγωσ-, ἱδρωσ-.

THE UNTHEMATIC CLASSES

365. *Root class* (**354.**1).—Here belong εἰμί (**333**), εἶμι (**334**), φημί, ἤμί, ἄημι (**349.**2*a*), ἧμαι (**343**), κεῖμαι (3 sg. κεῖται = Skt. çéte), ἐπί-στα-μαι 'understand' (from the weak grade of στᾱ- 'stand').

Middle forms from dissyllabic stems (**354.**1*a*), ἄγα-μαι, κρέμα-μαι, δέα-μαι, ἔρα-μαι, πέτα-μαι, δύνα-μαι (perhaps originally δύ-να-μαι of the *νᾱ* class with extension of *να* to verb stem), δίε-μαι, ἵε-μαι, ὄνο-μαι, εἴρυ-μαι.

Peculiarities of inflection have been mostly covered in **335–40**, **349.**2.

a. The imperfect of εἶμι (**334**) shows a great variety of forms, some of which are not certainly explained. 1 sg. ᾖα (IE *ēyṃ would give *ηια, then with loss of intervocalic ι, *ᾗα) with η after the analogy of ᾗμεν (Skt. *āima*), etc.; 2 sg. ᾔεισθα, 3 sg. ᾔει(ν), 3 pl. ᾔεσαν, like the pluperfect forms (of οἶδα) ᾔδησθα, ᾔδεισθα, ᾔδει(ν), ᾔδεσαν, as also the later 1 sg. ᾔειν like ᾔδειν. Hom. 1 sg. ᾔϊα, 3 sg. ᾔϊε, probably to be read ᾖεα, ᾖεε like ᾖδεα, ᾖδεε. Hom. aug-mentless forms 3 dual ἴτην, 3 pl. ἴσαν. Hom. thematic forms 1 sg., 1 pl. ἀνήϊον, 1 pl. ᾔομεν.

The subj., opt., and imperat. forms are all formed from the weak grade of the root, as ἴω, ἴοιμι, ἴθι, etc.

366. *Reduplicating class* (**354.**3).—τί-θη-μι, ἵ-στη-μι, δίδω-μι, ἵ-η-μι, κί-χρη-μι, δί-ζη-μαι. βί-βη-μι, ὀνί-νη-μι (verb stem ὀνᾱ-), etc. With inserted nasal (after the type λαμβάνω) πί-μ-πλημι, πί-μ-πρημι (so dial. κί-γ-χρημι = Att. κί-χρημι).

a. The imperfect of τίθημι, ἵημι, and δίδωμι have some forms that follow the analogy of the contract verbs. Thus 1 sg. ἐτίθην, ἵην, but 2 sg. ἐτίθεις, ἵεις, 3 sg. ἐτίθει, ἵει, and from δίδωμι, all three persons of the singular, ἐδίδουν, ἐδίδους, ἐδίδου (for *ἐδίδων, etc.).

367. *nu-class.*—Suffix νῡ, νυ (**354.**8).—δείκ-νῡ-μι, ἄγ-νῡ-μι, ὄρ-νῡ-μι, ὄμ-νῡ-μι, στόρ-νῡ-μι, ὄλλῡμι (*ὀλ-νῡ-μι).

Forms in -ννῡμι from stems ending in σ, as ἕννῡμι (from *ἐσ-νῡ-μι, with δσ restored by analogy; the normal development appears in Ion. εἴνῡμι; **203.**2*c*), σβέννῡμι (cf. σβεστός), ζώννῡμι (cf. ζωστός), gave rise to others in -ννῡμι from stems ending in a vowel, as στρώ-ννῡμι, στορέ-ννῡμι (cf. aor. ἐ-στόρε-σα), κορέ-ννῡμι, κερά-ννῡμι, πετά-ννῡμι, etc.

368. *nā-class.*—Suffix *νᾱ* (Att.-Ion. *νη*), *να* (**354.**7).—δάμ-νη-μι,
πέρ-νη-μι, πίτ-νη-μι, σκίδ-νη-μι, κίρ-νη-μι μάρ-να-μαι, πίλ-να-μαι.

These occur mostly in poetry or in the dialects, and the class is
not productive in Greek.

   a. The ι in πίτνημι, σκίδνημι, κίρνημι, πίλναμαι, beside ἐπέτεσα, ἐσκέδασα,
ἐκέρασα, ἐπέλεσα, is generally taken as parallel to that of πίσυρες, etc. (**121**),
but its frequency in this particular type is remarkable.

THE PRESENT CLASSES IN LATIN

369. The familiar classification of Latin verbs in four conjugations is in reality a classification of present stems, applying only
to those tenses which make up the present system. Except for
most verbs of the first conjugation, there is no uniformity in the
perfect system or the perfect passive participle within a given
conjugation. Perfects in *-vī* or *-uī*, reduplicated perfects, and
those with lengthened vowel occur in all four conjugations, perfects in *-sī* in all but the first.

In general, verbs of the first, second, and fourth conjugation
reflect IE *yo*-presents, either primary or denominative. Those of
the first and second correspond in the main to the Greek presents
in -αω and -εω; those of the fourth (including the *capiō-* type
of the third) to the various types of the Greek iota-class (e.g.
veniō: βαίνω) with some denominatives in -ιω. Those of the third
conjugation comprise the simple thematic presents and those
formed with other thematic suffixes. The irregular verbs contain
relics of unthematic inflection and have other peculiarities.

FIRST CONJUGATION

370. The first conjugation comprises the most productive
type of denominatives and a few primary verbs.

   1. The great mass are denominatives answering to G. -αω and
reflecting the IE *-āyo-* type (**356**). Though originally based upon
ā-stems, they are freely formed from stems of all kinds. Thus
cūrō (*cūra*), *plantō* (*planta*), *dōnō* (*dōnum*), *levō* (*levis*), *laudō* (*laus,
laudis*), *generō* (*genus*).

   2. The frequentatives, ending in *-tō, -sō, -itō, -titō*, and denoting
repeated or sometimes mere intensive action, are in origin de-

nominatives formed from the stem of the perf. pass. pple. of the simple verb. Thus *dictō* from *dictus* (*dīcō*), *versō* from *versus* (*vertō*), *habitō* from *habitus* (*habeō*). But with the development of a distinctive meaning they came to be felt as formed from the verb stem, and many were actually thus formed with -*itō*. Thus *agitō* (not **āctō* like *tractō*) from *agō*, *rogitō* (not **rogātō*) from *rogō*, and so in all frequentatives from verbs of the first conjugations.

Some of the old frequentatives lost their distinctive force and new frequentatives in -*itō* were formed from them, the so-called double frequentatives. Thus *cantō* has the same force as *canō* (and eventually displaced it, hence It. *cantare*, Fr. *chanter*, etc.), and from it was formed *cantitō* with real frequentative force; similarly *dictitō* from *dictō*, etc.

3. There are a few primary verbs from monosyllabic stems ending in -*ā*, as *fā-rī*, *nō*, *stō*. These belong to the IE root class (**354**.1), as clearly *fārī* (cf. G. φημί, Dor. φᾱμί), or in part to parallel *yo*-presents (so for *nō*, *nāre*, cf. Skt. *snā-ya-te* beside *snā-ti*). The 1 sg. *stō* is probably from **sta-yō* (IE **stə-yō*) or **stā-yō*, like Umbr. *stahu* 'sto', ChSl. *stojǫ*, 'sto', *stajǫ* 'sisto', but some of the forms may also be directly from the root like aor. G. ἔστην, Skt. *asthāt*.

4. There are also several primary verbs with presents only from dissyllabic stems ending in *ā*, as *secō*, *secāre* (*secuī*, *sectus*), *iuvō*, *iuvāre* (*iūvī*, *iūtus*), *domō*, *domāre* (*domuī*, *domitus*). Even among the verbs which show *ā* throughout there may be some that were originally primary verbs of this type, as probably *amō*.

371. *Inflection.*—The 1 sg. -*ō* is contracted from -*āō*, -*āyō*, parallel to -*eō*, -*iō* of the second and fourth conjugations. The *ā* of the other persons (shortened before -*t*, -*nt*, (**101**) is simply that of the stem in some primary verbs. In the denominatives it may be the result of contraction from *ā(y)e* in the 2 sg., 3 sg., and 2 pl. forms, whence with the support of the uniform *ā* of some primary verbs it spread to 1 pl. -*āmus* (from -*āyomos* we should expect -*ōmus*, **105**.2), 3 pl. -*ant*. See also **373**.

SECOND CONJUGATION

372. The second conjugation comprises primary verbs with stems ending in *ē*, denominatives, and a few causatives.

1. Primary verbs from monosyllabic stems ending in $\bar{e}$, as -*pleō*, -*plēre* (cf. G. aor. πλῆ-το, Skt. aor. *aprā-t* and rare pres. *prā-ti*), *neō*, *fleō*. Like the corresponding forms of the first conjugation, these belong to the IE root class (**354.**1*a*), or in part to parallel *yo*- presents, as *fleō* perhaps from *bhlē-yō (cf. ChSl. *blě-jǫ* 'bleat').

2. Primary verbs with presents only from dissyllabic stems ending in $\bar{e}$, as *videō, habeō, iaceō, sedeō, iaceō*, etc. This is a large class, in which, with some exceptions like *videō, habeō*, the intransitive force prevails. Note *iaceō, iacēre* 'lie' beside *iaciō, iacere* 'throw', *pendeō, pendēre* 'be suspended, hang' beside *pendō, pendere* 'suspend, weigh out'. Similar stems in -$\bar{e}$ with distinctively intransitive force are seen in the Greek aorists like ἐχάρην, etc.

a. The Latin situation, with present stem in -$\bar{e}$, though paralleled in some Germanic forms (Goth. *habaiþ*, OHG *habēt*), is the opposite of that observed in other IE languages and is presumably secondary. Elsewhere the stem in -$\bar{e}$ is found mostly in non-present forms, and is combined with presents of various classes but especially with those of the *yo*-class. Thus G. χαίρω, ἐχάρην, φαίνομαι, ἐφάνην, μαίνομαι, ἐμάνην, ChSl. *mǐnjǫ*, infin. *mǐněti* (*ě* from IE $\bar{e}$; *mǐně*-: G. μανη-), *viždǫ, viděti* (:L. *videō*), *seždǫ, seděti*, Lith. *sėdžu, sėdėti* (:L. *sedeō*).

It is often stated that this combination rests on dissyllabic stems ending in -$\bar{e}i$, whence -$\bar{e}$ and -*i* (with thematic vowel -*y-o-*) respectively. But it is probably a matter of parallel extensions of the simple root.

3. Denominatives, answering to G. -εω and reflecting the IE -*e-yo*- type (**356**). They are primarily from *o*-stems, but also from others. Thus *albeō* (*albus*), *claudeō* (*claudus*), *flōreō* (*flōs, flōris*), etc. They are not nearly so numerous as the Greek denominatives in -εω, owing to the greater expansion of the $\bar{a}$-stem denominatives.

4. Causatives, reflecting the IE -$\acute{e}$-*yo*- type (**357**). Thus *moneō* (cf. *meminī*), *torreō* (cf. Skt. *tarṣáyati*, caus. of *tṛṣ*-), *doceō* (cf. *decet*), *noceō* (cf. *necō, necāre*), *spondeō* (cf. G. σπένδω), probably *moveō, foveō*, and a few others.

373. *Inflection.*—The 1 sg. -*eō* is from -*eyō* of the denominatives and causatives, followed by the primary verbs, though here it may be in small part from -$\bar{e}$-*yō*. The $\bar{e}$ of the other persons (shortened before -*t*, -*nt*, **101**) is that of the stem in the primary verbs. In the denominatives and causatives it is the result of regular contraction in *-ēs*, *-et*, *-ētis* from *-eyesi*, etc., whence under the added influence of the primary forms it was extended to *-ēmus*, *-ent* (which cannot represent the phonetic development of *-eyomos*, *-eyonti*). Thus:

videō by analogy	*moneō* from **moneyō*
vidēs from **widē-si*	*monēs* from **moneyesi*
videt from **widē-ti*	*monet* from **moneyeti*
vidēmus from **widē-mos*	*monēmus* by analogy
vidētis from **widē-te*	*monētis* from **moneyete*
vident from **widē-nti*	*monent* by analogy

THIRD CONJUGATION

374. The third conjugation comprises a variety of thematic present formations.

1. *Simple thematic class* (**354.**2). Thus *legō*, *tegō*, *dīcō*, *dūcō*, *rudō*, *agō*, etc.

2. *Reduplicating thematic class* (**354.**4). Thus *si-stō*, *gi-gnō*, *serō* from **si-sō* (**74**a), *sīdō* from **si-sdō*, *reddō* from **re-di-dō* (cf. Osc. *didest* 'dabit'). Here also in origin *bibō* (cf. Skt. *pi-ba-ti*) from root *pō-* in *pō-tus*, though the explanation of the *b* is uncertain.

3. *Nasal infix class, thematic* (**354.**6). Thus *rumpō*, *linquō*, *findō*, *fundō*, *tangō*, etc.; with nasal extended to the perfect, *fingō* (*fīnxī*, but *fictus*), *stringō*, etc.; with nasal extended to perfect and perf. pass. pple. *iungō* (*iūnxī*, *iūnctus*), *cingō*, *plangō*, *unguō*, etc.

a. These are to be distinguished from verbs in which the nasal belongs to the root, as *pendō* (cf. *pondus*), *tendō*, etc.

4. *no-class* (**354.**8). Thus *sper-nō*, *cer-nō*, *si-nō*, *li-nō*, *tem-nō*. Here also in origin some presents in *-llō* from *-l-nō* (**200.**1), as *pellō*, *tollō*, *-cellō* 'rise' (cf. *collis* from **kol-nis*), perhaps *fallō* (with extension of *ll* to the perf. *fefellī*). But *ll* may come from other combinations than *ln* (**200.**1), and *per-cellō* 'strike down' (perf. *per-culī*) is probably from **per-cel-dō* with a *d*-extension of the root (cf. *clādēs*).

5. *sko-class* (**355.**1).—Thus *crē-scō*, *nō-scō*, *discō* from **di-dc-scō*

(cf. perf. *di-dic-ī*), *poscō* from **porc-scō*, with extension of *posc-* to perf. *poposcī* (cf. also Skt. perf. *papraccha* beside pres. *pṛcchati*).

From forms like *crēscō* the suffix acquired the force of becoming or beginning, and gave rise to the numerous class of inchoatives in *-ēscō, -īscō, -āscō*, formed from verbs, nouns, and adjectives, as *calēscō* (*caleō*), *dūrēscō* (*dūrus*), *obdormīscō* (*dormiō*), *vesperāscō* (*vesper*).

6. *yo-class* (**355**.2).—Presents of the type *capiō, capere* belong historically with the primary verbs of the fourth conjugation like *veniō, venīre*. They are traditionally classed in the third conjugation because of their agreement with it in the infinitive (which was the Roman basis of classification) and other forms. Such agreement is secondary. See **376**.

7. *Verbs in -uō*.—These include:

A few primary verbs from roots ending in *u*, as *suō* from **su-yō* (Goth. *siu-ja*), *ruō, fluō, struō*. Here also *solvō* from **se-luō* (cf. G. λύω), *volvō* from **weluō* (cf. G. ἐλύω).

Two primary verbs with thematic forms of *nu*-suffix (**355**.10), namely *mi-nuō, ster-nuō*, with *nu* extended to the perfect, etc.

Denominatives from *u*-stems (**356**), as *statuō* (*status*), *metuō* (*metus*).

8. *Presents in -tō-*.—Thus *pectō* (cf. G. πέκω and πεκτέω), *plectō* (cf. G. πλέκω), *flectō, nectō*. These have the appearance of containing a present suffix *-to-*, parallel to *-no-, -yo-*, etc. But there is little evidence for such an IE present suffix, since the Greek forms in π-τω are derived from -π- μω. Elsewhere we find rather a *t*-extension of the root which is generally not confined to the present stem but may be common to the whole verb system and derivatives, so that the form with added *t* is really a new verb stem. So OE *fleohtan*, OHG *flehtan*, cognate with L. *plectō*, OE *feohtan*, OHG *fehtan*, probably cognate with L. *pectō*, and many others in Germanic. The same may be true of the Latin forms, for example, *plec-t-* not only in *plectō* but also in *plexī* (**plect-sī*) and *plexus* (**plect-tos*, **190**), similarly *pec-t-* in *pectō, pexī, pexus*, as also in *pecten*.

9. There are other similar root extensions (or root increments, as they are sometimes called) that are generally characteristic of verb stems, rather than of present stems, e.g. IE *d* or *dh* and *s*. Thus L. *tendō, tetendī* from *ten-d-* beside *ten-* (G. τεν- in τείνω, Skt. *tan-*) in *ten-tus* (later *tēnsus*); L. *vīsō, vīsī, vīsus* from **weid-s-*, beside *videō, vīdī; quaesō*, earlier *quaes-sō*, beside *quaerō* from **quaisō*.

With such an *s*-extension are in some way connected, though their precise development is obscure, the intensives in *-essō*, like *capessō, -petessō*, and also the forms like *indicāssō* (**394**). The *s*-element very commonly has a desiderative or intensive force, notably in the Sanskrit desiderative class (see **388**).

FOURTH CONJUGATION

375. The fourth conjugation comprises primary verbs with presents of the *yo*-class and denominatives.

1. Primary verbs with *yo*-presents (**355.**2), with which belong those of the third conjugation like *capiō*.

THIRD CONJ.: *capiō, faciō, iaciō, 'rapiō, sapiō, fugiō, fodiō, -spiciō*, etc.

FOURTH CONJ.: *veniō, saliō, operiō* and *aperiō* (from **-weryō*), *re-periō, sepeliō, vinciō, farciō*, etc.

There is some fluctuation, especially in *morior* (*moritur*, but early L. *morīrī, morīmur*), *orior* (*oritur*, but *orīrī*), *potiō* (*potitur*, but *potīrī*).

2. Denominatives from *i*-stems and consonant stems (**356**) and by analogy from some others. Thus *fīniō* (*fīnis*), *partior* (*pars, partis*), *custōdiō* (*custōs, custōdis*), *serviō* (*servus*).

376. *Inflection.*—The 1 sg. *-iō* is from *-yō* (**180**) or, in the denominatives of *i*-stems, from *-i-yō;* likewise the 3 pl. *-iunt* from *-yonti* or *-i-yonti*. The *ī* of the other persons (shortened before *-t, -nt*, **101**) is inherited in the primary verbs like *veniō*, agreeing with that of the corresponding Slavic inflection (**355**). The denominatives follow the analogy of the primary inflection.

In the *capiō* type the stem in short *i* is also inherited, agreeing with that of the corresponding Lithuanian inflection (**355**). There is then only a secondary agreement between *capi-s, capi-t, capi-mus, capi-tis*, with orig. *i*, and *legis* from **lege-si*, etc. In *capere, caperem*, etc., the *e* may reflect a phonetic change (**74**a), though also easily explained as due to the analogy of *legere*, etc.

a. According to the view preferred here (it is disputed by some), both the *ī* of the *veniō* type and the *i* of the *capiō* type are inherited. But there are doubtless special factors in the distribution of the two types in Latin. It is observed that the *capiō* type is followed by most verbs with a short root syllable (*veniō* being one of the exceptions), while the *veniō* type is followed by one with a long root syllable or with two short syllables preceding the -*iŏ*. This may be in part connected with the IE distribution of *i* and *ī* and their relation to -*yo*- and -*iyo*- respectively. But it also suggests that iambic shortening in the second and third singular (e.g. *capis, capit* from **capīs, *capīt*) may have been a factor in spreading the *i*-type at the expense of the *ī*-type. In the Italic dialects the latter prevails, though Osc. *factud* from **faki-tōd* is clear evidence of the *i*-type.

377. The irregular verbs of Latin grammar are so classed because in one or another respect they do not conform to any of the four conjugations. The chief irregularity is the survival of some unthematic forms of the root class, like *est*, together with the present subjunctive in -*im* which is in origin an optative of the type which goes with the unthematic indicative (**419**). Another is the composite character of some of them, the combination of different roots making up the verb system, as *sum, fuī*, or *ferō, tulī*. Cf. the similar composite feature in some of the Greek verbs and in the comparison of adjectives (**216** with *a*).

It is only the first of these irregularities that applies to inflection proper and is entirely within the present system. But the other peculiarities are also considered here for convenience.

378. *sum: present indicative.*—Cf. the table of cognate forms in **333.** The analysis is plain for 2 sg. *es;* in Plautus *ess*, from **es-si;* 3 sg. *est* from **es-ti;* 2 pl. *es-tis* like G. ἐσ-τέ with strong grade of the root carried over from the singular (in contrast to Skt. *s-thá*), and with ending -*tis* for -*te* as usual (**339**). More difficult are 1 sg. *sum* from **som* (cf. Osc. s ú m), 1 pl. *sumus* from **somos*, and 3 pl. *sunt* from **sonti*, which have the appearance of thematic forms. The most probable starting-point (despite the fact that Oscan-Umbrian has 3 pl. *sent*, yet 1 sg. Osc. s ú m) is a 3 pl. **sonti*, to be recognized as an Italic or perhaps even IE (cf. ChSl. *sątĭ*) thematic by-form of the usual **senti* (**340.**2), like pres. pple. **sont*- beside *sent*- (Att. ὄντες, Dor. ἔντες). From this might be formed 1 sg. **som* (with secondary ending, or after some form with -*m* from -*mi*) and 1 pl. **somos*. But neither this nor any other explanation is entirely satisfactory.

Beside the usual *sumus*, the form *simus* after the usual type *legimus*, etc., came into partial use.

For imperf. indic. *eram* from **esā-*, see **387**; for fut. *erō* from **esō*, **393**.3; for pres. subj. *sim*, **425**.3. Beside imperf. subj. *essem* from **es-sē-* (**426**), also *forem* from **fu-sē-* (**76a**), like Osc. 3 sg. f u s í d (cf. also Umbr. imperat. *futu* in contrast to L. *estō*).

The perf. *fuī*, early *fūī*, is probably based on the aorist stem seen in G. ἔφῡν, Skt. 1 sg. *abhuvam*, 3 sg. *abhūt*.

The two roots that make up the Latin verb are IE **es-* and **bheu-*, just as in NE *is* and *be*.

379. *possum.*—The present system is based on a union of *pote* 'able' and the regular forms of *sum*, as *possum* from *pote sum* with syncope and assimilation of *ts* to *ss* (**193**), *potest* from *pote est* with elision. In early Latin the uncompounded forms are still in use, with either *potis* or *pote*. The former is the inherited nom. sg. masc., originally a noun = G. πόσις, Skt. *patis* 'lord, master', while *pote* is a nom.-acc. sg. neut. formed to this. But both are used indeclinably without regard to gender or number, as *potis est* or *pote est* 'it is possible', and *potis sunt* 'they can'.

The imperf. subj. *possem*, in place of the rare *potessem*, is due to the influence of *possum, possim;* so also the infin. *posse* in place of *potesse* (both forms in early Latin).

The perf. *potuī* belongs to a pres. *poteō*, of which the only relic in Latin is the pple. *potēns* used as an adjective, but which appears in Osc. p ú t í a d 'possit'.

380. *volō and compounds.*—1 sg. *volō* from **velō* (**80**.6), thematic form of **wel-mi* (cf. Lith. *pa-velmi*); thematic also 1 pl. *volumus* (for *u*, see **349**.1), 3 pl. *volunt*. Unthematic 3 sg. *vult*, earlier *volt* (**82**.5), from **wel-ti* (**80**.6; cf. Lith. *pa-velt*), similarly 2 pl. *vultis, voltis.*

The 2 sg. *vīs* (the connection of *vois* in the Duenos inscription is altogether doubtful) cannot be derived from **wel-si*, which would give *vell, vel* and probably is actually represented by the adverb *vel*. It is rather an isolated relic of another root of similar meaning, namely **wei-*, Skt. *vī-* (2 sg. *veṣi*) 'approach, seek, follow', Av. *vayeiti* 'pursues'.

To the unthematic type belong pres. subj. *velim*, imperf. subj. *vellem* from **vel-sē-*, infin. *velle* from **vel-se*.

For *sī vīs* 'if you please, please' the contracted *sīs* (cf. **171**) is common. After the analogy of this relation arose also **soltis*, early *sultis* beside *sī voltis*.

Nōlō is from **ne-volō* (probably through **novolō* by **92.2, 171**, though there are certain chronological complications), whence *nōl-* spread to nearly all the other forms, *nōlumus*, *nōlunt*, *nōlim*, *nōluī*, etc. But uncontracted forms prevailed in the second and third singular and second plural of the present indicative, with either the old *ne* or its substitute *nōn*, as early *nevīs*, *nevolt* beside *nōn vīs*, *nōn volt*, *nōn vultis*.

mālō is from *māvolō* (**105.2**), this from **mag(i)s-volō* (cf. *sēvirī* from *sex virī*, **207**). Early Latin has *māvolō*, *māvelim*, though more commonly *mālō*, *mālim*, and regularly *māllem*. Uncontracted *māvīs*, *māvolt*, *māvoltis*, like the corresponding forms of *nōlō*.

381. ferō.—In the present system, *fers*, *fert*, *fertis*, *fertō*, *ferre*, etc., have the appearance of being unthematic forms like Vedic *bhárti* beside usual Skt. *bhárati*. Yet the present of this root is normally thematic in the other IE languages, and even in Latin the pres. subj. *feram* (in contrast to *sim*, *velim*) is that which belongs to the thematic type. Hence, since vowel syncope is especially common after *r* (cf. *vir*, *ager*, *ācer*, etc., **109**), one suspects that the forms in question may after all be thematic in origin, e.g. *fers*, *fert* from **feris*, **ferit* (in spite of *geris*, *gerit*, etc., without such syncope).

The perfect is supplied by *tulī*, earlier *tetulī* (the reduplication was lost first in the compounds, then in the simplex), this from **tetolī* from the root of *tollō*. From another grade of the same root comes *lātus* from **tlātos* (**116, 126**).

382. eō.—Unthematic *īs* from **ei-si*, *it*, early *īt*, from **ei-ti*, and, with extension of the strong grade to the plural, *īmus* (in contrast to G. *ἴμεν*, Skt. *imás*), *ītis*. Similarly with *ī* from *ei*, *ībam*, *ībō*, imperat. *ī*, *ītō*, imperf. subj. *īrem*, infin. *īre*.

Pres. sub. *eam* of the thematic type. Forms parallel to *sim*, *velim* would be in part identical with indicative forms, as 1 pl. *imus*.

The perfect is *iī* (*īvī* rare until late), probably from **īyai* (as if Skt. 1 sg. mid. **īye;* cf. 3 pl. act. *īyur*), though there are various possibilities of analysis. 2 sg. *iistī* or contracted *īstī*.

383. *edō.*—Unthematic *ēs, ēst, ēstis,* imperat. *ēs, ēstō,* etc., imperf. subj. *ēssem,* infin. *ēsse,* 3 sg. pres. indic. pass. *ēstur.* All these are from *ēd-,* the lengthened grade of the root, which is also found in the present in Balto-Slavic. The differentiation from the forms of the verb 'to be' was doubtless a factor in the preference for these forms. The evidence for the long vowel is beyond reasonable question.

In *ēst, ēstis,* etc., with *st,* for which the normal phonetic development of dental+dental would give *ss* (**190**), the *t* is kept or restored under the influence of the usual endings. The perf. pass. pple. *ēsus* shows the normal phonetic development, but here also *comēstus* beside *comēsus.*

Pres. subj. *edim* of the unthematic type. Forms of the thematic type, *edam,* etc., are late, and still later thematic forms of the present indicative, as *edis, edit.*

384. *dō.*—From the Latin point of view the irregularity lies in the short *a* of most of the forms, as *damus, datis, dabam, darem, dare,* etc., by which they differ from those of *stāre* and the first conjugation in general. From the comparative point of view, on the contrary, the irregularity lies in the *ā* of *dās, dā.* For the root is **dō-,* as in G. δίδωμι and L. *dōnum,* with weak grade **dǝ-* from which come L. *damus,* etc. The total loss of *dō-* in the verb and the substitution of *dā-* in *dā, dās* is not fully explained. Perhaps it is nothing more than an assimilation of *ō* in quality only to that of the *a* in *damus,* etc.

Early L. pres. subj. *duim,* rarely *duam,* are from a collateral form of the root, namely **dōu-, *dou-* (cf. Umbr. *pur-douitu* 'porricito', Lith. *daviau* 'I gave'), whence *du-* (**110.**5) first in compounds like *perduim.*

385. *fīō.*—From **bhwiyō,* a *yo-* present from the weak grade of the root **bheu-* (L. *fuī,* etc.), like OIr. *-bíu,* OE *bēo* 'am', etc. It belongs with the primary verbs of the fourth conjugation, like *veniō*, but differs from them in having *ī* before a vowel (*fīō, fīunt, fīēbam, fīam*), except in *fierī, fierem* (and even here sometimes *fīerī, fīerem* in early Latin), and in the *ie* of these last forms as compared with *venīre, venīrem*. The *ī* of *fīō*, etc., is probably an extension of that in *fīs*, etc., such extension and also the persistence of the *ī* in contrast to the general rule (**103**) being favored by the fact that this was the only verb in *-iō* with accent on the *i*. That is, we may assume *fīō* for **fiō* after *fīs*, likewise *fīunt, fīam*, etc., then by further extension *fīēbam*, etc. Why there was only a restricted extension of *ī* to *fīerī, fīerem* in early Latin (where *fierī, fierem* are usual) is not clear. But for the later period it is significant that *fīerī, fīerēs, fīerēmus*, etc., could not stand in dactylic verse.

While *fīō* serves as the passive of *faciō*, it retains its active inflection except in the infin. *fierī*, which prevails already in early Latin, though the active form *fīere* is also attested. Early L. *fītur, fīēbantur* are quoted from Cato.

Only forms of the present system occur, the perfect being formed regularly from *faciō*, as *factus sum*, etc.

386. 1. *aiō.*—Pronounced *aiyō* and sometimes written *aiiō* (**179**.2). From **agyō* (cf. *ad-agium, prōd-igium*) like *maior* from **magyō* (**180**). Its early inflection was that of the fourth conjugation. So early L. *aīs, aīt*, and *aibam* from **aībam* beside *aiēbam*, like *audībam* (**387**). Later *ais, ait*, sometimes in two syllables, but usually in one syllable (with retention of the spelling, never *aes, aet*).

2. *inquam.*—*inquit* is from **in-squit*, with the weak grade of the root seen in *īnseque* 'say', OE *secgan* 'say', etc. Most of the forms are of the simple thematic type, as *inquis, inquit, inquimus, inque*, etc. But some, as *inquiunt, inquiēbat*, etc., follow the verbs in *-iō*, perhaps influenced by *aiunt*, etc. The 1 sg. *inquam* is best explained as originally subjunctive, 'let me say', hence 'I assert'.

THE IMPERFECT

387. The Greek imperfect agrees with the Sanskrit and reflects the IE imperfect. This was formed from the present stem with secondary endings, and with or without the augment, which finally became fixed in Greek as in Sanskrit. Thus G. ἔφερον = Skt. *ábharam*. Cf. paradigms **332–33,** and for the augment **350–51.**

In Italic there is no trace of this formation. The isolated L. *eram* is from *esā-, the root *es*- with an *ā* which sometimes occurs elsewhere in past tenses, as in Lith. *buvo* 'was' from *bhuāt (as if L. *fuat instead of *erat*).

Otherwise the tense sign is L. *-bā-* (with regular shortening before *-m*, *-t*, *-nt*, *-r*, **101**), from Italic *-fā-*, as shown by Osc. f u f a n s 'erant', which happens to be the sole example of the imperfect indicative in the Italic dialects. This Italic *-fā-* is probably from **-bhwā-*, with the weak grade of the same root as L. *fuit* and the same *ā* as in L. *eram* and Lith. *buvo* (see above).

a. Upon this basis the whole Latin formation has generally been regarded as one of periphrastic origin. This is still the most attractive view, despite the fact that there is no entirely satisfactory explanation of the part preceding the *-bam*. It cannot be merely the present stem, for, aside from the fact that this does not agree in the third conjugation (*legēbam*, but present stem *leg*ᵉ/*o*-), the present stem is only an abstraction, whereas periphrastic formations are combinations of actual words having an independent existence. Such a proposed derivation as *legēbam* from *legens-fām, that is, a combination with the pres. act. pple., is ideal from every point of view except the phonetic, but in that respect is too improbable. With *vidēbam*, *legēbam* may be compared the *frīgēfactō*, *calefīō* (*cale* from *calē* by iambic shortening), etc. which are obviously of periphrastic origin (cf. also *facit āre*, Lucr.), though the *ē*-forms are here also unexplained. With this support for *-ēbam*, one may regard the other forms as analogical extensions, namely *-ābam*, *-ībam* (in early Latin more frequent than *-iēbam*, as *audībam* beside *veniēbam*), and those that are apparently from the root as *ībam*, *dabam*, and Osc. f u f a n s . The problem is similar in the case of the future in *-bō* (**393.**i).

THE FUTURE

388. The existence of a distinctive future tense in the parent speech is doubtful. Future time might be expressed by the present indicative (as G. εἶμι 'I am going'), by the subjunctive (as G. ἔδομαι, πίομαι, are short-vowel subjunctives to unthematic ἔδμεναι, πίθι), or by certain *s*-formations with desiderative and future force. A suffix *-syo-* is common to the futures of Indo-

Iranian and Lithuanian, as Skt. *dāsyāmi*, Lith. *duosiu;* a suffix *-so-*
to those of Greek and the Italic dialects, as δείξω, Osc.-Umbr.
fust 'erit' (from **fūseti*), and to the early Latin forms like *faxō;*
while both of these are related to the reduplicated *s*-formations
of the Sanskrit desideratives, as *pi-pā-sāmi* 'I wish to drink', and
certain Irish futures.

GREEK

389. The future in -σω is formed with the suffix *-so-*, and is
allied to the other future and desiderative *s*-formations mentioned in **388.** This analysis is preferable to that according to
which the future is the short-vowel subjunctive of an σ-aorist
(**420**). For the agreement with the latter, while frequent, is only
partial and accidental. There are many futures in -σω without
corresponding σ-aorists, and even among verbs which have both
tenses formed with σ there is a significant difference in the case of
the stems ending in a liquid or nasal, as Att. τενῶ from **τενεσω*,
but ἔτεινα from **ἔτενσα*.

a. The consonant changes, the interchange of -ξω and -σω from verbs in -ζω,
the analogical retention of σ in λύσω, the usually long vowel before -σω, are
parallel to the situation in the σ-aorist, and will be discussed in that connection.

390. But the future of most verb stems ending in a liquid or
nasal is formed with -εσω and here the regular loss of intervocalic
σ is effective, hence -εω, Att. -ῶ, as τενέω, τενῶ, βαλέω, βαλῶ, etc.
The ε of this type belongs in origin to certain dissyllabic stems
(**127**) from which it was generalized. Similarly in Sanskrit all
roots ending in *r* or *ṛ*, whether or not they show a dissyllabic
stem in other forms, have the future in *-iṣya-*, as *kariṣyāmi* from
kṛ, and the desiderative in *-īrṣa-* or *-ūrṣa-* (with the *īr, ūr* which
belong to dissyllabic stems, **126**). One may also compare the fact
that in Latin most of the verbs that have perf. *-uī* (from *-ewai*)
and pple. *-itus* (from *-etos*) are from roots ending in a liquid or
nasal, as *molō, moluī, molitus, gignō, genuī, genitus, domō, domuī,
domitus.*

391. The so-called Attic futures are of similar character to the
preceding, in that they also are formed from dissyllabic stems end-

ing in a short vowel and have lost the σ. They differ from them in that they are formed from a greater variety of verb-stems and on the other hand are mainly characteristic of Attic, though some of them occur in Homer and elsewhere. In general they are Attic futures in -ῶ from verbs which in other dialects have the future in -σω. Thus τελῶ (also Hom. τελῶ beside τελέσω), καλῶ (also Hom. καλέω), ἐλῶ (also Hom. ἐλάω; pres. ἐλαύνω), σκεδῶ from -αω (pres. σκεδά-ννῡμι, aor. ἐσκέδα-σα; so from all in -αννῡμι and some in -εννῡμι), κομιῶ (pres. κομίζω; so from most in -ιζω). These may all be regarded as analogical extensions of the type which is general Greek in the case of βαλῶ, etc.

392. The "Doric future" in -σεω is the regular form in the West Greek dialects, as Delph. κλεψέω, etc. But some middle forms of this type occur also in Attic-Ionic. Thus Hom. ἐσσεῖται (beside ἔσσεται, ἔσεται, ἔσται), πεσέονται; Att. πεσοῦμαι, πλευσοῦμαι beside πλεύσομαι, φευξοῦμαι beside φεύξομαι, etc.

This type appears to be a blend of those in -σω and -εω (1 and 2), and that may be a sufficient explanation. In Attic-Ionic it was limited to a few middle forms influenced by the type Att. φανοῦμαι, while in West Greek it prevailed in the whole future system.

a. But a more specific source has been suggested, namely Hom. ἐσσεῖται, which is then explained as a blend of ἔσσεται and an *εἶται (from *ἔσεται, a 3 sg. subj. like L. erit) reflected by ἔσται with ἐσ- restored by analogy.

b. Hom. πεσέονται, Att. πεσοῦμαι are separated by some from this type and derived from *πετέομαι (cf. **391**). But there is nothing against the derivation from *πετσέομαι, since for metrical reasons σσ could not stand in the quotable Homeric forms.

LATIN

393. 1. The future in -bō, of the first and second conjugations and occurring sometimes in the fourth in early Latin in the form -ībō (dormībit, etc.), parallel to the imperfect in -ībam (**387**), is from an Italic -fō. It occurs in Faliscan (pipafo 'bibam'), but not in Oscan-Umbrian, where the future is formed with -so- like the Greek (**388**). This Italic -fō is probably from *-bhwᵉ/o-, with the weak grade of the same root as L. fuit and the thematic vowel, perhaps here the short-vowel subjunctive, like erō (3). That is, the origin of the formation is similar to that of the imperfect in -*bam*, with the same problem (**387**).

2. The future of the third and fourth conjugations is formed with the two Latin mood signs of the subjunctive (**425**), namely *ā* in the first person, *ē* in the other persons, as *legam*, *legēs*, etc., *veniam*, *veniēs*, etc.

3. The isolated *erō*, *eris*, etc., is from **esō*, etc., a present subjunctive of the short-vowel type (**419**).

394. Early L. *faxō*, *capsō*, etc., though commonly called future perfects, are simple futures formed with -*so*-, like the future in Greek and in Oscan-Umbrian (**388**). With them belong the subjunctives *faxim*, *axim*, *ausim* (with optative suffix, **425**.3).

In the forms like *indicāssō*, *negāssim*, etc., the precise source of the *ss* is uncertain, but they have some connection with the intensives like *capessō* and other *s*-formations like *quaesō* from **quaes-sō* (**374**.9).

That all these have nothing to do with the perfect system is shown by the passive forms like *faxitur*, *iussitur*, *turbāssitur*, also infin. *impetrāssere, reconciliāssere*.

THE AORIST

395. The distinctive IE aorist is the *s*-aorist formed from the root by the addition of *s* and the secondary endings. In Sanskrit there is gradation of the root syllable between the lengthened grade in the active and strong or weak grade (according to certain rules) in the middle. But it is unlikely that this reflects the original distribution. There is no gradation in Greek, the root keeping the same form throughout, usually the *e*-grade or the same grade as the present.

The other types of aorist have no positive characteristics distinguishing them from some imperfects belonging to the present stem. For a particular verb they are distinguished by a difference in the grade of the root or by the absence of the special suffix or other characteristic which marks its present stem. Thus in Sanskrit *asicam* is aorist, distinguished from imperf. *asiñcam* (present stem with nasal infix), while the similar *adiçam* is imperfect;

abudham is aorist (imperf. *abodham*), while *atudam* is imperfect. So in Greek aor. ἔτραπον but imperf. ἔγραφον, aor. ἔβην but imperf. ἔφην, aor. ἐγένετο but imperf. ἐλέγετο.

That is, in these types the aorist stem is distinguished from the present stem by contrast in a given verb, rather than by the presence of any formative element peculiar to the aorist as such.

It remains true, however, that the thematic formation with weak grade of the root and accent on the thematic vowel (**354**.2B), while occurring as a present stem, is much more commonly an aorist stem, and nearly always so in Greek.

In Latin the aorist was lost as a distinct tense. Such aorist forms as survived in the perfect will be discussed in that connection.

THE GREEK SIGMATIC AORIST

396. The Greek sigmatic aorist represents the IE *s*-aorist, but with an important innovation. Originally the secondary endings were added directly to the *s*, as 1 sg. -*s-m̥*, 2 sg. -*s-s*, 3 sg. -*s-t*, etc. Cf. Skt. 1 sg. *anāiṣam*, 2 sg. Vedic *anāis*, 3 sg. Vedic *anāis*, 1 pl. *anāiṣma*, 2 pl. *anāiṣṭa*, 3 pl. *anaiṣur*. For Greek we might expect, e.g. ἔλῦσα (-α from -*m̥*), *ἔλῦς, *ἔλῦς, *ἐλῦ(σ)μεν, *ἐλῦστε, ἔλῦσαν (-α from -*n̥t*, then -αν after -ον, etc.). From 1 sg. -σα and 3 pl. -σαν the σα spread to all the indicative forms except 3 sg. -σε, which has ε from the perfect or the thematic aorist; and further to the optative, the imperative (except 2 sg. -σον), and participle (though this may partly reflect an IE -*sn̥t*-), in fact to virtually the whole aorist system except the subjunctive.

397. 1. From roots or verb stems ending in a consonant the usual results of the combinations with σ are observed. Thus ἔγραψα (**191**), ἔδειξα (**192**), ἔπεισα from *ἐπειθ-σα (**193**). For -ξα and -σα from verbs in -ζω, see **360**.2*a*. ἔφηνα from *ἔφαν-σα (**203**.2), ἔστειλα from *ἔστελ-σα, and ἔφθειρα from *ἔφθερ-σα (**205**.2), but ἔκελσα, ὦρσα (**205**.1).

2. From verb stems ending in a vowel the retention of the intervocalic σ is due to the analogy of forms like ἔγραψα, etc. (see **165**).

3. The great majority of verb stems ending in a vowel have a

long vowel before -σα, as ἔλῡσα, ἐτίμησα (Dor. ἐτίμᾱσα), ἐφίλησα, ἐδήλωσα. In some this is the true form of the verb stem, as most obviously in the case of denominatives in -αω, where the short vowel in the present is secondary. But it is largely due to analogical extension from such inherited stem forms as φῡ-, δρᾱ-, πλη-, γνω-.

4. Those that have a short vowel before -σα are from stems ending in σ, as ἐτέλεσα (Hom. ἐτέλεσσα, pres. τελείω from *τελεσ-ψω, 179.1, 363.2), ἔζεσα, ἔτρεσα (363.2), ἔσβεσα, etc. (367); or from stems, mostly dissyllabic (127), ending in a short vowel, as ἐκάλεσα, ἐδάμασα, ἐστόρεσα, ὤμοσα, etc. (here also Hom. ἐκάλεσσα, etc., by analogy of ἐτέλεσσα). In some verbs there is fluctuation, as, from αἰνέω, Att. ᾔνεσα, but Hom. ᾔνησα.

THE GREEK UNSIGMATIC OR "SECOND" AORIST

398. *Thematic.*—Most of these belong to the type which has the weak grade of the root and the accent originally on the thematic vowel (354.2B). Thus ἔλιπον (λιπεῖν, λιπών), ἔφυγον, ἔτραπον, ἔδρακον, ἔσχον, ἐπτόμην, ἐσπόμην, ἔλαβον, etc. A few have the e-grade, as ἔτεκον, ἐγενόμην, ἔτεμον beside ἔταμον. The old accent belonging to the former type is preserved in the infinitive and participle (220, end), as λιπεῖν, λιπών, and is extended to the others, as τεκεῖν, τεκών. That is, in Greek it becomes a characteristic of the aorist, without regard to the original distribution.

A few have reduplication, as ἤγαγον (ἄγω), Hom. ἐκέκλετο (κέλομαι), λέλαθον (λήθω), etc. So, in origin, εἶπον, Hom. ἔειπον from ἔϝειπον (cf. ϝειπ- attested in many dialects, as Cret. 3 pl. subj. ϝείπōντι), this (see 92.1a) from *ἐϝευπον, corresponding to Skt. avocam, from IE *e-we-uqʷom (uqʷ the weak grade of *weqʷ, Skt. vac-, G. ϝεπ- in ϝέπος).

399. *Unthematic.*—These are mostly forms of the root class without gradation but with shortening of the vowel in the third plural, as ἔβην, ἔβλην, ἔγνων, 3 pl. ἔβαν, ἔγνον, etc. (see 349.2a). By analogy of these ἔστην also has ἔστημεν, instead of *ἔσταμεν parallel to ἔθεμεν, ἔδομεν (see below).

The aorists of τίθημι, δίδωμι, ἵημι are peculiar in having their singular, as ἔθηκα, ἔδωκα, ἧκα, formed from an extension of the root, the same that is seen in L. *faciō, fēcī* and in the κ-perfect (see **406**). They also preserve the old gradation, with weak grade outside the singular, as 1 pl. ἔθεμεν, ἔδομεν, εἷμεν (from *ἐ-εμεν*), 1 sg. mid. ἐθέμην, ἐδόμην, εἵμην. The oldest 3 pl. forms are ἔθεν, ἔδον, then Att.-Ion. ἔθεσαν, ἔδοσαν, but also ἔθηκαν, ἔδωκαν formed from the singular.

There is also a series of root aorists occurring only in the middle and mostly Homeric, as λύτο, χύτο, ἆλτο, πάλτο, γέντο, δέκτο, λέκτο.

400. There are several aorists in -α, the history of which is much disputed. Att. ἤνεγκα is in origin a perfect with "Attic reduplication", that is, ἤν-εγκα, exactly corresponding to Skt. perf. *ān-aṅça* from *aṅç-* 'attain'. Most dialects have ἤνεικα from a different root. ἔχεα (χέω) is based upon an old root aorist *ἔχεϝα (α from ṃ), *ἔχευς, *ἔχευ (cf. Skt. *açravam, açros, açroi*), that is, the active form to which belongs 3 sg. mid. χύτο. The α was extended from the first singular to the other forms after the analogy of the σ-aorist. Hom. ἔχευα beside ἔχεα is best explained as having ευ from the old *ἔχευς, *ἔχευ. Like ἔχεα is Hom. ἔκηα from *ἔκηϝα (pres. καίω from *καϝιω, fut. καύσω), and like ἔχευα are Hom. ἄλευαι, ἔσσευα. Arc. ἀπυδόας = ἀποδούς points to an *ἔδοϝα (cf. L. *duim*, **383**).

εἶπα beside εἶπον, rare in Homer (εἶπας, εἴπατε), but frequent in Attic, Ionic, and other dialects (cf. Cret. προϝειπάτō, Lac. προϝειπάhας) is hardly to be explained as an inherited by-form. It seems rather to be formed from εἶπον after the analogy of other aorists in -α. But the more special source, explaining why the α-form is so early and so widespread in this particular verb, is yet to be found. In later times such a shift is frequent, as ἦλθα for ἦλθον, similarly εὗραν, ἔφαγαν, etc. (as ἔφυγα, ἔφυγαν). (So regularly in Modern Greek, ἔφυγα, ἔφυγαν, etc.)

THE GREEK AORIST PASSIVE

401. The Greek aorist passive has two types, -ην and -θην, both with the active secondary endings.

The type in -ην is in origin simply an active unthematic aorist from a stem ending in η (IE *ē*), parallel to ἔβλην (Hom. ξυμβλήτην) beside mid. βλῆτο. Such stems very commonly had intransitive force, and frequently appear beside *yo-* presents which are also largely intransitive and furnished the Sanskrit present passive (**355.**2B, **372.**2*a*). Many of the Homeric forms might be classed as active (intransitive) forms and so translated, as ἐάγη 'broke', ἐκάη 'burned', μίγη 'mingled', ἐχάρη 'rejoiced', φάνη 'appeared'. The intransitive force came to be felt as passive only by contrast with active forms of transitive meaning.

The type in -θην is of disputed origin. But the most probable view is that the starting-point was the 2 sg. mid. ending IE -*thēs*, e.g. ἐδό-θης = Skt. *ádi-thās* from which arose the other forms, 1 sg. ἐδόθην, 3 sg. ἐδόθη, etc., after the analogy of the type in -ην, -ης, -η.

This type was better adapted to verb stems ending in a vowel, especially the great mass of denominative verbs, and already in Homer is many times more frequent than that in -ην. Occasionally both types occur from the same verb, as Hom. μιγήμεναι and μιχθήμεναι, ἐφάνην 'appeared', but ἐφάνθην 'was', ἐγράφην, late ἐγράφθην.

Forms like ἐγνώσθην may be derived from the *s*-aorist middle, as if ἐγνώσθης = Skt. *ajñāsthās*. But it is more probable that the σ here, as in ἔγνωσται (**407***a*), γνωστός, belongs with the widespread analogical extension of σ from forms derived from stems ending in σ or a dental.

The inflection of both types is the same as that of ἔβλην, etc., with η throughout except for the regular shortening before ντ, as in the participle and the old 3 pl. -εν. Hom. 3 pl. ἄγεν, κόσμηθεν, etc., beside -ησαν as in Attic.

THE PERFECT

402. The IE perfect was marked by the following characteristics.

1. Certain distinctive personal endings, as 1 sg. -*a*, 2 sg. -*tha*, 3 sg. -*e*, 2 pl. -*e* (probably, as indicated by Skt. -*a*, but forms of other languages reflect the usual -*te*), 3 pl. -*r* (indicated by Skt. -*ur*, L. -*ēre*, etc.; see **417.**6).

2. Shift of accent and gradation of root, with the same distribution as in the present of the root class, but here (from roots of the *e*-series) with the *o*-grade in the singular in contrast to the *e*-grade of the present (**349.**2). There was also a type with the lengthened grade of the root (*ē, ō,* or *ā*), though the original distribution of such forms is uncertain.

3. Reduplication, commonly consisting of the initial consonant of the root followed by *e* (**352.**3), was a prevailing, though not a universal, characteristic. The agreement between Skt. *véda,* G. οἶδα, L. *vīdī,* Goth. *wait,* together with other evidence, shows that there was an IE perfect type without reduplication.

Apart from the matter of reduplication, the main features of the IE perfect are illustrated by the accompanying table.

Skt.	G.	Goth.
véda	οἶδα	*wait*
véttha	οἶσθα	*waist*
véda	οἶδε	*wait*
vidmá	ἴδμεν (Hom.)	*witum*
vidá	ἴστε	*wituþ*
vidúr	(ἴσᾱσι)	*witun*

THE GREEK PERFECT SYSTEM

403. οἶδα.—This is the one Greek perfect which most faithfully reflects the IE formation in the gradation of the root syllable and in the addition of the endings directly to the root. The regular treatment of two dentals (**190**) accounts for 2 sg. οἶσθα, 2 pl. ἴστε, while 1 pl. Att. ἴσμεν, for earlier ἴδμεν as in Homer, is due to the influence of ἴστε. But the 3 pl. ἴσᾱσι is a new formation. It is from *ϝιδ-σαντι* (cf. also Att. εἴξᾱσι, 3 pl. of ἔοικα), whence Hom. ἴσσᾱσι beside ἴσᾱσι, Dor. ἴσαντι, formed to 3 pl. pluperf. *ϝιδ-σαν,* Hom. ἴσαν, which has -σαν from the σ-aorist. In Doric ἴσαντι gave rise to ἴσᾱμι, etc., after the analogy of ἴστᾱμι to ἴσταντι.

The *e*-grade appears in subj. εἰδῶ (Hom. εἰδέω, 1 pl. εἴδομεν), opt. εἰδείην, partic. εἰδώς (in Homer also fem. ἰδυῖα), fut. εἴσομαι, infin. Att. εἰδέναι (but Hom. ἴδμεν, ἴδμεναι), and in the pluperf. ᾔδη, Hom. ᾔδεα, 3 sg. ᾔειδει, from *ἠϝειδ- with η-augment (**351.**1).

404. *The "second perfect"*, λέλοιπα, *etc.*—The "second perfect" is so called because it is second in frequency to the "first" or κ-perfect; historically it is the earlier. As compared with the primitive οἶδα it shows two important innovations: First, the old gradation is given up, the grade of the singular being generalized in all the active forms. Second, the root syllable is followed by α in all the indicative forms with the exception of the 3 sg. -ε. This is similar to the spread of α in the σ-aorist (**396**), and probably the two processes went on simultaneously with mutual support. Here the source of the α is to be found, first of all, in the inherited 1 sg. -α, supported by the early 3 pl. -ατι (**340.**3) and by some forms like ἔσταμεν, τέθναμεν, etc., in which α belongs to the weak grade of the root (IE ə; cf. Skt. *tasthima* and the extension of *i* to *bubudhima*, etc.). With the generalization of the α, the old 3 pl. -ατι was mostly replaced by -α-ντι, whence Att.-Ion. -ᾶσι.

Roots of the *e*-series regularly show the *o*-grade, that is, the inherited grade of the singular, generalized. Thus λέλοιπα, πέποιθα, γέγονα, τέτροφα, etc. But from roots with ευ the only *o*-grade perfect form is Hom. εἰλήλουθα (cf. fut. ἐλεύσομαι) beside ἐλήλυθα with weak grade as in Attic. All others, as πέφευγα, etc., have the *e*-grade of the present.

A disguised *o*-grade form is Hom. δείδω from *δεδϝοια, beside δείδια (Att. δέδια) from *δεδϝια with weak grade from pl. δείδιμεν. In the Hom. forms the ει is only an indication of the original syllabic length of δεδϝ-.

A parallel gradation, ō:ē (**125**), is seen in ἔρρωγα (ῥήγνυμι), Hom. εἴωθα (ἔθω), and (with κ-type) Dor. ἔωκα (ἵημι).

Roots which have gradation between α and ᾱ, Att.-Ion. η (**123**a) show the latter in the perfect, as εἴληφα (λαμβάνω), ἔᾱγα (ἄγνυμι), πέφηνα (φαίνω from *φανιω), Hom. ἕᾱδε (ἀνδάνω).

Many Greek verbs show no gradation of the root, hence also γέγραφα, etc.

a. There are many scattered traces, mainly in Homer, of the earlier system exemplified by the inflection of οἶδα, namely forms with gradation of the root, or with endings added directly to the root, or with both features. Such are the so-called μι-forms of the perfect or pluperfect. Thus ἔοιγμεν, ἔϊκτην (ἔοικα), infin. γεγάμεν, pple. γεγαώς (γέγονα), μέμαμεν, μεμάᾱσι, μεμαώς (μέμονα), εἰλήλουθμεν (εἰλήλουθα), ἐπέπιθμεν (πέποιθα), δείδιμεν, Att. δέδιμεν (δείδω, above).

Sometimes there is gradation of the root in the participle, with weak grade in the feminine. Thus εἰδώς, ἰδυῖα ; μεμηκώς, μεμακυῖα ; ἀρηρώς, ἀραρυῖα.

405. *The aspirated perfect, Att.* κέκοφα, *etc.*—This is mainly Attic, though some examples occur in other dialects. It is un-known in Homer in the active (cf. κεκοπώς) but does occur in some 3 pl. mid. forms, as τετράφαται (τρέπω), ἔρχαται (εἴργω), ὀρωρέχαται (ὀρέγω), and that is clearly its starting-point. If one compares, for example, the perfect middle forms of τρῑβω, κόπτω, γράφω, as τέτρῑμμαι, κέκομμαι, γέγραμμαι, 2 sg.-ψαι, 3 sg. -πται, 2 pl. -φθε, or a similar series from roots ending in a guttural stop, one observes that owing to the regular changes in consonant combina-tions the differences in order are eliminated, that all roots ending in a labial stop have the same forms, likewise all ending in a guttural stop, etc.—except in the old 3 pl. -αται, where the original final stop of the root would properly remain unchanged. But the leveling common to all the other forms was, in the case of some roots ending in a labial or guttural, extended to the 3 pl. in -αται, and with generalization of the aspirate belonging to γράφω, τρέχω, etc., this being favored by the uniform 2 pl. -φθε or -χθε.

This is the situation indicated by Hom. τετράφαται, etc., and by other similar forms in Herodotus and Thucydides. From such forms (prior to their displacement by the periphrastic forms) the aspirate spread to the active, especially in Attic, as τέτροφα (τρέπω), κέκοφα (κόπτω), τέτριφα (τρῑβω), πέπομφα (πέμπω), δέδειχα (δείκνῡμι), πεφύλαχα (φυλάττω), etc. The type is rare in the early Attic writers, and spread from word to word without ever be-coming universal.

a. In the case of roots ending in a dental stop, the orders were still kept apart in the early period before the endings beginning with μ (cf. κεκαδμένος, κεκορυθμένος, **199**) and there was no analogical leveling in the third plural, like that in Hom. τετράφαται, and no aspirated perfect in Attic. But there was a curious extension of 3 pl. -δαται, -δατο from verb stems ending in δ as Hom., ἐρηρέδαται, ἐρηρέδατο (properly ἐρηριδ- to pres. ἐρείδω), to others as Hom. ἐρράδαται, ἐρράδατο (ῥαίνομαι), ἀκηχέδαται (1sg. ἀκάχημαι), ἐληλά-δατο (3 sg. ἐλήλατο).

406. *The κ-perfect*, τέθηκα, *etc.*—This is a type peculiar to Greek. Its primary evolution must belong to prehistoric Greek, for it is already established, within limits, in Homer and in the earliest records of other dialects. Yet certain stages of its growth are observable in the historical period.

The κ is the same as in three aorists ἔθηκα, ἔδωκα, ἧκα, and is in origin a root "increment" or extension, like that in L. *faciō, fēcī* (IE *dhē-*, *dhə-*, Skt. *dhā-*, G. θη- in τίθημι). Such an extension is a kind of suffix, but one that is not distinctive of any particular tense; it produces another form of the root which may run through all the tenses, as in L. *faciō* (and many others). Thus we may analyze ἔθηκα, τέθηκα from this point of view as ἔ-θηκ-α, τέ-θηκ-α, formed from an extended form of the root identical with that seen in L. *fēcī;* similarly ἧκα like L. *iēcī* (*iaciō*). Not necessarily just these forms alone, for which we find convenient parallels in Latin, but at any rate some few forms of this kind furnished the starting-point. In the first and third singular they offered convenient substitutes for forms in which the vowel endings were obscured by contraction with the final long vowel of the root, e.g. 1 and 3 sg. *τεθη, *δεδω (cf. Skt. *dadhāu, dadāu* with a *u*-extension; Vedic also -*ā*).

The κ-perfect started and was first established with stems ending in a long vowel (including forms like πλη-, βλη- from dissyllabic stems), and in the singular of the indicative. This last is indicated by surviving traces of such distribution in Homer and in various dialects. Thus Hom. βέβηκας, βέβηκε, but 3 pl. βεβάασι, inf. βεβάμεν, part. βεβαώς; τέθνηκε, but 3 pl. τεθνᾶσι, inf. τεθνάμεν, part. τεθνηώς; κέκμηκας, but part. κεκμηώς. Cf. also Boeot. 3 pl. ἀποδε-δόανθι, part. δεδώωση, Arc. 3 pl. [ϝο]φλέασι, etc. So even in Attic ἕστηκα, but pl. ἕσταμεν, etc., δέδοικα (in contrast to Hom. δείδω from *δεδϝοια, **404**), but still pl. δέδιμεν, etc.

From the singular the κ spread to the dual and plural and to all the active forms. From primary verbs the type spread to the denominatives in -αω, -εω, etc., with verb stem ending in a long vowel, and in general to verb stems ending in a vowel. This stage is already reached in Homer and in the early records of other dialects, except for the occasional survival of forms without κ as shown above.

In later times new κ-perfects were formed by analogy from verbs with stems ending in a consonant, as ἔφθαρκα formed to ἔφθαρμαι in place of ἔφθορα, ἔσταλκα formed to ἔσταλμαι, πέπεικα formed to πείσω, ἔπεισα (πείθω) and used in transitive sense in contrast to the older πέποιθα which goes with πείθομαι in meaning.

Many verbs show -ηκα from a secondary stem in η, after the analogy of βέβληκα, etc., as νενέμηκα (νέμω), τετύχηκα (τυγχάνω), μεμάθηκα (μανθάνω), and similarly λελάβηκα (λαμβάνω) in several dialects.

407. *The perfect middle.*—The endings are added directly to the root or verb stem, as originally in the active also (cf. οἶδα, **403**). In the original gradation, as seen in Sanskrit, the root had the weak grade as in the dual and plural of the active. In Greek this is often preserved in contrast to the generalized o-grade of the active. Thus τέτραμμαι (τρέπω) and τέθραμμαι (τρέφω) in contrast to τέτροφα, ἔφθαρμαι in contrast to ἔφθορα, and so ἔσπαρμαι, ἔσταλμαι, τέταται, κέχυται, ἔσσυμαι, πέπυσμαι, etc. But frequently the grade of the present stem is followed, as λέλειμμαι, πέπεισμαι, ἔρρηγμαι, in contrast to λέλοιπα, πέποιθα, ἔρρωγα, not to speak of the many cases like λέλεγμαι from verbs which show no gradation.

a. The numerous consonant changes before the endings are partly in accordance with the regularly phonetic processes, but partly due to analogical leveling (see **190, 191–93, 199**). Of chief importance is the analogical extension of σ which is regular in the third singular from stems ending in a dental stop or in σ, as πέπεισται (πείθω), τετέλεσται (τελέω from *τελεσ-μω), to the forms with μ-endings, as πέπεισμαι, τετέλεσμαι, and from these even to some stems ending in ν, as πέφασμαι (but 3 sg. πέφανται), or in a vowel, as τέτεισμαι (τίνω, fut. τεί-σω), ἔγνωσμαι (γιγνώσκω), etc. These last were favored by forms like ἔζωσμαι, ἔζωσται beside ἔζωμαι, ἔζωται (ζώννῡμι, root ζωσ-), which show leveling in opposite directions from 1 sg. ἔζωμαι (with regular loss of σ before μ), 3 sg. ἔζωσται.

408. *The pluperfect.*—This is a Greek formation, based on the inherited perfect, but its history is partly obscure. Some old dual and plural forms like Hom. ἐπέπιθμεν, ἐΐκτην, βέβασαν are simply forms of the perfect stem with augment or with secondary

endings, and in the pluperfect middle these are the only characteristics. But in the active the earliest forms of the singular,
namely 1 sg. -εα, 2 sg. -εας, 3 sg. -εε or -ει, as in Hom. ἤδεα, ἤδεε,
πεποίθεα, ἐπεποίθει, contain an element ε before the endings proper,
which are the same as in the perfect. The ε appears also before
the endings in the usual dual and plural forms, as ἐλελοίπεμεν,
etc., and in the perf. inf. λελοιπέναι. The source of this apparent
stem in ε is obscure. The derivation of Hom. ἤδεα from *ἤϝειδεσα
and the further comparison of L. pluperf. -eram (from -isā-) is
at best only a partial explanation.

The regular contraction of the old singular forms, -εα, etc.,
gives -η, -ης, -ει, and these, with dual -ετον, -ετην, pl. -εμεν, -ετε,
-εσαν, are the proper Attic forms of the best period. In later Attic
the ει of the third singular was extended by analogy, giving rise
to 1 sg. -ειν, 2 sg. -εις, dual -ειτον, -ειτην, pl. -ειμεν, -ειτε, and
eventually even -εισαν.

a. Hom. 2 sg. ἤειδεις, ἤδησθα, 3 sg. ἤδη are of different formation, being
from a stem ϝειδη- seen also in fut. εἰδήσω and parallel to L. *vĭdē-*.

409. *The future perfect.*—This is a Greek formation, simply a
future in -σω from the perfect stem. It is rare in the active, mainly
ἑστήξω and τεθνήξω from the perfects with present meaning ἕστηκα,
τέθνηκα. Middle forms are common, as λελείψομαι, γεγράψομαι,
etc.

THE LATIN PERFECT SYSTEM

410. The Latin perfect is a blend of the IE perfect and aorist,
both in form and in function. Apart from the uniformity in the
personal endings, it presents a variety of types, partly of perfect
and partly of aorist origin, while the commonest type, the *vī*-
perfect is a specifically Latin development.

a. The merging of the perfect and aorist belongs to the Italic period. But
Oscan and Umbrian show several formations that are unknown in Latin,
and conversely nothing corresponding to the Latin perfect in -*vī*.

411. *The reduplicated perfect.*—This represents the IE reduplicated perfect, in a few forms perhaps also the reduplicated aorist
(cf. *tetigī*, G. τεταγών). For the consonant of the reduplication in
general and for *stetī*, *spopondī*, see **352.4**.

The original vowel of the reduplication is preserved in *dedī*, *stetī*, *cecinī*, *cecīdī*, *pepulī*, *tetendī*, etc., But it is replaced by the vowel of the root syllable wherever this is *i*, *u*, or *o* in both the present and perfect, as in *didicī* (*discō*), *cucurrī* (*currō*), *pupugī* (*pungō*), *momordī* (*mordeō*), *spopondī* (*spondeō*), etc.

This is not a matter of phonetic assimilation, but an analogical extension of the relation observed in cases like *tetendī* (with inherited *te-*) to *tendō*, after which arose *momordī* to *mordeō* in place of *memordī*, *cucurrī* to *currō* in place of *cecurrī*, etc. In several cases the older forms with the orig. *e*-reduplication are quoted, as *memordī*, *pepugī*, *peposcī*, etc.

The loss of the reduplication in the majority of compounds is due to the vowel syncope so characteristic of Latin (**108**). In the few cases where the prefix ends in a short vowel the resulting two double consonants remain, as in *re-ttulī* (*tetulī*), *re-pperī* (*peperī*). But after a long syllable the double consonants are simplified, so that nothing is left of the reduplication, as in *at-tendī* (*tetendī*), *oc-cīdī* (*cecīdī*), etc. A few perfects of compounds retain the reduplication of the simplex, as those in *-didī* (*dedī*), *-stitī* (*stetī*), *-didicī*, *-poposcī*, and *-cucurrī* beside *-currī*.

The vowel of the root syllable is the same as in the present, or with its regular weakening, as in *cecinī* (*canō*), *cecīdī* (*caedō*), *pepulī* (*pellō*), etc. There is no trace of the original gradation.

412. In some verbs the loss of reduplication in compounds led to the use of a perfect without reduplication in the simplex. Thus *tetulī* (frequent in Plautus) was gradually replaced by *tulī*, *scicidī* by *scidī* (late), similarly *fidī* (late) from the frequent *-fidī*. The same explanation holds for *vertī*, *līquī*, and many others, though these appear thus without reduplication from the earliest period.

413. *Perfect with lengthened vowel of the root syllable.*—This is only a convenient heading for a series of forms of diverse origin.

In *vēnī*, *sēdī*, *lēgī*, *ēmī*, *ēdī* beside pres. *veniō*, etc., we have an inherited type with the *ē*-grade of the *e*-series, seen also in Goth. 1 pl. *qēmum*, *sētum*, etc. (1 sg. *qam*, *sat* with the *o*-grade). The original distribution of such forms, and whether they reflect an old perfect or aorist type, is uncertain.

A similar relation in other series ($\bar{a}:a$, $\bar{o}:o$) is partly inherited, as perhaps in *scābī* (*scabō*), *fōdī* (*fodiō*), and extended by analogy as in *cāvī* (*caveō*), *lāvī* (*lavō*), *mōvī* (*moveō*), *vōvī* (*voveō*), *iūvī* (*iuvō*), though these last are otherwise analyzed (as belonging to the *vī*-perfect) by some.

In *fēcī*, *iēcī* (cf. G. ἔθηκα, ἦκα) the *ē* represents the normal grade of the *ē*-series in contrast to the weak grade of the pres. *faciō*, *iaciō*. The same type is followed, but mostly by analogy, in *ēgī* (*agō*), *cēpī* (*capiō*), early L. *co-ēpī* (*apiō*) whence *coepī*, *frēgī* (*frangō*), *pēgī* (*pangō*).

In *vīdī* (*videō*), *līquī* (*linquō*), *vīcī* (*vincō*) the *ī* represents *oi* (cf. G. οἶδα, λέλοιπα, and **90**). So in *fūgī* (*fugiō*), *fūdī* (*fundō*), *rūpī* (*rumpō*) the *ū* presumably represents *ou* (cf. G. πέφευγα for *πέφουγα).

414. *The perfect in -sī.*—This is based on the IE *s*-aorist. Cf. *dīxī*, *clepsī*, like G. ἔδειξα, ἔκλεψα. It occurs only in primary verbs from roots ending in a stop consonant (including the nasals) or in *s*, or in a few cases has been formed by analogy. For the consonant changes, see **191–93**.

Forms in *-psī* from roots ending in a labial stop, as *scrīpsī* (*scrībō*), *clepsī* (*clepō*). So from roots ending in *m*, with the inserted *p* (**195**), as *sūmpsī* (*sūmō*), *-tempsī* (*temnō*).

Forms in *-xī*, from roots ending in a guttural stop, whether palatal or labiovelar, as *dīxī* (*dīcō*), *coxī* (*coquō*), *auxī* (*augeō*), *iūnxī* (*iungō*), *stīnxī* (*stinguō*), *vexī* (*vehō*, from *weĝh-*), *cōnīxī* (*cōnīveō*, from *kneig^{w}h-*, **153**), *fīxī* (early L. *fīvō*, from *dheig^{w}*; later *fīgō*). After the analogy of the relation between *fīxī* and *fīvō*, or the like, arose *vīxī* (*vīvō*) and *strūxī* (*struō*), which are not from roots ending in a guttural. But *flūxī* (*fluō*) is probably from a parallel form of the root (cf. early L. *cōnflugēs* and G. φλυγ- in φλύζω, φλύξαι, beside φλυ- in -φλύω).

Forms in *-ssī*, *-sī* are mostly from roots ending in a dental, as *-cussī* (*-cutiō*), *clausī*, early *claussī* (*claudō*), etc. So *iussī* (*iubeō*, from *yudh-*, **140**). Others are from roots ending in *n*, as *mānsī* (*maneō*), or in a guttural which is lost in the groups *lcs* or *rcs* (**207**.2), as *fulsī*, (*fulgeō* and *fulciō*), or in *s* which becomes *r* in the present, as *gessī* (*gerō*), *ussī* (*ūrō*), *hausī*, early *haussī* (*hauriō*), *haesī*, early *haessī* (*haereō*). So *pressī* (*premō*) must be from a **pres-* beside **prem-* (cf. **tres-* in Skt. *tras-*, G. τρέω beside **trem-* in L. *tremō*).

a. The vowel of the root syllable is usually the same as in the present, apart from the regular lengthening before *ns* or *nx* (**99.**2). But there are some differences. Thus *ussī* with the weak grade, probably under the influence of *ustus*, in contrast to *ūrō* from **eusō;* *cessī* in contrast to *cēdō*, which is perhaps from **cezdō* and so with secondary *ē*. The opposite relation, long vowel in the perfect beside short vowel in the present, appears in two classes of forms.

Those with *ī*, *ū*, from *ei*, *ou* (*eu*), the strong grade, just as in *dīxī*, *dūxī*, but here in contrast to weak grade in the present. Thus *dī-vīsī* (*di-vidō*), *mīsī*, early *meissei* (*mittō*, but this is probably from **meitō*, **mītō*, by **209**), *strūxī*, *flūxī* (*struō*, *fluō;* see above). So the earliest perfect form of *iubeō* (once *ioubeatis*, but probably an error) is 3 sg. *ioussit*, *iūssit* (written *iousit*, etc.), which would have yielded *iūsī* (cf. *meissei*, *mīsī*), but this was replaced by *iussī* under the influence of *iussus*.

Those with *ē* or *ā*, representing the lengthened grade and so parallel to forms like *lēgī* (*legō*) or *scābī* (*scabō*). Thus *rēxī* (*regō*), *tēxī* (*tegō*), *dī-lēxī*, etc., beside *collēgī*, etc. (*legō*), *trāxī* (*trahō*). There is definite evidence for the long vowel in these, but the statement that all perfects in *-exī* had the long vowel is unwarranted. There is no evidence for the long vowel in *vexī* (*vehō*), though it is often quoted as *vēxī* on account of Skt. *avākṣam*, ChSl. *věsŭ*.

Several of the perfects in *-sī* are secondary beside perfects of other types in the same verb. Thus *pānxī* beside *pepigī*, *pēgī* (*pangō*), *parsī* beside *pepercī* (*parcō*), *-pūnxī* beside *pupugī* (*pungō*), *sūmpsī* (*sūmō*) beside *ēmī* (*emō*) and an old *surēmī*.

Forms like *dīxtī*, *dīxem*, *dīxe*, beside *dīxistī*, *dīxissem*, *dīxisse*, are due to haplology (**40.**13), by which *sis* was reduced to *s*. If it were only a matter of vowel syncope, we should expect similar forms from other than *s*-perfects.

415. *The perfect in -vī or -uī.*—This is a type peculiar to Latin (it is not even Italic), just as the κ-perfect is peculiar to Greek, and its evolution was along similar lines. A *w*-element which in some few cases belonged to the root or to an extended form of the root spread to other roots ending in a long vowel (cf. *flē-vī*, *crē-vī*, *sprē-vī*, *sē-vī*, *lē-vī*, *sī-vī*, *scī-vī*, *trī-vī*, *pā-vī*, *strā-vī*, *nō-vī*), also to some dissyllabic stems ending in a short vowel (whence *monuī*, etc.; see below), and to the great mass of verb stems in *ā* and *ī* of the first and fourth conjugations.

a. But the more precise starting-point remains uncertain. According to one view the principal rôle was played by early L. *fūī* pronounced, with the natural glide between *ū* and the following vowel, as *fūvī* and occasionally so written. But neither this nor any of the various other possibilities suggested has won general acceptance.

The perfect in *-uī* is only a variety of that in *-vī*, being formed from stems ending in a short vowel which appear also in the participles in *-itus* (**437.**2), that is, *-uī* from **-e-wai* with the same weakening as in *ēluō, dēnuō,* etc. (**110.**5).

The perfect in *-uī* is combined with that in *-sī* in *messuī (metō)* for **messī*, perhaps due to the influence of early *seruī (serō* 'sow'), and in *nexuī (nectō)* for early *nexī,* like *texuī (texō).*

416. *The shorter forms of the perfect in -vī.*—Some of the "contracted" forms are the result of actual contraction, while others arose by analogy. Where *v* stood between like vowels, it was subject to loss, with resulting contraction of the vowels, as in *dītis* beside *dīvitis,* etc. (**171**). Such parallel forms as *audīvistī—audīstī, audīvissem—audīssem, audīvisse—audīsse, dēlēvērunt—dēlērunt, dēlēveram—dēlēram,* led to others like *nōvistī—nōstī, nōvērunt—nōrunt, nōvisse—nōsse,* and those of the first conjugation which are naturally the most frequent, *amāvistī—amāstī, amāvērunt—amārunt, amāveram—amāram, amāvisse—amāsse,* etc.

In perfects in *-īvī* the contracted forms remain restricted to those which had the sequence *īvi.* There are no forms in *-īrunt, -īram,* etc., parallel to *amārunt, amāram, amārō, amārim,* but rather *audiērunt, audieram, audierō, audierim,* and with these belongs 1 sg. *audiī.* These are probably not derived from the forms with *v,* but arose after the analogy of *iī* with its compounds, which is earlier than *īvī* and not originally of the *vī*-type (**382**).

The shorter forms, especially those of the first conjugation, are quotable from early Latin (cf. *conioura(s)se,* 186 B.C.) and are more common than the full forms in the classical period. But the details of relative frequency are too involved to be presented here.

417. *The endings of the Latin perfect.*

1. *First singular.*—*-ī,* early *-ei* (inscr. *fecei,* etc.), is from a 1 sg. ending IE *-ai,* represented in Skt. 1 sg. perf. mid. *-e,* as *bubudhé,* also in ChSl. *vědě* 'I know', in form = L. *vīdī.*

2. *Second singular.*— *-istī*, early *-istei*, is to be analyzed as *-is-tī*, as also 2 pl. *-is-tis*. The first part belongs in origin to an s-aorist stem, the same which underlies the other tenses of the Latin perfect system (**418**). The second part is from the 2 sg. perf. ending *-tha* (Skt. *-tha*, G. *-θa*, **402**), remade into *-tei*, *-tī* after the analogy of the first singular.

3. *Third singular.*—The earliest forms have *-ed*, as inscr. *fhefhaked*, *feced*, like Osc. d e d e t , etc., with the secondary ending *-d* from *-t* (**337**), which belonged to such forms as were thematic aorists in origin, like Osc. k ú m b e n e d , and was added by analogy to the original perfect ending *-e*.

The *-īt* in Plautus and Terence (also inscr. *-eit*) has (besides the generalized *-t* for earlier *-d*) the long vowel after the analogy of the first singular.

Since we cannot determine whether this *-īt* displaced the form with short vowel or was only one preferred by the early poets, it is uncertain whether the later *-it* comes from *-īt* with the regular shortening (**101**), or represents the old *-ed*.

4. *First plural.*— *-imus* has the same *-mus* from *-mos* as the other tenses (**338**), while the preceding *i* may be explained in various ways and is very likely of various sources. It may be in part the weakening of *a* = IE *ə* belonging to the weak grade of certain roots, and correspond to the *i* of Skt. *-ima*, for example, in *dedimus* = Skt. *dadima*.

5. *Second plural.*— *-istis* is *-is-tis*, with the same *-is-* as in the second singular (above, 2), and with the same *-tis* as in other tenses (**339**).

6. *Third plural*—Three forms, *-ēre*, *-ērunt*, and *-ĕrunt*. The *-ĕrunt*, frequent in poetry and also reflected in the Romance forms, is probably from *-is-ont*, with the same *is* as in 2 sg. *-is-tī*, etc.

Of the other two forms it is clear that *-ēre* cannot come from *-ērunt*, but that *-ērunt* may easily be explained as formed from *-ēre* after the analogy of the frequent 3 pl. *-unt* (or more specifically after *-ĕrunt*).

In fact, *-ēre* contains an inherited ending belonging to a group of 3 pl. *r*-endings (parallel to the 3 pl. *nt*-endings) which are common in Indo-Iranian and are now attested also for Tocharian and Hittite. So, in the perfect, Skt. 3 pl. act. *-ur*, 3 pl. mid. *-ire* (where *-re* is parallel to *-nte* from *-ntai*), Toch. *weñār*, Hitt. *kueṇṇir*. In the L. *-ēre* the *re* may be from *-ro*, parallel to the secondary middle ending *-nto*, and the preceding *ē* may belong in origin to verb stems ending in *ē*. But such details are uncertain.

418. *The other tenses of the Latin perfect system.*—These are all based upon a combination of the Latin perfect stem with an *is*-element (the same as in *-is-tī*, *-is-tis* of the perf. indic.), which represents a variety of the *s*-aorist stem, similar to the Skt. *iṣ*-aorist, as *abodhiṣam*, etc. (But the latter comparison is less perfect than it looks, for the Skt. forms contain in part IE *-əs-*, like G. ἐδάμασα. Cf. also ἐκάλεσα. There were types with different vowels originally belonging to the verb stem, and of these Latin reflects that in *-is-*.)

1. *Pluperfect indicative.*— *-eram* from *-isā-* (**74a**), with the same preterite *ā* as in *eram* (**387**) or perhaps formed after the analogy of the latter.

2. *Future perfect indicative.*— *-erō* from *-is^e/o-*, with the same short-vowel subjunctive as in *erō* (**419**), or perhaps formed after the analogy of the latter. The 3 pl. *-int* instead of *-unt* is from the perfect subjunctive.

3. *Perfect subjunctive.*— *-erim* from *-isī-*, with the optative *ī* (**425.3**). In early Latin the forms *-īs*, *-īt*, *-īmus*, *-ītis* prevail, as against *-is*, *-it*, *-imus*, *-itis* in the future perfect. But later there was much confusion, forms with *ī* in the future perfect and conversely with *i* in the perfect subjunctive. For *faxim*, etc., see **394**.

4. *Pluperfect subjunctive.*— *-issem* from *-is-sē-* with the same *sē* as in the imperfect subjunctive (**426**).

THE SUBJUNCTIVE AND OPTATIVE

419. Survey of the mood signs.

	Subjunctive	Optative
A. From thematic stems	IE ē/ō (?) Skt *ā* G. η/ω L. *ā, ē*	IE *oi* Skt. *e*, Goth. *ai* G. οι L. —— Cf. 3 sg. Skt. *bháret*, Goth. *baírai*, G. φέροι
B. From unthematic stems	IE *e/o* Skt. *a* G. ε/o, later η/ω L. -ō, *is*, etc. Cf. Skt. 3 sg. *asat* to indic. *asti* G. Hom. ἴομεν, βήσομεν, dial. ποιήσει, etc. L. fut. *erō*, and fut. perf. in -*erō*	IE *yē/ī* (*yē* in sg., *ī* in dual, pl.) Skt. *yā/ī* (*yā* in act., *ī* in mid.) G. ιη/ι L. (*iē*), *ī* Cf. Skt. 3 sg. act. *syắt*, 3 sg. mid. *duhītá* G. εἴην from *ἐσιην, εἶμεν from *ἐσῑμεν. Early L. *siem, siēs*, etc., later *sim, sīs*, etc.

a. For the subjunctive of Type A, owing to the difference between Greek and Latin and the ambiguity of the Skt. *ā*, the IE type is somewhat uncertain. But probably it was a combination of the stem vowel *e/o* with the *e/o* of the subj. of unthematic stems, hence with contraction ē/ō, as in G. η/ω, but with generalization of the *ē* in Latin. The *ā*, common to Italic and Celtic is a different element, identical with the *ā* which appears in past tenses of the indicative, as L. *eram* (387). It was originally employed with the verb stem. Cf. early L. *advenat, attigās, abstulās*, which are properly aorist subjunctives.

b. The IE *oi* in the optative of Type A is from *o-ī*, made up of the stem vowel *o* and the weak grade of the suffix *yē/ī* of Type B.

THE GREEK SUBJUNCTIVE

420. *From unthematic stems.*—The original type is that with ε/o, which was generally replaced by the more distinctive η/ω belonging to the thematic stems. Many of the old "short-vowel subjunctive" forms occur in Homer and various dialects, especially in the σ-aorist. Thus, in Homer, ἴομεν (ἴμεν), φθίεται (ἔφθιτο), ἄλεται (ἄλτο), εἴδομεν (οἶδα), πεποίθομεν (πέποιθα), and from σ-aorists, βήσομεν, ἀλγήσετε, ἀμείψεται, etc.; in inscriptions, Ion. ποιήσει, Cret. ἀδικήσει, etc. (-σει was doubtless Homeric also, but was not saved by metrical difference from correction to the later -ση).

So also from stems ending in a long vowel, as Hom. γνώομεν, στήομεν (στείομεν), θήομεν (θείομεν), whence with quantitative

metathesis (**98**.3), Hom. στέωμεν, θέωμεν, Att. στῶμεν, θῶμεν. So
in aor. pass. *λυθήομεν (cf. Hom. τραπείομεν, δαμήετε), Ion.
λυθέωμεν, Att. λυθῶμεν.

Attic has δύνωμαι, ἐπίστωμαι, κρέμωμαι, from δύναμαι, etc., as if
thematic stems.

a. A different formation, with long vowel corresponding to a short
vowel in the indicative, occurs in some dialects, as Mess. τίθηντι beside indic.
τίθεντι, Cret. δύναμαι beside indic. δύναμαι, etc.

421. *From thematic stems.*—Formed with η/ω corresponding
to ε/ο of the indicative. The 2 sg. -ης and 3 sg. -η are formed to
the indic. -εις, -ει (**336–37**), parallel to the relation of 2 pl. -ητε
to indic. -ετε. In Homer there are also forms of the singular with
μι-endings added, ἐθέλωμι, ἐθέλησθα (cf. τίθησθα, etc. **336**), ἐθέλησι.
In the 3 pl. -ωντι (Att. -ωσι) and mid. -ωνται, the ω is preserved
by the analogy of -ωμεν, -ωμεθα from the usual shortening before
ντ.

a. There is no sufficient evidence for the survival of a more original 3 sg.
-η from -ητ, with the ending added directly to η (cf. Skt. -āt). The dialect
forms in -η may stand for the usual -η.

THE GREEK OPTATIVE

422. *From unthematic stems.*—Formed with ιη/ι from IE yē/ĭ.
Thus εἴην from *ἐσιην, εἶμεν from *ἐσῖμεν, εἶεν from *ἐσιμεν
(ending -ent, **340**.2), all with the strong grade of the root in contrast to Skt. *syām*, early L. *siem, siēs*, etc. From stems ending in
a vowel, τιθείην, ἱσταίην, διδοίην, pl. τιθεῖμεν, ἱσταῖμεν, διδοῖμεν.
The retention of ι in εἴην, τιθείην, etc., is due to the analogy of
εἶμεν, τιθεῖμεν, etc.

The inherited distribution of strong forms in the singular and
weak forms in the dual and plural is maintained in Homer with
only one exception, σταίησαν = σταῖεν. But in Attic the singular
stem form is often carried over into the plural, as εἴημεν, εἴητε,
less often εἴησαν; θείημεν, δοίημεν, etc.

By analogy of διδοίην, διδοῖμεν were formed φιλοίην, μισθοίην
to φιλοῖμεν (from φιλέ-οιμεν), μισθοῖμεν, and further τιμῴην (from
*τιμαοιην). For the singular of contract verbs this is the usual
Attic type, though forms in -οῖμι, -οῖς and especially -οῖ also

occur. In Homer only φιλοίη, φοροίη. Attic has also σχοίην to pl. σχοῖμεν, which in contrast to the corresponding form of all other thematic aorists, as λίποιμεν, agrees in accent with δοῖμεν, etc. Conversely sometimes 3 sg. mid. τιθοῖτο, θοῖτο (for τιθεῖτο, θεῖτο) after φιλοῖτο.

Presents in -νῡμι regularly follow the thematic type, as δεικνύοιμι. But there are a few forms with ῡ, from νι, as Hom. 3 sg. δαινῦτο,, 3 pl. δαινύατο.

423. *From thematic stems.*—Formed with -οι-, IE -oi-, as φέροις, φέροι = Skt. *bháres, bháret,* Goth. *bairais, bairai.*

The earliest 1 sg. form was -οια (from *-oyṃ or *-oiyṃ, see below), as long since assumed and now attested by Arc. ἐξελαύνοια. This was replaced by -οιμι, as φέροιμι, with the substitution of the familiar ending of εἰμί, etc. The 3 pl. φέροιεν, etc., is parallel to εἶεν, etc., with -εν from -ent (**422**). In 3 pl. mid. Hom. γενοίατο, but Att. φέροιντο, like -νται for earlier -αται (**344.**6).

a. There is no evidence to show whether 3 pl. -εν is inherited from *-ent only in εἶεν, etc., and is analogical in φέροιεν, etc. (in place of an *-a from *-ṇt), or whether *-ent belonged to both classes. Sanskrit has an r-ending, namely -ur, in both.

b. The apparent retention of intervocalic y as ι in -οια, -οιεν, -οιατο may be easily explained as due to the analogy of οι in the other forms, φέροιμεν, etc.; similarly τιθείην after τειθεῖμεν, etc. So also in Skt. 1 sg. *bháreyam,* 3 pl. *bháreyur,* instead of -ayam, etc., the e may be from *bháret, bhárema,* etc. But taken together (cf. also θείην, Skt. *dhéyam*), they seem to point to IE -oiyṃ, -əiyṃ, etc., as if after vowel stems the y of the suffix was pronounced in both syllables.

424. *From the σ-aorist.*—The usual type, λύσαιμι, λύσαις, λύσαι, etc., is obviously formed from the stem in -σα- (after its spread at the expense of -σ-, **396**) after the analogy of the thematic forms φέροιμι, λίποιμι, etc.

An earlier type is represented by the forms in -ειας, -ειε, -ειαν, which are common in Homer and in Attic, with traces in other dialects. The corresponding 1 sg. -εια, 1 pl. -ειμεν, 2 pl. -ειτε are quoted by grammarians. The source of this type is much disputed, but it appears to reflect an old formation in -sei- from -se-ī-, parallel to the usual thematic -oi- from -o-ī-. The 1 sg. -εια would then be parallel to -οια (**423**), and from this the -ειας, -ειε would be formed with the endings of the indicative.

THE LATIN SUBJUNCTIVE

425. The Latin subjunctive is a blend of the IE subjunctive and optative, both in form and in its uses. The distribution of the mood signs (all of which are long vowels, with the regular shortening before -*m*, -*t*, -*nt*, -*r*, **101**) is as follows:

1. -*ā*- in the present subjunctive of the second, third, and fourth conjugations.

2. -*ē*- in the present subjunctive of the first conjugation, and in the imperfect and pluperfect subjunctive of all conjugations.

In the present subjunctive of the first conjugation the -*ē*- is from -*āyē*, that is, -*āy-ē*- from the stem -*ayo*- (not -*ā-yē*- as an optative). This became first (with loss of intervocalic *y*, **178**) -*āē*-, seen in Osc. *deiuaid*, etc., then with contraction L. -*ē*-.

3. -*ī*- of the IE optative in the present subjunctive of several irregular verbs, as *sim, velim, edim*, and in the perfect subjunctive of all conjugations.

a. The only trace of the old gradation *yē/ī* is in the early L. *siem, siēs, siet, sīmus, sītis, sient*. The singular forms contain the orig. -*yē*-, like G. εἴην, Skt. *syām*, while the 3 pl. *sient* is not from **s-yē-nt* but from **s-y-ent* with ending -*ent* as in G. εἶεν (cf. also Skt. *s-y-ur*). Even early Latin has also *sim, sīs, sit, sīmus, sītis, sint*, with generalized *ī* and in other verbs only such forms. The generalization of the *ī* probably began in the plural, *sient* yielding to *sint*, and then extended from the whole plural to the singular.

426. The imperfect subjunctive is formed with -*sē*-, as *essem* from *es-sē*-, *vellem* from **vel-sē*-, *ferrem* from **fer-sē*-, *amārem* from **amā-sē*- and so, with rhotacism, in all four conjugations.

The further analysis of this -*sē*- has been much disputed. But the simplest view, and one to which there is no valid objection, is that it is an *ē*-subjunctive of an *s*-aorist stem. If we understand the latter in its function as a past tense (in the indicative) and the former in its future value, we have a future of the past, which is a rational basis for the actual uses of the tense.

For the perfect and pluperfect subjunctive, see **418**.3, 4.

THE IMPERATIVE

427. The imperative has no special mood sign like the subjunctive and optative. Some of the endings are the same as the secondary endings of the indicative, so that the forms are of the so-called injunctive type (**326**a). So some 2 sg. forms (**428**.2) and the 2 pl. forms like G. φέρετε, L. *legite*, Skt. *bhárata*, with the regular secondary ending IE -*te* (**339**). There are no proper imperative forms of the first person.

428. *The second singular active.*

1. The bare stem, the commonest type. So regularly from thematic stems, as IE **bhere*, G. φέρε, Skt. *bhára*, G. λέγε, L. *lege*, etc. Here also, with loss of final vowel, L. *dīc, dūc, fac* (beside *dīce, dūce, face* in early Latin), and *fer*.

From unthematic stems, G. ἴστη (but τίθει, δίδου from **τιθε-ε*, **διδο-ε* after thematic type), δείκνῡ, Dor. ἄνστᾱ, etc., L. *es, ī* from **ei*.

The L. -*ā*, -*ē*, -*ī* of the first, second, and fourth conjugations are likewise forms of the bare stem, but, like other forms of these conjugations, partly thematic and partly unthematic, e.g. *vidē* with inherited *ē*, but *monē* from **moneye*.

2. With secondary ending -*s*. G. θές, δός, ἔς, σχές.

3. With special ending, G. -θι, Skt. -*dhi*, -*hi*, IE -*dhi*. This belongs only to unthematic stems.

G. ἴσθι 'be', with prothetic vowel (**106**) from **σ-θι* (cf. Av. *zdī*, but Skt. *edhi* from **az-dhi*), ἴσθι 'know' (cf. Skt. *viddhí*), ἴθι (cf. Skt. *ihí*), φαθί, στῆθι, γνῶθι, Hom. κλῦθι (cf. Skt. *çrudhí*), δίδωθι, ὄρνυθι (beside δείκνῡ; cf. Ved. *sunuhí* and *sunú*), etc.

This remains the regular ending in the aorist passive, as φάνηθι, etc., or, with dissimilation of aspirates (**132**), λύθητι, etc.

4. The rare πίει, ἄγει, δίδοι are probably nothing more than the stem forms with an added particle ι. But some regard the first two as relics of an IE 2 sg. -*ei* and forerunners of the 2 sg. -*εις* (otherwise **336**).

5. The ον in the σ-aorist, λῦσον, etc., is of obscure origin.

429. Forms with G. -τω, L. -*tō* (early L. -*tōd*, Osc. -*tud* = -*tōd*), Skt. (mostly Vedic) -*tād*, IE -*tōd*. This ending is probably in origin the ablative singular of the pronominal stem *to-, used adverbially and attached to the verb stem in its imperative use (**428**.1), *bhere *tōd, *bheretōd—the result being a form which had the force of a future imperative and was not restricted in person or number. The Sanskrit forms are used mainly with future force, like the Latin, and most commonly as second singular but also not infrequently as third singular and as second plural.

In Greek the inherited -τω is restricted to the third singular. From it were formed the 3 dual -των (in place of the secondary ending -τᾱν, -την), and the 3 pl. -ντων, etc.

There are various 3 pl. formations, namely:

-των, with added secondary ending, as Att.-Ion. ἔστων

-ντω, after the analogy of -ντι, in many dialects, as φερόντω, τιθέντω, ἔντω

-ντων, with double pluralization, a combination of the two preceding types, in Attic-Ionic and several other dialects, as φερόντων, τιθέντων, etc.

-τωσαν, with the same expansion of -σαν from the σ-aorist as elsewhere (**340**.4), in late Attic, as φερέτωσαν, ἔστωσαν

In Latin the -tō serves as second and third singular of the future imperative, and new plurals are formed from it, 2 pl. -tōte with the inherited ending -te as in the present imperative, 3 pl. -ntō after the analogy of -nt, as feruntō from *ferontōd, like G. dial. φερόντω.

430. *The Greek middle and the Latin passive endings.*—In the second singular both Greek and Latin (in the present) reflect the IE secondary ending -so, as G. τίθεσο, φέρου from *φερεσο (see **344**.2a), L. sequere (**347**.2). In the second plural the endings are the same as in the other moods, G. -σθε, L. -minī. Likewise the Greek 2 dual -σθον.

In Greek, after the analogy of the relation of -σθε to act. -τε, was formed 3 sg. -σθω to act. -τω, and from this again 3 dual -σθων, parallel to act. -των, and 3 pl. -σθων, etc.

There are various 3 pl. formations, as in the active.

-σθων, parallel to -των in Att.-Ion. ἔστων, but here the commonest type, as φερέσθων, etc.

-(ν)σθω, parallel to -ντω, in Arg. ποιγραφάνσθō, Epid. φερόσθō.

-(ν)σθων, parallel to -ντων, in early Att. ἐπιμελόσθōν

-σθωσαν, parallel to -τωσαν, in late Attic

For L. -tor, -ntor, see **347**.3, 6. Beside -tor, also early L. -minō, as fruiminō, formed from the same stem as 2 pl. -minī (**347**.5) after the analogy of act. -tō.

THE INFINITIVE

431. As already stated in **329**.1, the infinitive is in origin a case form which has become attached to the verb system, and, while the use of such verbal nouns had doubtless begun in the parent speech, no particular set of forms was yet stabilized as infinitives. In Vedic Sanskrit the forms that may be classed as infinitives (thirty-five different types in the Rigveda) include a great variety of noun stems and of cases, but conspicuous among the former are root nouns, stems in -tu-, s-stems, and n-stems, and among the latter the dative and locative singular.

Just as there is great diversity in the infinitive forms among the IE languages in general, so there is no agreement between Greek and Latin, or between Latin and Oscan-Umbrian, and even within Greek there is much diversity among the dialects.

Owing to this diversity, the variety of possibilities, and the lack for the most part of cogent equations, the analysis of the Greek and Latin infinitives is difficult and can hardly go beyond certain probabilities.

432. *The Greek infinitives.*—The infinitive middle has uniformly -σθαι. But the infinitive active has different endings for thematic and unthematic stems, and dialectic variety within each class.

1. *From thematic stems.*—Att.-Ion. -ειν (ει = ē, **96**), in some dialects -ην, both by contraction from -εεν (to be understood in Hom. ἰδέειν before consonants). This may be from either *-εσεν or *-ειεν (hardly *-εϝεν which would have left some trace of the ϝ in the dialects). If we choose the former, we may call it a locative singular without ending (**230**.9) of a stem in -sen- (a combination of s- and n-stem), and compare Vedic -sani (neṣáṇi, from nī-, etc.).

But many dialects have simply -εν, as φέρεν, ᾶγεν and some of
these even from verbs in -εω, as Arg. πωλέν.

2. *From unthematic stems.*—Att.-Ion. (also Arc.-Cypr.) -ναι,
in part -εναι and -ϝεναι(?). Thus τιθέναι, διδόναι, perf. εἰδέναι,
aor. θεῖναι from *θεεναι, δοῦναι from *δοεναι, Cypr. δοϝέναι. This
last (cf. Vedic *dāváne*) is probably to be analyzed as δο-ϝέναι, but
possibly as δοϝ-έναι (cf. L. *duim*, etc., 383). Att.-Ion. εἶναι, Arc.
ῆναι may be from *ἐσ-ναι or from *ἐσεναι.

The type rests on an *n*-stem case form parallel to that of Hom.,
Lesb. -μεναι (cf. Vedic -*mane*) and to the *s*-stem form of the aor.
infin. -σαι (cf. Vedic -*ase*), and the ending in all these is probably
an old dative. For this is the natural analysis of the Vedic forms
and it is unlikely that the Greek forms are different, despite the
evidence that points also to an IE dat. ending -*ei* (230.6).

-μεν in Homer and many dialects is a locative singular without
ending, like Vedic loc. sg. *karman*, etc. (230.9). Cret. -μην and
Rhod. -μειν are blends of -μεν with thematic -ην or -ειν.

Hom. -μεν and -μεναι are sometimes extended to thematic
stems, as εἰπέμεν, εἰπέμεναι beside εἰπεῖν. Similarly Boeot. φε-
ρέμεν, Thess. ὑπαρχέμεν.

3. For -σαι of the σ-aorist see above, 2. By analogy also εἶπαι
to εἶπα, etc.

4. *The infin. mid. in.* -σθαι.—Probably related in some way to
the frequent Vedic -*dhyāi*, though all details are uncertain. According to a possible analysis the σ belongs to a nominal σ-stem,
while -θαι answers to Skt. -*dhe* in çrad-dhe, dat. sg. of a noun in
-*dh*-, the weak form of IE *dhē*—for example, εἴδεσ-θαι (εἶδος),
then felt as εἴδε-σθαι.

433. *The Latin infinitives and supine.*

1. *The present infinitive active.*—The ending is -se, as in *es-se*,
ferre from *fer-se*, *velle* from *vel-se*, *amāre* from *amā-se* and so
with rhotacism in, all four conjugations. This -se is from *-si
(74b), loc. sg. of an s-stem.

Perf. infin. -*isse*, that is, -*is-se* with the same *is* as in -*istī*,
-*issem*, etc. (418).

2. *The present infinitive passive.*—The -*ī* of the third conjuga-

tion may be regarded as a dat. sg. of a root noun, and the -*rī* of the other three conjugations as a dat. sg. of an *s*-stem, like G. aor. infin. -σαι.

Early L. *laudārier*, *dīcier*, etc., appear to be formed from the -*rī*, -*ī* with the addition of -*er* and regular shortening of the vowel (103). But while one could readily understand the addition of an -*r* after the analogy of other passive forms, an -*er* is difficult to explain. The true analysis remains doubtful.

3. The other infinitives are periphrastic. In the future active the simple -*tūrum* is more common than the -*tūrum esse*, and is thought by some to be the earlier and itself an infinitive (derived from supine in -*tū* + *erom* = Osc. *ezum* 'esse'). But this view is not followed here.

The future passive -*tum īrī* is based on an active -*tum īre* (the supine with *īre*, cf. *eō questum* 'I am going to cry', Plautus), which was made passive by converting *īre* into the (otherwise unknown) passive form *īrī*.

4. The supine is formed with the suffix -*tu*-, the same that appears in nouns of action like *cantus*, *adventus*, etc. Acc. sg. -*tum*, corresponding to the regular infinitive of classical Sanskrit, abl. sg. or dat. sg. -*tū* (there is no early inscriptional example to show whether the form was -*tūd* or -*tou*), and rarely dat. sg. -*uī*.

THE PARTICIPLES

434. *The active participles in -nt-.*—The IE active participle of all tenses except the perfect was formed from the tense stem with the suffix -*nt*-. Thus, from the thematic stem, G. φέροντ-, L. *ferent*-, Skt. *bhárant*-, Goth. *bairand*-, Lith. *vežant*-, etc. Most of the forms point to -*ont*- (just as in 3 pl. -*onti*), but in Latin this appears only in the oblique cases of *iēns*, *euntis*, etc., otherwise -*ent*-. Whether this latter reflects an inherited thematic -*e-nt*- beside -*o-nt*- or has been taken over from an unthematic -*ent*-, -*n̥t*- (see following) is uncertain. That the participles of the thematic type had -*n̥t*- originally is, despite the situation in Sanskrit, the most unlikely view.

a. After unthematic stems ending in a consonant there was gradation of the suffix, as IE **s-ént-* (cf. 3 pl. **sénti*), weak **s-ṇt*, Skt. acc. sg. *sántam*, gen. sg. *satás*, nom. sg. fem. *satî*. There are traces of this in a few G. dialect forms. Thus, nom. pl. Dor. ἔντες (for *ἔντες, like 3 pl. ἐντί for *ἐντί, 340.2), fem. ἔασσα, ἴαττα (from *ἄτια=Skt. *satî*, with ε from other forms). But the usual forms are of the thematic type, as ἐών, ἐόντος, fem. ἐοῦσα, or Att. ὤν, ὄντος, οὖσα.

435. *The Greek perfect active participle.*—The IE suffix was *-wes-* with gradation. Cf. Av. nom. sg. *vīdvå*, acc. sg. *vīdvåṇhəm* (from *-vās-*), Skt. nom. sg. *vidván,* acc. sg. *vidvåṅsam* (both with second-ary *n*, from another class), voc. sg. Vedic *vídvas*, gen. sg. *vidúṣas*, nom. sg. fem. *vidúṣī*.

So in Greek nom. sg. masc. *-ως* from *-ϝως, nom.-acc. sg. neut. *-ος* from *-ϝος, and fem. *-υια* from *-υσια=Skt. *-uṣī*, Lith *-usi*.

The other masc. and neut. forms are from a stem *-(ϝ)οτ-*. This may reflect a parallel IE suffix *-wet-* (cf. Goth. *weidwōps* 'witness'; but the Skt. *-vat-* forms appear to be late and to be explained otherwise), but its large rôle in the inflection of the pple. is pe-culiar to Greek and probably connected with the otherwise ob-served spread of *τ*-stems, especially in neuters (**250–52**).

a. In the Aeolic dialects the perfect participle follows the thematic *ντ*-type, as Lesb. κατεληλύθοντος, Thess. πεφειράκοντες, Boeot. ϝεϝυκονομειόν-των. So Hom. κεκλήγοντες.

436. *The Latin future active participle in -tūrus.*—The suffix is formally identical with that in the adjective *mātūrus*, and related to that in feminines like *nātūra, cultūra*, also to that in the de-siderative verbs like *parturiō*. These rest on a combination of the suffix *-tu-* (cf. the supine) with *-ro-*, *-rā-*, etc., giving a *-turo-* as indicated by *parturiō* as well as *-tūro-, -tūrā-*. Cf. G. γλαφυρός, ἰσχυρός, L. *figūra* (**470.**5). The future force develops from the notion of 'what is to be' (*futūrus*), 'to do' (*factūrus*), etc. Likewise the allied desiderative force of the verbs.

437. *The Latin perfect passive participle and the Greek verbal adjective in -τος.*

1. These are formally identical with each other and with the Sanskrit passive participle in *-tá-*. They reflect an IE verbal adjective formed with *-to-* from the root or verb stem, rather than

from a tense stem like the regular participles, and not belonging to any tense system or strictly to any voice. It indicated the object or person as being in a situation resulting from the action expressed by the verb. From transitive verbs it would usually have passive force, but it might also be formed from intransitive verbs.

In Sanskrit and Latin the force is usually passive, but not always. Thus Skt. *gatás* 'gone', *bhūtás* 'been', *sthitás* 'standing', *patitás* 'fallen', L. *pōtus* 'having drunk', *cēnātus* 'having dined', *iūrātus* 'having sworn'.

The Greek verbal adjectives in -τος may have passive force, as γραπτός 'written' just like L. *scrīptus*, or active force, as ῥυτός 'flowing', or may indicate possibility, as ὁρᾱτός 'to be seen, visible'.

2. The formation originally had accented suffix and, from primary verbs, the weak grade of the root, as regularly in Sanskrit. In Greek and Latin many forms show the inherited weak grade, as G. κλυτός, L. *inclutus* (Skt. *çrutás*), G. στατός, L. *status* (Skt. *sthitás*), L. *dictus* (Skt. *diṣṭás*), *ductus, ustus*, etc.; or, from dissyllabic stems, G. τλητός, Dor. τλᾱτός, L. *lātus*, etc. (126). But many show a different grade, mostly conforming to that of the present, or in Latin sometimes to that of the perfect. Thus G. γευστός (but L. *gustō*, -āre, Skt. *juṣṭás*), ζευκτός, L. *scrīptus, fīsus*, etc., or *ēsus, ēmptus, lēctus*, with the same grade as the perf. *ēdī, ēmī, lēgī*. For *lēctus, tēctus, tāctus*, etc., see also 99.2d. For L. *ūnctus*, with nasal from the present stem, see 374.3.

The Latin forms in -*itus* are mostly from roots ending in a liquid or nasal, or rather from their dissyllabic stems which appear also in the perfect in -*uī* (415) and the Greek futures in -εω (390). In *monitus* from the causative *moneō* (372.4) the *i* may represent IE *i* as the weak grade of the causative suffix (so Skt. -*ita*- in causatives). But in most cases it is the weakening of an earlier *e*, though this may stand in the place of an IE ə. Thus for *genitus* the immediate source is **genetos* (cf. Osc. G e n e t a í , G. γενέτης) though in theory we should assume an IE **ǵenətos* (126). So *tacitus* (cf. Umbr. *taśes*), *molitus, domitus*, etc.

L. -*ūtus* regularly from verbs in -*uō*, as *tribūtus, minūtus*. So *solūtus, volūtus* to *solvō, volvō* from **se-luō, *weluō* (G. ἐλύω), and by analogy *secūtus, locūtus* to *sequor, loquor*. In vulgar Latin this spread to many other verbs, hence It. *veduto, venuto*, Fr. *vu, venu*, etc.

3. In forms from roots ending in a consonant the usual changes in consonant groups (190) are observed. Thus, from roots ending in a dental, G. πιστός (πείθω), L. *fissus* (*findō*), *clausus* (*claudō*), etc.

In Greek, from forms like πιστός, ζωστός (cf. Av. yāsta-), the σ spread to some stems ending in a vowel, as γνωστός, etc., just as in the aor. pass. (**401**) and perf. mid. (**407**).

In Latin the great majority of the forms in -sus are thus derived from roots ending in a dental. From these the -sus spread by analogy to others. In verbs having an s-perfect this was especially favored by pairs like clausī, claussus, hence fīxus (fīgō, fīxī), flūxus (fluō, flūxī), mulsus (mulgeō, mulsī), mānsus (maneō, mānsī), etc. But also in others, as cēnsus (censeō, cēnsuī; but Osc. ancensto 'incensa'), lāpsus (lābor; here perhaps special influence of cāsus 'fallen'), pulsus (pellō; cf. early L. pultō, -āre, from *pultus), falsus (fallō), etc. The s may come from a dental combination in percu̇sus (if percellō is from *-celdō, **374**.4), plexus (plectō, **374**.8), amplexus (amplector).

438. *The middle participle.*—IE -meno- with gradation, G. -μενο-, Skt. -māna- (from thematic stems; otherwise -āna-), Av. -mana-, -mna-, etc. Cf. G. φερόμενος, Skt. bháramāṇas. For the accent, see **219**. In the perfect, -μένος from -μενός (cf. Skt. -āná-), regularly in forms of dactylic ending (**219**) like γεγραμμένος, and by analogy in λελυμένος, etc.

439. *The Latin gerundive.*—This is a formation peculiar to Italic. It occurs in Oscan-Umbrian (with nn from nd), e.g. Osc. ú p s a n n a m 'operandam', Umbr. pihaner 'piandi'. It cannot be identified with any productive category in the other IE languages. One can only compare certain scattered forms showing an nd-suffix without well-defined value, as L. glāns, glandis 'acorn' (*glā-nd-, cf. G. βάλα-νος), ChSl. želądǐ 'acorn' (*gʷela-nd-i-), Lith. balandis 'dove' (:bal-tas 'white'), valanda 'while' (from the same root as L. volvō), rakanda 'a kind of basket' (:renku, renkti 'collect'), etc., also the verb ChSl. bądą 'become' formed from a *bhu-ndo- (cf. L. -bundus).

Similar forms in -ndo-, with adjectival-participial value, must have furnished the starting-point of the type which became so productive in Latin. Its earliest force was substantially that of a simple active or middle participle, as it appears in oriundus 'rising', volvendus 'rolling' (volvenda diēs 'time rolling on'), lābundus 'slipping', etc., and similarly in secundus (lit. 'following':sequor), rotundus (lit. 'rolling':rota 'wheel').

This developed along two lines into the more distinctive uses which came to prevail. From transitive verbs it was used with retention of the active force, but in agreement with the logical object (or better, both in the same construction), as in *cupiditās bellī gerendī* 'desire of war, of the carrying on' = 'desire of carrying on war'. Or it was used with the force of 'that which is to do, to be done', as in *bellum gerendum est* 'war is to carry on, to be carried on'. This use as a "future passive participle" or "participle of necessity" is a secondary one, just as the corresponding use of the Sanskrit gerundives in *-ya-* is only a specialized use of the same suffix as employed in adjectives.

a. In the third and fourth conjugations the original type is that in *-undus* from *-ondo-s*, as *dīcundus, faciundus*. That in *-endus*, as *dīcendus, faciendus*, which also occurs even in early Latin (*exdeicendum, faciendum* in SC de Bacch.), and in Umbrian (*anferener* 'circumferendi'), and which eventually prevails, is due to the influence of the pres. act. pple. in *-ent-*. But always *eundum*, just as *euntis*. And *secundus, rotundus*, not being felt as participles, were unaffected.

440. *The Latin gerund.*—This consists simply of certain case forms (gen., dat., acc., abl., sg.) of the gerundive, in its earlier active value, used as verbal nouns. Such use is perhaps a purely Latin development, although the absence of examples in Oscan-Umbrian may easily be accidental.

a. In late Latin the gerund, in the ablative form, came to be used freely as an indeclinable present participle, and is the source of the present participle in the Romance languages (It., Sp. *amando*, Fr. *amant*).

WORD FORMATION

441. By word formation is meant the formation of the word as a unit as distinct from its inflectional variations. For nouns and adjectives the unit is the stem, so that here word formation is equivalent to stem formation. In the case of the verb, the formation of tense stems is always treated as a part of inflection, and even the formation of secondary verb stems (denominatives, etc.) has been given above in that connection. Several other matters belonging to word formation have also been discussed already, such as the comparison of adjectives, and the formation of certain noun or adjective stems which constitute distinct declensional types.

It remains to consider the formation of nouns, adjectives, and adverbs, and the principles of composition. But the subject is so complex and involved in detail that nothing more can be attempted here than a skeleton survey with a few illustrative examples.

DERIVATION OF NOUNS AND ADJECTIVES

442. Some nouns and adjectives have stems that are identical with verbal roots. But the great majority are formed by means of added suffixes of derivation.

Some suffixes can be shown to be in origin independent words forming the second member of compounds. Thus NE -*ly* comes from a word *līc* 'body, form', as in OE *eorþ-līc* 'having the form of the earth, earthly'. Similarly the suffixes in NE *wis-dom, child-hood, up-ward*, etc. So in the temporal adjectives formed from adverbs, like L. *diūtinus* 'long', Skt. *nūtana-*[1] 'present' (464.12), the suffix is probably from the root **ten-* 'stretch'. Cf. also G. -ωδης, **497**.

But the great majority of the suffixes which are common to the IE languages were already in the parent speech mere formative elements, the remoter origin of which is entirely beyond our reach.

---

[1] In this chapter Sanskrit nouns and adjectives are quoted mostly in their stem forms (with hyphen; some nom. sg. forms without hyphen).

443. 1. One distinguishes primary derivatives or primary suffixes, when the derivation is from a root or verb stem, and secondary derivation or secondary suffixes, when the derivation is from another noun or adjective stem. Many suffixes are used prevailingly in one way or the other, but there is no hard-and-fast line, and some are common as both primary and secondary suffixes.

2. One may also distinguish between productive and unproductive (or living and dead) suffixes. Thus in English abstracts derived from adjectives the suffix -*ness* in *darkness, happiness,* etc., is very productive, while *warmth, depth,* etc., are formed with an old inherited suffix which is no longer productive. An IE suffix -*ti*- is very productive in Greek, where it is represented by some five thousand words in -σις, whereas in Latin it is inherited in some words like *pars, gēns,* but as a productive suffix is replaced by its extension -*tiōn*-, as *āctiō,* etc. (**486**).

444. It is a frequent phenomenon that an element which belongs to the stem to which the suffix is added becomes attached to the latter in analogical formations, so that a new form of the suffix, independently productive, is created. Thus in Latin after forms like *silvā-nus* 'of the forest' (*silva*), were formed others like *urb-ānus* 'of the city' (*urbs*), with a new suffix -*āno*-, under which we now, for convenience, group also *silvānus.* Similarly, or starting in part from verbal *ā*-stems, L. -*āris, -ālis, -ābilis,* etc.

Similarly in composition. After G. κακοῦργος 'evildoing' from κακο-(ϝ)εργός was formed παν-οῦργος 'villainous'.

In this way arose many suffixes that are compounded of others, as L. -*tiōn* (*āctiō,* etc.) originating in the addition of an *n*-suffix to words formed with the -*ti*- suffix. In the following such compounded suffixes are generally grouped according to the final element, but sometimes according to the first, when this brings out the more important relationship, as that between L. -*tiōn*- and -*ti*-, or between G. -τήριον and -τήρ, L. -*tōrium* and -*tor.*

445. *Back-formations.*—Ordinarily one word is formed from another by the addition of a suffix. Thus from L. *cūra* 'care' is formed (with the suffix -*yo*-, **356**) the verb *cūrō,* and from the verb stem *cūrā-* again *cūrātor, cūrātio*. But L. *pugna* 'fight', instead of being the source of the verb *pugnō* 'fight', is rather formed from it after the analogy of *cūra* beside *cūrō*, etc., while *pugnō* is a denominative from *pugnus* 'fist', the sequence being *pugnus* 'fist', *pugnō* ('use the fist') 'fight', *pugna* 'fight'.

Ordinarily the feminine is formed to the masculine, and the plural to the singular. But G. ἑταῖρος 'companion' in place of earlier ἕταρος is formed from the more important ἑταίρᾱ 'female companion' (orig. *ἑταρ-ι̯α), just as NE *widower* from the inherited *widow*. L. *decemvir* from pl. *decemvirī* the official 'ten men', like NE *tenpin* from *tenpins*. L. *duumvir, triumvir* from pl. *duumvirī, triumvirī*, these from gen. pl. *duumvirum, triumvirum*.

Such cases where the usual relation is reversed are conveniently known as back-formations. Those like L. *pugna* from the verb are also called postverbal formations or postverbals.

446. In describing the semantic character of derivatives, the following classes are of especial importance.

Nouns of agency, or agent nouns for short, denoting the doer of the action expressed by the verb, as NE *maker*, L. *victor*, etc. While these generally denote persons or at least living beings, they may also come to be applied to inanimate objects, for example, utensils, as G. κρᾱτήρ 'mixer, mixing bowl', ῥαιστήρ 'hammer' (cf. NE *boiler*, *strainer*, etc.).

Nouns of action, action nouns, or verbal abstracts, denoting the action expressed by the verb, like the English verbal nouns *doing, singing*, etc. But such verbal abstracts are very frequently employed in a concrete sense, as in NE *a (newspaper) clipping*, or L. *cantus*, orig. 'the act of singing', but commonly 'song'. Of the many suffixes that may form verbal abstracts, some keep closer than others to the original force and form the more distinctively abstract classes.

Qualitative abstracts, nouns derived from adjectives and denoting the quality expressed by the adjective, as NE *goodness*, L. *bonitās* 'goodness', G. νεότης 'youth'. These may also be used concretely, as NE *a youth, many kindnesses*.

Diminutives, secondary nouns or adjectives denoting something smaller than what is expressed by the word from which they are derived. Words of this type are often used without reference to actual size, as terms of affection or ridicule. Sometimes they lose all distinctive force, are equivalent in meaning to their source words, and even displace the latter in common use.

Other more specific classes which may be indicated by special suffixes are:

Patronymics, denoting a person's family descent

Words denoting a person's country, nationality, or native town

Words denoting a person's trade or occupation

Words denoting means or instrument, or place

447. In the following the derivative suffixes will be classified by form, but with an indication of their uses, so far as these are at all distinctive. Frequently the uses of a suffix are so various that no statement regarding them is worth while, and the examples are left to speak for themselves.

ROOT STEMS

448. Root stems, with or without gradation.

G. πούς, ποδός 'foot', L. pēs, pedis, Skt. pắt, padás

G. ὄψ, ὀπός 'voice', L. vōx, vōcis, Skt. vắk, vācás

G. κλώψ, κλωπός 'thief' (κλέπ-τω 'steal')   φλόξ, φλογός 'flame' (φλέγω 'burn')

θήρ, θηρός 'wild beast'   θρίξ, τριχός 'hair'

L. dux, ducis 'leader' (dūcō 'lead')   lēx, lēgis 'law'

lūx, lūcis 'light'   pāx, pācis 'peace'

Often as the second part of compounds.

G. σύ-ζυξ, σύ-ζυγος 'spouse', L. con-iux, con-iugis (iungō 'join')

G. χέρ-νιψ, χέρνιβος 'water for washing the hands' (νίζω 'wash')

L. in-dex, in-dicis 'informer, sign', iū-dex, iūdicis 'judge' (*in-dic-, iūs-dic-, from the root of dīcō orig. 'point out')

au-spex, au-spicis 'observer of omens' (avis 'bird', speciō 'watch')

au-ceps, au-cupis 'fowler' (avis 'bird', capiō 'seize')

VOWEL SUFFIXES

449. -o- and -ā-.

1. In Greek the derivatives with -o- comprise mainly action nouns with accent on the root syllable and agent nouns with accent on the suffix, while the derivatives with -ā- are mostly action nouns with accent on the suffix. A similar relation is observed in Sanskrit, as çása- 'order', çāsá- 'orderer'. But there are many exceptions in both Greek and Sanskrit.

From roots of the e-series the o-grade is most common, but other grades also occur, as in στέγη 'roof', λώπη 'covering', δίκη 'right', φυγή 'flight', ζυγόν 'yoke'.

τροχός 'wheel' (τρέχω 'run')	τρόχος 'course'	
τροφός 'nurse' (τρέφω 'nourish')		τροφή 'nourishment'
φορός 'bringing in' (φέρω 'bring')	φόρος 'tribute'	φορά 'crop'
τροπός 'thong' (τρέπω 'turn')	τρόπος 'turn, manner'	τροπή 'turning'
ἀοιδός 'singer' (ἀείδω 'sing')		ἀοιδή 'song'
ἀρχός 'leader' (ἄρχω 'lead, begin')		ἀρχή 'beginning'
	στόλος 'equipment, expedition' (στέλλω 'send') λόγος 'speech' (λέγω 'speak')	στολή 'equipment, garment' σπουδή 'haste' (σπεύδω 'hasten')

a. The compound masculine agent nouns in -ās, -ης, like παιδοτρίβης 'gymnastic master', Ὀλυμπιονίκης 'victor at the Olympic games', are ultimately based upon feminine action nouns of the usual type (see **525**).

2. In Latin the type occurs in a number of words, but is not productive as in Greek.

coquus 'cook' (*coquō* 'cook') *procus* 'suitor' (*precor* 'ask')
dolus 'deceit' (cf. G. δόλος) *iugum* 'yoke' (*iungō* 'join', cf. G. ζυγόν)
fuga 'flight' (*fugiō* 'flee', cf. G. φυγή) *toga* 'cloak' (*tegō* 'cover')

There are also some masculine agent nouns formed with -ā-, mostly compounds like *agricola* 'farmer', but also *scrība* 'writer', etc.

3. The most widespread use of the suffixes -o- and -ā- is in combination, in the common type of adjectives, like G. σοφός, σοφή, σοφόν, L. bonus, bona, bonum (280).

450. -i-. G. τρόχις 'runner' (τρέχω 'run').

δῆρις 'fight' (δέρω 'flay')   ὄφις 'serpent' (Skt. ahi-)

ὄϝις (Att. οἶς) 'sheep', L. ovis (Skt. avi-)   L. anguis 'serpent'

avis 'bird'   neut. mare 'sea'

Adjectives.—Rare in Greek, common in Latin (see **283**)

G. τρόφις 'stout'   L. dulcis 'sweet'   turpis 'base'

451. 1. -u-. G. πῆχυς 'forearm' (Skt. bāhu-).

γένυς 'chin',   γόνυ 'knee' (Skt. jānu)   δόρυ 'beam, spear' (Skt. dāru 'wood')

L. manus 'hand'   acus 'needle'   genu 'knee'   pecu 'cattle' (Skt. paçu)

Adjectives.—Greek only. ἡδύς 'sweet, pleasant' (Skt. svādu- 'sweet')   γλυκύς 'sweet'   ταχύς 'swift'.

2. -ū-. G. νέκῦς 'corpse'   ἰσχύς 'strength'   πληθύς 'crowd'. Cf. the root stems ὀφρῦς 'brow' (Skt. bhrús, bhruvás), σῦς, ῦς, L. sūs.

452. G. -ευς. For stem and declension, see **269**. Very productive type, partly primary agent nouns, but especially secondary derivatives denoting one's office, occupation, home. The ultimate source of this type is obscure.

βασιλεύς 'king'   ἱερεύς 'priest'   γραμματεύς 'secretary'

ἱππεύς 'horseman, knight' (beside ἱππότης)   φονεύς 'murderer'

Μεγαρεύς 'Megarian'

453. Suffix -ī-/-yā, G. -ια/-ιᾱ-. Forms feminine nouns and especially the feminine of participles and adjectives, from cons. stems and u-stems (see **237**).

-yo-[1]

454. -yo- furnishes the most productive type of IE adjectives, some primary (cf. G. ἅγιος 'holy' to ἅζομαι 'worship', Skt. yajya- 'to be worshiped' to yaj- 'worship'), but mostly secondary derivatives from nouns and denoting any sort of relationship to the

---

[1] That is, -yo- (or -io-) and -yā (or -iā). So in the succeeding captions, like -mo-, -no-, etc., the corresponding ā-stem forms are to be understood as included.

latter. In derivatives from *o*-stems the *o* is dropped before the suffix. There are also many nouns, which are in part only the adjective forms in substantive use.

This suffix is one most frequently combined with others, giving rise to a great variety of compound suffixes. Some of these will be mentioned here, others in connection with their first element.

455. 1. *Adjectives.*—G. πάτριος, L. *patrius*, Skt. *pitriya-* 'paternal' (πατήρ, etc.).

G. φίλιος 'friendly' (φίλος 'dear')   τῑμιος 'honored' (τῑμή 'honor')

πλούσιος 'rich' (πλοῦτος 'wealth')   L. *rēgius* 'royal' (*rēx* 'king') *noxius* 'harmful' (*noxa* 'harm')

Patronymic use in Hom. Τελαμώνιος (and frequently in the Aeolic dialects), and in the Latin gentile names *Claudius*, *Tullius*, etc.

2. *Nouns.*—Neuter and feminine abstracts.

G. σφάγιον 'victim' (σφάζω 'slaughter')   ἐρείπια 'ruins' (ἐρείπω 'throw down')

L. *studium* 'zeal' (*studeō* 'be zealous')   *gaudium* 'joy' (*gaudeō* 'rejoice')   *coniugium* 'wedlock' (*coniux* 'spouse')

But G. -ιον is most common in diminutives, as παιδίον 'small child' (παῖς, παιδός), ἀσπίδιον 'small shield' (ἀσπίς, -ιδος). From forms like the last arose -ιδιον, as ξιφίδιον 'dagger' (ξίφος 'sword').

G. σοφίᾱ 'wisdom' (σοφός 'wise')   μανίᾱ 'madness' (μαίνομαι 'rage')

ἡγεμονίᾱ 'sovereignty' (ἡγεμών 'leader')   L. *invidia* 'grudge' (*invideō* 'grudge')

audācia 'boldness' (*audāx* 'bold')   *miseria* 'misery' (*miser* 'wretched)

In Latin also *-iēs* in similar abstracts, as *faciēs* 'form, face' (*faciō* 'make'), *speciēs* 'look' (*speciō* 'look'). For the relation to *yā*-stems, see **273.**

Greek masculines in -ιᾱs are formed on the basis of feminine abstracts like the above, as νεανίᾱς 'a youth' from *νεανίᾱ 'youth'.

456. *-eyo-*, G. *-εos*, Att. *-οῦs*, L. *-eus*. Adjectives denoting material.

G. χρύσεos 'golden' (χρῡσός 'gold')   Hom. λίθεos 'of stone' (λίθos 'stone')

L. *aureus* 'golden' (*aurum* 'gold')   *ferreus* 'of iron' (*ferrum* 'iron')

Cf. Skt. *hiraṇyaya-* 'golden' (*hiraṇya-* 'gold')

The suffix *-no-* is also used in the same way, as Att. λίθινos 'of stone', L. *fāginus* 'of beech' (*fāgus* 'beech'). Hence, by combination with the preceding, G. *-ινεos*, L. *-neus*, as:

Hom. ἐλάϊνεos 'of olive wood' (ἐλαία 'olive tree')

L. *eburneus* 'of ivory' (*ebur* 'ivory')

Among other Latin combinations with *-eus* are *-āceus* (**502.2**), *-āneus* (**464.9**). For G. *-λεos* see **472.4**.

457. Greek adjectives in *-αιos*, *-ειos*, *-οιos*.

-αιos. Mostly from ā-stems, but extended by analogy to others. Probably from loc. sg. *-αι+ιο-*.

δίκαιos 'just' (δίκη 'right')   ἀγοραῖos belonging to the ἀγορά
σπουδαῖos 'earnest' (σπουδή 'zeal')   νησαῖos 'insular' (νῆσos 'island')   'Αθηναῖos 'Athenian' ('Αθηνᾶ)

-ειos. From o-stems, cons. stems, and nouns in *-εύs*.

οἰκεῖos 'of the house' (οἶκos 'house')   ἀνδρεῖos 'manly' (ἀνήρ 'man')

βασίλειos 'royal', neut. βασίλειον 'palace' (βασιλεύs 'king')

From *-ηιos*, as in Ionic and other dialects (οἰκήιos, ἀνδρήιos, βασιλήιos), and this in part at least from *-ηϝιos* (cf. Boeot. καρυκέϝιos), that is, *-ηϝ-ιos* from nouns in *-εύs*.

-οιos. αἰδοῖos 'venerable' (αἰδώs 'shame'), but mostly in the pronominal derivatives denoting kind, as οἶos, ποῖos, ἀλλοῖos, etc. These latter are probably from loc. sg. *-οι+ιο-*.

-wo-

458. *-wo-* forms adjectives, including a considerable group denoting color, and some nouns. G. *-ϝos* or *-ϝᾱ* are directly attested only for words that occur in early dialect inscriptions, but are to be assumed for many others (**176**).

G. βίος 'life', L. vīvus, Skt. jīva-, Lith. gyvas 'living', from IE
*gʷī-wo- (152)

Boot. καλϝός, Hom. κᾱλός, Att. καλός 'beautiful'

Cor. ξένϝος, Hom. ξεῖνος, Att. ξένος 'stranger'

Arc. κόρϝᾱ, Hom. κούρη, Att. κόρη 'maiden'

*μόνϝος, Hom. μοῦνος, Att. μόνος 'alone'

*ὄλϝος, Hom. οὖλος, Att. ὅλος 'whole', L. salvus 'well, safe'

λαι(ϝ)ός, σκαι(ϝ)ός, L. laevus, scaevus 'left'

L. parvus 'small'   calvus 'bald'   ·helvus 'yellow'   flāvus
'golden'

L. fulvus 'tawny'   rīvus 'stream'   clīvus 'slope'   silva
'forest'   arvum 'field'

459. L. -ĭvus, -tīvus. nocīvus 'harmful' (noceō 'harm'), aestīvus
'of summer' (aestus 'heat'). Mostly -tīvus, formed from the perf.
pass. pple., and then independently productive.

captīvus 'captive' (capiō 'take')   fugitīvus 'fugitive' (fugiō 'flee')
statīvus 'stationary' (stō 'stand')

So the names of the cases, nōminātīvus, genetīvus, etc. (which
are translations, partly mistranslations, of the Greek), and other
grammatical terms.

NASAL SUFFIXES

460. -mo-.

1. *Adjectives.*—G. θερμός 'warm' (cf. θέρος 'summer') L.
formus 'warm' (cf. Skt. gharma- 'heat').

G. ἔτυμος 'true' (cf. ἐτε(ϝ)ός 'real')   φαίδιμος 'shining' beside
φαιδρός   κύδιμος 'glorious' beside κῡδρός (-ι- beside -ρο- as
in cpd. κῡδι-άνειρα)

μάχιμος 'warlike' (μάχη 'battle')

G. -σιμος, from abstracts in -σις, as χρήσιμος 'useful' (χρῆσις 'use'),
στάσιμος 'stationary' (στάσις 'standing')

L. almus 'nourishing, kind' (alō 'nourish')   firmus 'firm',
līmus 'sideways'

a. For L. -mus, -imus, -timus, -simus in superlatives, see **295**; for -mus in
ordinals, **318.**

2. *Nouns.*—G. θῡμός 'spirit, temper', L. fūmus 'smoke',
Skt. dhūma- 'smoke, vapor'.

G. ἄνεμος 'wind', L. *animus* 'soul' (cf. *anima* 'wind, breath, life')

G. ἁρμός 'joint' (ἀραρίσκω 'join, fasten'), L. *armus* 'shoulder,' neut. pl. *arma* 'fittings, arms'

G. φήμη, L. *fāma* 'report' (φημί, *fārī* 'say')

G. γνώμη 'intelligence, opinion' (γιγνώσκω 'know')

μνήμη 'memory' (μιμνήσκω 'remind')　　L. *forma* 'shape'　*flamma* 'flame'　　*gemma* 'bud, gem'

G. -τμος, -θμος, -σμος (fem. -τμη, -θμη, -σμη), starting from verb stems ending in a dental or with dental increment, and with analogical extension of σ as in perf. mid. πέπεισμαι, etc. (407)

ἐρετμόν 'oar' (cf. ἐρέτης 'rower')　　σταθμός 'station' (ἵστημι 'stand')　　δασμός 'division, tribute' (δατέομαι 'divide')

ῥυθμός 'rhythm' (ῥέω 'flow')　　θεσμός 'law', Dor. τεθμός (τίθημι 'set')　　ὀσμή 'smell', Hom. ὀδμή (ὄζω 'smell')

461. -men-.

1. *Masculines.*—G. -μην and -μων, L. -*mō*, gen. -*mōnis*. Agent nouns and action nouns.

G. ποιμήν 'shepherd'　　λιμήν 'harbor'

ἄκμων 'anvil'　　τέρμων 'boundary'　　ἡγεμών 'leader' (ἡγέομαι 'lead')

τελαμών 'strap for carrying' (ἔτλην, ἐτάλασα 'bear')

L. *sermō* 'discourse'　　*pulmō* 'lung'

2. *Neuters.*—G. -μα, gen. -ματος (**250**), L. -*men*. Originally action nouns, but most frequently denoting the result of the action. One of the most productive types in Greek, the number running to several thousands.

G. ὄνομα, L. *nōmen*, Skt. *nāma* 'name'　　G. τέρμα 'goal', L. *termen* 'boundary'

G. πρᾶγμα 'act' (πράσσω 'do')　　ποίημα 'a work, poem' (ποιέω 'make')

G. μνῆμα 'monument' (contrast μνήμη 'memory')　　δέρμα 'skin' (δέρω 'flay')

L. *flūmen* 'stream' (*fluō* 'flow')　　*fragmen* 'fragment' (*frangō* 'break')

sēmen 'seed' (*serō* 'sow', root *sē-*)

3. Combined with -*to*-, in -*m̥to*-, L. -*mentum*.

fragmentum 'fragment' beside *fragmen*   *alimentum* 'nourishment' (*alō* 'nourish')

ōrnāmentum 'ornament' (*ōrnāre* 'adorn')   *testāmentum* 'testament, will' (*testor* 'testify')

Here perhaps also G. -ματα in plural of -μα (**250***a*).

4. Combined with -*io*- in L. -*mōnium*.

alimōnium 'nourishment' (*alō* 'nourish')   *mātrimōnium* 'mar-
riage state' (*māter* 'mother')

So fem. -*mōnia*, as *parsimōnia* 'thriftiness' (*parcō* 'spare')

462. -*meno*- and -*mno*. Mostly in middle participles (**438**).
A few nouns, as:

G. στάμνος 'jar' (ἴστημι)   βέλεμνον 'missile'

λίμνη 'lake' (cf. λιμήν 'harbor')   ποίμνη 'herd' (cf. ποιμήν
'shepherd')

L. *fēmina* 'a female, woman' (lit. 'one who gives suck', cf. G.
θῆλυς 'female', θῆσθαι 'suck, suckle')

463. -*en*- and -*yen*-.

1. G. -ην (-ενος or -ηνος) and -ων (-ονος or -ωνος), L. -ō (*inis* or
ōnis).

G. ἄρρην, -ενος 'male'   τέρην, -ενος 'tender'

αὐχήν, -ένος 'neck'   πευθήν, -ῆνος 'inquirer, spy' (πεύθομαι 'learn')

τέκτων, -ονος 'craftsman, carpenter' (Skt. *takṣan*-, **160**)   εἰκών,
-ονος 'image' (ἔοικα, εἰκ- 'be like')

ἀγών, -ῶνος 'assembly, contest' (ἄγω 'bring')   L. *carō, carnis,*
'flesh'   *homō, -inis* 'man'

G. -ων, -ωνος and L. -ō, -ōnis are productive in designations of
persons, especially derogatory epithets.

G. γάστρων 'glutton' (γαστήρ 'belly')   φύσκων 'fat-belly' (φύσκη
'sausage')

L. *comedō* 'glutton' (*comedō* 'eat up')   *labeō* 'big-lip' (*labium*
'lip')   *praedō* 'robber' (*praeda* 'booty')

lēnō 'pander'   *caupō* 'tavern-keeper'

G. -ών, -ῶνος, beside -εών, in words denoting place.

ἀνδρών 'men's apartment' (ἀνήρ 'man')   παρθενών 'maidens'
apartment' (παρθένος 'maiden')

ἱππών 'stable' (ἵππος 'horse')   οἰνών 'wine-cellar' (οἶνος 'wine')

ἀμπελών 'vineyard' (ἄμπελος 'vine')   δαφνών 'laurel-grove'
(δάφνη 'laurel')

2. L. *-iō, -iōnis*. Masc. agent nouns and fem. abstracts.
centuriō, decuriō 'head of a centuria, decuria'
histriō 'actor'   *lūdiō* 'stage-player'
legiō 'body of soldiers, legion' (*legō* 'gather, select')
regiō 'direction, region' (*regō* 'direct')
occīdiō 'slaughter' (*occīdō* 'slay')

a. More productive in the combination *-tiō, -tiōnis* (486). Other combinations of *-en-* are *-men-* (461); *-gen-*, L. *-gō* (505); *-den-*, L. *-dō*, G. *-δων* (496; L. *-tūdō*, 488).

For neuters formed with an *n*-suffix (apart from *-men-*, 461.2), mostly with nom.-acc. sg. in *-r*, see 251.

464. *-no-*. This furnishes one of the most productive types of adjectives (in Sanskrit they serve mostly as passive participles), also many nouns of all genders. From combinations with the preceding stem arise many varieties, of which the most productive types are G. *-ινος*, L. *-ānus* and *-īnus*.

1. G. δεινός 'fearful' (δέδοικα 'fear').
σεμνός 'revered' (σέβομαι 'revere')   στυγνός 'abhorred' (στυγέω 'abhor')
L. *dignus* 'worthy' (*decet* 'is fitting')   *magnus* 'great' (cf. G. μέγας 'great')
plēnus 'full' (*-pleō* 'fill'; cf. Skt. *pūrṇa-*, Lith. *pilnas*, but G. πλήρης 'full')
G. ὕπνος, L. *somnus* 'sleep' (cf. Skt. *svapna-* and see 80.2, 119.3)
G. τέκνον 'child' (τίκτω 'bear', ἔτεκον)   ποινή 'punishment' (cf. Slav. *cěna* 'reward')
L. *dōnum* 'gift' (*dare* 'give', orig. root **dō-* as in G. δίδωμι; cf. δῶρον 'gift')
lāna 'wool' (cf. Skt. *ūrṇā-* 'wool')

2. G. *-avos* (from *-n̥o-*, beside *-no-*).
πιθανός 'probable' (πείθω 'persuade')   στεγανός 'covered' (στέγω 'cover')
στέφανος 'crown' (στέφω 'put round')   κτέανον 'property' (κτάομαι 'possess')

δαπάνη 'expense' (δάπτω 'devour')

3. G. -ᾱνος, -ηνος in derivatives of place names in Asia Minor, as Σαρδιᾱνός 'of Sardis', Περγαμηνός 'of Pergamum', and of non-Greek origin.

4. G. -ινος. πεδινός 'level' (πεδίον 'plain').

ἀνθρώπινος 'human' (ἄνθρωπος 'man')

Adjectives of time, as:

χθεσινός 'of yesterday' (χθές 'yesterday') περυσινός 'of last year' (πέρυσι 'last year')

Adjectives of material (with recessive accent), as:

λίθινος 'of stone' (λίθος 'stone') ξύλινος 'wooden' (ξύλον 'wood')

5. G. -ῑνος, mostly in derivatives of place names, as:

Βυζαντῖνος 'of Byzantium', Ταραντῖνος 'of Tarentum' (but this probably from L. -ῑnus)

6. G. -εινος (orig. -εσ-νο- from σ-stems). ἀλγεινός 'painful' (ἄλγος 'pain').

ὀρεινός 'mountainous' (ὄρος 'mountain') ταπεινός ('low')

7. G. -ῡνος, -ῡνη. κίνδῡνος 'danger' αἰσχύνη 'shame' (αἶσχος 'shame').

8. G. -συνος, -σύνη. δουλόσυνος 'enslaved', δουλοσύνη 'slavery' (δοῦλος 'slave').

εὐφροσύνη 'mirth' (εὔφρων 'merry') δικαιοσύνη 'justice' (δίκαιος 'just')

Those in -σύνη are feminine abstracts from adjectives or nouns, denoting quality or condition, like those in -της, -τητος. Probably from -τυνος (cf. 141b), with -no- added to the abstract suffix -tu-, and parallel to the Sanskrit neuter abstracts in -tvana- beside -tva-, as patitvanam 'wedlock' (pati- 'husband').

9. L. -ānus. Adjectives originally formed from ā-stem nouns, then from others.

Rōmānus 'Roman' (Rōma) silvānus 'of the forest' (silva) urbānus 'of the city' (urbs)

mundānus 'of the world' (mundus) montānus 'of the mountains' (mons)

Also *-āneus*, as *subterrāneus* 'underground' (*sub terrā*, **526**), *mediterrāneus* 'inland' (*medius, terra*)

10. L. *-īnus* (adj.) and *-īna*.

canīnus 'of a dog' (*canis*)   *equīnus* 'of a horse' (*equus*), *marīnus* 'of the sea' (*mare*)

fēminīnus 'of a woman' (*fēmina*)   *Latīnus* 'Latin' (*Latium*)

rēgīna 'queen' (*rēx* 'king')   *gallīna* 'hen' (*gallus* 'cock')   *ruīna* 'fall, ruin' (*ruō* 'fall down')

opificīna, officīna 'workshop' (*opifex* 'artisan')   *medicīna* 'healing' (*medicus* 'physician')

disciplīna 'instruction' (*discipulus* 'pupil')   *doctrīna* 'teaching' (*doctor* 'teacher')

11. L. *-ūnus* and *-ūna*.

tribūnus 'head of a tribe, tribune' (*tribus* 'tribe')   *fortūna* 'chance, fortune' (*fors* 'chance')

12. L. *-(t)ernus, -(t)urnus, -tinus*. Mostly adjectives denoting time.

hodiernus 'of today' (*hodie*), *hesternus* 'of yesterday' (*herī*) *diurnus* 'daily' (*diēs*)

diuturnus, diūtinus 'long-continued' (*diū*)   *crāstinus* 'of tomorrow' (*crās*)

For those in *-tinus* cf. Skt. *hyastana-* 'of yesterday' (*hyas* 'yesterday'), Lith. *dabartinas* 'of the present' (*dabar* 'now').

465. *-ni-* and *-nu-*. L. *ignis*, Skt. *agnis*, Lith. *ugnis* 'fire'.

L. *collis* 'hill' from **col-ni-s* (Lith. *kalnas* 'mountain' with *-no-*) cpd. adj. *commūnis* 'common', *immānis* 'huge'

G. λιγνύς 'smoky flame'   θρῆνυς 'footstool'

L. *sinus* 'fold'   *pīnus* 'pine'

r-SUFFIXES

466. *-ter-, -tor-* (or sometimes *-er-, -or-*). Agent nouns and nouns of relationship. For gradation and inflectional types, see **249**.

1. G. δοτήρ, L. *dator*, Skt. *dātar-* 'giver' (δίδωμι, etc. 'give').

G. σωτήρ 'savior' (σῴζω 'save')   ῥήτωρ 'speaker' (ἐρέω, ἐρρήθην 'say')

L. *amātor* 'lover' (*amō* 'love') *victor* 'victor' (*vincō* 'conquer')
scrīptor 'writer' (*scrībō* 'write'); with -*sor* from roots ending in a
dental (190), *dēfēnsor* 'defender' (*dēfendō* 'ward off, defend')
tōnsor 'barber' (*tondeō* 'shear')

By analogy formed also from nouns:

iānitor 'one who keeps the door' (*iānua*) *gladiātor* 'one who
uses the sword' (*gladius*)

In Latin this is the most productive suffix of agent nouns. But
not in Greek, where it comes to be replaced by -της, Dor. -τᾱς
(484). Forms in -τηρ occur in poetry, and the dialects, where
Attic has -της, as Hom. ἐθελοντήρ 'volunteer' = Att. ἐθελοντής,
dial. δικαστήρ, κριτήρ = Att. δικαστής, κριτής. The older type
appears also indirectly in the derivatives like ψάλτρια fem. of ψάλτης 'harper', or δικαστήριον 'court' beside δικαστής 'judge'.

In Attic, -τηρ survives in σωτήρ, as a fixed epithet, otherwise in
names of implements or utensils, which were agent nouns in
origin but no longer felt as such (like the personal agent nouns),
as κρᾱτήρ 'mixer, mixing-bowl' (κεράννῡμι 'mix'), ῥαιστήρ 'hammer' (ῥαίω 'smash').

2. G. πατήρ, L. *pater*, Skt. *pitar-* 'father'.

G. μήτηρ, L. *māter*, Skt. *mātar-* 'mother' G. φράτηρ 'member
of a brotherhood', L. *frāter*, Skt. *bhrātar-* 'brother'

G. θυγάτηρ, Skt. *duhitar-* 'daughter' L. *soror*, Skt. *svasar-* 'sister'

So G. ἀνήρ, Skt. *nar-* 'man'

For neuters formed with an *r*-suffix in nom.-acc. sg., beside *n*-suffix in
the other cases, see 251.

467. G. -τήριος, -τήριον, L. -*tōrius*, -*tōrium*. Originally formed
with -*yo*- from the agent nouns, but in part independently productive.

Adjectives.—G. σωτήριος 'preserving' (σωτήρ 'savior').
θελκτήριος 'charming' (θελκτήρ 'charmer') L. *imperātōrius* 'of
a general' (*imperātor*)
dictātōrius 'of a dictator' (*dictātor*)

Nouns.—Denoting especially place, but also means, etc.

G. δικαστήριον 'court' (δικαστήρ, δικαστής 'judge', cf. above), ἐργαστήριον 'workshop' (ἐργάζομαι 'work')

θελκτήριον 'a charm' (θέλγω 'charm')   L. audītōrium 'lecture-hall' (audītor 'hearer')

praetōrium 'tent or house of the praetor'

468. -tro- and -dhro-. Mostly neuter nouns (with some masc. and fem.), denoting the action, or especially, means, instrument, or place.

1. -tro-. G. ἄροτρον L. arātrum 'plow' (ἀρόω, arō, -āre 'plow').

G. λουτρόν 'bath' (λούω 'wash')   λύτρον 'ransom' (λύω 'release') θέατρον 'theater' (θεάομαι 'look on')

φέρετρον 'quiver' (φέρω 'bear')   L. feretrum 'bier' (ferō 'bear')

rāstrum 'rake' (rādō 'scrape')   rōstrum 'beak' (rōdō 'gnaw')

χύτρᾱ 'pot' (χέω 'pour')   παλαίστρᾱ 'wrestling place' (παλαίω 'wrestle')

ῥήτρᾱ 'compact' (ἐρέω, ἐρρήθην 'say')   L. mulctra 'milk-pail' (mulgeō 'milk')   fenestra 'window'

A few masculines, partly agent nouns, formed from the neuter type.

G. ἰᾱτρός 'physician' beside dial. ἰᾱτήρ (ἰάομαι 'heal')   δαιτρός 'carver' (δαίω 'divide')

L. culter 'knife'

2. -dhro-. G. -θρον, L. -brum (**134,** but see **473.2a**). For L. -crum (from -clo-, -tlo-), see **473.1**.

G. βάθρον 'base' (βαίνω 'step')   ἄρθρον 'joint' (ἀραρίσκω 'fit')

βάραθρον 'pit' (βιβρώσκω 'swallow')   crībrum 'sieve' (cernō 'separate')

G. κρεμάθρᾱ 'basket for hanging things' (κρεμάννῡμι 'hang')

G. ὄλεθρος 'destruction' (ὄλλῡμι 'destroy')

469. -tero-. In words of contrasted relations and (Greek and Sanskrit) comparatives (see **294**).

470. -ro-. Mostly adjectives, with a few nouns of all genders.

1. G. ἐρυθρός, L. ruber 'red' (cf. Skt. rudhira-).

G. λαμπρός 'bright' (λάμπω 'shine')   μακρός 'long' (cf. μῆκος 'length')   ὑγρός 'wet'

L. *niger* 'black'   *integer* 'whole' (*tangō* 'touch')

G. ἀγρός, L. *ager*, Skt. *ajra-* 'field'

L. *vir* 'man' (cf. Skt. *vīra-*, IE *$w\breve{\imath}$-ro-*)   G. νεκρός 'corpse' (cf. νέκυς 'corpse')   L. *mūrus* 'wall'   G. δῶρον 'gift' (δίδωμι 'give')

G. ἕδρᾱ 'seat' (ἕζομαι 'sit', root ἑδ-), ἔχθρᾱ 'hatred' (adj. ἐχθρός 'hated', cf. ἔχθος 'hate').

2. G. -αρος (from -ρο-, like -ανος from -ρο-, **464**.2; cf. Skt. *rudhira-* 'red').

λιπαρός 'oily, shiny' (cf. λίπος 'fat')   στιβαρός 'sturdy' (στείβω 'tread on')   βλέφαρον 'eyelid' (βλέπω 'look')

a. From -ιο- derivatives of such forms (cf. ταλάριον beside τάλαρος 'basket') arose the dimin. -αριον, παιδάριον 'little child' (παῖς 'child'), κυνάριον 'puppy' (κύων 'dog').

3. *-ero-*. G. ἐλεύθερος, L. *līber* 'free'.

G. φανερός 'visible, manifest' (φαίνω 'show')   φοβερός 'terrible' (φόβος 'terror')

L. *miser* 'wretched'   *tener* 'delicate'

a. Interchange of -ερος, -αρος in Att. ἱερός, Dor. ἱαρός 'holy'; μιερός, μιαρός 'defiled', σκιερός, σκιαρός 'shady'.

4. G. -ηρος (or -ᾱρος). ἀνιᾱρός 'grievous' (ἀνιάω 'grieve'). πονηρός 'toilsome' (πονέω 'toil')   λῡπηρός 'painful' (λῡπέω 'pain')

5. G. -υρος and -ῡρος. λιγυρός 'shrill' (λιγύς 'shrill').

φλεγυρός 'burning' (φλέγω 'burn')   ἰσχῡρός 'strong' (ἰσχῦς 'strength')

Cf. L. *satur* 'full' (*satis* 'enough'), *satura* 'mixture'; *figūra* 'form' (*fingō* 'form'). Cf. also L. *-tūrus* and *-tūra* (**489**).

471. *-ri-* and *-ru-*. G. ἄκρις, ὄκρις 'summit', beside ἄκρος 'highest', L. *ocris* 'mountain', *ācer* 'sharp', stem *ācri-*, beside *ācro-* in early Latin.

Conversely L. *sacer*, stem *sacro-*, in early Latin also *sacri-* (both stems in Oscan-Umbrian)

L. *celer* 'swift', *pauper* 'poor'   *imber* 'shower'   *febris* 'fever'

L. *fūnebris* 'of a funeral' from **fūnes-ri-* (*fūnus* 'funeral', *fūnestus* 'fatal')   *muliebris* 'of a woman' from **mulies-ri-* (*mulier* 'woman'; see **202.**2)

For L. *-āris* from *-ālis*, see **474**.3

G. δάκρυ 'tear'; cf. L. *lacrima* 'tear', early *lacruma, dacruma*, that is, *dacru-ma*

l-SUFFIXES

472. *-lo-*. Adjectives, and nouns of all genders. Diminutive force is very common in Latin, but only occasional in Greek.

1. G. τυφλός 'blind' (τύφω 'raise a smoke').

στρεβλός 'twisted' (στρέφω 'turn') τύλος, τύλη 'swelling, lump' (cf. L. *tumeō* 'swell')

φῦλον 'race', φῦλή 'tribe' (φύω 'produce')

L. *pendulus* 'hanging' (*pendeō* 'hang') *crēdulus* 'credulous' (*crēdō* 'believe') *bibulus* 'fond of drink' (*bibō* 'drink')

figulus 'potter' (*fingō* 'fashion') *angulus* 'corner' *famulus* 'servant'

vinculum 'bond' (*vinciō* 'bind')

a. These Latin forms, and the diminutives in *-ulus* (2), are in part from *-elo-* (**80**.6, **82**.3), belonging with G. *-ελος* (5).

2. *Diminutives*.—L. *albulus* 'whitish' (*albus* 'white').

longulus 'longish' (*longus* 'long') *fīliolus* 'small son' (*fīlius* 'son')

rēgulus 'chieftain' (*rēx* 'king') *agellus* 'small field' (*ager* 'field')

tabella 'tablet' (*tabula* 'tablet') *homullus* 'manikin' (**homon-lo-*, *homō* 'man')

Also, from combination with *-ko-* suffix, *-culus*, etc. (to be distinguished from *-culum* in primary derivations denoting instrument or place, **473**.1).

articulus 'joint' (*artus* 'joint') *aedicula* 'chapel' (*aedēs*) 'temple')

ōsculum 'kiss' (*ōs* 'mouth')

G. (Boeot. inscr.) πάϊλλος 'little boy' (**παϊδ-λος*, παῖς, παιδός 'boy'), after which was formed also κόριλλα 'little girl' (κόρη 'girl').

3. G. -αλος (from -l̥o-, parallel to -ανος, -αρος, **464**.2, **470**.2.)

τροχαλός 'running' (τρέχω 'run') ὁμαλός 'level' (ὁμός 'same')

διδάσκαλος 'teacher' (διδάσκω 'teach') κεφαλή 'head'

πέταλον 'leaf' (πετάννυμι 'spread out')

4. G. -αλέος. From preceding in combination with -εος. Mainly in poetry.

θαρσαλέος 'bold' (θάρσος 'boldness')   κερδαλέος 'crafty (κέρδος 'gain')

ἀργαλέος 'painful' (by dissim. from *ἀλγαλέος, ἄλγος 'pain')

5. G. -ελος. εἴκελος 'like' (ἔοικα 'am like').

εὐτράπελος 'easily turning' (τρέπω 'turn')   νεφέλη 'cloud' (νέφος 'cloud'; cf. L. *nebula* 'mist')

6. G. -ηλος (or -ᾱλος). σῑγηλός, Dor. σῑγᾱλός 'silent' (σῑγάω 'be silent', σῑγή 'silence').

ὑψηλός 'high' (ὕψι 'high')   κάπηλος 'huckster'

θυηλή 'offering' (θύω 'offer')   Cf. L. -*ālis* and -*ēlis* (**474**.3, 4)

7. G. -ιλος, -ῑλος. ποικίλος 'many-colored'   στρόβῑλος 'top'.

8. G. -υλος. ἀγκύλος 'curved' (ἄγκος 'bend').

δάκτυλος 'finger'   σταφυλή 'bunch of grapes'

With diminutive force, ἀρκτύλος 'young bear' (ἄρκτος 'bear')
μικκύλος (μικκός 'small')

παχυλός in adv. παχυλῶς 'roughly' (παχύς 'thick')

a. Hence also in combination with -ιο- and with hypocoristic doubling (**209***a*), the diminutives in -υλλιον, as εἰδύλλιον 'idyl' (εἶδος 'form'), ἐπύλλιον 'scrap of poetry' (ἔπος 'poetry,').

9. G. -ωλος. φειδωλός 'thrifty, a miser' (φειδώ 'thrift', φείδομαι 'spare').

εὐχωλή 'prayer' (εὔχομαι 'pray')   εἴδωλον 'image' (εἴδομαι 'resemble')

473. -*ilo*- and -*dhlo*-. Parallel to -*tro*- and -*dhro*- (**468**).

1. -*ilo*-, Italic -*klo*- (**200**.3; cf. Osc. p u k l u m 'filium'. Pael. *puclois*: Skt. *putras* 'son'), whence L. -*culum*, or, by dissimilation when added to words containing *l*, L. -*crum*.

L. *pōculum* 'cup' (*pō*- 'drink' in *pōtus* 'drunk')   *piāculum* 'expiation' (*piō* 'expiate')

vehiculum 'carriage' (*vehō* 'carry')   *perīculum* 'trial, danger' (cf. *perītus* 'experienced')

lucrum 'gain' (*luō* 'pay')   *simulācrum* 'likeness, image' (*simulō* 'make like')   *sepulcrum* 'tomb' (*sepeliō* 'bury') *a.* Although the anaptyxis is attested from a very early period, as in *pōcolom,* where Plautus also has *pōculum,* yet in most words Plautus has usually forms without anaptyxis, as *perĭclum, saeclum.* This in contrast to dimin. *-culus,* always dissyllabic, the vowel here not being anaptyctic (**472.**2).

2. *-dhlo-,* G. *-θλο-,* L. *-bulum, -bula.*

G. γένεθλον, γενέθλη 'race' (γίγνομαι 'be born', cf. γένεσις, γενέτης) θέμεθλα (pl.) 'foundations' (cf. θεμέλιος, θέμις); here also by dissimilation G. φύτλον 'plant', φύτλη 'race' (φύω 'produce')

χύτλα (pl.) 'water for bathing, libations' (χέω 'pour')

L. *fābula* 'narrative' (*fārī* 'speak')   *fībula* 'clasp, pin' (*fīgō* 'fix')

stabulum 'stall' (*stō* 'stand')   *vocābulum* 'name' (*vocō* 'call')

pābulum 'fodder' (*pāscō* 'feed')

a. Some of the forms in *-brum, -bra* probably also belong here (rather than from *-dhro-,* **468.**2), by dissimilation as in *-crum* beside *-culum.* Thus *dolābra* 'mattock' (*dolō* 'hew'), *candēlābrum* 'candlestick' (*candēla* 'candle'), *vēlābrum* 'name of a street in Rome', *lābrum* 'basin' (from **lavābrum, lavō* 'wash'). The fact that so many of the forms in *-brum* have *l* in a preceding syllable (cf. also *flābra, dēlūbrum, pollubrum,* etc.) makes this probable.

474. L. *-li-.* Adjectives, with some used as nouns. From IE *-lo-,* with transfer to *i*-declension (**283**).

1. *-ilis. similis* 'like' (G. ὁμαλός 'level'), *humilis* 'low' (*humus* 'ground', G. χθαμαλός 'low', χθών 'ground').

gracilis 'thin'   *agilis* 'active' (*agō* 'move')   *facilis* 'do-able, easy' (*faciō* 'do')

fragilis 'breakable, frail' (*frangō* 'break')

Hence also *-tilis, -silis,* formed from the perf. pass. pple., as: *coctilis* 'baked' (*coquō* 'cook, bake')   *fictilis* 'made of clay' (*fingō* 'fashion')   *missilis* 'missile' (*mittō* 'send, throw')

2. *-bilis.* From *-bli-,* Italic *-fli-,* with transfer from *-flo-,* IE *-dhlo-,* seen in nouns in *-bulum* (**473.**2). Cf. *stabilis* 'steady' (*stō* 'stand') beside *stabulum* 'stall'. Primary derivatives, and mostly with distinctive passive force (quality of being loved, lovable, etc.), as also some of those in *-ilis* (*agilis,* etc., above).

crēdibilis 'credible' (*crēdō* 'believe')   *mōbilis* 'movable' (*moveō* 'move') *amābilis* 'lovable' (*amō* 'love')   *dūrābilis* 'lasting' (*dūrō* 'last')

laudābilis 'praiseworthy' (*laudō* 'praise')   *-ābilis* very productive, and the source of NE *-able* in *lovable*, etc.

3. *-ālis*. Secondary derivatives, originally from *ā*-stems, but widely productive.

animālis 'having life' (*anima* 'life'), neut. *animal* (**101**) 'living thing, animal'

mortālis 'subject to death, mortal' (*mors* 'death')   *rēgālis* 'royal' (*rēx* 'king')

Neut. pl. in names of festivals, as *Bacchānālia, Saturnālia, Vestālia*, etc.

Here also *-āris*, by dissimilation.

populāris 'of the people, popular' (*populus* 'people')   *mīlitāris* 'of soldiers, military' (*mīles* 'soldier')

cōnsulāris 'of a consul' (*cōnsul*)   *familiāris* 'of the family, intimate' (*familia* 'family')

exemplar (**101**) 'pattern, copy' (*exemplum*)

4. *-ēlis, -īlis, -ūlis*. Secondary derivatives.

fidēlis 'faithful' (*fidēs* 'faith')   *crūdēlis* 'cruel' (*crūdus* 'bloody, raw')

cīvīlis 'of a citizen' (*cīvis* 'citizen)   *hostīlis* 'of an enemy' (*hostis* 'enemy')   *servīlis* 'slavish' (*servus* 'slave')

Neut. *-īle*, mostly in words denoting place (some of these from verbs)   *sedīle* 'seat' (*sedeō* 'sit')   *cubīle* 'bed' (*cubō* 'lie down')

ovīle 'sheep-fold' (*ovis* 'sheep')   *bovīle* 'ox-stall' (*bōs* 'ox')

equīle 'horse-stall' (*equus* 'horse')

tribūlis 'fellow tribesman' (*tribus* 'tribe')   *cu(r)rūlis* 'of a chariot' (*currus* 'chariot'; **208.4**)

a. The long vowel is peculiar in *-īlis, -īle* from *i*-stems (*cīvīlis, ovīle*) where we should expect *-i-lis*, and in *-ūlis* from *u*-stems (*tribūlis*) where we shou.d expect *-u-lis*. The situation is the same as in *-īnus, -ūnus* (*canīnus, tribūnus*, etc., **464**.10, 11) and some others. Such forms of the suffix may owe their long vowel to the influence of the productive *-ālis, -ānus*, etc.—or perhaps rather, since there are some such forms in other languages (cf. Lith. *akýlas* 'sharp-sighted' from *akìs* 'eye'), to a similar influence of IE *-ālo-, -āno-* beginning in the parent speech.

DENTAL SUFFIXES

t-SUFFIXES

475. -*t*-.

1. Added to roots ending in a vowel in the type corresponding to root stems from roots ending in a consonant (**448**) and likewise most common in compounds. Cf. Skt. *viçva-ji-t-* 'all conquering' (*ji-* 'conquer'), *madhu-kr̥-t-* 'honey-making' (*kr̥-* 'make').

G. verbal adjectives in -*ās*, -*ηs*, -*ωs*, gen. -*ᾱτος*, etc. Some with active, but most with passive force. Mainly confined to poetry.

νεοκρᾱs 'newly mixed' (κεράννῡμι 'mix')   προβλής 'jutting out' (προβάλλω 'put forth')

ὠμοβρώs 'eating raw flesh' (βιβρώσκω 'devour')

L. *sacerdōs* 'priest' (*dō-* 'give')   *locuplēs* 'rich' (*pleō* 'fill')

superstes 'surviving' (*stō-* 'stand')   *comes* 'companion' (*eō* 'go') *pedes* 'one who goes on foot'

2. G. -*ηs*, -*ητος*, mostly agent nouns.

κέλης 'courser' (κέλλω 'drive')   γόης 'sorcerer' (γοάω 'howl') λέβης 'basin'

L. -*es*, gen. -*itis* or -*etis*. *teges* 'mat' (*tegō* 'cover')   *eques* 'horseman' (*equus* 'horse', cf. G. ἱππότης)

mīles 'soldier' (but this type not always to be distinguished from compounds like *comes*, *pedes*, above, 1).

3. L. -*ās*, -*ātis* in words denoting rank or origin.

optimās 'aristocrat' (*optimus* 'best')   *cuiās* 'of what country?' (*cuius* 'whose?')   *Arpīnās* 'of Arpinum'

  a This belongs here, though the gen. pl. is usually -*ium*. Cf. -*tāt*-, following. The origin of the type is obscure, but it probably started from some primary derivatives.

4. For G. secondary -*τ*- in neuters and elsewhere, see **250–52**.

476. -*tāt*-. G. -*της*, -*τητος*, Dor. -*τᾱs*, -*τᾱτος*, L. -*tās*, -*tātis* (gen. pl. -*um* and -*ium*), Skt. -*tāt*- (and -*tāti*-). The most productive type of qualitative abstracts derived from adjectives or nouns.

G. νεότης 'youth' (νέος 'young')   L. *novitās* 'newness' (*novus* 'new')

G. φιλότης 'friendship' (φίλος 'friend')   κακότης 'badness'
(κακός 'bad')

γλυκύτης 'sweetness' (γλυκύς 'sweet')   L. *bonitās* 'goodness'
(*bonus* 'good')

cīvitās 'citizenship' (*cīvis* 'citizen')   *lībertās* 'freedom' (*līber*
'free)

iuventās 'youth' (*iuvenis* 'young')   *tempestās* 'time, storm'
(*tempus* 'time')

Cf. L. *-tūs, -tūtis* and *-tūdo, -tūdinis*, with same force (**488**)

477. *-nt-*. Regularly in active participles (**434**). A few nouns
of participial origin, as the inherited G. ὀδούς, L. *dēns*, Skt. *dant-*
'tooth' (from **ed-* 'eat'), G. γέρων 'old man' = Skt. *jarant-* 'infirm,
old' (from *jar-* 'waste away'). Others of obscure history, as ἱμάς
'strap', ἀνδριάς 'statue'.

λέων 'lion', δράκων 'dragon', ἄκων 'javelin', θεράπων 'attendant'
are orig. *ν*-stems (cf. fem. λέαινα, δράκαινα, etc.) with transfer to
ντ-declension.

478. L. *-antia, -entia*. Abstracts formed with *-iā-* from participles in *-ant-, -ent-*, like similar abstracts from other adjectives
(as *audācia* from *audāx*, **455.**2).

ignōrantia 'ignorance' (*ignōrāns* 'ignorant')   *ēlegantia* 'refine-
ment' (*ēlegāns* 'fastidious')

intellegentia 'intelligence' (*intellegēns* 'discerning')   *sapientia*
'wisdom' (*sapiēns* 'knowing')

patientia 'patience' (*patiēns* 'enduring')   *sententia* 'opinion'
(**sentēns*, cf. *sentiēns* 'feeling, thinking)

479. *-went-*, G. *-fεντ-*, Skt. *-vant-*. Added to noun stems, forming adjectives meaning 'possessed of, abounding in'. Skt. *rūpa-*
vant- 'beautiful' (*rūpa-* 'form, beauty'), G. χαρίεις 'graceful'
(χάρις 'grace'). For inflection, see **286**.

-ᾶεις, Att.-Ion. *-ηεις*, mostly from ᾱ-stems, but by analogy from
others

τῑμήεις 'honored' (τῑμή 'honor')   κοτήεις 'wrathful' (κότος
'wrath')

τελήεις 'perfect' (τέλος 'end, completion')

-ιεις, only χαρίεις 'graceful' (χάρις 'grace')

-οεις, originally from o-stems, but by analogy from others. Most productive type

δολόεις 'wily' (δόλος 'wile')   μελιτόεις 'sweet' (μέλι, μέλιτος 'honey')   δακρυόεις 'tearful' (δάκρυ 'tear')

-ωεις, εὐρώεις 'moldy' (εὐρώς 'mold'), and a few others

Adjectives of this type are almost exclusively poetical, only a few being used in prose, as χαρίεις. Hence the retention of the uncontracted forms and of σσ in fem. χαρίεσσα even in Attic.

But certain forms, used substantively as technical names or place names, were ordinary prose words and show the normal phonetic development.

πλακοῦς 'flat cake' (πλάξ 'flat')   τυροῦς 'cheese-cake' (τυρός 'cheese')

μελιτοῦττα 'honey-cake' (μέλι 'honey')   οἰνοῦττα 'wine-cake' (οἶνος 'wine')   Ὀποῦς, Σκοτοῦσσα

480. L. -ōsus. Adjectives derived from nouns. Perhaps from -o-went-to-, with -to- extension of the preceding -went- (cf. L. -mentum beside -men, **461.**3), and generalization of the type derived from o-stems (G. -όεις).

formōsus (formōnsus also attested) 'shapely' (forma 'shape')

vīnōsus 'wine-bibbing' (vīnum 'wine'), verbōsus 'wordy' (verbum 'word')

dolōsus 'crafty' (dolus 'guile')   nivōsus 'snowy' (nix 'snow')

bellicōsus 'war-loving' (bellum 'war', but in form from adj. bellicus)

a. For ō from owe, see **92.**2d; for loss of n, **202.**3. But it is strange that the spelling with n is attested only for formōnsus. The above analysis is doubted by many.

481. L. -ēnsis. Adjectives, many of them also used substantively, derived from nouns denoting place, especially names of towns. History obscure, but probably from a combination -ent-ti-.

castrēnsis 'of the camp' (castra)   circēnsis 'of the circus' (circus)

Cannēnsis 'of Cannae'   Narbōnēnsis (Narbō, -ōnis), Hispani-ēnsis (Hispania)

-iēnsis (after the analogy of Hispaniēnsis, etc.), Athēniēnsis (Athenae), Carthāginiēnsis (Carthāgō, -inis)

482. *-to-*. 1. G. verbal adjectives in *-τος*, and L. perf. pass. pple. in *-tus*, *-sus*, **437**. Ordinals, **318**. Superlatives, **291**.

2. L. adjectives of participial origin, but not felt as part of the verb system, even if the verb existed.

altus 'high' (*alō* 'nourish')   *certus* 'sure' (*cernō* 'distinguish')
lautus 'neat, splendid' (*lavō* 'wash')   *grātus* 'pleasing'
lātus 'broad'   *mūtus* 'dumb'

3. Adjectives formed from nouns, after the analogy of participles of denominative verbs which might be felt in direct relation to the original nouns.

L. *barbātus* 'bearded' (*barba* 'beard')   *hastātus* 'armed with a spear' (*hasta* 'spear')

aurītus 'long-eared' (*auris* 'ear')   *nāsūtus* 'with long nose' (*nāsus* 'nose')

rōbustus 'hardy' (*rōbur* 'oak')   *honestus* 'honored' (*honōs, honor* 'honor')

G. *θυσανωτός* 'tasseled' (*θύσανος* 'tassel') and some others in *-ωτός*

4. Nouns of all genders, mainly verbal abstracts (or with derived concrete sense).

G. *κοῖτος, κοίτη* 'couch' (*κεῖμαι* 'lie')   *φόρτος* 'load' (*φέρω* 'bear')
θάνατος 'death' (*θνῄσκω* 'die')   *βροντή* 'thunder' (*βρέμω* 'roar')
ἀρετή 'excellence' (*ἀραρίσκω* 'fit')   *μελέτη* 'care' (*μέλει* 'is a care')

L. *lectus* 'couch'   *hortus* 'garden'   *porta* 'gate'

From nouns, *iuventa* 'youth,' *senecta* 'old age', beside more usual *iuventās, iuventūs, senectūs*. Many are simply the participial forms in substantive use, as *fossa* 'ditch' (*fodiō* 'dig'), *pūnctum* 'point' (*pungō* 'prick').

L. *-ētum*, originally from verb stems in *ē*, as *acētum* 'vinegar' (*acēscō* 'turn sour'), but productive in nouns of place, especially place where a plant grows.

rosētum 'rose bed' (*rosa*)   *vīnētum* 'vineyard' (*vīnum*), *pīnētum* 'pinegrove' (*pīnus*), *cupressētum* 'cypress grove' (*cupressus*)

483. L. *-(o* or *u)lentus*. Adjectives derived from nouns.

vīnolentus 'drunken' (*vīnum* 'wine')   *violentus* (also *violēns*) 'violent' (*vīs* 'strength')

opulentus (also *opulēns*) 'wealthy' (*ops*, pl. *opēs* 'wealth')
fraudulentus 'cheating' (*fraus* 'fraud')   *corpulentus* 'fleshy'
(*corpus* 'body')

a. Origin uncertain. Probably extension of *nt*-stems (cf. *violēns*, *opulēns*),
and possibly starting from compounds of *olēns*, pple. of *oleō* 'smell', as **vīno-
lēns*, then with loss of literal meaning, as in G. *-ώδης* (**497**). Or, also through
nt-stems, from adjectives of the type *bibulus*, *crēdulus* (**472.**1).

484. G. *-της* (gen. sg. Att. *-του*), Dor. *-ᾱς*. The most productive type of agent nouns, replacing *-τηρ* (**466**). Also secondary
derivatives denoting the person occupied with, etc.

κριτής 'judge' (κρῑ́νω 'decide')   δικαστής 'judge, juryman'
(δικάζω 'pass judgment')

κλέπτης 'thief' (κλέπτω 'steal')   ποιητής 'maker, poet' (ποιέω
'make')

μαθητής 'pupil' (μανθάνω 'learn')   ἱκέτης 'suppliant' (ἱκνέομαι
'approach')

ναύτης 'sailor' (ναῦς 'ship')   οἰκέτης 'house-servant' (οἶκος
'house')

δημότης (dial. δᾱμέτᾱς like οἰκέτης) 'one of the people' (δῆμος
'people')

τοξότης 'bowman' (τόξον 'bow')   πολῑ́της 'citizen' (πόλις 'city')
στρατιώτης 'soldier' (στρατιά 'army')

-ᾱτης, -ητης, -ῑτης, -ωτης in words denoting one's native place
Τεγεᾱ́της, Αἰγῑνήτης, Ἀβδηρῑ́της, Ἰταλιώτης

a. *-τᾱ-* is an extension of the *-t-* used in verbal adjectives and agent nouns,
and especially common in compounds (**475.**1). For the transfer to *ā*-stem,
perhaps due in part to the existence of feminine abstracts in *-tā-* (cf. L.
iuventa 'youth,' **482.**4), cf. compounds like παιδοτρίβης (**525**), and patronymics in *- ιδης* (**493**).

b. The distribution of agent nouns in *-της* in Homer indicates that their
main starting-point was in compounds, whence they spread to derivatives of
denominative verbs, and lastly to derivatives of primary verbs, in place of
-τηρ. The substitution of *-της* went farthest in Attic, while *-τηρ* often survived in poetry and in dialects (see **466**).

c. The agent nouns form their feminine in *-τρια* or *-τρις* (*-ιδος*), belonging
with the older *-τηρ*.

ψάλτης 'harper' fem. ψάλτρια   αὐλητής 'flute-player' fem. αὐλητρίς
μαθητής 'pupil' fem. μαθήτρια or μαθητρίς

The secondary nouns form their feminine in -τις (-ιδος). πολῑτης 'citizen' fem. πολῖτις, οἰκέτης 'house-servant' fem. οἰκέτις. So also some that are agent nouns in origin. ἱκέτης 'suppliant' fem. ἱκέτις, ἐργάτης 'workman' fem. ἐργάτις.

485. -ti-, Skt. -ti-, G. -τις, -σις, L. *vestis, mēns*, etc. Mostly verbal abstracts, with a few agent nouns.

G. βάσις 'slipping, slip' (βαίνω 'step, walk'), Skt. *gati-* 'going, gait' (*gam-* 'go')

G. ῥύσις 'flowing' (ῥέω 'flow'), Skt. *sruti-* 'flowing' (*sru-* 'flow')

G. θέσις 'placing' (τίθημι 'place')   πίστις 'trust' (πείθομαι 'trust')

ζεῦξις 'yoking' (ζεύγνῡμι 'yoke')   βλάψις 'injury' (βλάπτω 'injure')

L. *mēns* 'mind' (*meminī* 'remember'), Skt. *mati-* 'thought, mind' (*man-* 'think')

L. *mors* 'death' (*morior* 'die'), Skt. *mṛti-* 'death' (*mṛ-* 'die')

L. *vestis* 'clothing' (IE *wes- G. ἕννῡμι, Skt. *vas-* 'clothe'), *hostis* 'stranger, enemy', *pars* 'part', *fōns* 'spring'

G. -τις is retained after σ (πίστις, etc.) and in some others, as μάντις 'seer', φάτις 'saying' (also φάσις). But mostly -σις, (-ξις, -ψις) by phonetic change (**141**) and analogical extension. This is the most productive type of verbal abstracts in Greek, running to some five thousand words. In Latin the suffix survives as -*tis*, or more often with syncope, as in *mors*, etc., but as a productive suffix it is replaced by its extension -*tiō*. Cf. following.

486. L. -*tiō*, -*tiōnis*. Combination of the inherited -*ti*- with an *n*-suffix, especially -*iō*, -*iōnis* (**463.**2). Productive type of verbal abstracts. Form of verb stem and phonetic changes the same as in the perf. pass. pple.

āctiō 'action' (*agō* 'do, act')

lectiō 'reading' (*legō* 'read')   *mōtiō* 'motion' (*moveō* 'move')

sessiō 'sitting' (*sedeō* 'sit')   *ratiō* 'account' (*reor* 'reckon')

audītiō 'hearing' (*audiō* 'hear')   *accūsatiō* 'accusation' (*accūsō* 'accuse')

probātiō 'approval' (*probō* 'approve')

487. -*tu*-, Skt. -*tu*-, G. -τυς, L. -*tus*. Like -*ti*-, mostly in verbal abstracts.   Comparatively rare in Greek, productive in Latin. Originally mostly masculine in contrast to fem. -*ti*-, and so regularly in Latin, but feminine in Greek.   For -τύs instead of -τυs, see **268**.

G.   βοητύs 'shouting' (βοάω 'shout')   γραπτύs 'scratching' (γράφω 'scratch, write')

ἐδητύs 'food' (ἔδω 'eat')   numeral derivatives, τριττύs, etc. (**322**), ἥμισυς 'half', Dor. ἥμιτυς (cf. L. *sēmi*- 'half')

neut. ἄστυ 'city' (cf. Skt. neut. *vāstu* 'abode')

L. *cantus* 'singing, song' (*canō* 'sing')   *adventus* 'arrival' (*adveniō* 'arrive')

vīsus 'sight' (*videō* 'see')   *exercitus* 'army' (*exerceō* 'exercise, train')

fluctus 'wave' (*fluō* 'flow')   *mōtus* 'motion' (*moveō* 'move')

-*ātus*, originally from denominatives of the first conjugation, became productive in secondary derivatives denoting office or official body.

cōnsulātus 'consulship' (*cōnsul*)   *iūdicātus* 'office of judge' (*iūdex*)

magistrātus 'magistracy' (*magister*)   *tribūnātus* 'tribuneship' (*tribūnus*)   *senātus* 'senate' (*senex* 'old man')

equitātus 'cavalry' (*eques* 'horseman')

488. L. -*tūs*, -*tūtis*, and -*tūdō*, -*tūdinis*.   Combination of the inherited -*tu*- with -*t*- and with the type -*dō*, -*dinis* (**496**).   Since there is no sufficient evidence of a parallel IE -*tū*-, the *ū* is probably due to analogy, namely -*tūs*, -*tūtis* after -*tās*, -*tātis* (**476**), and -*tūdō* after -*ēdō*, -*īdō*, -*ūdō*.   Used, like -*tās*, in forming qualitative abstracts from adjectives or nouns.

iuventūs 'youth' (*iuvenis* 'young')   *senectūs* 'old age' (*senex* 'old man')

virtūs 'manliness' (*vir* 'man')   *servitūs* 'servitude' (*servus* 'slave')

altitūdō 'height' (*altus* 'high')   *magnitūdō* 'greatness' (*magnus* 'great')

longitūdō 'length' (*longus* 'long')   also, by analogy, from verb stems, *valētūdō* 'health' (*valeō* 'be strong')

cōnsuētūdō 'custom' (*cōnsuēscō* 'accustom')

489. L. *-tūrus* and *-tūra*. Combination of *-tu-* with a *-ro-*
suffix. Cf. especially *-ūro-* (**470.**5).

-tūrus. Future active participle (**436**).

-tūra. Verbal abstracts denoting action, often result or occupation. From the last use, felt in relation to agent nouns in *-tor*, it
came to be formed directly to nouns in *-tor*, in the sense of office.

nātūra 'birth, nature' (*nāscor* 'be born')   *cultūra* 'cultivation'
  (*colō* 'cultivate')

scrīptūra 'writing' (*scrībō* 'write')   *pictūra* 'painting' (*pingō*
  'paint')

mercātūra 'trade' (*mercor* 'trade'; cf. *mercātor* 'trader')

praetūra 'praetorship' (*praetor*)   *quaestūra* 'quaestorship' (*quaes-
  tor*)

cēnsūra 'censorship' (*cēnsor*)

490. *-tio-* (or *-tyo-*, Skt. *-tya-*), G. *-σιος* (dial. also *-τιος*, **141**a),
-σιον, *-σιᾱ*, L. *-tius*, *-tium*, *-tia*, and, with transfer to fifth declension, *-tiēs*. Originally adjectives formed with the *-yo-* (*-io-*)
suffix from words containing one of the *t*-suffixes. But substantive
use prevails in Latin.

G. *ἐνιαύσιος* (Delph. *ἐνιαύτιος*) 'yearly' (*ἐνιαυτός* 'year')   *πλούσιος* 'wealthy' (*πλοῦτος* 'wealth')

δημόσιος 'public' (*δημότης* 'one of the people')   *συμπόσιον* 'drink-
  ing-party' (*συμπότης* 'fellow-drinker')

θυσίᾱ 'sacrifice' (*θύτης* 'sacrificer')   *προδοσίᾱ* 'betrayal' (*προ-
  δότης* 'betrayer')

L. *propitius* 'favorable' (*prope* 'near')

comitium 'place of meeting', *exitium* 'ruin', *initium* 'beginning'
  (cpds. of *-i-t-* 'going', cf. *comes* 'companion')

nūntium 'news' (**novo-ventiom* 'new-coming'), hence *nūntius*
  'messenger'

grātia 'thanks' (*grātus* 'pleasing')   *molestia* 'trouble' (*molestus*
  'troublesome'

Hence *-tia* and *-tiēs* in qualitative abstracts from adjectives or
nouns.

dūritia, dūritiēs 'hardness' (*dūrus* 'hard')   *mollitia, mollitiēs*
'softness' (*mollis* 'soft')
amīcitia 'friendship' (*amīcus* 'friendly')   *pueritia* 'childhood'
(*puer* 'boy')

d-SUFFIXES

491. The *d*-suffixes play only a small rôle in most of the IE
languages, but furnish some very productive types in Greek, as
-ας, -αδος, -ις, -ιδος, and the patronymics in -αδης, -ιδης.

492. -*d*-. Rare in Latin, productive in Greek.

1. L. *lapis, -idis* 'stone'   *capis, -idis* 'bowl'
mercēs, -ēdis 'wages'   *pecus, -udis* 'head of cattle'
palūs, -ūdis 'swamp'   *custōs, -ōdis* 'guard'

2. G. -ας, -αδος. A few masc. or fem., as φυγάς 'exile' (φεύγω
'flee'), but mostly feminine.

λαμπάς 'torch' (λάμπω 'shine')   νιφάς 'snow-flake' (νείφω 'snow')
δειράς 'ridge' (cf. δειρή 'neck')   Θεστιάς 'daughter of Thestius'

Numeral collectives, τριάς etc. (**322**), with α from ṃ as in
δεκάς (cf. Skt. *daçat-*, IE **dekṃt-*) and ἑπτάς, but with unexplained
d for *t* (cf. **315a**, end).

3. G. -ις, -ιδος. Very productive type, spreading at the expense of orig. *i*-stems.

ἔρις 'strife' (acc. sg. ἔριν)   ἐλπίς 'hope'   ἀσπίς 'shield'

Territory.—Ἀργολίς, Θηβαΐς, Μεγαρίς 'territory of Argos,
Thebes, Megara'.

Denoting women's native place.—Μεγαρίς 'Megarian woman'
(fem. of Μεγαρεύς).

Θηβαΐς 'Theban woman' (fem. of Θηβαῖος)   Περσίς 'Persian
woman' (fem. of Πέρσης).

Feminine patronymics.—Πριαμίς 'daughter of Priam'.

Ἀτλαντίς 'daughter of Atlas'   Νηρηΐδες 'daughters of Nereus'

493. Greek patronymics in -δης (Dor. -δᾱς), namely -ιδης (the
most common form), -αδης, -ιαδης, and in dialects also -ωνδᾱς or
-ονδᾱς.

Hom. Πριαμίδης (Πρίαμος)   Νεστορίδης (Νέστωρ)
Ἱπποτάδης (Ἱππότης)   Ἀσκληπιάδης (Ἀσκληπιός)
Πηλεΐδης and Πηληιάδης (Πηλεύς)

Such forms are real patronymics in Homer, but in later times are merely a common type of personal names without patronymic force, as Θουκυδίδης, Ἀλκιβιάδης, Boeot. Ἐπαμεινώνδας.

a. The starting-point of this type, peculiar to Greek, is probably to be sought in the feminine patronymics in -ις, -ιδος and -ας, -αδος (492.2, 3), where the patronymic use is only one aspect of the fem. δ-stems which grew to such proportions from a small nucleus of IE d-stems. Thus from Πριαμίς 'daughter of Priam' was formed the masc. Πριαμίδης 'son of Priam'. Cf. the masculine agent nouns παιδοτρίβης, etc. (525).

494. G. (-ιδεος, -ιδεᾱ) -ιδοῦς, -ιδῆ, and -ιδεύς, allied to the patronymic names.

ἀδελφιδοῦς 'nephew', ἀδελφιδῆ 'niece' (ἀδελφός 'brother')
υἱδεύς 'grandson' (υἱός 'son')   λυκιδεύς 'wolf's whelp' (λύκος 'wolf')
ἀετιδεύς 'eagle's young' (ἀετός 'eagle')

495. G. -άδιος and -ίδιος, from adverbs or adverbial phrases.

διχθάδιος 'divided' (διχθά 'in twain')   ἀμφάδιος 'public' (ἀμφαδον 'openly')
ἐγχειρίδιος 'in the hand' (χείρ 'hand')   παραθαλασσίδιος 'by the sea' (θάλασσα 'sea')
ἐντοσθίδια 'entrails' (ἔντοσθε 'within')

496. -den-, G. -δων, L. -dō, -dinis. Mostly verbal abstracts denoting a physical or mental state.

G. μελεδών 'care' (μέλει 'is a care')   σηπεδών 'rottenness' (σήπω 'rot')
ἀλγηδών 'pain' (ἀλγέω 'suffer')   ἀχθηδών 'distress' (ἄχθομαι 'be weighed down')
L. dulcēdō 'sweetness' (dulcēscō 'become sweet')   torpēdō 'numbness' (torpeō 'be torpid')
cupīdō 'desire' (cupiō 'desire')   libīdō 'pleasure, lust' (libet 'pleases')
hirūdō·'leech'   testūdō 'tortoise' (testu 'earthen pot')
For -tūdō, see **488**.

a. In Greek, beside μελεδών, also μελεδώνη 'care' and μελεδωνός 'keeper'. A further related suffix is -δανος, ῥῑγεδανός 'causing to shiver' (ῥῑγέω 'shiver'), ληθεδανός 'causing to forget' (λήθομαι 'forget'). In Homer also -δνος, μακεδνός 'tall' (cf. μακ-ρός 'long'), ὀλοφυδνός 'lamenting' (cf. ὀλοφύρομαι 'lament').

497. G. -ωδης. Originally compounds containing the root of ὄζω 'smell', as εὐώδης 'fragrant,' hence from 'smelling of' to 'having the character of, like'.

ποιώδης 'grassy' (ποία 'grass')   σφηκώδης 'wasplike' (σφήξ 'wasp')
λυσσώδης 'raging' (λύσσα 'rage')   πρεπώδης 'proper' (πρέπει 'is fitting')

498. L. -idus. Adjectives, from verbs and nouns (often uncertain which).

cupidus 'eager' (cupiō 'desire')   tepidus 'warm' (tepeō 'be warm')
timidus 'afraid' (timeō 'fear')   lūcidus 'bright' (lūceō 'be light', lūx 'light')
fūmidus 'smoky' (fūmus 'smoke')   gelidus 'icy' (gelu 'ice')

a. There are various possible, and perhaps actual, sources of this type. It may combine IE -do- and -dho-, may possibly include some compounds of IE *dō- 'give' or *dhē- 'put' (e.g. lūcidus, fūmidus).

499. L. -bundus and -cundus. Adjectives, with about the force of an active participle. Cf. the related gerundive, **439.**

moribundus 'dying' (morior 'die')   tremebundus 'trembling' (tremō 'tremble')
errābundus 'wandering' (errō 'wander')   fācundus 'eloquent' (fārī 'speak')
īrācundus 'wrathful' (īrāscor 'be angry')   fēcundus 'fruitful' (fē- in fēmina 'woman')

dh-SUFFIXES

500. The IE dh-, G. θ- suffixes are relatively unimportant, and are mostly connected with the root increment which appears also in verbal forms, as G. πλήθω 'be full' beside πίμπλημι 'fill', πλήρης 'full', stem πλη-.

1. -θ-. ὄρνῑς 'bird', ὄρνῑθος (acc. ὄρνιν), extension of an ι-stem, beside Dor. ὄρνιξ, ὄρνῑχος with guttural stem. κόρυς 'helmet', κόρυθος.

2. -θος. κάλαθος 'basket'   κύαθος 'cup'   ψάμαθος 'sand'.

3. -νθ-, -νθος. Place names like Τίρυνς (gen. Τίρυνθος), Κόρινθος, Ὄλ·νθος, etc., are of pre-Greek origin. So also, in part at least, the

appellatives, mostly names of plants, fruits, etc., as ἐρέβινθος 'chickpea', τερέβινθος a kind of tree, ὄλυνθος 'winter-fig'.

a. For -θμος, -θρος, -θλος, see **460**.2, **468**.2, **473**.2.

GUTTURAL SUFFIXES[1]

501. -*k*-.

1. *Greek.*—λίθαξ, -ακος 'stony' (λίθος 'stone').

λεῖμαξ, -ακος 'meadow' (beside λείμων)

κόλαξ -ακος 'flatterer'   θώραξ, -ᾱκος 'breastplate'

κύλιξ, -ικος 'cap'   κῆρυξ, -ῡκος 'herald'

Diminutive or derogatory.—μεῖραξ, -ακος 'young girl' (beside μειράκιον 'young boy'), νέᾱξ, -ᾱκος 'young fellow' (νέος 'young').

2. *Latin.*—Adjectives in -*āx*, -*ācis* (productive), -*ōx*, -*ōcis*, and -*īx*, -*īcis*, denoting personal characteristics.

audāx 'daring' (*audeō* 'dare')   *rapāx* 'rapacious' (*rapiō* 'seize')

tenāx 'tenacious' (*teneō*)   *vorāx* 'voracious' (*vorō* 'devour')

atrōx 'cruel' (*āter* 'black, dismal')   *ferōx* 'fierce' (*ferus* 'wild')

vēlōx 'swift' (*volō*, -*āre* 'fly')   *fēlīx* 'happy' (orig. 'fruitful':
  fēlō 'suckle')   *pernīx* 'active, swift'

Nouns, *vertex*, -*icis* 'whirl, peak' (*vertō* 'turn')

appendix, -*icis* 'addition' (*appendō* 'weigh out')   *cornīx* -*īcis* 'crow'

Productive -*trīx*, -*trīcis*, feminine of agent-nouns in -*tor*.

creātrīx, *genetrīx*, *imperātrīx*, *tōnstrīx*, *victrīx*, fem. of *creātor*, *genitor*, *imperātor*, *tōnsor*, *victor*

502. -*ko*-. G. -κος, L. -*cus*. Mainly adjectives derived from nouns.

1. *Greek.*—θηλυκός 'feminine' (θῆλυς 'female').

ὀστακός 'lobster' (ὀστέον 'bone', Skt. *asthan*-; here -ακος from -ṇ-*ko*-)

φάρμακον 'drug'   σκιακός 'shadowy' (σκιά 'shadow')

καρδιακός 'pertaining to the heart' (καρδίᾱ 'heart')

κῡριακός 'pertaining to the lord' (κύριος 'lord')

Κορινθιακός 'Corinthian' (beside Κορίνθιος, from Κόρινθος)

-ικός. Partly inherited IE -*iqo*- (L. -*icus*, Skt. -*ika*-, Lith. -*ikas*, etc.), not confined to derivatives of *i*-stems. Rare in Homer, except in ethnica like Τρωϊκός, Πελασγικός, but appearing later

---

[1] The rare and mostly unproductive labial suffixes are omitted.

with increasing frequency, until it becomes in Attic prose the most productive adjective suffix.

φυσικός 'natural' (φύσις 'nature')   μουσικός 'musical' (μοῦσα 'muse')

ἱππικός 'of horses' (ἵππος 'horse')   ἀστικός 'of the city' (ἄστυ 'city')

βασιλικός 'royal' (βασιλεύς 'king')

-τικός from neut. τ-stems, agent nouns in -της, and verbals in -τός.

μαθηματικός 'fond of learning' (μάθημα 'learning')   κριτικός 'critical' (κριτής 'judge')

πρᾱκτικός 'practical' (πρᾱκτός 'to be done')

2. Latin.—paucus 'few' (cf. G. παῦρος 'few').

prīscus 'ancient' (prius 'before')

-icus (cf. G. -ικός, above; Osc. t ú v t í k s 'publicus' from toutā- 'people', m ú í n í k ú 'communis').

cīvicus 'of a citizen (cīvis 'citizen')   modicus 'moderate' (modus 'measure')

bellicus 'of war' (bellum 'war')   Italicus 'Italian' (Italia)

-ticus (by combination with -to- suffix).

rūsticus 'of the country' (rūs 'country')   domesticus 'of the home' (domus 'home')

fānāticus 'inspired' (fānum 'shrine')

-īcus. amīcus 'friendly, friend' (amō 'love').

antīcus 'in front' (ante 'in front')

-ūcus. cadūcus 'falling' (cadō 'fall').

mandūcus 'chewing, a chewer' (mandō 'chew')

-icius, -īcius (by combination with -ius).

patricius 'patrician' (pater 'father')   tribūnicius 'of a tribune' (tribūnus 'tribune')   novīcius 'new' (novus 'new')

-tīcius (from pple. in -tus).

fictīcius 'fictitious' (fictus 'feigned')   adventīcius 'foreign' (adventus 'arrived')

-āceus (by combination with -eus, 456).

rosāceus 'of roses' (rosa 'rose')   crētāceus 'of chalk' (crēta 'chalk')   farrāceus 'of spelt' (far, farris 'spelt') *a.* There are a few forms with *qu*, formed from adverbs, and quite distinct from the above. *antīquus* 'ancient' (*ante* 'before'), *longinquus* 'remote' (*longē* 'afar'), *propinquus* 'neighboring' (*prope* 'near'). They are related to Sanskrit forms like *pratyañc-*, *pratīc-* 'backward' (*prati* 'over against'), and are compounds in origin.

503. G. *-ίσκος*, fem. *ίσκη*, in diminutives. Originally adjectives related to a productive type of adjectives in Germanic and Balto-Slavic, as NE *childish*.

παιδίσκος, παιδίσκη 'young boy', 'young girl' (παῖς 'boy', 'girl')

ἀνθρωπίσκος 'manikin' (ἄνθρωπος 'man') νεανίσκος 'youth' (νεανίας 'youth')

504. *-g-*. Rare. G. ἅρπαξ, *-αγος* 'rapacious'.

μάστιξ, *-ῑγος* 'whip' ἄντυξ, *-υγος* 'rim'

Stem with preceding nasal, in *-γγ-*, in words denoting hollow shape.

φάλαγξ 'phalanx' λάρυγξ 'larynx' σάλπιγξ 'trumpet' σύριγξ 'pipe'

505. *-gen-*, L. *-gō*, *-ginis*. Combination of *-g-* and *n-* suffixes, parallel to *-den-*, L. *-dō*, *-dinis*. Related to the adjectives in *-āx*, *-ācis*, etc., **501.**2.

imāgō· 'likeness, image' (cf. *imitor* 'imitate') *vorāgō* 'abyss' (*voro* 'swallow'; cf. *vorāx*)

virāgō 'manlike woman' (*vir* 'man') *vertīgō* 'dizziness' (*vertō* 'turn')

orīgō 'source, origin' (*orior* 'arise') *prūrīgō* 'itching' (*prūriō* 'itch')

aerūgō 'copper-rust' (*aes* 'copper') *lānūgō* 'down' (*lāna* 'wool')

506. *-gho-*, G. *-χος*, in diminutives.

στόμαχος 'throat', later 'stomach' (στόμα 'mouth') νηπίαχος 'childish' (νήπιος 'childish')

ὁρτάλιχος 'chick' (ὁρταλίς 'chicken') Dor. πύρριχος 'reddish' (πυρρός 'red')

S-SUFFIXES

507. *-s-*. 1. Neuters in *-os*, *-es-*, G. *-os*, *-εος* (Att. *-ους*), L. *-us*, *-eris* or *-oris* (**254**). Verbal abstracts.

G. γένος, L. *genus*, Skt. *janas-* 'race, family' (G. γίγνομαι 'be born', L. *gignō* 'beget, bear', Skt. *jan-* 'beget')

G. μένος 'courage, rage, purpose' (cf. Skt. *manas* 'mind', from *man-* 'think')

ψεῦδος 'lie' (ψεύδομαι 'lie')   κράτος 'strength'

θράσος 'boldness'   L. *foedus* 'treaty' (*fīdō* 'trust')

pondus 'weight' (*pendō* 'weigh')   *tempus* 'time'   *corpus* 'body'

2. Adjectives, nom. sg. masc. fem. in *-ēs*, G. *-ηs* (**256**). Derived from the neuters in *-os*, and mostly compounds.

εὐγενής 'well-born' (γένος)

εὐμενής 'well-disposed' (μένος)   ψευδής 'lying' (ψεῦδος)

3. Masc. or fem. nouns in *-ōs*, G. *-ωs*, L. *-or* (early *-ōs*), *-ōris* (**255**). Rare in Greek, but in Latin productive in verbal abstracts, mostly denoting a quality or condition.

G. αἰδώς 'shame', ἠώς 'dawn'   L. *amor* 'love'   *honor* 'honor'
  dolor 'pain'   *timor* 'fear'   *labor* 'toil'   *tumor* 'swelling'
  vapor 'steam'

4. *-yes-* in comparatives (**291-93**).

5. *-wes-* in perfect active participle (**435**).

508. Other IE *s*-suffixes, as *-so-*, *-sā-*, are rare, and with only scattered relics in Greek or Latin. In Greek suffixes containing σ, other than those mentioned above, the σ is from τ in *-σιs* (**485**), *-σιος*, *-σια* (**490**), *-σιμος* (**460**), *-συνος*, *-συνη* (**464**.8); or from κι, τι, etc., in *-σσος*, *-σσα* and partly in words in *-σος*, *-σα*. But some of these last may reflect IE *-so-*, *-sā-*.

In Latin, *-sus* is almost wholly from *-to-* after a dental or by analogical extension (**437, 482**); similarly *-ōsus* (**480**), and probably *-ēnsis* (**481**).

SURVEY

509. *Survey of the formation of certain classes of derivatives.*— It must be repeated here that several of these classes overlap, and furthermore that but few suffixes are restricted in use to any one class.

Greek	Latin
1. Agent nouns:	
-της (*-του*) **484**, fem. *-τρια*, *-τρις* **484**c	
	-tor **466**, fem. *-trīx* **501**.2
-τηρ, *-τωρ* **466**	

2. Other designations of persons by occupation, personal characteristics, etc.:

-ευς **452**

-ων **463**.1   -ŏ **463**.1, -iŏ **463**.2

3. Designations of persons according to their native town or country:

-ιος **454**   -ānus, -īnus **464**.9, 10

-αιος **457**   -icus **502**.2

-ευς **452**   -ēnsis **481**

-κος **502**   -ās **475**.3

-της **484**, fem. -τις **484**c

-ις (-ιδος) fem. **491**.3

-ᾱνος, -ηνος, -ῑνος **464**.3, 5

4. Patronymics:

-ιδης, -(ι)αδης **493**

fem. -ας (-αδος), -ις (-ιδος)

     492.2, 3

-ιος **455**.1   -ius **455**.1

5. Diminutives:

-ιον **455**.2   -lus, -culus **472**.2

-ιδιον **455**.2

-αριον **470**.2a

-υλλιον **472**.8

-ισκος **503**

6. Verbal abstracts, denoting action, state, result, whence also concrete force. The most distinctively abstract types are given first:

-σις **485**   -tiŏ **486**

-η **449**, -ιᾱ **455**.2   -iŏ **463**.2, -ia, -iēs **455**.2

-ις -(ιδος) **491**.3   -tus **487** -tūra **489**

                             -or **507**.3

-δων **496**   -dŏ **496**

-μα **461**.2   -men, -mentum **461**.2, 3

7. Nouns denoting means, instrument, or place:

-τρον, -θρον **468**   -trum **468**.1   -brum **468**.2, **473**.2a

                             -bulum **473**.2 -culum, -crum **473**.1

-τηριον **467**   -tŏrium **467**

-ων **463**.1   -īle **474**.4

8. Qualitative abstracts:

-της (-τητος) **476**   -tās **476**   -tia, -tiēs **490**

-συνη **464**.8   -tūs, -tūdŏ **488**

-ιᾱ **455**.2   -ia **455**.2

9. Adjectives of most general use:

-ιος **454**.1

-ικος **502**

-αιος, -ειος **457**

-ius **454**,1

-ānus, -īnus **464**.9, 10

-ālis, -āris **474**.3

10. Adjectives of material:

-εος **456**

-ινος **464**.4

-eus **456**

-nus, -neus **456**

11. Adjectives of time:

-ινος **464**.4

-ternus, -tinus **464.**12

FORMATION OF ADVERBS

510. The majority of adverbs are simply case forms used adverbially. Others are formed with certain distinctively adverbial endings, some of them inherited from the parent speech, not corresponding to any known case forms. Still others, including those that have come to be used mainly as prepositions, are isolated forms without any distinctive formative element. Some adverbs are merely prepositional phrases which have come to be felt as single words.

511. *Case forms.*—All of the cases, except the vocative, may be used adverbially. Such use of the accusative is the most widespread, that of the nominative the least frequent. But the most productive types of Greek and Latin adverbs are of ablative origin.

1. *Acc. sg. neut.*—G. πρῶτον 'at first', σήμερον 'today', αὔριον 'tomorrow', πολύ 'much', μέγα 'greatly', μᾶλλον 'more', σοφώτερον 'more wisely' (and so regularly from comparatives).

L. *prīmum* 'at first', *secundum* 'beside', *multum* 'much', *cēterum* 'for the rest', *vērum* 'truly, but' (*vērus* 'true'); *plūs* 'more', *melius* 'better' (and so regularly from comparatives); sometimes from *i*-stems (usually *-iter*), *facile* 'easily', *impūne* 'without punishment'.

Here also the temporal adverbs and conjunctions derived from pronominal stems, *dum, tum, num, nunc* (**num-c*), *cum*, early *quom*, with *m* instead of the orig. *d* retained in the conjunction *quod*.

Likewise, from pronominal *i*-stems, *im*, *interim* 'meanwhile',
ōlim 'formerly', *enim* 'for' *illim, illinc* (**illim-c*) 'thence', *hinc*
(**him-c*) 'hence'. The ablative force in the last three is secondary,
probably absorbed from *dē hinc*, etc.

2. *Acc. pl. neut.*—πολλά 'often', μεγάλα 'greatly' (beside sg.
πολύ, μέγα), ἀλλά 'otherwise, but' (from ἄλλος 'another'), μάλιστα
'most', σοφώτατα 'most wisely' (and so regularly from superlatives,
in contrast to acc. sg. from comparatives).

Probably here also, by analogy, the much-discussed τάχα
'quickly, perhaps' (ταχύς), ὦκα 'swiftly' (ὠκύς), σάφα 'plainly'
(σαφής), μάλα 'very', ἄμα 'at the same time'.

L. *multa, cētera* (beside sg. *multum, cēterum*), *quia* 'because' (from
the *i*-stem of *quis, quid*)

3. *Acc. sg. fem.*—G. μακράν 'far', πέραν 'beyond', δίκην 'after
the manner of, like', δωρεάν 'freely'.

L. *clam* 'secretly', *palam, cōram* 'openly'; the pronominal adverbs *tam, quam, iam, nam, -dam.* Cf. the acc. pl. *aliās* 'at
other times', *forās* 'out of doors'.

L. *partim* 'partly' (the orig. acc. of *pars*, otherwise replaced by
partem); hence by analogy *fūrtim* 'secretly' (*fūr* 'thief'), *cursim*
'quickly', etc.

4. *Abl. sg.*—G. -ω from -ōd in Doric adverbs of place whence,
ὅπω 'whence', etc., Delph. οἴκω 'from the house'.

Hence (or in part. from instr. sg. -ō), with addition of adverbial
-*s* (cf. ἀμφί-ς, L. *ab-s*, etc.), -ως in καλῶς 'well', etc., the most common adverbial type.

L. -ō, early -ōd. *prīmō* 'at first', *tūtō* 'safely'; with iambic
shortening (**102**) *modo* 'only', *cito* 'quickly'.

a. The pronominal adverbs of place whither, as *quō, eō*, early *hōc, illō(c)*,
istō(c), usually *hūc, illūc*, etc., are of different but uncertain origin.

L. -ē, early -ēd. *altē* 'highly', *cārē* 'dearly', *facillimē* (early
facilumēd) 'most easily', the usual type from adjectives of the
first and second declension; with iambic shortening *bene* 'well'
(*bonus* 'good'), *male* 'badly'.

L. -ā, early -ād. *suprā* 'above' (early *suprād*), *dextrā* 'on the
right', *aliā* 'otherwise'; pron. adv. *eā, quā, hāc*, etc.

5. *Loc. sg.*—G. οἴκει 'at home', ἐκεῖ 'there', Dor. ὅπει 'where' (=Att. ὅπου). L. *domī* 'at home', *humī* 'on the ground', *hīc* 'here', *illīc* 'there'.

G. οἴκοι 'at home', 'Ισθμοῖ 'at the Isthmus', ποῖ 'whither'. In dialects also -υι, as Dor. ὅπυι 'whither' (IE. *qʷu-*, 308.3), Lesb. πήλυι 'afar'

G. (dat.-loc.) λάθρᾳ 'secretly', κοινῇ 'in common', πῇ 'how'

Cf. loc. pl. θύρᾱσι 'at the doors', 'Αθήνησι 'at Athens' (234.3)

6. *Gen. sg.*—ποῦ 'where', αὐτοῦ 'at the very place', ὁμοῦ 'at the same place'. This type, denoting 'place where', is peculiar to Attic-Ionic.

7. *Instr. sg.* in. -ō, -ē, -ā (229). G. ἄνω 'above', κάτω 'below', πώ-ποτε 'ever' (Lac. πή-ποκα), ὅπη 'where, how', κρυφῇ 'secretly'.

8. *Nom. sg.*—G. πύξ 'with the fist', ἀναμίξ 'promiscuously', ἅπαξ 'once', ἐγγύς 'near'.

L. *versus* 'toward', *adversus* 'opposite', *praeceps* 'headlong'

Such adverbs were originally adjectives in agreement with, or nouns in apposition to, the subject.

512. *Other adverbial endings. Greek.*

1. -θεν, -θε, -θα, -θι. Related to *dh*-endings elsewhere, as Skt. *kuha*, Av. *kudā* 'where?', Skt. *iha*, OPers. *idā* 'here'.

-θεν, place whence. οἰκόθεν 'from home', πόθεν 'whence?', 'Αθήνηθεν 'from Athens'

-θι, place where. Hom. οἴκοθι 'at home', πόθι 'where?', ἄλλοθι 'elsewhere'

-θεν, -θε, -θα, added to adverbs and prepositions

πρόσθεν, πρόσθε, Dor. πρόσθα 'before', but ἔνθα 'there' with -θα in all dialects

2. -σε, place whither, mostly from pronouns. ἄλλοσε 'to another place', ὁμόσε 'to the same place'.

3. -δε, -δον, etc. Related to L. -de, -dam, etc. (513.3), all from a pronominal stem *do-*.

-δε, place whither. οἰκόν-δε 'to one's home', also οἴκαδε (from *οἴκα acc. sg. of an old cons. stem), φύγαδε 'to flight', πόλιν-δε 'to the city', 'Αθήναζε 'to Athens' (from -ας-δε, 203.1, 204.3)

-δον. ἔνδον 'within', σχεδόν 'almost', ἐμβαδόν 'on foot' (ἐμβαίνω 'go on')

-δα. κρύβδα 'secretly' (κρίπτω 'hide'), μίγδα 'in confusion' (μίγνυμι 'mix')

-δην, Dor. -δāν. κρύβδην 'secretly', μίγδην 'in confusion', κλήδην 'by name' (καλέω 'call')

-ινδην, Dor. -ινδāν. πλουτίνδην (choose) 'according to wealth' (πλοῦτος 'wealth'), 'from the wealthy', ἀριστίνδην 'from the best' (ἄριστος 'best')

4. -ις, -ιν, in adverbs of time. Att. αὖθις, Ion. αὖτις Cret. αὖτιν 'again', Att.-Ion. πάλιν 'back, again'.

So -κις, -κι, -κιν in numeral adverbs, τετράκις, Lac. τετράκιν, etc.

5. -τε, -τα, -κα in pronominal adverbs and conjunctions of time. ὅτε, τότε, πότε, Lesb. ὅτα, etc., Dor. ὅκα, etc.

6. -κας, distributive. ἑκάς orig. 'by oneself', hence 'far off', ἀνδρακάς 'man by man'. Cf. Skt. ekaças 'one by one', dviças 'by twos'.

513. *Other adverbial endings. Latin.*

1. -*ter.* Inherited in forms like *inter* 'between' (cf. Skt. *antar*), *praeter* 'beside' (*prae*), *subter* 'beneath' (*sub*), *propter* 'near' (*prope*), where it is related to -*tero-* in words of contrasted relations, *dexter*, etc. (**294**). Hence it came to be used freely in forming adverbs from adjectives, as *breviter* 'briefly' (*brevis* 'short'), *graviter* 'heavily' (*gravis*), *firmiter* 'firmly' (*firmus*), *audācter* 'boldly' (*audāx*).

2. -*tus*, from -*tos*. *intus* 'within', *funditus* 'from the bottom' (*fundus*), *antīquitus* 'from of old' (*antīquus*), *penitus* 'inwardly'. Cf. G. ἐντός 'within', ἐκτός 'without', Skt. *tatas* 'thence', *sarvatas* 'from all sides'.

3. -*de*, -*dem*, -*dam*, -*dum*, -*dō*. Related to G. -δε, -δον, etc., all from a pronominal stem **do-*.

quamde 'than', *inde* 'thence' (**im-de*, for *im* see **306**), *unde* 'whence' (**um-de*, cf. *umquam;* or formed after *inde*)

tandem 'at last' (*tam*), *prīdem* 'long ago', *quidem* 'indeed', *totidem* 'so many'. Cf. *īdem* (**306.2**)

quondam 'once' (*quom*). Cf. *quīdam* 'a certain one'
dūdum 'a while ago', *interdum* 'for a time'
quandō 'when' (*quam*), early *endō* 'in'

4. *-bi*. *ibi* 'there', *ubi* 'where', early *ibei*, *ubei*. From *-dhi* (G. *-θι*) with *ei* from loc. adverbs; *b* from *dh* regularly in *ubi* (**140**), and by analogy in *ibi*. Cf. Osc. p u f 'ubi'.

5. *-per*. *semper* 'always', *nūper* 'recently'.

6. *-r* in *cūr*, early *quōr*. Cf. Lith. *kur* 'where', Skt. *kar-hi* 'when', NE *here, there, where*, OE *hēr*, etc.

514. *Adverbs from prepositional phrases.*

G. *ἐνῶπα* 'face to face' (*ἐν* = *εἰς*, **324**a), *ἐκποδών* 'out of the way' (*ἐκ ποδῶν*), hence by analogy *ἐμποδών* 'in the way'

L. *admodum* 'to full measure, fully' (*ad modum*), *obviam* 'in the way' (*ob viam*), whence the adj. *obvius*, *dēnuō* 'anew' (*dē novō*, **110.**5), *sēdulō* orig. 'without guile' (*sē dolō*), then 'carefully, busily', whence adj. *sēdulus*

a. Whether such phrases are felt and written as single words depends mainly on the degree of their detachment from the literal meaning of the phrase, but in part on formal differences, as the accent of *ἐκποδών* or the vowel changes in *dēnuō*, *sēdulō*.

COMPOSITION

515. Composition is the formal union of two or more words in one. Compounds are marked as such by certain formal peculiarities, such as a single word accent, various phonetic changes, and especially, in the earlier and most widespread types of noun compounds, the appearance of the stem form as the first part. They are also generally distinguished by a more intimate union in sense, a specialized application as compared with that of the words when used separately. Thus in English, though here the more conspicuous marks of composition (the old stem forms) have disappeared, a *blackbird* is distinguished in both accent and sense from a *black bird*.

The semantic union of a word group tends to result in formal composition, of a kind sometimes known as juxtaposition as distinguished from the older type of stem composition. But it does not necessarily so result. It may be a question if and when certain combinations were felt as compounds, and the writing of them as such or separately may be only a fluctuating convention. Thus usually Διόσκουροι but sometimes Διὸς κοῦροι, Hom. καρηκομόωντες or κάρη κομόωντες (an ancient dispute), L. *aquaeductus* or *aquae ductus*. L. *rēs pūblica* 'commonwealth, state' is a unit in meaning but since it keeps the inflection of both parts, as gen. *reī pūblicae* (in contrast to G. Νεάπολις, gen. Νεᾱπόλεως), it is generally written separately.

a. Mere semantic unification of a group of words may constitute a sort of psychological composition, but not necessarily linguistic composition in any reasonable use of the term. Thus in current English idiom *house of ill fame* is as much a unit in sense as its equivalent *brothel*, but common sense rebels against calling it a compound. Yet this would be the logical result of the extension which some scholars give to the notion of composition.

516. The commonest type of nominal compounds, in which the first part is a noun or adjective stem form, reflects a type that was fully established in the parent speech and must go back to a remote period before the full development of inflection, when the stem was not a mere abstraction but a form in actual use.

A corresponding type with a verbal stem as first part, if it existed in the parent speech, was comparatively rare (**522**).

Certain compounds with inseparable prefixes are inherited from the parent speech, notably those with the negative prefix, IE *ṇ-*, the weak form of the full *ne*.

The commonest type of verbal compounds, those with adverbial prefixes, the "prepositional compounds", mostly arose independently in the several languages, by increasingly fixed juxtaposition. The parts are still separable in Vedic Sanskrit and Homeric Greek.

Although noun composition is an inheritance from the parent speech, as shown by the agreement in the type of stem compounds and by the rôle of composition in the IE system of personal names (**527**), the various IE languages differ greatly in the degree in which such composition is employed. It is carried to the extreme in Sanskrit, with its many artificially constructed compounds of monstrous length. There is a notable contrast between the wealth of compounds in Greek and their scarcity in Latin. Many of the compounds used by Latin authors are either borrowed directly from the Greek or obviously modeled after them.

The verbal compounds, however, are common in Latin, as in Greek.

The syntactical relation of the parts is most commonly that in which the first part modifies the second. So regularly in verbal compounds, and in the most widespread type of noun and adjective compounds. But there are also less frequent types in which the parts are co-ordinate or the first governs the second.

NOUN AND ADJECTIVE COMPOUNDS

MEANING

517. Accordingly to the syntactical relation of the parts and the meaning of the whole, one distinguishes certain classes of compounds. Such a classification is useful for our analysis, but it must not be understood as a rigid system of which the speakers were conscious. The very range and vagueness of the relations is a characteristic of composition. Some compounds may be analyzed in more than one way. Thus G. ἰᾱτρό-μαντις as 'physician and seer' (copulative) or as 'physician-seer' (descriptive with first part a noun in attributive relation). So φιλό-ξενος probably rests on the possessive type as 'one who has strangers dear', but was doubtless felt as 'loving strangers' (see **522** with *a*).

1. *Copulative compounds.*—The parts are co-ordinate, and may be more than two.

G. ἀρτό-κρεας (late) 'bread and meat', δώ-δεκα 'twelve'

L. *su-ove-taurīlia* 'sacrifice of a swine, sheep, and bull', *quattuor-decim* 'fourteen'

2. *Determinative compounds.*—The first part modifies the second. These include:

A. *Descriptive compounds.*—The first part is an adjectival or adverbial modifier.

ἀκρό-πολις 'upper city, citadel'   ἄ-κακος 'not evil'

σύν-δουλος 'fellow-slave'   πρό-γονος 'forefather'

L. *angi-portus* 'narrow passage, lane'   *in-grātus* 'unpleasant'
con-iux 'spouse'   *per-facilis* 'very easy'

B. *Dependent compounds.*—The first part is a noun stem, or more rarely an actual case form, depending on the second part.

G. λογο-γράφος 'speech-writer'   στρατηγός 'army-leader, general'   οἰκο-γενής 'born in the house, homebred'   Διόσ-κουροι 'sons of Zeus'   ὁδοι-πόρος 'wayfarer'

L. *armi-ger* 'armor-bearer'   *agri-cola* 'farmer'   *parti-ceps* 'sharing'   *aquae-ductus* 'aqueduct'

a. In the great mass of determinative compounds the relation of the parts is as above. But there are some in which this is inverted and the second part modifies the first. These are formed directly from certain phrases in the formal likeness of the usual type. So G. ἱππο-πόταμος, 'river-horse' (for earlier ἵππος ποτάμιος), ἀξιό-λογος 'worthy of mention' (ἄξιος λόγου), ἰσό-θεος 'god-like' (ἴσος θεῷ), late L. *domn-aedius* 'landlord' (*dominus aedium*), *domni-funda* 'landlady' (*domina fundī*).

The second part is governed by the first also in the type with verbal form as first part (**522**) and in those arising from prepositional phrases (**524**).

3. *Possessive or mutated compounds.*—These are in origin determinative noun compounds which through their use as epithets in apposition to other nouns have come to gain adjectival force, 'possessed of'. Cf. epithets like *red-breast* of the bird having a red breast, *block-head*, *one-eye(d)*, *lion-heart(ed)*.

G. ἠώς ῥοδο-δάκτυλος 'dawn the rose-fingered, rosy-fingered dawn' λεοντο-κέφαλος 'lion-headed'   ὠκύ-πους 'swift-footed' εὐ-τυχής, δυσ-τυχής 'having good (bad) fortune'

ἄ-παις 'having no child'   τρί-πους 'having three feet, tripod'

L. *magn-animus* 'great-souled'   *ūn-oculus* 'one-eyed'   *bi-pēs* 'two-footed'

a. In Sanskrit the possessive compounds are distinguished in accent from the determinative, as *yajña-kāmá-* 'desire of sacrifice', but poss. *yajñá-kāma* 'having desire of sacrifice'. This difference appears in Greek in certain words, where it has become associated with active or passive meaning of the second part. λαιμο-τόμος 'throat-cutting' but λαιμό-τομος 'with throat cut', πατροκτόνος 'slayer of one's father' but πατρόκτονος ('having a father as one's slayer'=) 'slain by one's father', λιθο-βόλος 'throwing stones', but λιθό-βολος 'pelted with stones'.

FORM

FIRST PART THE STEM OF A NOUN OR ADJECTIVE

518. The stem was originally the same as that of the uncompounded word. But there are many analogical substitutions,
especially a great spread of the *o*-stem at the expense of others,
and, in Greek, also some extension of the *ā*-stem.

A final stem vowel is elided, when the second part begins with a
vowel. But there are some few traces of an earlier system of contraction, such as occurs in Sanskrit (**526***a*).

519. *Greek.*—μονο-μάχος 'one who fights alone' (μόνος), μόν-αρχος
'one who rules alone, monarch'.

ὑλο-τόμος 'wood-cutter' (ὕλη; cf. Dor. ὑλᾱ-τόμος)

δικο-λόγος 'pleader' (δίκη)   φυσι-ο-λόγος 'student of nature'
(φύσις)   ἰχθυ-ο-φάγος 'fish-eating' (ἰχθύς)

μητρ-ό-πολις 'mother city' (μήτηρ)   ἀγαλματ-ο-ποιός 'sculptor'
(ἄγαλμα)

νῑκη-φόρος 'victory-bringing' (νῑκη)

θανατή-φορος 'death-bringing' (θάνατος)

μαντι-πόλος 'inspired' (μάντις)   ἀστυ-νόμος 'city magistrate'
(ἄστυ)

σελασ-φόρος 'light-bringing' (σέλας)

When the second part once began with ϝ or σ, the final vowel of
the first part is not elided but remains or is contracted with the
following. Hom. κακο-εργός, Att. κακοῦργος 'evil-doing' (*κακο-ϝερ-
γος, cf. ϝέργον), hence by analogy also παν-οῦργος 'knave'; κληροῦχος
'one who holds an allotment' (*κληρο-σοχος, cf. ἔχω from *σεχω,
162*a*), and so Att. πολιοῦχος 'city-protecting' (but Ion. πολιήοχος,
Dor. πολιᾱοχος, πολιᾱχος from πολιᾱ-).

520. *Latin.*—The first part generally ends in *i*, with elision if
the second part begins with a vowel. This *i* represents mostly the
o of *o*-stems, by weakening in medial syllable (**110.**2), but also in
part the *i* of *i*-stems, with its extension to cons. stems in Latin.
It wholly displaces the *ā*- of *ā*-stems (there are no Latin forms
parallel to Gr. νῑκη-φόρος), and with some exceptions the *u*-stem
and cons. stem forms.

armi-ger 'armor-bearer' (*arma*)   *agri-cola* 'farmer' (*ager*)

ūni-versus 'all together' (*ūnus*)   *ūn-animus* 'of one mind'
parti-ceps 'sharing' (*pars, partis*)   *corni-ger* 'horned' (*cornu*)
frātri-cīda 'fratricide' (*frāter*)   *tubi-cen* 'trumpeter' (*tuba*)
manu-pretium 'wages' (*manus*)   *iūdex* 'judge' (**ious-dic-, iūs*)

   a. Forms like *Aeno-barbus, mero-bibus,* etc., follow the analogy of compounds borrowed from Greek, like *philo-sophus, hippo-dromus.*

FIRST PART A CASE FORM

521. G. Νεάπολις (*νέᾱ πόλις*), gen. Νεᾱπόλεως.

Διόσ-κουροι 'sons of Zeus'   Ἑλλήσ-ποντος 'Helle's sea'   Πελοπόννησος (Πέλοπος νῆσος 'Pelops' island')
πυρί-καυστος 'burnt in fire'   δορί-κτητος 'won by the spear'
πᾱσί-φιλος 'dear to all'   νουν-εχής 'having understanding'
L. *aquae-ductus* 'aqueduct'   *senātūs-cōnsultum* 'decree of the
   senate'

   a. Compounds of this kind occur also in the other IE languages. But they represent a later and less widespread type than that with a stem form as first part. Most of them have arisen in the historical period from a union of words used separately. The fact of composition may be shown by some difference in form from that of the words used separately, as in Πελοπόννησος in contrast to Πέλοπος νῆσος, or gen. Νεᾱπόλεως in contrast to νέᾱς πόλεως. When there is no formal difference, apart from the matter of accent which may be unknown, it may be a question if and when composition is to be recognized, e.g. L. *aquae-ductus* or *aquae ductus* (see **515**).

FIRST PART A VERB FORM

522. G. φέρ-ασπις 'shield-bearing'.

φερέ-νῑκος 'carrying off victory'   ἀρχέ-κακος 'beginning mis-
   chief'
ἀρχέ-λᾱος 'leading the people' (cf. Μενέ-λᾱος)
δακέ-θῡμος 'biting the heart'   μῑσό-δημος 'hating the people'
μῑσ-άνθρωπος 'man-hating', λιπο-στρατίᾱ 'desertion of the army'
φυγό-μαχος 'shunning battle'
σωσί-πολις 'saving the state'   στησί-χορος 'establishing the
   chorus'
ἑλκεσί-πεπλος 'trailing the robe, with long train'

   a. This type of compound is common in Greek, but in the other IE languages it is rare or of late appearance. It is a question whether in forms like φερέ-νῑκος the first part is to be regarded as a verbal stem form, parallel to the noun stem in the more usual type of compounds, or as the same form in its imperative use. For compounds based upon imperative phrases occur in Sanskrit, and such is believed to be the origin of the modern types like NE *pick-pocket, break-fast*, Fr. *porte-manteau*, etc.

In the forms like φυγό-μαχος the *o* is due to the analogy of the common type with noun stem as first part.

The forms like σωσί-πολις were associated with the σ-aorist stem and also with the abstracts in -σις, but the real origin of the σι is obscure.

FIRST PART AN ADVERBIAL PREFIX

523. Most of these prefixes are identical with adverbs and prepositions in independent use. Others occur only in composition and are known as inseparable prefixes.

　　1. *Separable.*—G. εἰσ-οδος 'entrance', σύν-δουλος 'fellow-slave'. περι-καλλής 'very beautiful'　　ὕπ-αρχος 'under-officer'
With possessive force, ὑπό-ξυλος 'having wood underneath', ἐπί-χαλκος 'covered with bronze', ἔν-θεος 'inspired' ('having god within')
L. *con-lībertus* 'fellow-freedman', *prae-nōmen* 'fore-name'
per-facilis 'very easy'; with possessive force, *prae-ceps* 'head-foremost'

　　a. But the great majority of compounds with adverbial prefix are merely derivatives of compound verbs, like NE *undertaking* from *undertake*.

　　2. *Inseparable.*—Negative prefix IE *ṇ-* (orig. weak form of IE *ne*, see **115**), G. ἀ-, αν-, L. *in-*.

G. ἀ or ἁ- copulative (properly ἁ = Skt. *sa-*, IE *sm̥-*, related to ἅμα 'together', ὁμός 'common'; ἀ first by dissimilation, then extended) ἅ-πᾱς 'all together', ἄ-λοχος 'wife' (having the same bed, λέχος), ἀ-κόλουθος 'attendant' (κέλευθος 'way'), ἀ-τάλαντος 'of the same weight'

G. δυσ- 'ill-'. δυσ-μενής 'ill-disposed, hostile' (cf. Skt. *dur-manās*). Cf. εὐ- 'well-' (though this occurs separately as εὖ), εὐ-μενής 'well-disposed'

L. *vē-* 'without', *vē-cors* 'senseless'

FIRST PART A TRUE PREPOSITION

524. Compounds arising from a prepositional phrase, or prepositional-phrase compounds as they have been termed, are the true prepositional compounds and are not to be confused with the preceding class in which the first part is an adverbial modifier. They are very common, especially in Greek, and sometimes show an added suffix or change of the noun stem.

G. παρά-δοξος 'contrary to opinion' (παρὰ δόξαν)

ὑπό-στεγος 'under the roof' (ὑπὸ στέγης)

ἐπι-θαλάσσιος 'dwelling by the sea' (ἐπὶ θαλάσσῃ)

κατά-γειος 'underground (κατὰ γῆς)

L. ob-vius 'in the way' (ob viam)   dē-mēns 'out of one's mind'
   (dē mente)

ē-gregius 'distinguished' (ē grege)   ē-normis 'irregular, huge'
   (ē normā)

prō-cōnsul orig. 'one who acts in the place of the consul (prō
   cōnsule)

sub-terrāneus 'underground' (sub terrā)

SECOND PART

525. The second part is a noun or adjective stem, but it may be one that appears only in composition and not in independent use.

G. λογο-γράφος 'speech-writer' and others in -ποιός, -μαχος, -φαγος, etc.

L. armi-ger 'armor-bearer' and others in -fer, -fex, -ficus, etc., in which the second part is a verbal noun not occurring alone

G. εὔ-φρων 'cheerful' beside φρήν 'mind', ἀ-πάτωρ 'fatherless' beside πατήρ 'father', εὐ-μενής 'well-disposed' beside μένος with difference in gradation

Fem. ā-stems normally become o-stems in masc. and neut. forms, as G. ἄ-τῑμος 'dishonored' (τῑμή), L. in-glōrius 'without fame' (glōria).

But in Greek some appear as masc. ā-stems, as χρῡσο-κόμης 'golden-haired', παιδο-τρίβης 'gymnastic teacher' (τριβή 'practice', τρίβω 'rub'), 'Ολυμπιονῑκης 'victor at the Olympic games'. Such forms came to be associated with the corresponding verbs, and others were formed directly from a verb, as those in -πώλης, -μέτρης, -άρχης beside -αρχος, etc.

In Latin some compounds of ā- and o-stems become i-stems, as *bi-fōrmis* 'double' (*fōrma*), *ē-normis* (**524**), *in-ermis* 'unarmed' (*arma*), *bi-iugis* 'yoked two together' (*iugum*) beside *in-ermus*, *bi-iugus*.

Compounds of cons. stems generally retain the cons. stem, as G. ἄ-παις 'childless' (παῖς, παιδός), εὐδαίμων 'fortunate' (δαίμων), L. *quadru-pēs* 'quadruped' (*pēs*, *pedis*), *prae-ceps* 'headlong' (*caput*). But some become *o*-stems, as G. ἄν-υδρος 'without water' (ὕδωρ), L. *per-iūrus* 'oath-breaking' (*iūs*).

Compounds are sometimes formed with an added suffix, especially *-yo-*. G. ἐπι-θαλάσσιος, L. *ē-gregius*, etc. (**524**). L. *in-iūrius* 'unlawful' (*iūs*), *bi-ennium* 'period of two years' (*annus*), *bi-nocti-um* 'period of two nights' (*nox*, *noctis*), *medi-terrāneus* 'inland' (*terra*).

526. *Vowel lengthening in Greek.*—When the word forming the second part began with α, ε, ο, followed by a single consonant, the vowel is frequently lengthened to the corresponding ᾱ (Att.-Ion. η), η, ω.

ἀν-ώνυμος nameless' (ὄνομα)   ἀν-ώμαλος 'uneven' (ὁμαλός)

στρατ-ηγός, Dor. στρατ-ᾱγός 'general' (ἄγω)

παν-ήγυρις 'national assembly' (ἀγορά)

εὐ-ήνεμος 'with fair wind' (ἄνεμος)   φιλ-ήρετμος 'fond of the oar' (ἐρετμός)

a. This has its origin in certain forms in which the long vowel was the result of contraction with the vowel of the preceding stem, before such contraction which prevailed in the parent speech, as in Sanskrit, was replaced by the later system of elision (**518**). So ὠμηστής 'eating raw flesh' (ὠμο-ἐδ-) like Skt. *āmād-* of the same meaning (*āma-ad*), with IE contraction; similarly στρατᾱγός, etc., and by analogy ἀν-ώμαλος, etc.

PERSONAL NAMES

527. Composition is characteristic of the system of personal names which prevails in Greek and the other main branches of the IE family, except the Italic, and which must be an inheritance from the parent speech.

Thus, with the word for 'horse' as first or second part, G. Ἵππ-αρχος, Ἄρχ-ιππος, Skt. *Açva-sena-*, *Bṛhad-açva-*, Av. *Vīrāspa-*, OPers. *Vištāspa* (Ὑστάσπης), Gall. *Epo-rēdii*, OIr. *Each-cenn;*

with 'wolf' G. Λυκό-φρων, Ἀρπά-λυκος, Skt. *Vṛka-karman-*, OE
Wulf-fređ, Bēo-wulf; with 'renowned', G. Κλυτο-μήδης, Περι-
κλυτος, Skt. *Çruta-karman-*, OHG *Hlud-wig* (NHG *Ludwig*, Fr.
Louis); with 'glory', G. Κλεό-βουλος, Περι-κλῆς, Skt. *Su-çravas-*,
Slav. *Slavo-bor, Bole-slav.*

The names are not formed from any and every word, but rather
from a limited number which are conventionally employed in the
system of nomenclature, and which may therefore be termed
name words. Certain of these may be especially popular in a given
language, dialect, or family. In Greek there are several hundred
different names formed from ἵππος, while in Germanic there are
virtually none from 'horse', but very many from 'wolf'.

Names of successive generations often show one name word in
common, in different combinations, as son and father in G. Κλεο-
μέδων Κλε-αρέτου, Δωρό-θεος Θεο-δώρου, etc.; OE *Ethel-bald, Ethel-
bert, Ethel-red*, sons of *Ethel-wulf.*

Of the Greek name words some are used only in the first part
of names, some only in the second, but many in either. Examples
are numerous of parallel names with the same two name words in
reverse order, as Ἄρχ-ιππος, Ἵππαρχος ; Φιλό-δημος, Δημό-φιλος.

Nearly all the various classes of compounds, according to form
and meaning, are represented. Thus Δημο-σθένης (lit. 'having the
strength of the people'), a possessive compound with first part a
noun stem (517.3), Φανό-δικος (lit. 'showing justice'), with first
part a verbal form governing the second (522). But while originally
the names were like any other compounds in having an appropriate sense, the familiar name words came to be combined conventionally without any consciousness of the resulting sense or
nonsense. In the well-known passage of Aristophanes (Clouds,
60 ff.), Strepsiades, who wished to name his son Φειδωνίδης after
the grandfather, and his wife, who wanted a name with ἵππος,
compromised on Φειδιππίδης.

For the names in -αδης, -ιδης, orig. patronymic, but no longer
so in historical names like Θουκυδίδης (from Θεο-κύδης), see 493.

528. From the compound names, which form the main body
of the Greek system, were formed short names containing only

the first or second part, or sometimes the first part with the beginning of the second, with perhaps an added suffix. These are in origin pet-names, which however are not felt as such but have gained an independent status, like NE *Eliza* beside *Elizabeth.*

Ἱππίας, Ἵππων beside Ἵππ-αρχος, Ἱππο-κράτης, etc., Φείδων beside Φειδο-κράτης, etc., Φίλιος, Φιλέᾱς, Φιλάκων, etc., beside Φιλό-δωρος, etc., Δημοσθᾱς (late) beside Δημο-σθένης

The painter Ζεῦξις is called Ζεύξιππος in Plato, and there are some other examples of short and full name attested for the same person. But generally the short names have become quite independent of the full names. Cf. Ἱππίας brother of Ἵππαρχος.

But not all the Greek short names are of such origin. There are many which did not originate in compound names but were from the outset simple descriptive epithets, used first as nicknames. Thus Πλάτων (πλατύς 'broad, flat'), which in the case of the great philosopher displaced his original name Ἀριστο-κλῆς, Στράβων (στράβων 'squinter'), Πάχης (παχύς 'stout, fat').

a. Whether simple or compound, the Greek name was a single name. While there was a tendency to repeat the same name or a part of the name in the family, there were no true family names like the Roman gentiles.

The official title of a Greek citizen consisted of his own name, followed by that of his father expressed by the genitive or in some dialects by the old patronymic adjective in -ιος, and generally a designation of his native town, or if an Athenian, his deme. Thus Δημοσθένης Δημοσθένους Παιανιεύς.

529. In Italic the IE system of compound names was displaced in prehistoric times. Latin and the Italic dialects agree in a system of praenomina and gentile names, with the father's name expressed by the genitive. The only differences are the order and the usual addition of *f.* (*filius*) to the genitive in Latin. The further addition of a cognomen is mainly Latin.

L. M. *Tullius* M. f. *Cicero*

Osc. V . P ú p i d i i s V . 'Vibius Popidius son of Vibius'

Umbr. T . T . K a s t r u ç i i e (gen. sg.) 'of Titius Castrucius, son of Titus'

The praenomina are mostly of obscure etymology, but clearly original short names of the same type as G. Πλάτων.

The gentiles are in origin patronymic adjectives derived from the father's name, like Hom. Τελαμώνιος, but becoming fixed as family names. *Tullius* was orig. 'the son of Tullus', as NE *Johnson* was orig. 'John's son'.

VERBAL COMPOUNDS

530. The only widespread type of verbal composition is that with adverbial prefixes, most of them identical with forms that are used independently as adverbs or prepositions, in short, the "prepositional compounds". The situation in Vedic Sanskrit and Homeric Greek, where the parts are still separable (the so-called τμῆσις 'cutting, severance'), shows that the formal union belongs mainly to the history of the individual languages.

Forms like G. οἰκοδομέω, L. *aedificō* 'build' are not really compounds of a noun stem with a verb, but are rather derivatives of a compound noun, as οἰκο-δόμος, *aedifex*.

Others have arisen from juxtaposition, as L. *bene-dīcō* 'bless', *manū-mittō* 'set free', *animadvertō* 'attend to' (*animum advertō*). So *cale-faciō* 'make hot' (*cale faciō* in early Latin), *candē-faciō* 'make white', etc., which came to be felt as derived from verbs in *-eō*.

a. Latin inseparable prefixes with verbs are:

amb-, am- 'about': G. ἀμφί
an- 'in' (rare): Umbr. *an-,* G. ἀνά
dis- 'apart', from IE* *di-*, beside* *dwi-* (**313.2**)
por- 'forth': *prō*
re-, red- 'back'
sē-, sēd- 'apart' (early L. also as preposition 'without'), orig. 'by one's self': *sē* reflexive.

APPENDIX

SELECTED BIBLIOGRAPHY

(WITH ABBREVIATIONS EMPLOYED)

PERIODICALS

AJA = American Journal of Archaeology

AJP = American Journal of Philology

BSL = Bulletin de la Société de Linguistique

BB = (BEZZENBERGER'S) Beiträge zur Kunde der indogermanischen Sprachen

Ber. Berl. Akad. = Sitzungsberichte der preussischen Akademie der Wissenschaften zu Berlin

CP = Classical Philology

CQ = Classical Quarterly

CR = Classical Review

CW = Classical Weekly

Ger.-Rom. Monatsschrift = Germanisch-romanische Monatsschrift

Glotta, Zeitschrift für griechische und lateinische Sprache

Gött. gel. Anz. = Göttingische gelehrte Anzeigen

Gött. Nachr. = Nachrichten von der königlichen Gesellschaft der Wissenschaften zu Göttingen

Idg. Jhb. = Indogermanisches Jahrbuch

IF = Indogermanische Forschungen

IF Anz. = Anzeiger für indogermanische Sprache und Altertumskunde

KZ = Zeitschrift für vergleichende Sprachforschung, begründet von A. KUHN

Language, Journal of the Linguistic Society of America

MSL = Mémoires de la Société de Linguistique

Rev. de ph. = Revue de philologie

Rev. ét. gr. = Revue des études grecques

RhM = Rheinisches Museum für Philologie

Riv. di fil. = Rivista di filologia

Riv. IGI = Rivista Indo-Greco-Italica

TAPA = Transactions of the American Philological Association

Woch. klass. Ph. = Wochenschrift für klassische Philologie

ZDMG = Zeitschrift der deutschen morgenländischen Gesellschaft

Z. rom. Ph. = Zeitschrift für romanische Philologie

GENERAL LINGUISTICS

BLOOMFIELD. Introduction to the Study of Language. New York, 1941.

BOAS. Handbook of American Indian Languages. Washington, 1911.

GRAFF. Language and Languages. New York, 1932.

JESPERSEN. Language. London, 1922.
———. Philosophy of Grammar. London, 1924.
MEILLET. Linguistique historique et linguistique générale. Paris, 1921.
OERTEL. Lectures on the Study of Language. New York, 1902.
PAUL. Prinzipien der Sprachgeschichte. 5th ed. Halle, 1920.
SAPIR. Language. New York, 1921.
STURTEVANT. Linguistic Change. Chicago, 1917.
———. An Introduction to Linguistic Science. New Haven, 1947.
VENDRYES. Le langage. Paris, 1921.
WHITNEY. Life and Growth of Language. New York, 1878.

INDO-EUROPEAN

BRUGMANN. Grundriss = Grundriss der vergleichenden Grammatik der indogermanischen Sprachen. 2d ed. Strassburg, 1897–1916.
———. KVG = Kurze vergleichende Grammatik der indogermanischen Sprachen. Strassburg, 1903.
HIRT. Idg. Gram. = Indogermanische Grammatik. Heidelberg, 1921–29.
MEILLET. Introd. = Introduction à l'étude comparative des langues indo-européennes. 7th ed. Paris, 1934.
WALDE. Vergleichendes Wörterbuch der indogermanischen Sprachen, herausgegeben und bearbeitet von JULIUS POKORNY. Berlin und Leipzig, 1930.

GREEK AND LATIN

KRETSCHMER. "Die Sprache," in GERCKE und NORDEN, Einleitung in die Altertumswissenschaft, 3d ed. Leipzig, 1923.
MEILLET et VENDRYES. Traité de grammaire comparée des langues classiques. 2d ed. Paris, 1927.
STURTEVANT. Pronunciation of Greek and Latin. Chicago, 1920.
WACKERNAGEL. Vorlesungen über Syntax mit besonderer Rücksicht von Griechischem. Basel, 1920.

GREEK

GOODWIN. Greek Grammar. Revised by C. B. GULICK. Boston, 1930.
HIRT. Handbuch der griechischen Laut- und Formenlehre. 2d ed. Heidelberg, 1912.
KIECKERS. Historische griechische Grammatik. Sammlung Göschen, 1925–26.
KÜHNER-BLASS = KÜHNER. Ausführliche Grammatik der griechischen Sprache. 3d ed. Part I, revised by BLASS. Hannover, 1892.
MEILLET. Aperçu = Aperçu d'une histoire de la langue grecque. 3d ed. Paris, 1930.

SCHWYZER. Griechische Grammatik, auf der Grundlage von Karl Brugmanns griechischer Grammatik. Vol. I. Munich, 1939.

SMYTH. Greek Grammar for Colleges. New York, 1920.

THUMB in STREITBERG's Geschichte der indogermanischen Sprachwissenschaft 1.2. Strassburg, 1916.

BOISACQ. Dict. étym. = Dictionnaire étymologique de la langue grecque. Heidelberg-Paris, 1916.

GREEK DIALECTS

BECHTEL. Die griechischen Dialekte. Berlin, 1921–24.

BUCK, Gr. Dial. = Introduction to the Study of the Greek Dialects. 2d ed. Boston, 1928.

THUMB. Handbuch der griechischen Dialekte. Heidelberg, 1909. 2d. ed. revised by KIECKERS. Vol. I, 1932.

SCHWYZER. Dialectorum graecarum exempla epigraphica potiora. Leipzig, 1923.

LATIN

ERNOUT. Morphologie historique du latin. 2d ed. Paris, 1927.

KENT. The Sounds of Latin. Language Monographs XII, 1932.

————. The Forms of Latin. 1946.

KIECKERS. Historische lateinische Grammatik, mit Berücksichtigung des vulgärlateinischen und der romanischen Sprachen. Dorpat, München, 1930+.

LINDSAY = LINDSAY. Latin Language. Oxford, 1894.

MEILLET. Esquisse d'une histoire de la langue latine. 2d ed. Paris, 1931.

NIEDERMANN. Précis de phonétique historique du latin. Paris, 1931.

————. Historische Lautlehre des Lateinischen. Heidelberg, 1911.

SOMMER. Hdb. = Handbuch der lateinischen Laut- und Formenlehre. 2d ed. Heidelberg, 1914.

————. Erläut. = Kritische Erläuterungen zur lateinischen Laut- und Formenlehre. Heidelberg, 1914.

STOLZ. Historische Grammatik der lateinischen Sprache, I. Leipzig, 1895. [Still important for Latin word-formation.]

STOLZ-DEBRUNNER = STOLZ. Geschichte der lateinischen Sprache. Revised by DEBRUNNER. Berlin, 1922.

STOLZ-LEUMANN = STOLZ. Lateinische Grammatik. 5th ed. Revised by LEUMANN.

ERNOUT et MEILLET. Dictionnaire étymologique de la langue latine. 2d ed. Paris, 1939.

WALDE. Lateinisches etymologisches Wörterbuch. 3d ed. Revised by J. B. HOFMANN. Heidelberg, 1930+.

ITALIC DIALECTS

BUCK. Osc.-Umbr. Gram.=A Grammar of Oscan and Umbrian. New printing with brief additions and corrections. Boston, 1928.

CONWAY. The Italic Dialects. Cambridge, 1897.

VON PLANTA. Grammatik der oskisch-umbrischen Dialekte. Strassburg, 1892–97.

NOTES AND REFERENCES[1]

1. On the term Indo-European, Buck, CR 18. 399 ff.

4. Whitney, Sanskrit Grammar. Wackernagel, Altindische Grammatik.

5. Jackson, Avesta Grammar. Reichelt, Awestisches Elementarbuch. Meillet, Grammaire du vieux perse, 2d ed., revised by Benveniste.

6. Hübschmann, Armenische Grammatik. Meillet, Altarmenisches Elementarbuch.

7. Jokl, in Streitberg's Geschichte der idg. Sprachwissenschaft 2. 3. 121, with references.

8. Pedersen, Vergleichende Grammatik der keltischen Sprachen. Thurneysen, Grammar of Old Irish (Dublin, 1946). Vendryes, Grammaire du vieil-irlandais.

9. Streitberg, Urgermanische Grammatik. Streitberg, Gotisches Elementarbuch. Jespersen, Growth and Structure of the English Language.

11. Leskien, Litauisches Lesebuch. Endzelin, Lettische Grammatik. Trautmann, Altpreussische Sprachdenkmäler.

12. Meillet, Le slave commun. Vondrák, Vergleichende Slavische Grammatik. Leskien, Altbulgarische Grammatik.

13. Kretschmer, Einleitung in die Geschichte der griechischen Sprache (fundamental work on the languages of Asia Minor, etc., but antedating the most important discoveries). Friedrich, Altkleinasiatische Sprachen, in Ebert's Reallexikon der Vorgeschichte. Articles in Schrader's Reallexicon der indogermanischen Altertumskunde and Pauly-Wissowa. On Lycian and Lydian, cf. also Meriggi, Festschrift Hirt 2. 257 ff.

Hoffmann, Die Makedonen. Numerous controversial articles by Hatzidakis, Kazarof, and others.

14. Sieg und Siegling, Tocharisch, Ber. Berl. Akad. 1908, 915 ff. Meillet, Le Tokharien, Idg. Jhb. 1. 1 ff. Sieg, Siegling, und Schulze, Tocharische Grammatik. Lane, CW 1941, 194 ff. Benveniste, Festschrift Hirt. 2. 227 ff. Pedersen, Tocharisch.

15. Sturtevant, Hittite Grammar. Sturtevant, Hittite Glossary. Friedrich, Altkleinasiatische Sprachen, in Ebert's Reallexikon der Vorgeschichte. Friedrich, Hethitisch und kleinasiatische Sprachen, in Streitberg's Geschichte der idg. Sprachwissenschaft 2. 5. 1.

For an early branching-off of Hittite (also Luwian, Lydian, etc.) from a Proto-IE or Indo-Hittite, cf. (after Forrer) Kretschmer, Glotta 14. 300, and especially Sturte-

---

[1] For most of the matters discussed in the main part of the book it is sufficient to refer once and for all to the Schwyzer and the Stolz-Leumann with their bibliographies.

vant, Hittite Grammar 29 ff., Language 15. 11 ff., Laryngeals 23 ff. Adversely, Benveniste, Bonfante, Pedersen, and many others cited at length by Bonfante, CP 39. 51 ftn. and JAOS 64. 170 ftn. But cf. the remark in this book, p. vii.

16. Debrunner in Ebert, Reallexikon der Vorgeschichte IV. 510 ff. Buck, CP 21. 1 ff. Blegen, AJA 32. 146 ff. Nilsson, Homer and Mycenae 64 ff. J. L. Myres, Who Were the Greeks?

19, 20. Buck, Grk. Dial. 1–14, with references 295. Schwyzer 75 ff.

16–21. Buck, Grk. Dial. 1–14, 154–61, with references 295 ff. Meillet, Aperçu, *passim.*

22. Thumb, Die griechische Sprache im Zeitalter des Hellenismus. Moulton, Grammar of New Testament Greek. Blass-Debrunner, Grammatik des neutestamentlichen Griechisch.

24. Conway, Whatmough, and Johnson, Prae-Italic Dialects of Italy. Whatmough, Foundations of Roman Italy. Etruscan. Sktusch, Etruskische Sprache in Pauly-Wissowa. Eva Fiesel, Etruskisch, in Streitberg's Geschichte der idg. Sprachwissenschaft 2. 5. 4. Ligurian, Whatmough, Harvard Studies in Classical Philology 38. 1 ff.

25–27. Buck, Osc.-Umbr. Gram. 1–21, with references 353 ff.

29. Diehl, Altlateinische Inschriften, 3d ed. Ernout, Recueil des textes latins archaiques.

30. Budinsky, Ausbreitung der lateinischen Sprache. Wartburg, Die Entstehung der romanischen Völker.

31–33. Grandgent, Introduction to Vulgar Latin. Meyer-Lübke, Einführung in das Studium der romanischen Sprachwissenschaft.

34. Ernout, Les éléments étrusques du vocabulaire latin, Bull. Soc. Ling. 30. 1, 82 ff. Weise, Die griechischen Wörter im Latein. Ernout, Les éléments dialectaux du vocabulaire latin. Dottin, La langue gauloise, passim. Brüch, Einfluss der germanischen Sprachen auf das Vulgärlatein.

41–63. Cf. the works on general linguistics cited above, p. 364.

42. The postulate of the "invariability of the phonetic laws" ("Ausnahmslosigkeit der Lautgesetze") goes back to Leskien, Declination im Slavischlitauischen und Germanischen (1876), Einl. p. xxviii. It was taken up with enthusiasm, as a guiding principle, by most of the then younger generation of scholars, though also rejected by some. In 1901 it was remarked (Wheeler, TAPA 32. 6) that "few herald it in the abstract, few disregard it in the concrete". For recent discussion, cf. E. Hermann, Lautgesetz und Analogie (1931), with the review by L. Bloomfield in Language 8. 220 ff.

43. Jespersen, Language 255 ff.

On the geographical theory, cf. also the conclusion of Boas (Hdb. Am. Ind. Lang. 52), "I do not believe that detailed investigations in any part of the world would sustain this theory."

Criticism of the substratum theory. Jespersen, Language 191 ff. Wagner, Z. rom. Ph. 40. 286 ff., 385 ff. Rohlf, Ger.-Rom. Monatsschrift 18. 37 ff.

The ease theory is the one that is most prominent in early works, and is also made the most of by Jespersen, Language 26 ff.

44. Taylor, The Alphabet. Mason, The Art of Writing. Diringer, The Alphabet (1948). Gelb, The Theory of Writing (in preparation).

46. For the numerous examples of spelling pronunciation in English, cf. also Jespersen, Modern English Grammar 1, Index, under "Spelling-pronunciations".

49–52. Bréal, Essai de sémantique (also in English, as Semantics, Studies in the Science of Meaning). Greenough and Kittredge, Words and Their Ways in English Speech. Meillet, Ling. hist. et ling. gén. 230 ff. Nyrop, Das Leben der Wörter. Sperber, Einführung in die Bedeutungslehre. Buck, Dictionary of Selected Synonyms in the Principal Indo-European Languages (in press).

53. Sapir, Language 127 ff.

55–57. Jespersen, Language, 367 ff. Oertel and Morris, Nature and Origin of Indo-European Inflection, Harvard Studies 16. 63 ff.

61. Hempl, Language Rivalry and Speech Differentiation in the Case of Race-Mixture, TAPA 29. 31 ff.

63. Buck, Language and the Sentiment of Nationality, Amer. Pol. Sci. Rev. 10. 44 ff.

64. For the Egyptian origin of the Phoenician alphabet, cf. Gardiner, Journal of Egypt, Arch., and of the extensive subsequent discussions, especially Ullman, AJA 31. 311 ff. with table on p. 314; and Sprengling, The Alphabet, Its Rise and Development from the Sinai Inscriptions. But the importance of the Sinaitic script as a connecting link has come to be doubted, and at any rate the statement in the text is too positive. The precise source of the North Semitic alphabet is still unsettled. Cf. Diringer, The Alphabet 195 ff. especially 199 ff.

65–68. Kirchhoff, Studien zur Geschichte des griechischen Alphabets. Roberts, Introduction to Greek Epigraphy. Larfeld, Griechische Epigraphik. Roehl, Imagines inscriptionum graecarum antiquissimarum. Kern, Inscriptiones graecae. Buck, Grk. Dial. 302 ff.

Kirchhoff's map, while needing revision in some details, shows the distribution of the main types, and is so familiar that one speaks of the "blue" (East Greek), "red" (West Greek), and "green" (Cretan, etc.) alphabets.

The earliest Phoenician inscription from Byblos, formerly attributed to the 13th century, is not earlier than c. 1000 B.C. Cf. Albright, JAOS 67. 154.

69. Hammarström, Beiträge zur Geschichte des etruskischen, lateinischen und griechischen Alphabets. Ullman, The Etruscan Origin of the Roman Alphabet and the Names of the Letters, CP 22. 372 ff. Photograph of the Massiliana tablet in AJA 30. 218.

71. Schulze, Ber. Berl. Akad. 1904. 760 ff. Hammarström, Ullman in citations to **69.** For English names, Sheldon, Harvard Stud. in Phil. 1. 75 ff., 2. 155 ff. For the history and name of Y, Buck, Manly Anniversary Studies 340 ff.

79.2. Variously classified and explained. Lindsay 229. Sommer, Hdb. 57 ff. Stolz-Leumann 57 ff., 96.

80.4, 5. The preceding *w* is taken here as the primary factor, as in 2,3, though the change is further conditioned by the quality of the following vowel (cf. *bonus, bene*). Classed as a plain assimilation by Sommer, Hdb. 114, with inclusion of doubtful cases like *homō, modus* which may perfectly well be inherited *o*-grade forms, and without regard to the countless exceptions to such assimilation. Similarly Stolz-Leumann 96.

83.2. The usual explanation, but a doubtful one, is that the change took place in the syllable before the accent, e.g., *cavēre*, whence by analogy *caveō*. Stolz-Leumann 61.

88. Further details and problems of Att. ā, η, Schwyzer 185 ff.

90b. Sommer's phonetic explanation of *poena*, etc. (Hdb. 76 ff., Erläut. 20 ff.), is too complicated to carry conviction, and even so leaves *moenia* as admittedly archaistic. The view preferred in the text is also that of Lindsay 246, Wackernagel, KZ 33. 55, Solmsen, KZ 37. 11, Conway, CR 17. 364, Marouzeau, MSL 17. 272.

90e. For the current explanation of L. *oboediō*, cf. Stolz-Leumann 87.

99.2c. Against the assumption of general lengthening before *gn*, Buck, CR 15. 311 ff.

99.2d. Against "Lachmann's Law," accepted in modified form by Sommer, Hdb. 122 ff. and Stolz-Leumann 105, cf. Buck, CR 27. 122; Kent, Language 4. 181 ff.

102a. Lindsay, 210 ff.

116. For retention of the symbols r̄, etc., cf. also Language 2. 106.

116, 127a. On στρωτός, ἔμολον, etc., Schwyzer 361 f.

127a. Forms like βλη-, πλη- are the starting-point for the numerous secondary stems in η, as in σχήσω (ἔχω), μελήσω (μέλω), ἐθελήσω, ἠθέλησα, ἠθέληκα (ἐθέλω), βουλήσομαι, βεβούλημαι (βούλομαι) νενέμηκα (νέμω), ἐψήσω, ἥψησα, ἐψητός (ἕψω), εὑρήσω, εὕρηκα (εὑρίσκω, and so from several others in -ισκω), μαθήσομαι, μεμάθηκα (μανθάνω, and so from several others in -ανω). Much less common is the extension from δρα-, τλα-, etc., to a secondary stem in ā, Att.-Ion. η, as in ὀνήσω, Dor. ὀνάσω (ὀνίνημι) or from γνω-, στρω-, etc., to a secondary stem in ω, as in πέπτωκα (πίπτω), ἀλώσομαι, ἑάλων, ἥλων, ἑάλωκα, ἥλωκα (ἀλίσκομαι), ἥβλωσα, ἥμβλωκα (ἀμβλίσκω).

129. Mention should have been made of occasional alternation in the orders, especially in root finals. Thus **pāg-* in G. πήγνῡμι, Dor. πάγνῡμι, L. *pangō, pepigī*, etc., but **pāk̑-* in G. πήσσω, πάσσαλος (-κι-, **182**), L. *pāx pācis, paciscor*, etc. In some roots such alternations run through many of the IE languages, while in others a variant form may appear only in some dialect (e.g., G. κλέπτω, κλοπή, but Mess. κεκλεβώς). Cf. Schwyzer Griech. Gram. p. 333.

129.3. Other views on the stages of the Italic development are cited in Stolz-Leuman 137 ff.

131. For native Latin aspiration, Sommer, Hdb. 200 ff., Erläut. 72 ff., Stolz-Leumann 131.

142. Lindsay 286 ff. Sommer 176. Stolz-Leumann 128.

189. Details on assimilation in Latin compounds, Buck, CR 13. 156 ff.

189–210. Besides the changes described, there are certain widespread instances of initial doublets, especially *st/t, sp/p*, etc. Thus G. στέγος (cf. Lith, *stegti* 'to roof') beside τέγος (cf. L. *tegō, toga*, NHG *Dach* 'roof,' etc.), G. πῦρός and dial. σπῦρός, etc. Cf. also *sw/s* in the reflexive pronoun (**297, 300**) and the numeral for six (**313**.6), and *tw/t* in the pronoun of the second person (**297, 298**).

201.3. Schwyzer 283 f.

212, 216. Sturtevant and Kent, TAPA, 46. 129 ff.

218-220. Schwyzer 371 ff. with references.

223. For the extensive controversial literature on the character of the Latin accent, cf. references in Stolz-Leumann 184–89. Add Frank, CQ 4. 35 ff. (on the doubtful cogency of the statements of the Roman writers), Fraenkel, Iktus und Akzent im lat. Sprechvers. Debrunner, IF 48. 314 ff.

Even the old initial stress accent (**221**) is now being denied by advocates of the pitch accent. While a certain dominance of the initial syllable is of course admitted, to account for the vowel syncope and weakening in other syllables, it is claimed this had nothing to do with stress. But as this dominance was obviously not one of quantity, it is difficult to see what else it could be than one of stress. It must have been some phonetic actuality, not a psychological phantom.

227a. Against *Pomplio* as dual (Sommer, Hdb. 348), Meister, Lat.-Gr. Eigennamen 1. 99; Wackernagel, Vorles. über Syntax 1. 77; Stolz-Leumann 255.

229-30. Brugmann, Grundriss 2. 122 ff. Wackernagel, Altind. Gram. 3. 28 ff. (with full citation of the literature).

229, 238, 239.7. For the abl sg. IE. *-ōd, -ēd* are assumed here, but it must be admitted that *-ōt, -ēt* are equally possible, since the Italic final *d* may come from final *t* (212.3), the Skt. final *t* and *d* are interchangeable (e.g. *vṛkāt, vṛkād*), and the cognate forms of other languages are equally ambiguous in this respect. If the ending is ultimately connected with the adverbial *-tos* (513.2), this, of course, favors *t*.

237a. Solmsen, Beiträge zur griech. Wortforschung 238 ff.

260. L. *sēdēs*, etc., are taken as *ē*-stems and compared with the isolated Skt. nom. sg. *panthās*, acc. sg. *panthām*, by Meillet, Indian Stud. in Honor of C. R. Lanman 3 ff., and Pedersen (see ref. to **273**).

273. Pedersen, La cinquième déclinaison latine, with criticism by Leumann, Glotta 18. 255.

282a. πολλο- from πολυ-λο-. Thurneysen, IF 21. 176. Schwyzer 265.

286. Buck, CP 16. 367 ff.

299.3. For Att.-Ion. ἡμῖν, ὑμῖν and the prosody of the Homeric forms, cf. Sommer, Glotta, 1. 219 ff., IF. 30. 415 ff.; Witte, Glotta 2. 8 ff., RhM 68. 217 ff.

304.1. Sommers' derivation from gen. sg. *q͏ʷosyo*, etc., accepted by many, is to me phonetically improbable. The derivation from possessive adjective, as in the text, is a very old view, often independently revived (so in my Osk. Vocalismus 151 ff., without knowledge that it went back to Aufrecht, KZ 1. 232; later by Brugmann and others) and still preferred by many. Sturtevant, TAPA 44. 99 ff. Herbig, IFAnz. 37. 27 ff.

307a. Sturtevant, Relatives in Indo-European and Hittite, Curme Volume of Linguistic Studies 141 ff. Fowler, Origin of the Latin *qui*-Clauses, Language 7. 14 ff.

325. 346. 416.6. Charpentier, Die verbalen *r*-Endungen der idg. Sprachen. Edith Claflin, AJP 48. 157 ff.; Language 5. 232 ff. For Hittite *r*-forms, Sturtevant, Hittite Gram. 264 ff.

327b. Wackernagel, Studien zum griechischen Perfektum. Chantraine, Histoire du parfait grec.

336. On φέρεις, Schwyzer 661.

387. Perophrastic origin doubted by Petersen, Language 3. 175 ff., 8. 133 ff. Cf. also Leumann, IF 42. 60 ff., Glotta 18. 257 ff.

405*a*. Schwyzer 672.

439. Quite otherwise Miss Hahn, TAPA 74. 279 ff.

441 ff. Word-formation. For IE, Brugmann, Grundriss 2. 1. For Greek, De-brunner, Griechische Wortbildung. Chantraine, La formation des noms en grec ancien, Paris, 1933. Buck and Petersen, Reverse index of Greek nouns and adjectives. For Latin, Stolz, Historische Grammatik der lateinischen Sprache 365 ff.

522*a*. Type σωσί-πολις, recent discussion by Specht, Glotta 20. 31 ff.

527. Brugmann, Grundriss 2. 117 ff. Fick-Bechtel, Griech. Personennamen.

INDEX

OF GREEK AND LATIN WORDS[1]

[1] The references are to pages.

τυροῦς 334
τυφλός 328

ὑβρίζω 262
ὑγρός 326
ὕδωρ 134
ὑϊδεύς 341
υἱός 139, υἱύς 198, υἱάσι 46
ὑλοτόμος 356
ὑμεῖς 219
ὑμέτερος 220
ὕμμε, ὕμμες 219
ὑμός 220
ὑός 139
ὕπαρχος 358
ὑπέρ 50, 134, 237
ὕπνος 82, 109, 146, 322
ὑπό 99, 134, 237
ὑπόξυλος 358
ὑπόστεγος 359
ὗς 132, 316
ὕστερος 134
ὑψηλός 329
ὗ ψιλόν 76

φαίδιμος 319
φαίνω 142, 262, ἔφηνα 85, 151, 282,
    πέφηνα 287, πέφασμαι 290, ἐφάνην,
    ἐφάνθην 285
φάλαγξ 345
φανερός 327
Φανόδικος 361
φάρμακον 343
φάσκω 264
φάτις 337
φέβομαι 260
φεῖ 76
Φειδιππίδης 361
φειδωλός 329
Φείδων 362
φερένϊκος 357
φέρετρον 326
φέρω 81, 85, 121, 123, 131, 242, 245–
    46, 249, 250, 257, 260, φέροιμι 300,
    φέρουσα 112, 179, 189, οἴσω 216,
    ἤνεγκα, ἤνεικα 216, 284
φεύγεσκον 264

φεύγω 109, 257, 260, ἔφυγον 109, 257,
    283, πέφευγα 120, 287
φήμη 85, 320
φημί 113
φήρ 128
φθάνω 263
φθείρω 142, 262, ἔφθειρα 152, 282,
    ἔφθορα, ἔφθαρκα 290
φθίνω 131, 263, φθίεται 298
φιλέω 259, 264, 265, φιλοίην 299
φιλήρετμος 360
φίλιος 317
φιλομμειδής 132
φιλόξενος 354
φιλότης 333
φλεγυρός 327
φλόξ 314
φοβερός 327
φοβέω 260, 264
φόβος 52
φονεύς 316
φόνος 109, 129
φορά 315
φορός, φόρος 315
φόρτος 335
φράτηρ 121, 325
φρᾱτρίᾱ 35
φρήν 109, 110, 189
φροῦδος 134
φρουρά 134
φσέφισμα 144
φύγαδε 350
φυγάς 340
φυγή 315
φυγόμαχος 357
φυλάσσω 140, 261, πεφύλαχα 288
φῦλή 328
φῦλον 328
φυσικός 344
φυσιολόγος 356
φύσκων 321
φύτλον, φύτλη 330
φωνέω 264
φωνή 113
φῶς 190

LATIN